Abraham Lincoln
From Skeptic to Prophet

Abraham Lincoln
From Skeptic to Prophet

Wayne C. Temple

Mayhaven Publishing

Mayhaven Publishing
P. O. Box 557
Mahomet, IL 61853
U. S. A.

Copyright 1995 © Wayne C. Temple
First Edition - First Printing 1995
Illústrations by Lloyd Ostendorf
Halftones by Frank Scott, Allied Printing, Farmer City, IL
Printing: Superior Printing, Champaign, IL
Binding: Dekker, Grand Rapids, MI
Library of Congress Catalog Number: 95-76060
ISBN   1-878044-36-2

Dedicated To
Professor Richard Nelson Current
and the memory of
Professor Frederick Charles Dietz
(May 23, 1888—May 6, 1987)
Who Were Greatly Admired by the Author
While a Student at the University of Illinois

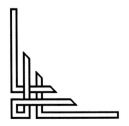

Foreword

I met the author in the winter of 1981. I was an undergraduate student at North Central College in Naperville, Illinois and he was the Deputy Director of the Illinois Archives. I had received the Richter Fellowship for undergraduate research and was beginning my formal study of Mary (Todd) Lincoln. Dr. Temple was recommended to me by Dr. Ralph McGinnis of Eastern Illinois University. Dr. McGinnis said Dr. Temple would be of great assistance to me. He most certainly was. He generously opened his files and suggested a dozen contacts—including several other world-class historians. He also spent many hours discussing my research and challenging my inquiry. It was the educational experience of a lifetime—until now. Working with this manuscript has surpassed even that exciting time.

The author's astute insights and meticulous research have, for over half a century, informed, assisted, and inspired students, historians, and writers. This book is one of many Dr. Temple has written about Lincoln. He has contributed to many others. He brings to each his unique experience assisting Lincoln biographers James G. Randall and Ruth Painter Randall, editing the *Lincoln Herald*, his tenure with the Illinois State Archives, and many other distinguished posts. He is, of course, the recipient of many awards.

Abraham Lincoln, From Skeptic to Prophet is the result of a lifelong study of Abraham Lincoln, especially his spiritual and religious views. The author's fellow historians and those new to the study of Lincoln will find fresh information and much clarification within this book. The rich details of history that pique our interest and lift our spirits are entwined within this volume. It has been the greatest pleasure and privilege to have served as its editor and publisher.

Doris R. Wenzel
Mahomet, Illinois
January 8, 1995

The house, similar to Lincoln's Springfield home, in which the First Presbyterian Church was organized.

Acknowledgments

This project has stretched out over thirty years, and many of those who originally assisted with this difficult project have passed from this earth. Nevertheless, their names are listed here in remembrance of their vital assistance. To the best of the author's memory, the following persons—living and dead—are respectfully acknowledged for having performed vital services in the research of this volume:

Terry Alford, Anne R. Ashmore, Janice K. Broderick, Christabelle Brown, Michael Burlingame, Mary Carey, Linda Clark, J. Winston Coleman, Jr., Carolyn S. Denton, G. Fay Dickerson, Georgia M. Dudley, Richard E. Dunn, Jennifer Ericson, Kathleen C. Eustis, Bonnie Jean Everhart, Peggy M. Farrow, Linda Garvert, Mary Jane Ginter, Charles H. Glatfelter, Dorothy Graebel, Robert Graham, James C. Holmes, King V. Hostick, Roger D. Hunt, Ruth Hutchcraft, Gordon P. Irvine, Dolores M. Johnson, Paul Kallina, Stanley T. Kusper, Jr., Dorothy Lanham, Tom Lapsley, Charles S. Longley, Robert W. Lyle, Larry Morrison, Leslie Nash, George M. Oldenbourg, Lloyd Ostendorf, James S. Patton, Kenneth E. Pettit, Mark Plummer, Boyd Reese, Judith P. Reid, Lesley M. Richmond, Sally A. Robertson, L. Eugene Rubley, Herbert C. Ruckmick, Lori E. Scherr, Thomas F. Schwartz, William Shlifka, Kathy Shurtleff, Alto & Hilda Sneller, Barbara M. Soper, Sunderine Temple, Jacquelyn H. Thomas, Robert D. Uteg, Alex. Weir, Doris R. Wenzel, Quintin Mathias Porter, Robert Zinsmeister, Jr., and Ann V. Todd.

A number of scholarly institutions have been of great assistance: Illinois State Archives, Illinois State Historical Library, Illinois State Library, and the Lincoln Library in Springfield, Illinois. Certain staff members of The Library of Congress have aided the author, too. Their individual names are mentioned above.

Table of Contents

Drawing by Lloyd Ostendorf

Abraham and Mary Lincoln talk with the Rev. Dr. James Smith in front of the First
Presbyterian Church in Springfield, Illinois

Introduction

For many years, this author has sifted slowly through voluminous collections of primary source materials in order to tell the story of Abraham Lincoln's experience with religion. It has proved to be a most interesting but difficult quest, for Lincoln lived an extremely complicated life and kept so many of his personal thoughts buried within his keen mind and refused to share them. Even so, it has been possible to uncover a number of important documents which have never been cited previously in a study of Lincoln's theological beliefs. In addition, Mary Todd's church affiliations have been searched out and described here, because this cultured Kentucky lady certainly exerted a tremendous influence upon her highly-inquisitive husband. Also, the church experiences of the Lincoln children have been examined in detail. Actually, this study might be considered a biography of the Lincolns.

So that all interested readers may be fully aware of the author's prejudices in this matter, it is only proper to reveal the author's own religious background. As a young lad he was baptized (March 29, 1936) into the First Baptist Church of Richwood, Ohio. On April 14, 1957, he and his late wife, Lois, joined the First Presbyterian Church in Springfield, Illinois. There, the author was ordained a Deacon on January 19, 1958. Following a six-year hiatus away from this city, he returned. He was installed again as a Deacon on December 13, 1964, served as Vice Chairman of the Board, and later became Chairman. On January 7, 1968, he received ordination as an Elder. In recent years he has not been a regular attendant.

In Springfield, Illinois, the author is a Life Member of St. Paul's Lodge No. 500, Ancient, Free & Accepted Masons. He is also a Life Member and a Thirty-third Degree Scottish Rite Mason as well as a Knight Templar in the York Rite (a Christian organization), and a Knight in the Order of the Red Cross of Constantine. He also holds membership in Ansar Temple, Ancient Arabic Order, Nobles of the Mystic Shrine, and sat for six years on the Board for the Shrine Hospitals of North America.

In his capacity as an Elder, the author preached in First Church on February 8, 1970, February 9, 1975, and March 21, 1976. While escorting distinguished guests, it has been his privilege to sit with them in the Lincoln Family Pew, No. 20, which now stands in the sanctuary of the current building at the northwest corner of Seventh and Capitol.

Upon occasion, the author has also delivered sermons in other churches. On April 20, 1975, he spoke to the Unitarian Universalistic Abraham Lincoln Fellowship at 215 West Elliott in Springfield, Illinois. He preached on January 11, 1976, for the Bicentennial service of the First Congregational Church in Springfield, Illinois. Another personal highlight in his career occurred when he occupied the renown pulpit of the New York Avenue Presbyterian Church in Washington, D. C., during the afternoon of February 16, 1975. During the morning worship service, he and his wife were allowed to sit in the Lincoln Pew, No. B 14.

For these few sermons, the author has generally chosen a text related to Lincoln's religious faith. As his research progressed slowly but steadily, it finally became evident to him that Lincoln actually uttered many prophetic statements and functioned for his Nation reflecting the patterns of the prophets of old. He, too, dreamed dreams. He oftentimes pointed out the many visions recorded in the Holy Scriptures. Senator Stephen A. Douglas once accused Lincoln of wanting to go into the Senate on his "qualifications as a prophet." And Lincoln even foresaw his own tragic assassination through a shocking revelation which came to him one night in 1865 while he lay sleeping fitfully in the historic White House. Thus, it seems only proper to call him an inspired prophet.

Some, including those who follow the teachings of The Church of Jesus Christ of Latter-day Saints, insist that God has sent prophets to this troubled Earth whenever mortals found themselves in dire need of inspired leadership. In the years just before and after 1861, the Union discovered itself to be in just such a critical situation. Into the very midst of this fratricidal dilemma the Sovereign Grand Architect of the Universe seems to have dispatched the incomparable Abraham Lincoln as a savior and prophet.

Father Abraham undoubtedly recognized the role he had been foreordained to play in this drama. For example, on his way toward Washington to be inaugurated, he revealed to anxious listeners in New Jersey that he would "be most happy indeed if I shall be an humble instrument in the hands of the Almighty . . . ."

Once firmly established in the seat of power, President Lincoln proceeded to lead his troubled people out of the wilderness at the sacrifice of his own precious life. Like Moses, he did not live to see the "promised land."

But though Lincoln eventually thought of himself as God's own servant, he never inscribed his name upon the membership roll of any denomination. Actually, he seems to have started life as a doubter or skeptic. However, his faith and belief gradually matured until he could utter on August 14, 1862, that "It is difficult to make a man miserable while he feels he is worthy of himself, and claims kindred to the great God who made him." Yes, he came to believe there was a God who created the Earth and mankind. Yet Lincoln declined to give allegiance to any one church or group of worshippers. It would seem that Abraham Lincoln's religion lay far above the arguments and dogma of denominations.

It is the author's hope that he can somewhat explain why Lincoln never formally joined any one organized religious body. Just what did Lincoln think of organized religion? We shall never know for certain, but Lincoln's frequent references to God and his acknowledgment of suffering fellow men exceeded that exhibited by most clergymen who touched his all-too-brief mortal existence. Both ministers and laymen in Lincoln's day—with self-righteous authority—seemed bent on establishing numerous pietistic rules governing the admission of members and the complete regulation of their lives once they entered a spiritual fold.

To trespass against these stern ecclesiastical codes quickly brought embarrassing public censure or dismissal from the congregation. For instance, some Ruling Elders of the Presbyterian Church poked brazenly into the personal lives of parishioners at the first veiled hint of wrongdoing brought to their sharp ears by despicable gossip. If they themselves lacked the physical courage to make the investigation, the Elders generally shoved that awesome responsibility off into the minister's trained hands.

What constituted some of these heinous crimes? Well, dancing, for one. Many churches, among them the Presbyterian, deemed social dancing a deadly sin. Would Lincoln have asked for membership knowing the penalty for dancing? He had attended dances—even served at least once as a manager. Lincoln would never have allowed some sanctimonious inquisitor to probe blindly into his private actions. Lawyer Lincoln once declared the "higher matter of eternal consequences" for each person's earthly shortcomings should be left between that human and his "maker."

It seems highly unlikely that as an astute politician, Lincoln would add his name to the membership of one denomination and risk offending all the other religious orders and churches. Other reasons for Lincoln's non-membership are outlined in the following pages. In conclusion, however, it is the author's opinion that Mr. Lincoln exhibited the most truly religious attitudes of any man who ever sat in the august Executive Mansion.

February 12, 1995   Springfield, Illinois
Wayne C. Temple, Ph. D., F.R.S.A., Chief Deputy Director, Illinois State Archives

Drawing by Lloyd Ostendorf

President-elect Abraham with his family in Pew No. 20 of the
First Presbyterian Church in Springfield, Illinois.

Lincoln's "Political Religion"

Abraham Lincoln's love and respect for the law was almost a religion to him. He declared on January 27, 1838: "Let reverence for the laws, be breathed by every American mother, to the lisping babe, that prattles on her lap—let it be taught in schools, in seminaries, and in colleges—let it be written in Primers, spelling books, and in Almanacs—let it be preached from the pulpit, proclaimed in legislative halls, and enforced in courts of justice. And, in short, let it become the *political religion* of the nation and let the old and the young, the rich and the poor, the grave and the gay, of all sexes and tongues, and colors and conditions, sacrifice unceasingly upon its altars." Laws, Lincoln declared, "should be religiously observed."

Abraham Lincoln's Address Before the Young Men's Lyceum of
Springfield, Illinois, January 27, 1838.
Also in Basler, ed., *The Collected Works of Abraham Lincoln*, I, 112.

Photo by Alto and Hilda Snells

Little Pigeon Church

Thomas and Abraham Lincoln constructed the Little Pigeon Baptist Church in Perry County, Indiana, where they lived.

Chapter One—Genesis

Neither shall thy name any more be called Abram, but thy name shall be Abraham;
for a father of many nations have I made thee.
And I will make thee exceeding fruitful, and I will make nations of thee, and Kings
shall come out of thee.

Genesis 17:5-6

For years prior to his becoming nationally famous, numerous persons and careless newspaper editors often spelled Lincoln's first name as "Abram." With his soft Kentucky drawl, one can readily understand why this noisome error occurred. But as the newly-chosen Republican candidate for President of the United States, Lincoln quickly complained to one gentleman who had misspelled his name in print: "It seems as if the question whether my first name is 'Abraham' or 'Abram' will never be settled." "It is 'Abraham'," he insisted.[1]

Eventually, most interested citizens knew the name of the tall Illinois lawyer who emerged from out of the midwest to become the first Republican President. Soon the beleaguered North referred to their courageous leader as "Father Abraham." If one counts the Northern States as "nations," he, too, became a leader of "many nations." No doubt Union soldiers and civilians alike called him "Father Abraham" because of certain passages in the Bible. In those days, fewer books existed for readers to peruse, and most literate persons knew the Holy Word extremely well. Over time, the fascinating story of Lincoln's inspirational life has influenced countless struggling people in countries all over the world. Kings and leaders have followed his sage advice through the written word.

Many writers and speakers have claimed the immortal Abraham Lincoln as a member of their own particular denomination, but he never formally united with any church. Even some ordained gentlemen of the cloth have tried to make Lincoln a secret member of their congregation, saying they had baptized him in this creek or that.[2] Their assertions are false. In addition to political considerations, our Sixteenth President shied away from joining organizations, no matter how worthy.

The lack of church membership certainly does not bar a person from spiritual beliefs. We must examine Lincoln's religious heritage in order to understand this great man's spiritual thoughts and actions. What were his religious roots?

The name Lincoln comes from the British Isles. Native Britons, before the coming of the Romans, had established a settlement which they called Lindun, one hundred and twenty miles north of London. Within the first century after the birth of Christ, the Roman Empire expanded from the Continent into England and soon built a fortress for its legions at this spot which they called Lindum. When the Roman soldiers marched farther north to fight the Scots, this settlement became a municipality or "colonia"—thus the name Lindocolonia. Gradually, the spelling of the town was shortened simply to Lincoln. In fact, some early residents in this municipality identified themselves as being from Lincoln. In the *Doomsday Book* there is an Alfred de Lincoln listed in 1086. He was an Anglo-Saxon but had married a Norman woman, evidently a descendant of the victorious Normans who had crossed the English Channel in 1066. By the "de," one might assume that he had accepted the French spelling of his name, meaning "from Lincoln."

In the 13th Century, there were Lincolns at Great Yarmouth on the east coast of Norfolk, bordering on the North Sea. Being from this area, they might have had ancestors who were Celts, Britons, Anglo-Saxons, Danes, or Norman French. This question cannot be answered. But here we do find one William de Lincoln. These early Lincolns must have practiced Roman Catholicism since that was the established religion at that time. However, when Henry VIII, who reigned from 1509-47, disestablished the Roman Catholic Church and became head of his own Church of England, the Lincolns must have conformed to the new religion of their Sovereign. They did not accept the return to Roman Catholicism during Queen Mary's reign (1553-58) because in Norwich many Lincolns revolted and as a result a few were hanged, drawn and quartered.

President Lincoln's direct line of ancestors came from Swanton Morley and Hingham in Norfolk. His first known progenitor was one Robert Lincoln of Hingham who died in 1543. His son, Robert, Jr., died in 1556. His son, Richard, who spelled his name "Lincolne," was a churchwarden from 1599 to his death in 1620. Richard's eldest son, Edward, being disinherited, moved to Hingham and died in 1640. Edward's son, Samuel Lincoln, was baptized in St. Andrew's Church at Hingham on August 24, 1622. Prior to this date, Queen Elizabeth I (1558-1603) had returned the state religion to the Church of England, and yet her successor, James I from Scotland (1603-25) had given encouragement to Roman Catholics, and his Bishops tried to reintroduce some old Catholic usages, especially in the placing of the communion

Bust of Abraham Lincoln in St. Andrew's Church.

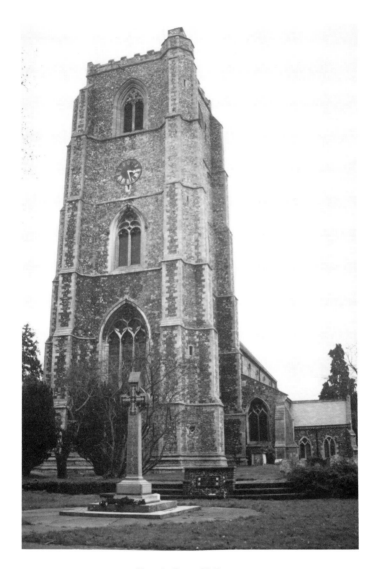

Photo by Peggy M. Farrow

St. Andrew's Church, Hingham Parish, County of Norfolk, England. Here, Samuel Lincoln was baptized Aug. 24, 1622. He emigrated to Massachusetts and became the first American ancestor of Abraham Lincoln.

See also M. E. Lonsdale, *Hingham and St. Andrew's Church* (Wymondham, Norfolk: Geo. R. Reeve, Ltd., n. d.).

table, etc. Charles I (1625-49) was even worse as far as the Anglicans were concerned. As a result, the Lincolns and their minister, Robert Peck, became extremely unhappy with these Popish practices and joined the dissenters in their parish who wanted to purify the church and thus became "Puritans." By this time, many of the Lincolns in Hingham were yeomen, minor gentry or even gentlemen. Those closely-related Lincolns living in Swanton Morley worshipped in All Saints Church.

Not being the eldest son of Edward Lincoln, Gentleman, Samuel Lincoln could look forward to little or no inheritance. So, he became apprenticed to Francis Lawes, a weaver of Norwich, and left for New England with his master on April 8, 1637. They went to Salem, Massachusetts, but Samuel had two brothers already living in Hingham, Massachusetts, and soon departed to join them. There, he worshipped in the Old Ship Church which for a time was under the leadership of Robert Peck. Samuel died in 1690.

Evidently, Samuel came from a long line of independent-thinking and strong-willed forefathers, because he married Martha Lyford, a daughter of the Rev. John Lyford who had been a minister with the Pilgrims but had been expelled from their colony for his misbehavior. In addition, he was even said to have favored Episcopal services.

In 1657, Samuel and Martha had a son named Mordecai. He was the first Lincoln to have the name Mordecai, and it came from his mother's side of the family. He became a noted and wealthy iron worker. Mordecai (1657-1727) married Sarah Jones, daughter of Abraham Jones. They named one of their sons Abraham Lincoln (1688-1745) after the wife's father, and here is the first use of the name Abraham in the Lincoln clan. He moved to Monmouth County, New Jersey with his older brother, Mordecai, Jr. (1686-1736). The latter married Hannah Saltar and they ended up in Berks County, Pennsylvania. Their first son was named John Lincoln (1716-1788). He would marry and move to Rockingham County, Virginia.

Lincoln divulged that the paternal side of his ancestral line stemmed from Quaker stock, "though in later times they have fallen away from the peculiar habits of that people."[3] For years Lincoln scholars shook their unbelieving heads and replied solemnly that Father Abraham simply had not known his lineage and knew not whereof he spoke. Apparently, these disbelievers did not search the original records for verification or disproof. Then, in recent years, David S. Keiser of Philadelphia finally ascertained that Abraham Lincoln had been right all along in his recital of family tradition. In the minutes of Concord Meeting (Concordville, Pennsylvania) he discovered that Enoch Flower and Rebecca Barnard had married in 1713—at some date prior to April 8—after having their intentions published twice in Meeting. Enoch, a weaver whose father had toiled as a farmer, and his wife, raised a daughter named Rebecca who married John Lincoln on July 5, 1743. Thus, the President's great, great grandparents were both Quakers.[4]

From Berks County, Pennsylvania, the Lincolns migrated to Rockingham County, Virginia, as Abraham later stated.[5] "Virginia John" Lincoln, as his kinsmen called him, settled on Linville Creek about 1767. From his will, we know that he professed to be a Christian. In fact, he probably had changed his denominational loyalty from Quaker to Baptist.[6]

"Virginia John's" son, Captain Abraham Lincoln (1744-1786) followed the Baptist persuasion and lies buried in the Long Run Baptist Church Cemetery of Jefferson County, Kentucky, eighteen miles east of Louisville. When the old stone church was replaced by a brick structure, the new building was constructed over his grave in 1844. Abraham's wife, Bathsheba Lincoln, is interred in the First Regular Baptist Church's Mill Creek Cemetery in Hardin County, Kentucky,[7] despite the fact she was Episcopalian. This may have been due to the fact that the Baptist Church was the closest church available. Their son, Thomas Lincoln (1778-1851) is known to have preferred the Baptist faith, being a member of the Little Mount Separate Baptist Church in Kentucky.[8] And yet a Methodist Episcopal minister, the Rev. Jesse Head, performed the ceremony which united Thomas with Nancy Hanks on June 12, 1806. But Head was probably chosen merely because he was a fellow cabinetmaker and readily available.

In 1816, Thomas removed with his spouse and little brood to a wild frontier territory about to become the new State of Indiana. There, in Perry County in southwestern Indiana, Thomas Lincoln received a contract to supervise the building of the Little Pigeon Baptist Church in 1821, for Thomas, like Christ's earthly father, also labored as a carpenter as well as a farmer. Young Abraham helped his sire with this construction.

Two years later, on June 7, 1823, Thomas joined this small church by submitting a letter from the Little Mount Separate Baptist Church back in Kentucky. His second wife, Sarah Bush Johnston Lincoln, united, too, with this Indiana congregation—but by experience. Just five days afterwards, Little Pigeon's congregation chose the craftsman Thomas Lincoln as one of its Trustees, and eventually the callow Abraham started to work there as a

Photo by Peggy M. Farrow

All Saints Church, Swanton Morley, County of Norfolk, England. This was where some of Abraham Lincoln's early ancestors worshipped.
See also *Rev. R. N. Usher, M. A., Swanton Morley Church*
(Norwich: Soman-Wherry Press, 1945).

Photo Courtesy of Captain John B. McCollister

Capt. Abraham Lincoln's widow, Bathsheba, lies buried in the old First Regular Baptist Church's Mill Creek Cemetery which is now called the Lincoln Memorial Cemetery on the Fort Knox Military Reservation in Kentucky. Her stone reads:

"BATHSHEBA OR BERSHEBA LINCOLN
WHOSE GRANDSON WAS THE SIXTEENTH PRESIDENT OF THE UNITED STATES, MARRIED CAPTAIN ABRAHAM LINCOLN IN VIRGINIA, ACCOMPANIED HIM OVER THE MOUNTAINS TO KENTUCKY, WORKED BY HIS SIDE TO CREATE A LANDED ESTATE,
UNTIL HE WAS KILLED BY THE INDIANS IN MAY, 1786."

In the base of the tombstone is a piece of stone from the Lincoln Tomb at Springfield, Illinois, presented by Gov. William G. Stratton on May 18, 1960.

sexton. On April 10, 1824, Thomas was appointed to attend a church conference and on October 9 of that year was named to a church discipline committee to investigate a married couple who had separated. He helped support the church by donating corn. However, in September 1828, he resigned from his trusteeship. He even thought of leaving this church with a letter of dismission but was convinced to remain a member. Although Abraham Lincoln's sister, Sarah, had added her name to the membership roll of Little Pigeon Baptist Church on April 4, 1826, Abraham did not.

Abraham Lincoln's childhood began in a Christian home where both parents and his sister worshipped regularly as members of the Baptist faith. Neighbors recalled years later that young Abraham sometimes went to church but not always. Did he believe in a Supreme Being at this time? We shall never know. Nevertheless, the stepmother, Sarah, subsequently announced to an inquirer that she believed in Heaven and that she expected to join her husband, Thomas, and her stepson, Abraham, there some day. Sarah also declared that "Abe" had been a good boy. A neighbor, Elizabeth Crawford, remembered "Abe" as being a very moral and kind youth. Honesty and fairness became an early part of his very being.[9]

During 1860-1861, while he was posing in the St. Nicholas Hotel at Springfield, Illinois, for the noted Cincinnati sculptor, Thomas D. Jones, the topic of discussion between the Model and the Modeler turned to religion. Artist Jones disclosed that he sometimes felt a deep curiosity about a person's faith. To this casual remark Lincoln replied, "Well, what do you think of mine?" Jones ventured a guess that judging from the "peculiar characteristics" of Lincoln's face he originated from the Hard-Shell Baptist persuasion. "You are right," Lincoln readily admitted, "my father was a member of the Baptist Church, but I am not."[10]

Abraham Lincoln made his acquaintance with the Bible at a very early age. Thomas Lincoln owned a family Bible. Not only did Abraham see one at home in his cabin, but also in the primitive schools of the frontier. The Bible became a textbook for him. "We had no reading book," Lincoln revealed, "and we read out of the Bible." "The class would stand up in a row," explained Lincoln, "the teacher in front of them, and read verses, turn about."[11]

Upon one occasion during the Civil War, President Lincoln related a humorous story to Senator John Brooks Henderson, from Missouri, concerning this part of his early schooling. Lincoln remembered that while queued up before one teacher, certainly in Indiana, the lesson in reading that particular day had been taken from that portion of the Bible which dealt with the Hebrews in the fiery furnace (Daniel 3:12-30). "As none of us were very good readers," admitted the President, "we were in the habit of counting ahead and each one practicing on his particular verse. Standing next to me was a red-headed, freckled-faced boy, who was the poorest reader in the class. It so fell out that the names of the Hebrew children appeared in his verse. He managed to work through Shadrack, fell down at Meshack, and went all to pieces at Abednego. The reading went on, and in due course of time came round again, but when the turn came near enough for the boy to see his verse, he pointed to it in great consternation, and whispered to me, 'Look! there come them three d[amne]d fellers again.'" Immediately after finishing this droll tale, Lincoln pointed toward a White House window and exclaimed to Senator Henderson, "And there come those three same fellows." Henderson peered out the casement and saw Senators Benjamin F. Wade, Thaddeus Stevens and Charles Sumner coming up the walk. For days, they had been badgering the President to issue a proclamation of emancipation for the Negroes, and it appeared that they were calling upon Lincoln once more to plead this same cause.[12]

It is quite possible that Lincoln and his youthful companions often perused the Old Testament even when not working on a school assignment. Here, they could quietly relish numerous erotic passages which dealt with rather explicit sexual matters. There was practically no other handy printed source which could fulfill their prurient curiosity about the opposite sex. Furthermore, there was small risk that they would be reprimanded or punished for reading the Bible.

It seems safe to say that the first truly large church building which young Abraham Lincoln ever saw was in New Orleans. When he was just nineteen years of age, he floated into the historic and picturesque old city on a flatboat during the year 1828. He came ashore on the east side of Jackson Square, and the magnificent St. Louis Cathedral stands in all its glory on the opposite side. Although this basilica is a Roman Catholic edifice, the inquisitive flatboatman probably examined its architecture inside and out. And he must have asked about its history, also. It was, and still is, one of the unforgettable landmarks in the "City That Care Forgot," although it has been greatly altered since Lincoln's day.

If young Abraham Lincoln, while living in southern Indiana, did not put the local ministers upon a pedestal, there was one preacher that he greatly admired—from a great distance. This was Rev. Mason Locke Weems (1759-

1825) who had written a life of George Washington. Weems, had been ordained in Maryland as an Anglican Church priest, but he later worked as a book salesman. In "the earliest days" of his "being able to read," Abraham Lincoln somehow acquired a copy of this book by "Parson" Weems and simply devoured it from beginning to end. It was a very patriotic volume, telling—among other things—of the great political struggles and armed battles during the American Revolution. This very readable story also imparted moral lessons to the impressionable young Lincoln. He never forgot it or its author. At a very tender age, Weems' work started Lincoln to thinking about liberty and how we had obtained our national independence. It, no doubt, influenced his later stand against slavery.[13]

Abraham Lincoln's first teacher in Kentucky at the Knob Creek School was Zachariah Riney, a.Roman Catholic. Although this scholar's religious beliefs do not seem to have greatly influenced young Abraham, the experience probably made him more tolerant of other denominations. His own uncle, Mordecai Lincoln, had married Mary Mudd, a Catholic, but there is little evidence that the two Lincoln families visited each other very often.[14]

There is an old tradition that just before Nancy (Hanks) Lincoln died on October 5, 1818, she called Sarah and Abraham to her bedside and admonished them to be good children, to be kind to their father and to each other. She hoped they both would continue to live their lives as they had been taught and would love, revere and worship God. One of the spiritual leaders of the local Baptist Church, Young Lamar, prayed over the body of Nancy Lincoln as she was interred in a crude grave near the cabin. However, this same family tradition relates that the Lincolns wanted a minister to conduct a regular funeral ceremony for Nancy. So, it is said, little Abraham himself indited a letter to the Rev. David Elkin at the Little Mount Baptist Church back in Kentucky and petitioned him to come and perform the rites of burial over his mother's last resting place. In due course, the Rev. Elkin did appear in southern Indiana to visit relatives and gave a funeral sermon for Nancy Lincoln. It would seem that the Lincolns of Indiana years conducted their simple lives within the confines of the Baptist religion.[15]

References

1   Lincoln to George Ashmun, Springfield, Ill., June 4, 1860, in Roy P. Basler, Marion D. Pratt and Lloyd A. Dunlap, eds., *The Collected Works of Abraham Lincoln* (New Brunswick: Rutgers Univ. Press, 1953), IV, 68.

2   Jim R. Martin, *The Secret Baptism of Abraham Lincoln* (Sesser, Ill.: Jim Martin Printing, 1987).

3   Autobiography written for John L. Scripps, ca. June, 1860, in Basler, ed., *The Collected Works*, IV, 60-61.

4   J. Henry Lea and J. R. Hutchinson, *The Ancestry of Abraham Lincoln* (Boston: Houghton Mifflin Co., 1909); William E. Barton, *The Lineage of Lincoln* (Indianapolis: The Bobbs-Merrill Co., 1929); David S. Keiser, "Quaker Ancestors for Lincoln," *Lincoln Herald*, LXIII, 134-137 (Fall, 1961); Francis E. Wylie, "Missing Lincoln Link Found, With Certain Mysteries," *Genealogy Digest*, XIX, 15-18 (Summer, 1988); Edward Steers, Jr., "Lincoln's Ancestry: A New Document," *Lincoln Herald*, XCI, 13-16 (Spring, 1989).

5   Basler, ed., *The Collected Works*, IV, 60.

6   John W. Wayland, *The Lincolns in Virginia* (Staunton, Va.: McClure Print. Co., 1946), 35, 48.

7   *Ibid.*, 48; Charles H. Coleman, "Lincoln's Lincoln Grandmother," *Jour. Ill. State Hist. Soc.*, LII, 80 (Spring, 1959); R. Gerald McMurtry, *The Kentucky Lincolns on Mill Creek* (Harrogate: Lincoln Memorial Univ., 1939), 60, 51; Harvey H. Smith, *Lincoln and the Lincolns* (N. Y.: Pioneer Publications, 1931), 33, 68, 74.

8   Louis Austin Warren, *Lincoln's Parentage & Childhood* (N. Y.: Century Co., 1926), 243.

9   Warren, *Lincoln's Youth: Indiana Years* (N. Y.: Appleton, Century, Crofts, 1959), 87, 115, 121; Emanuel Hertz, ed., *The Hidden Lincoln* (N. Y.: The Viking Press, 1938), 292, 350, 353, 366.

10 T. D. Jones, "Recollections of Mr. Lincoln," Cincinnati *Commercial*, Oct. 18, 1871, p. 4, cc. 5-6. See also Wayne C. Temple, *Abraham Lincoln and Others at the St. Nicholas* (Springfield: St. Nicholas Corp., 1968).

11 Basler, ed., *The Collected Works*, II, 94-96; Isaac N. Phillips, ed., *Abraham Lincoln By Some Men Who Knew Him* (Bloomington: Pantagraph Printing Co., 1910), 67.

12 Phillips, ed., *Abraham Lincoln*, 66-69. Henderson (1826-1913) took his seat in the Senate on January 29, 1862, and must have heard Lincoln's anecdote

shortly after this date but before September 22, 1862, when Lincoln issued his Emancipation Proclamation to take effect on January 1, 1863.

13   Basler, ed., *The Collected Works*, IV, 233-234.

14   Warren, *Lincoln's Parentage & Childhood*, 213, 221.

15   Warren, *Lincoln's Youth*, 54-56.

Drawing by Lloyd Ostendorf
Courtesy of Phillip H. Wagner

When Abraham Lincoln tied up his flatboat at New Orleans in 1828,
he saw the magnificent St. Louis Cathedral, a basilica of the Roman Catholic Church.

"At twenty one I came to Illinois," declared Abraham Lincoln to his friend Jesse W. Fell. In passing through Vincennes, Indiana, he went by St. Francis Xavier Roman Catholic Church whose white-spired architecture must have caught his attention. Just a little more than a year later, Abraham struck off on his own. Like a piece of flotsam or jetsam, he drifted slowly ashore at the struggling pioneer village of New Salem, which never had three hundred people in it, and for the first time in his life enjoyed an independent career.[1] His experiences there atop that river bluff were not unlike those of a college student away from home. In fact, New Salem on the Sangamon River turned out to be his alma mater, a place where he read new books, studied difficult subjects—such as surveying and law—and conversed with quaint backwoods philosophers like John A. Kelso. His military service in the Black Hawk War and his later duty in the Illinois State Militia were even similar to a student's R.O.T.C. service.

Quite naturally, like so many curious and probing freshmen, Lincoln started to question many of the false trappings and incongruities of orthodox religions. Some of his close New Salem friends even thought young Lincoln talked like an agnostic. Some local members of the Baptist faith had erected a log building for a church just one mile southwest of New Salem on Greene's Rocky Branch. Lincoln did not attend their worship meetings. On weekdays, William Mentor Graham (1800-1886), who signed his name simply "Mentor" Graham, taught school in this same structure. Graham, himself, had been raised as a Baptist. But the independent Lincoln did not attend school here. He studied on his own. Of course, he probably borrowed books from Mentor Graham if he possessed any which the inquisitive Lincoln desired to read.[2]

Countless thousands of developing striplings have gone through this same period of doubting. For example, at the age of fifteen summers, Robert Browning—who later won wide renown as a famous poet—militantly challenged, publicly, the whole basis of Christianity. And yet, in due time, he regained his belief in God and later presented his own son for baptism.[3] In 1841, Browning put these words into one of the little songs which Pippa sings in the drama *Pippa Passes*: "God's in His heaven—All's right with the world!" Browning's faith had returned.[4]

Lincoln described this important period of his life as being one in which he "inclined to believe in what I understand is called the 'Doctrine of Necessity'—that is, that the human mind is impelled to action, or held in rest by some power, over which the mind itself has no control; and I have sometimes . . . tried to maintain this opinion in argument."[5]

To further elaborate on his personal beliefs on March 9, 1832, Abraham Lincoln stated to the voters of his county that he greatly favored learning to the point that "every man may receive at least, a moderate education, and thereby be enabled to read the histories of his own and other countries . . . being able to read the scriptures and other works, both of a religious and moral nature, for themselves."[6] Young Lincoln—even then called "Honest Abe"—placed a great value on morality and the lessons to be learned from the Bible, even though he did not attend church much or desire to affiliate with a particular denomination.

As Lincoln grew to manhood in various rude, frontier cabins, the one book that was available to him was the Bible. This volume he read and reread until he knew the Holy Word as few of his contemporaries did and as even fewer of our contemporaries probably know it today. His wife would later report in writing that the Scriptures were "a book so very dear to <u>him</u>, and which it was his delight to read . . . ."[7]

A close friend, Charles Maltby, who aided Lincoln as an assistant when both clerked in a tiny general store owned by Denton Offutt at New Salem, declared: "Lincoln, at this period of his life, was not a religious man." "He was not a member of any church," said Maltby, "nor did he subscribe to any religious creed, but deep in his heart and nature was implanted a religious structure which was truly perfect." Maltby discovered that Lincoln "had read and studied the Bible much, in his childhood and youth." This old colleague vouched that Lincoln also believed in God. To explain why he did not unite with a religious body, Lincoln promised that "When any church will inscribe over its altar as its sole qualification for membership, the Savior's condensed statement of the substance of both law and gospel: 'Thou shalt love the Lord thy God with all thy heart, and with all thy soul, and with all thy strength, and thy neighbor as thy self,' that church I will join with all my heart and all my soul." Lincoln later repeated this excuse to the Honorable Henry Champion Deming (1815-1872), a member of Congress.[8]

Of course, Lincoln referred to the First and Second Commandments found in St. Mark 12:30-31, as well as other places in the Bible. It would appear that the logical "Railsplitter" could not abide ministers, congregations and theocratic assemblies which proclaimed ritual, dogma, and creeds above truth, moral right, law and the simple love of God and fellowmen.

Even as a young man, Lincoln upon occasion exhibited a broad streak of fatalism in his religious beliefs. In speaking about the inheritance given the American people by their heroic founding fathers, he declared that their blessings would continue on "to the latest generation that fate shall permit the world to know."[9] Note that he did not attribute the future to God but rather to "fate."

On July 4, 1842, Lincoln revealed to his intimate friend, Joshua Fry Speed, that he "always was superstitious," too. Yet he thought of himself as one of God's instruments. "God made me one of the instruments of bringing your Fanny and you together, which union, I have no doubt He had foreordained," Lincoln divulged. Then, once again Lincoln mentioned fate. "I was drawn to it as by fate," admitted Lincoln.[10] Here is an additional mention of predestination which permeated his very being. This belief became much more prominent when his national responsibilities as President of the United States became very heavy upon his shoulders.

With the passage of time, Lincoln perhaps somewhat modified his belief in fate and superstition. And yet, Mary Lincoln admitted to William H. Herndon, as late as 1866, that her late husband's philosophy had been "what is to be will be, and no [prayers] of ours can arrest nor reverse the decree."[11] Henry C. Whitney, an old circuit companion, also thought that Lincoln had remained a fatalist to the end.[12]

While living at New Salem, it would appear that Abraham Lincoln did not have a very high opinion of all ministers of the gospel. At least we know that he held the Rev. Peter Cartwright in very low esteem. Cartwright, a boisterous circuit-riding Methodist preacher, freely mixed blind religion with local politics. On August 6, 1832, he had defeated Lincoln at the polls for a seat in the Illinois General Assembly at Vandalia. Later, in 1846, when Lincoln ran against him for Congress, Cartwright whispered around the district that Lincoln was an infidel. This backwoods preacher had perhaps also used this same electioneering tactic back in 1832, but in 1846 Lincoln beat him.

At any rate, on May 30, 1834, the Rev. Cartwright printed a very prejudiced article in the *Christian Advocate and Journal*, a Methodist publication. It called for ardent Methodists to come out west and become teachers in the common schools. For Whigs, like Lincoln, who advocated the separation of Church and State, such a biased religious plea was anathema.

In a reply—authored by Lincoln on September 7, 1834, but published over the name of Samuel Hill, a New Salem neighbor—the author answered Cartwright with blistering and satirical words. Because Abraham Lincoln had been elected as a State Representative on August 4 of that year, he certainly did not wish his authorship to be known. Besides, Sam Hill had been publicly berated and humiliated by Cartwright. So the former certainly gave permission for Rep. Lincoln to use his name. In this way, Hill obtained some measure of revenge against Cartwright, too.

The writer, in answering Cartwright, declared that if he thought that Cartwright's "article was written with a view to aid the true religion in any shape, I should not meddle with it; or, if I could conceive that it was intended to vindicate the character of the 'West,' I should be the last to censure it." However, the writer was completely satisfied that the article was merely a despicable political device or maneuver. Furthermore, he identified Cartwright as being "a most ab[a]ndoned hypocrite (I will not say in religion— for of this I pretend to know nothing—but) in politics, I venture to handle it without restraint."

The author proceeded to state: "the people in this country are in some degree priest ridden." He pointed out that old Uncle Peter bestrided the poor people more than any one else in the region. He possessed "one of the largest and best improved farms in Sangamon [C]ounty." But how had he obtained it? "Only by the contributions he has been able to levy upon and collect from a priest ridden church." "It will not do," exclaimed the writer, "to say he has earned it 'by the sweat of his brow.'" This was a favorite expression used by Lincoln to renounce those who did not work for the bread they ate. Lincoln continued to use this quotation from Genesis 3:19 the rest of his life. It goes: "In the sweat of thy face shalt thou eat bread . . . ." Although Cartwright "may sometimes labor, all know that he spends the greater part of his time in preaching and electioneering."

In addition, the writer divulged that Cartwright had publicly boasted of "mustering his militia, alluding to the Methodist Church, and marching and counter-marching them in favor of or against this or that candidate—why, this is not only hard riding, but it is riding clear off the track, stumps, logs and blackjack brush, notwithstanding." Abraham Lincoln had received a Captain's commission in the 31st Regiment of the Illinois State Militia on December 20, 1832, and certainly was familiar with the annual muster and drill of his Rifle Company. "For a church or community to be priest ridden by a man who will take their money and treat them kindly in return is bad enough in all con-science;" said the writer, "but to be ridden by one who is continually exposing them to ridicule by making a public boast of his power to ho[odwink] them, is insufferable." Cartwright had "two sets of opinions, one for his religious, and one for his political friends; and to plat them together smoothly, presents a task to which his feverish brain is incompetent."[13]

Abraham Lincoln certainly inscribed this piece against the Rev. Mr. Cartwright, and it gives a clear picture of Lincoln's attitude toward men-of-the-cloth at this period of his life. Since it was released without his name being attached to it, he could speak his private thoughts freely. His disdain for Rev. Cartwright was one more reason why the young Abraham Lincoln stayed far away from church services. New Salem proved no different than his earlier experiences with unlettered clergymen. He definitely disliked preachers who dabbled in politics and herded their pastoral flocks like so many unthinking sheep, shaping their minds to suit some religious dogma, political cause, or both.

As a footnote to this story, it can be proved that the Rev. Mr. Cartwright purchased 655.75 acres of land between the years of 1826 and 1833. It lay in Township 17 North, Range 7 West of the Third Principal Meridian, near Pleasant Plains in Sangamon County. This area was later named Cartwright Township.[14]

References

1   Basler, ed., *The Collected Works,* III, 512; II, 327.

2   *Ibid.,* IV, 61-62. In Lincoln's autobiography written for John L. Scripps, he listed all the teachers that he ever had. Mentor Graham is not mentioned! See also Wayne C. Temple, *Lincoln and the Burners at New Salem* (Springfield: Phillips Bros., 1985), 12-13. Graham certainly greatly exaggerated his association with Abraham Lincoln's self-education. Evidently, there was some defect in Mentor Graham's character, because it seems that when he applied to become a member of Clinton Lodge No. 19, A. F. & A.M., at Petersburg, Illinois, he was rejected by the Brothers! *Proceedings of the Grand Lodge of Ilinois 1840-1850* (Freeport: Journal Print., 1892), 349-350.

3   John Maynard, "Robert Browning's Evangelical Heritage," *Browning Institute Studies* (N. Y.: The Browning Institute, 1975), III, 5, 12-13.

4   I passed through such an experience, too. After enrollment in a course at the University of Illinois entitled "A Literary Study of the Bible," I traveled gleefully home for Christmas vacation in 1948 and expounded to my genial father upon the unreliability of the Scriptures. This quiet man with huge shoulders and blue eyes had been forced to quit school after the eighth grade, but within his greying head lay a brilliant mind, and he eagerly read everything at hand—including his own son's college texts. As a Deacon and Trustee of the First Baptist Church in Richwood, Ohio, such a revelation from his only heir must have been anathema to him. Nevertheless, he merely shook his wise old head and predicted that eventually such youthful ideas would change for the better. They did, gradually. However, I probably find more solace in Masonry than in formal religious services.

5   Basler, ed., *The Collected Works,* I, 382.

6   *Ibid.,* I, 8.

7   Mrs. A. Lincoln to Mrs. Off and Mrs. Baker, Washington, D. C., May 16, 1865, in Justin G. Turner and Linda Levitt Turner, eds., *Mary Todd Lincoln: Her Life and Letters* (N. Y.: Alfred A. Knopf, 1972), 230.

8   Charles Maltby, *The Life and Public Services of Abraham Lincoln* (Stockton, Cal.: Daily Independent Steam Power Print., 1884), 32, 42; Henry Champion Deming, *Eulogy of Abraham Lincoln* (Hartford: A. N. Clark & Co., 1865), 42. Lincoln said he could not join "without mental reservation."

9   Basler, ed., *The Collected Works*, I, 108.

10   *Ibid.,* I, 289.

11   Hertz, ed., *The Hidden Lincoln*, 406.

12   Henry C. Whitney, *Life on the Circuit With Lincoln* (Boston: Estes & Lauriat, 1892), 267.

13   Article headed "For the Beardstown Chronicle, New Salem, Sept. 7th, 1834," in *Beardstown Chronicle, And Illinois Military Bounty Land Advertiser*, Nov. 1, 1834, p. 1, cc. 1-2; Douglas L.Wilson, "A Most Abandoned Hypocrite," *American Heritage*, XLV, No. 1, pp. 36-49 (Feb.-Mar., 1994); Prof. Wilson has examined the accounts of two New Salem residents, Caleb Carman and John McNamar, who told Billy Herndon that A. Lincoln had indeed written a newspaper article about Peter Cartwright and signed another's name to it. When the two statements are intermeshed, they show that the story was published between 1833 and 1836 in the *Beardstown Chronicle* and signed by Samuel Hill. Exactly correct. For Lincoln's militia duty, see Wayne C. Temple, *Lincoln-Grant: Illinois Militiamen* (Springfield: Illinois Military and Naval Dept., 1981), 16-20.

14   Federal Tract Book No. 695, p. 523, MS., Illinois State Archives.

Drawing by Dr. Lloyd Ostendorf

From Augustus Koch's "Bird Eye View of Springfield, Illinois," published in 1873.

When the congregation of the First Presbyterian Church moved into their new structure on the same large lot, their initial building was sold to the Springfield Mechanics' Union. In April of 1852, this old church edifice housed, temporarily, the classrooms of Illinois State University. Here, Robert T. Lincoln attended classes. No doubt his parents also visited this place upon occasion, but they never worshipped here.

Chapter Three—Revelation

On the fifteenth of April in 1837, Lincoln took a quiet leave from the small, dying village of New Salem and established his residence in the growing town of Springfield. Only a month and a half earlier it had been voted the capital of Illinois, thanks to the gigantic efforts of Lincoln himself and other legislative cohorts from Sangamon County, referred to as "The Long Nine" because of their unusually tall height. Here, he found a more refined culture than he had previously experienced in the unpolished New Salem.

"I've never been to church yet," confessed Lincoln in a letter written to Mary S. Owens from Springfield on May 7, 1837, "nor probably shall not be soon." "I stay away," he explained, "because I am conscious I should not know how to behave myself." If he was not jesting, Lincoln may have implied that he had not been to a church service for a long time. There was nothing wrong with his public deportment. Since 1834, this rising politician had sat in the General Assembly at Vandalia where he held the respect and admiration of his fellow legislators as floor leader of his Whig Party. About eight months after writing the letter to Mary Owens, Lincoln delivered an address on January 27, 1838, before the Young Men's Lyceum which met in the Baptist Church on the southwest corner of Seventh and Adams streets in Springfield. This was on a Saturday evening, and his topic was "The Perpetuation of Our Political Institutions," but at least Lincoln lectured in a church building and conducted himself with complete and proper decorum.[1] But this was not a religious meeting.

While speaking to the Lyceum, Lincoln alluded to civil and religious liberty which had been won by those who participated in the American Revolution. These accomplishments "will be read of, and recounted, so long as the bible shall be read," declared Lincoln, utilizing the Bible in his remarks. It was often an important source for his public addresses.

On December 26, 1839, Lincoln again drew a religious and political parallel by referring to the Bible. "The Savior of the World," Lincoln pointed out, "chose twelve disciples, and even one of that small number, selected by superhuman wisdom, turned out a traitor and a devil." "And," he continued, "it may not be improper here to add, that Judas carried the bag—was the Sub-Treasurer of the Savior and his disciples."

Actually, the true reason Lincoln quoted the Bible quite frequently but did not attend church lay closer to the fact that he had not found any comfort in a formal worship service which stressed precise rituals, dogmas and catechisms. Nor had he had a "religious experience" often required of prospective members before they could be declared "saved" and allowed to join. But some of his intimate friends suspected that Lincoln remained outside the fold for another reason. Joshua Fry Speed, with whom Lincoln shared a small bedroom during his first days in Springfield, recalled that when he first knew Lincoln, "in early life, he was a skeptic." Speed explained that Lincoln "had tried hard to be a believer, but his reason could not grasp and solve the great problem of redemption as taught."[2] James H. Matheny, who served as his best man, thought Lincoln had "been an infidel in his former life" but that after he rubbed shoulders with men and women of learning changed his impression of formalized religion.[3] A roommate in legislative days, John Todd Stuart, Lincoln's first law partner and a cousin to Mary Todd, related that in "the earliest part of his life" Lincoln seemed to have been an "infidel" but later changed his views.[4]

While addressing the Springfield Washington Temperance Society at noon on February 22, 1842, in the Second Presbyterian Church on the west side of Fourth Street, north of Monroe, Lawyer Lincoln readily admitted in complete candor that he was "not a church member." Yet in this same year, Lincoln is known to have participated in an event commonly associated with formal religious and fraternal practice. His old and trusted friend, Bowling Green, who had been a Justice of the Peace at New Salem during Lincoln's residence there, died suddenly near his old farm home on the evening of February 13, 1842, as a result of apoplexy. Born in North Carolina in 1787, he had eventually come to Clary's Grove about 1819. Much later, he acquired the Northwest Quarter of Section 25 in Township 18 North, Range 7 West of the Third Principal Meridian, a tract just north of New Salem which itself lay in the Southwest Quarter of this same section. Lincoln used the law books of Bowling Green and "practiced" before his court upon occasion. Although a leader of the local Democrats, Green supported Lincoln in his races for the General Assembly, and they became fast friends.

Because the weather that February proved to be extremely cold and the roads impassable, it was decided to inter Bowling Green in a small cemetery near his house but to defer burial ceremonies until later in the year. Having been an active and prominent Mason, his widow, Nancy (Potter) Green, and Masonic friends determined to have a memorial service in better weather. In 1826, Green had attended a meeting of the Grand Lodge of Illinois when it met in Vandalia, quite a distance to travel in those days. Since there was not as yet a Lodge in Petersburg, it fell to Springfield Lodge No. 4 to conduct the Masonic last rites. On September 3, 1842, this Lodge and other members of the Craft assembled in the Green home where Dr. Francis A. McNeill (Jan. 1, 1809—Feb. 3, 1872) preached the sermon. McNeill was not only a Methodist minister but he was also a physician as well as an officer of Lodge No. 4. In fact, the following year he would become the Master of his Lodge. An active Whig and a personal friend of Abraham Lincoln, it was probably he who implored Lincoln, on behalf of the Green family, to accompany the Springfield Lodge members out to the spot of the ceremonies and to deliver the eulogy on Brother Green. One later account of this event reported that the emotional Lincoln was moved to tears and could not finish his brief memorial address. Nevertheless, Abraham Lincoln had witnessed a Methodist minister give a burial service, and he had watched the Masonic Fraternity conduct its last rites for a departed Brother. The latter is quite impressive. Those participating Freemasons, no doubt, marched to the grave site from the Green residence. At a later date, both Bowling and Nancy Green's bodies were removed to Oakland Cemetery at Petersburg.[5]

A powerful feminine influence towards formal religious observance stepped into Abraham Lincoln's life when Mary Ann Todd (1818-1882) of Lexington, Kentucky, arrived suddenly in Springfield, Illinois, during the fall of 1839. Like Lincoln, she bore a very Biblical first name. Mary had come to visit with her sister, Elizabeth Porter Todd, the proud wife of Ninian Wirt Edwards, the son of a governor. Elizabeth had been married since February 18, 1832. Mary and Abraham later became engaged to marry; however, the fearful and doubting Lincoln broke the engagement on January 1, 1841, and the bridegroom-to-be quickly slipped into a deep mental depression.

Since a change of scene might assist him to recover, the extremely unhappy Lincoln paid a visit to the home of Joshua Fry Speed, called "Farmington," near Louisville, Kentucky, during the late summer of 1841. There, Joshua's mother, Lucy G. Speed, presented Lincoln with a Bible and told him to read it for solace. While writing to Mary Speed, Joshua's half sister, on September 27, 1841, Lincoln asked her to "Tell your mother that I have not got her 'present' with me [he was on the circuit]; but that I intend to read it regularly when I return home. I doubt not that it is really, as she says, the best cure for the 'Blues' could one but take it according to the truth." Note Lincoln's last statement: "could one but take it according to the truth." Certainly that was a rather doubting remark. Lincoln was still suffering from the "blues." Yet he never forgot Lucy's kindness. On October 3, 1861, while President, he sent her an autographed photograph of himself, known as 0-55, with these words inscribed under it on the mounting: "For Mrs. Lucy G. Speed, from whose pious hand I accepted the present of an Oxford Bible twenty years ago."[6]

Meanwhile, Mary Todd continued to reside with the Edwardses. Because this proud family preferred the Episcopal faith, Mary attended services at St. Paul's, on the southeast corner of Third and Adams, with her socially-prominent host and hostess. Custom in that era decreed that guests participate in the worship activities of the household which sheltered them. However, there is no document in the original records of the Cathedral Church of St. Paul to indicate that Mary Todd was ever confirmed or baptized into the fellowship of this stately church.

After Joshua Fry Speed finally and rather reluctantly married his Fanny Henning on February 15, 1842, he reported to his old friend Lincoln that marriage, after all, was all right. This encouraged Lincoln to seek again the company of Miss Todd. Dr. Anson G. Henry, Lincoln's physician, advocated that he again start dating Mary. However, the Ninian Edwardses proved rather cool to this renewed proposition. So, Simeon and Eliza L. Francis arranged for Mary and Abraham to meet clandestinely at their home on the southeast corner of Jefferson and Sixth. They had no children and plenty of room in their residence for the lovers to be together, undisturbed.

Simeon Francis, proprietor and editor of the *Sangamo Journal,* was a close political ally of Lincoln's. He had been born on May 8, 1796, in Wethersfield, Connecticut. He migrated to New Haven where he learned the art of printing. Then, he went to New London and published the *New London Gazette* with a partner named Clapp. Here, he married Eliza Rumsey on December 26, 1820. He followed the Episcopalian faith and also held membership as a Master Mason in Union Lodge. In June of 1824, Francis and his wife left for Buffalo where he published the *Buffalo Emporium.* Their next move came in 1829 when they became residents of Springfield, Illinois. In this town, he and his brother, Allen Francis, who was to become Consul at Victoria, later began to publish the *Sangamo Journal* which soon became known as the *Illinois State Journal.* A Whig, Simeon Francis grew to be a close friend and political ally of Abraham Lincoln when the latter moved into town in 1837. But in 1856, the Francises sold their newspaper to Baker & Bailhache.

After the sale, Simeon operated a mercantile trade before going out to Portland, Oregon, in 1859. During the summer of 1860, Thomas J. Dryer, editor and owner of *The Oregonian*, left his desk to campaign throughout the state for Abraham Lincoln. Thus, it came about that Simeon Francis became the acting editor of this paper. When Dryer carried the election returns to Washington, D. C., the President gave him an appointment as Commissioner to the Sandwich Islands—now called the Hawaiian Islands. As a result, Francis continued as editor under the new owner until President Lincoln appointed him a Paymaster in the Regular Army with the rank of Major, a handsome office, indeed. His commission was dated August 3, 1861, but Major Francis did not assume his responsibilities until April of 1862. His duty station was Fort Vancouver, Washington Territory. He retired with half pay on October 18, 1867, and died at his home in Portland, Oregon, on October 25, 1872. His body was conveyed back to the military cemetery at Ft. Vancouver. However, in 1883, it was reburied in Riverview Cemetery at Portland. His widow succumbed April 30, 1893, and was interred beside her husband. She was approximately eighty-five years of age.

Exactly what went on in the Springfield house of the Francises during these secret trysts between Abraham and Mary is unknown. There may have been very little chaperoning done by Simeon or Eliza Francis in the months which followed. Later, O. H. Browning confided to J. G. Nicolay on June 17, 1875, that Mary Todd was indeed the "aggressor" in this courtship (See this interview in the John Hay Papers at Brown University.) Therefore, she may have, in desperation, compromised the shy Lincoln. Anyhow, suddenly—very suddenly—Miss Todd and Lincoln announced one morning that they would be married that very day! No amount of unwanted advice from the Edwardses could dissuade them from "getting hitched" that same evening. Lincoln hurried to the C. W. Chatterton & Bro. Jewelry Store (Charles W. & George W. Chatterton) on the west side of the Public Square and purchased a wide-band wedding ring of Etruscan gold. He then—or at some later date—directed the jeweler to inscribe these words inside it: "A. L. to Mary, Nov. 4, 1842. Love is Eternal." Next, the couple called upon Rev. Mr. Charles Dresser and engaged him to marry them. While Mary was inviting only a few confidantes to stand up with her, Abraham was petitioning James Harvey Matheny, another of his Masonic friends, to be his best man. "Jim," he explained, "I shall have to marry that girl."

"Lincoln," Matheny reported, "looked and acted as if he were going to the slaughter." While dressing at his boarding house, Lincoln was asked by five-year-old Speed Butler, son of Lincoln's landlord, William Butler, where he was going so dressed up. "To hell, I suppose," replied the nervous Lincoln.

Was Abraham Lincoln reporting a true fact when he told Jim Matheny that he *had* to marry Miss Todd or was he merely expressing his desperate resignation to marriage with its unknown and feared consequences? One shall never know for sure, but those inquisitive, prying and meddlesome Springfield busybodies, who always counted on their fingers from the date of a wedding until the first child was born, must have gossiped behind closed doors about the Lincolns. Robert Todd Lincoln arrived promptly on August 1, 1843, *exactly* nine months to the day after the unexpected marriage of his unlike parents. At least once, Lincoln mentioned Robert's birth with a rather strange statement. In writing to his intimate friend, Joshua Fry Speed, on October 22, 1846, Abraham revealed that Robert "has a great deal of that sort of mischief, that is the offspring of much animal spirits." If Lincoln hinted that "animal spirits" had led to his conception, what did he mean? That is, indeed, a most interesting question.

As requested, the Rev. Charles Dresser performed the single-ring ceremony in the impressive Edwards' home just off Second Street.[7] To have asked any other minister to join them in holy matrimony at the Edwards mansion would have been an insult to Mary's benefactors who had housed and fed her since 1839. Ninian Edwards even considered himself Mary's guardian because she was female and single, although she was nearly twenty-four years of age. Nor did Lincoln and Mary consider having a judge officiate. In those genteel days, it was generally customary for the bride to be married in her parent's home. However, it would have been very impractical and costly for dependent Mary and impecunious Abraham to have journeyed back to the Todd residence on West Main in Lexington, Kentucky, where the bride's rather-disliked stepmother reigned supreme in the household of Robert S. Todd. Also, it appears from this couple's actions that time was of the essence. They would brook no delay whatsoever.

When Abraham Lincoln stood before the Edwards' fireplace to take Mary Ann Todd as his wife, it was probably the very first time that he had witnessed an Episcopal wedding service. From an original copy of *The Book of Common Prayer According to the Use of the Protestant Episcopal Church in the United States* (Philadelphia: Carey & Hart, 1836) in the Harvard College Library, we know what the rather unreligous bridegroom experienced that evening. The appropriate chapter is reproduced here:

The Form of Solemnization of Matrimony

The laws respecting Matrimony, whether by publishing the Bans in Churches, or by License, being different in the several States; every Minister is left to the direction of those Laws, in every thing that regards the civil contract between the Parties.

And when the Bans are published, it shall be in the following form:-I publish the Bans of Marriage between <u>M</u>. of . . . ., and <u>N</u>. of . . . . If any of you know cause or just impediment, why these two persons should not be joined together in holy Matrimony, ye are to declare it. (This is the first, second, or third time asking.)

At the day and time appointed for Solemnization of Matrimony, the Persons to be married shall come into the body of the Church, or shall be ready in some proper house, with their friends and neighbours; and there standing together, the Man on the right hand, and the Woman on the left, the Minister shall say,

Dearly beloved, we are gathered together here in the sight of God, and in the face of this company, to join together this Man and this Woman in holy Matrimony; which is commended of Saint Paul to be honourable among all men; and therefore is not by any to be entered into unadvisedly or lightly; but reverently, discreetly, advisedly, soberly, and in the fear of God. Into this holy estate, these two persons present come now to be joined. If any man can show just cause, why they may not lawfully be joined together, let him now speak, or else hereafter for ever hold his peace.

And also speaking unto the Persons who are to be married, he shall say,

I require and charge you both (as ye will answer at the dreadful day of judgment, when the secrets of all hearts shall be disclosed) that if either of you know any impediment, why ye may not be lawfully joined together in Matrimony, ye do now confess it: For be ye well assured, that if any persons are joined together otherwise than as God's words doth allow, their marriage is not lawful.

<u>The Minister, if he shall have reason to doubt of the lawfulness of the proposed Marriage, may demand sufficient surety for his indemnification; but if no impediment shall be alleged or suspected, the Minister shall say to the man,</u>

<u>M</u>. Wilt thou have this Woman to thy wedded Wife, to live together after God's ordinance, in the holy estate of Matrimony? Wilt thou love her, comfort her, honour and keep her, in sickness and in health; and forsaking all others, keep thee only unto her, so long as ye both shall live?

<u>The Man shall answer,</u> I will.

<u>Then shall the Minister say unto the woman,</u>

<u>N</u>. Wilt thou have this Man to thy wedded Husband, to live together after God's ordinance, in the holy estate of Matrimony? Wilt thou obey him, and serve him, love, honour, and keep him, in sickness and in health; and forsaking all others, keep thee only unto him, so long as ye both shall live?

<u>The Woman shall answer,</u> I will.

<u>Then shall the Minister say,</u>

Who giveth this Woman to be married to this Man?

<u>Then shall they give their Troth to each other in this Manner. The Minister receiving the Woman at her Father's or Friend's Hands, shall cause the Man with his right Hand to take the Woman by her right Hand, and to say after him as followeth:</u>

I <u>M</u>. take thee <u>N</u>. to my wedded Wife, to have and to hold, from this day forward, for better for worse, for richer for poorer, in sickness and in health, to love and to cherish, till death us do part, according to God's holy ordinance;and thereto I plight thee my Troth.

<u>Then shall they loose their Hands, and the Woman with her right Hand, taking the Man by his right Hand, shall likewise say after the Minister,</u>

I <u>N</u>. take thee <u>M</u>. to my wedded Husband, to have and to hold, from this day forward, for better for worse, for richer for poorer, in sickness and in health, to love, cherish, and to obey, till death us do part, according to God's holy ordinance; and thereto I give thee my Troth.

Then shall they again loose their Hands; and the Man shall give unto the Woman a Ring. And the Minister taking the Ring shall deliver it unto the Man, to put it upon the fourth Finger of the Woman's left Hand. And the Man, holding the Ring there, and taught by the Minister, shall say,

With this Ring I thee wed, and with all my worldly goods, I thee endow: In the name of the Father, and of the Son, and of the Holy Ghost. Amen.

Then the Man leaving the Ring upon the fourth Finger of the Woman's left Hand, the Minister shall say,

Let us pray.

Our Father, who art in Heaven, Hallowed be thy Name; Thy Kingdom come;Thy Will be done on Earth, as it is in Heaven; Give us this day our daily bread; And forgive us our trespasses, as we forgive those who trespass against us; And lead us not into temptation; But deliver us from evil. Amen.

O Eternal God, Creator and Preserver of all mankind, giver of all spiritual grace, the author of everlasting life; send thy blessing upon these thy servants, this man and this woman, who we bless in thy name; that as Isaac and Rebecca lived faithfully together, so these persons may surely perform and keep the vow and covenant betwixt them made, (whereof this Ring given and received is a token and pledge,) and may ever remain in perfect love and peace together, and live according to thy laws, through Jesus Christ our Lord. Amen.

Then shall the Minister join their Right Hands together, and say,

Those who God hath joined together, let no man put asunder.

Then shall the Minister speak unto the Company:

Forasmuch as <u>M</u>. and <u>N</u>. have consented together in holy Wedlock, and have witnessed the same before God and this company, and there to have given and pledged their troth, each to the other, and have declared the same by giving and receiving a Ring, and by joining hands; I pronounce that they are Man and Wife; in the name of the Father, and of the Son, and of the Holy Ghost. <u>Amen.</u>

<u>And the Minister shall add this Blessing:</u>

God the Father, God the Son, God the Holy Ghost, bless, preserve and keep you: The Lord mercifully with his favour look upon you, and fill you with all spiritual benediction and grace; that ye may live together in this life, that in the world to come ye may have life everlasting. <u>Amen.</u>

Although Mary Todd had just been married by an Episcopal priest, she never considered herself an Episcopalian. It is true that as a child she had attended primary school in Ward's Academy at Lexington, Kentucky, and it had been operated by Dr. John Ward, a former Episcopal Bishop. However, through her Scottish ancestors, Mary's religious roots stretched back deeply into the Presbyterian form of worship. Her prominent father, Robert Smith Todd (1791-1849), a Mason, signed the constitution of the McChord Presbyterian Church in Lexington, Kentucky, on January 31, 1818—the year of Mary's birth—and occupied Pew No. 15. In 1826, the congregation elected him a Trustee. During Mary's youth, this church stood at 184 Market Street and eventually became known as the Second Presbyterian.[8] Blue-Grass relatives later revealed that Mary not only went to Sunday School there but also attended the regular worship program in the sanctuary.[9] Now, for the first time, it is possible to name one of the persons who shaped her bright young mind in Sunday School classes. David Austin Sayre (1793-1870), instructed her, and none other than President Lincoln himself reported this fact after conversing with his wife concerning a letter of request mailed to her during the Civil War from Sayre in Lexington.[10]

Sayre had been born near Madison, New Jersey, and learned the silver-smithing trade. Then, in 1811, he followed his master to Lexington, Kentucky, where he eventually became a banker of great wealth and the founder of Sayre School, still in operation. By 1828, Sayre had accepted the office of Trustee in the Second Presbyterian Church where the Todds attended, and the following year he started teaching Sunday School there. When a separate structure to house Sunday School classes became necessary, David A. Sayre donated the money for its erection in 1834.[11] This banker's nephew, Lewis Albert Sayre (1820-1900), studied at Transylvania University in Lexington until he graduated in 1839.[12] Mary Todd no doubt met him, because in the fall of 1881 when she suffered so greatly with her back, she journeyed to New York and placed herself under the expert care of this same Dr. Lewis A. Sayre, by then one of the most renown surgeons of the day.[13]

As the tender sapling is shaped and restrained by guide wires, so the mature tree generally grows. Therefore, Mary (Todd) Lincoln certainly considered herself a Presbyterian and probably longed to take her tall, distinguished husband to divine services in a church of that denomination at Springfield. Although her children began arriving within nine months after her marriage and kept her extremely busy, she must have recalled the happy hours spent in a Sunday church service and longed for that solace again. "Mollie," as Lincoln sometimes called her, no doubt talked to her man about religion. It had once been a vital part of her upbringing.

Even before her marriage to Abraham, Mary had commenced visiting with Mrs. James L. Lamb as early as June of 1841.[14] James Lamb had been ordained as an Elder of the First Presbyterian Church of Springfield on June 4, 1835.[15] He taught the Young Ladies' Bible Class. Mary Todd sat in this study group as early as 1842, vouched Mrs. Goyn A. Sutton. However, it would appear that the recently-married Mary Lincoln also kept a tentative connection with the Episcopal Church. "Aunt" Ruth Stanton, a black woman who professed to have worked at times for Mary, related that Lincoln's wife acted as the hostess every Thursday for the Episcopal Church ladies who gathered to sew for the poor and that young master Robert Todd Lincoln, born August 1, 1843, attended Sunday School at the Episcopal Church for a time.[16]

At first, the independent Lincoln quietly ignored his pretty wife's religious influence. Being a politician as well as a lawyer, he soon encountered the prejudice and unfair political campaign tactics whereby a rival often tries to drag the subject of religion into the contest against his opponent. In March of 1843, Lincoln attempted to gain his party's nomination as its candidate for the Seventh District's Congressional race. After his defeat, Lincoln sat down dejectedly on the twenty-sixth and wrote a friend concerning the encounter: "My wife," explained Lincoln, "has some relatives in the Presbyterian and some in the Episcopal Churches, and therefore, wherever it would tell, I was set down as either the one or the other, whilst it was every where contended that no ch[r]istian ought to go for me, because I belonged to no church, was suspected of being a deist, and had talked about fighting a duel."[17] No doubt it had been a bitter experience for him. He quickly discovered—to his sorrow—that professing Christians could be just as mean and spiteful as "infidels."

While the unhappy Lincoln vented his political frustrations, he also disclosed information relating to his in-laws and their religious preferences. Note that he mentioned his wife's relatives and not Mary herself. She, as yet, had not joined a denomination. Her Presbyterian relatives were, among others, her grandmother, Elizabeth R. Parker, her father and stepmother in Lexington, and Dr. John Todd, her uncle in Springfield who was also a Freemason. Her sisters, Mrs. Edwards and Mrs. Wallace, favored the Episcopal Church.

Elizabeth (Todd) Edwards had been baptized as an adult at St. Paul's in Springfield on August 1, 1841, and confirmed on that same date by Bishop Philander Chase.[18] However, Elizabeth's husband, Ninian Wirt Edwards, delayed joining this church until January 20, 1858, at which time he was confirmed by the Right Reverend Bishop Henry John Whitehouse (1803-1874) and the Rector, Louis P. Clover. The Edwardses did not accept halfway measures. Both waited for a bishop to confirm them. Nor did the aristocratic Todds allow the Edwardses to surpass them in anything. Lincoln himself hinted at this fact once during the Civil War while interviewing David Tod, the Governor of Ohio, "You are perhaps aware, Governor," remarked the President, "that my wife is a member of the Todd family of Kentucky, and they all spell their name with two d's. How is it that you use but one?" "Mr. President," replied Tod in mock seriousness, "God spells his name with one d, and one is enough for the governor of Ohio."[19]

Yet prior to his conversion, nobody ever accused Ninian W. Edwards of being an "infidel" as some had Lincoln, his brother-in-law. Of course, Ninian attended St. Paul's for years without actually putting his famous name on the official roster of communicant members that had been confirmed. Another sister of Mary Lincoln's, Frances Jane (Todd) Wallace, finally allowed herself to be confirmed at St. Paul's on April 7, 1850.[20] Back in that staid century, serious folks did not rush into church membership. Many waited until they reached middle age, or beyond, before coming forward for Jesus Christ. Still, these same people had often attended some church regularly. As a result, numerous churches in those years carried but a small number of members on their rolls, while the congregation on any given Sunday far exceeded that sparse number many times over. Often, these men and women who were not members agonized over the question of whether or not they were worthy to be called Christians. Others attempted mightily to discover if they really felt a call from God to become one of His followers.

To explain his position on religion, Lincoln issued a handbill to the voters of the Seventh Congressional District on July 31, 1846. "Fellow citizens," he began. "A charge having got into circulation in some of the neighborhoods of this District, in substance that I am an open scoffer at Christianity, I have by the advice of some friends concluded to notice the subject in this form." "That I am not a member of any Christian Church, is true," Lincoln admitted; "but I have never denied the truth of the Scriptures; and I have never spoken with intentional disrespect of religion in general, or of any denomination of Christians in particular." The Rev. Peter Cartwright, an itinerant Methodist circuit rider and his Democratic opponent in the race for Congress, had conducted an insidious whispering campaign against Lincoln, telling anybody who would listen that his Whig adversary was an infidel.

Openly, Lincoln no longer espoused infidelity, but he was still a fatalist, and sometimes waxed very sad. For example, in late October and early November of 1844, he had returned to Southern Indiana where he had been raised. This visit resulted in some fine poetry from Lincoln's facile pen in early 1846. It is of an excellent nature, and yet it appears to reveal Lincoln's melancholy attitude as well as some very large segments of fatalism.

> My childhood-home I see again,
> And gladden with the view,
> And still as mem'ries crowd my brain,
> There's sadness in it too.
>
> O memory! thou mid-way world
> 'Twixt Earth and Paradise,
> Where things decayed, and loved ones lost
> In dreamy shadows rise.

Lincoln explained sadly that he found many of his former friends gone.

> I hear the lone survivors tell
> How nought from death could save,

Till every sound appears a knell,
And every spot a grave.

I range the fields with pensive tread,
And pace the hollow rooms;
And feel (companions of the dead)
I'm living in the tombs.

Later in 1846, Lincoln once more continued his poetry composition. Two stanzas convey his poetic philosophy of life and death where the sun seems to be God, and death is a prince independent of God.

To drink it's [sic] strains, I've stole away,
All stealthily and still,
Ere yet the rising God of day
Had streaked the Eastern hill
O death! Thou awe-inspiring prince,
That keeps the world in fear;
Why dost thou tear more blest ones hence,
And leave him [Matthew Gentry] ling'ring here?

Lincoln would seem here to question God's wisdom as well as His power to control Death who might be construed as the Prince of Darkness or Satan.

At this point in his life, Lincoln declined to make a firm decision on his personal commitment to any one church. But he did proclaim that the "higher matter of eternal consequences" should be left between a man and "his Maker."[21]

Three years later, an event occurred which began to change his entire religious thinking. Sometime during the middle part of October in 1849, Abraham Lincoln and his little family departed from Springfield, Illinois, on a long circuitous journey to Lexington, Kentucky, his wife's old home town. Much of this lengthy trip took place aboard slow-but-luxurious river steamers on the wide, smooth Mississippi and Ohio and probably required a week of restful traveling. For the Lincolns it proved to be an excursion of both joy and extreme sadness. Abraham, Mary and the two children, Robert and Eddie, steamed south to visit relatives in the beautiful Blue-Grass region of central Kentucky which Mary remembered so well with great fondness.

There, they would sojourn with the Todds and perhaps even see Henry Clay again. Mary Lincoln could proudly show off her tall, successful husband, a recent Congressman, to old and new friends. But this extended vacation came about not for social reasons but rather as the result of necessity: to settle the estate of Mary's father, Robert Smith Todd, who had died in his fifty-ninth year at one a. m. on July 17, 1849.[22] That terrible killer, cholera, had suddenly ended his exemplary life, and now his disputed financial affairs must be settled in court. Lincoln, the brilliant trial lawyer, had been retained to represent the four married daughters residing in Springfield—Mary (Mrs. Abraham Lincoln), Elizabeth (Mrs. Ninian Wirt Edwards), Frances (Mrs. William Smith Wallace), and Ann (Mrs. Clark Moulton Smith). Their harassed stepmother found herself involved in a nasty family lawsuit and needed expert legal aid in handling the complicated Todd holdings since she had been named administrix.

Luxurious Lexington, known then as the "Athens of the West," stood forth majestically as one of the prominent cultural centers of the United States. As the observant Lincoln first approached the comfortable Todd residence, he would notice immediately that it had been constructed of red brick in a Modified-Federal style of practical architecture. If his own wooden house back in Springfield had been two complete stories high, its floor plan would have resembled Mary's old home. Like their equals in town, the Todds possessed a large and diverse library at their pleasant dwelling on West Main Street. In these inviting quarters, Lincoln eagerly browsed in spare moments.[23] At times he even scribbled comments in the margins of the books that he perused there. As usual, he turned the pages slowly but mastered everything which he examined. He appreciated any person who would let him read a volume that pleased his literary fancy.

Whenever one is thrust into a confrontation with the actual death of a dear friend or loved one, the mind oft turns to thoughts of the hereafter and seeks religious consolation. Consequently, Lincoln perhaps sought out writings to assuage his feeling of sadness at the recollection of Mary's father's death.

As soon as Lincoln opened one of the impressive spiritual tomes in the Todd library, the author's name immediately attracted his keen attention. The Rev. James Smith, D. D., had written it. The son of Peter and Margaret (Bruce) Smith, Dr. Smith, a large stout man, had been born in Glasgow, Scotland, on May 11, 1798. His father (Jan. 1771-June 22, 1807), earned a profitable living as a West India merchant; his mother died giving him birth.

When James' father suddenly died, too, his Uncle Hugh Smith raised him. Although this guardian offered him a position in business, James expressed no interest in it. Yet he did obtain a fine education, but not at Glasgow College. There is no record in this old institution's archives of his attendance.

When James Smith attained his majority, he demanded that he receive his inheritance which was in due course presented to him by the uncle. Immediately, he married his sweetheart, Elizabeth Black, at Culross. She had been born on June 14, 1799. Deciding to try his hand at merchandising, James took his bride to New York City but later moved on to Cincinnati where their first child, Eliza, was born in 1820. After suffering financial reverses, Smith moved to southern Indiana in 1824 and began to teach school and write.

A confirmed Deist, he enjoyed discussing religion and attending camp meetings to make fun of the preachers. However, when he heard the Rev. James Blackwell, (1800-1875), James Smith became converted, and was licensed to preach by the Logan Presbytery of the Cumberland Presbyterian Church in Kentucky on October 13, 1825. On April 4 the following year, he was transferred to the new Indiana Presbytery and formally ordained April 3, 1829.

Sometime in 1830 or 1831, the Rev. Smith moved to Henderson, Kentucky, where he preached, but he soon moved on to Nashville, Tennessee, late in 1831. There, he began to write even more, becoming co-editor of *The Revivalist*. After buying out his partner, Smith changed the name of this publication to the *Cumberland Presbyterian*. He already had edited the works of the Reverend James McGready as well as a collection of Evangelical hymns. By 1835, he had completed and published a history of the Cumberland Presbyterian Church.

Smith became the stated clerk of the General Assembly in 1834 and served in this capacity until 1840. In 1838 the General Assembly approved Smith as a Trustee of Cumberland College. He had already raised funds for this institution which finally started at Lebanon, Tennessee. But after several arguments and losses in the publishing business for the Church, Rev. Smith left the Cumberland organization and joined the regular Presbyterians at Nashville on October 25, 1844. On February 16, 1845, he started his ministry at Shelbyville, Kentucky. It was from here that he transferred to Springfield, Illinois. He may have received his honorary Doctor of Divinity Degree from Cumberland College; their early records do not list such degrees, however.

Initially, Smith preached in the First Presbyterian Church of Springfield on Wednesday night, March 14, 1849, and every evening thereafter for the rest of the week. Shortly after these trial sermons, he was formally accepted by the congregation. The Board of Trustees voted him a salary of $1125 plus a rent-free manse. Dr. Smith was installed at 3:00 p.m. on April 11. In those days, evening devotional, or prayer, meetings were conducted on Friday nights in the basement of the church. Sabbath services took place, of course, in the sanctuary on the main floor.

Dr. Smith, a Democrat with Southern views but not a secessionist, had brought a rather large family with him: Elizabeth (Black) Smith, his wife; and their children: Margaret, Mary, Ann F., Helen, Hugh and James Bruce. In addition, the household included their married daughter, Eliza Wallace, and her children: David Wallace and James Wallace, plus a male and female servant born in the Madeira Islands: John Degam and Antonia Gomes.[24]

Lincoln certainly knew that Rev. Dr. Smith served as a pastor of the First Presbyterian Church on the southeast corner of Third and Washington streets back in Springfield. At that time, Illinois' Capital City numbered only 4,533 inhabitants. On further examination of the title page, Lincoln saw: *The Christian's Defense, Containing a Fair Statement, and Impartial Examination of the Leading Objections Urged by Infidels Against the Antiquity, Genuineness, Credibility and Inspiration of the Holy Scriptures; Enriched with Copious Extracts from Learned Authors.*

Indeed, it appeared to be a weighty book, not only from its typical, lengthy, title page so popular in that era, but also from its very thickness. Its publisher, J. A. James of Cincinnati, had bound the two volumes into one cover in 1843, the first part containing 312 pages and the second 364. Dr. Smith had compiled it from his voluminous notes for his lengthy debates in April of 1841 at Columbus, Mississippi, with a skeptic by the name of C. G. Olmsted. By special arrangement, these two indefatigable debaters spoke for hours each night for eighteen weary nights. One antagonist would open for one hour; then the other would reply for two hours, after which the first speaker could have half an hour for rebuttal. For fairness, they rotated the openings. Perhaps Lincoln remembered this exact arrangement when he later challenged Douglas to debate in 1858.

Quite naturally, Lawyer Lincoln could not possibly finish this long argumentative work before he departed for Springfield. But this learned minister's hard logic seems to have impressed him greatly. Dr. Smith dealt with all the usual objections which infidels raise against the Bible. Furthermore, he artfully attempted to refute them one after another. So, when Lincoln arrived home on the evening of November 15,[25] he determined to complete his reading of this monograph. Upon seeing his old friend and fellow lawyer Thomas Lewis (1808-1900), a Trustee of the First Presbyterian Church and later an Elder, Lincoln told him about finding *The Christian's Defense* while in Lexington and asked if Lewis could introduce him to Dr. Smith. He had partially mastered this study, said Lincoln, and desired to conclude his reading of these volumes and also make the acquaintance of Rev. Smith. Lincoln supposedly declared that the author's argument had forced "him to change his views about the Christian religion."

Tom Lewis, a prominent figure on the Square, promptly "took Dr. Smith to Mr. Lincoln's office and introduced him, and Dr. Smith gave Mr. Lincoln a copy of his book, as I know, at his own request," reported Lewis.[26] James Smith corroborated this testimony by relating that it had been a "high honor" to place his book into Lincoln's eager hands. As any competent lawyer might do, Lincoln carefully examined its reasoning and proofs and soon observers avowed he had come to believe Dr. Smith's thesis.[27]

Lincoln toted Smith's big tome home with him and reverently placed it in his bookcase at Eighth and Jackson. There, his son, Robert Todd Lincoln, observed it many times among that special collection of reading material owned by his father.[28] Father Abraham must have cherished it greatly, because he possessed only an unpretentious library at home. Borrowing satisfied many of his library requirements. He became the first patron of the Illinois State Library when it opened its doors on December 16, 1842.[29] His brother-in-law, Ninian W. Edwards, stated that Lincoln confessed to him at that time: "I have been reading a work of Dr. Smith on the evidences of Christianity, and have heard him preach and converse on the subject, and I am now convinced of the truth of the Christian religion."[30] To the great satisfaction of Rev. Smith, "Mr. Lincoln did avow his belief in the Divine authority and inspiration of the Scriptures . . . ," revealed this scholarly minister.[31] While Dr. Smith's statement appears to be correct, it is most doubtful that Abraham Lincoln declared his belief in "the Christian religion" at this time or the divinity of Christ.

Evidently, Lincoln not only pondered *The Christian's Defense* very minutely but also became better acquainted with Dr. Smith. Then, while Lincoln continued to plumb Christianity, his second son, Edward Baker

Lincoln, fell gravely ill. Except for Robert, the Lincoln offspring never exhibited strong constitutions. After fifty-two days of severe physical suffering[32] little Eddie succumbed at 6:00 a.m. on Friday, the first day of February, 1850.[33] Chronic consumption had taken his precious life.[34]

Both doting parents experienced severe soul-rending anguish at their heavy loss of a lovable son not yet four years of age. Nevertheless, funeral arrangements had to be made. In their hour of extreme grief, they turned their tearful and sleepless eyes to the Rev. Dr. James Smith. With tender sympathy and deep understanding, the good Doctor consoled the mournful husband and wife and then at 11:00 a.m. on February 2 conducted the funeral obsequies in the joyless Lincoln home.[35] From that average brown frame cottage on the northeast corner of Eighth and Jackson, the sorrowful cortège moved off slowly to Hutchinson's Cemetery, about eight blocks west of the Public Square where Springfield High School now stands. John Hutchinson had begun selling his cemetery lots on June 28, 1843, so this graveyard had existed for less than seven years.[36]

Mary Lincoln generally grew very unsettled—sometimes hysterical—under such trying circumstances, and Abraham Lincoln probably shed voluminous tears at the interment in Lot No. 490. When the heartbreaking ceremonies had at last been concluded, the helpful Rev. Dr. James Smith could recount, with a sigh of relief, that he had "buried their dead." Mary Lincoln later stated that Eddie's death had directed her husband's heart "toward religion."[37] He certainly considered attending a local church.

In the "seasons of sorrow" which followed this soul-searing event, Dr. Smith moved even closer to the distraught Lincolns and "administered to them those consolations which the Gospel of the Son of God can alone communicate . . . ."[38] He had not been long at the First Presbyterian Church, having been formally installed on April 11, 1849.[39] Like both Abraham and Mary Lincoln, Smith brought strong Kentucky ties to Springfield. His previous ministry had been performed in that state. For this obvious reason, the Lincolns certainly felt a warm kinship with him. Then too, Mary Lincoln had numerous friends and even some relatives in the First Presbyterian Church. Her prominent uncle, Dr. John Todd (1787-1865), for example, had been elected an Elder on June 22, 1849.[40]

As has been stated, James Smith had been a Deist, something like Lincoln, but had changed his mind and become a devout Christian. Smith's tombstone would later record that he was "A sinner saved by grace." Rev.

Smith professed himself to be an Old School Presbyterian clergyman. A Plan of Union had begun in 1801 when the Presbyterians merged their missionary ventures with those of the New England Congregationalists. Yet, as so often happens in any shaky alliance, an uncompromising schism developed in 1837 with the Presbyterians splintering into the Old School and the New School. Those adhering to the New School of thought continued to work closely with the Congregationalists in home and foreign missions, temperance, and anti-slavery programs. Those favoring the Old School organization insisted upon a completely separate agency of their own for missionary as well as evangelistic labors. However, the two factions also quarreled bitterly over the Confession of Faith. They interpreted certain articles much differently. The Old School observed the confession as they always had, while the New School made rather radical changes in their interpretation. Among the disputed points were: (1) Doctrine of Imputation whereby the sin of Adam was imputed to his descendants; (2) Doctrine of Atonement whereby Christ died in order to purchase reconciliation with God and satisfy divine justice; (3) Doctrine of Justification of men before God, making them just or righteous and the law by which individuals were judged; (4) Doctrine of Regeneration whereby original sin was removed and in its place was implanted the holy principle which led to obedience; and (5) Doctrine of Ability of men to obey commands of God through divine grace.

In the field of missions, the New School patronized the American Home Missionary Society and entrusted the work of foreign missions completely to the American Board of Foreign Missions. They also favored the Presbyterian Education Society, a branch of the American Education Society. On the other hand, the Old School used the General Assembly's Board of Education and Home Missions and established a Board of Foreign Missions which reported to the General Assembly.

Men and women of Scotch-Irish and Scottish extraction tended to join the Old School camp whose focus centered upon Princeton Seminary.[41] Having excellent leadership, the Old School group quickly achieved an efficient system of church government. This body functioned with remarkable unity until the bitter Civil War exploded in the United States. Immediately, the Old School officials announced loudly that their loyalties lay with the North. Having no other choice, really, members of the Old School down in Dixie seceded and formed their own federation of the Presbyterian Church.

The First Presbyterian Church as it appeared in 1903.

This photo is from the Seventy-Fifth Anniversary Booklet celebrating
the organization of First Church.

Following Eddie's death, the Lincolns began to sample the sermons
of Dr. Smith. Mrs. John Todd Stuart recalled that the Lincolns soon became
"regular attendants." But because they had not as yet purchased a pew, they
sat in the "Amen Corner" among the free pews.[42] By definition, the "Amen
Corner" is a conspicuous place in a sanctuary where worshippers fervently
express their approval of the minister's words by exclaiming "Amen." Such a
location would seem to be in keeping with Mary Lincoln's own opinion of her
social position in the community.

This was the very first church congregation in town; it had been
organized on January 30, 1828, in the private home of Dr. John Todd, who
then resided in a two-story frame dwelling on the south side of Washington

Street, between First and Second. It was later moved to the north side of this street where it was renumbered 116 East Washington. This prominent physician was also a Mason.[43] At first, church services had to be held in a log schoolhouse standing at the corner of Second and Adams. This little Presbyterian congregation of approximately twenty souls had no building of its own, and only six members lived in Springfield. The rest of the group had homes at Indian Point, twenty miles or so north of town. As a result, services were sometimes conducted in that community, too. Furthermore, they had no permanent minister.

The Reverend John G. Bergen, however, came to Springfield to become the pastor of this little flock during the winter of 1828-29. One of his first sermons called for the worshippers "to rise up and build a house for God." A building committee immediately began to lay plans. They selected Lot 3 in Block 15 of the Old Town Plat, a choice location on the southeast corner of Third and Washington. Although they quickly raised approximately $1,200 in cash, they found themselves unable to pay all of the expenses required to purchase the lot and also construct the building. Very generously, the owners of the land volunteered to wait for their money until the edifice had been completed and more funds accumulated.

On August 15, 1829, the cornerstone was duly laid for a structure which measured 45' by 30' and centered within the south 40 feet of the lot. Thomas Brooker burned the brick on the site and faced the church toward Third Street. It was probably one of the first brick sanctuaries in Illinois. Upon completion, the structure was dedicated on November 21, 1830. None other than Andrew McCormick installed the steps and finally received his $21 on February 14, 1832. He would later sit with Lincoln in the Legislature as one of the famous "Long Nine."

At last the congregation paid off the indebtedness and sought to secure title to the land. William and Jane Iles of Bath County, Kentucky, the absentee owners, donated half of Lot 3 to the Church and asked a mere $25 for the other half. This amount the trustees raised and gave to the grantors. By Illinois law, however, church property was to be held for the said members by the county commissioners. So, on January 10, 1833, the deed for this church property was executed in favor of Thomas Moffett, Josiah B. Smith, and Reuben Harrison, the Sangamon County Commissioners.[44]

As its membership expanded, the First Presbyterian Church determined to erect a new building. James L. Lamb, as chairman of the building committee, on February 8, 1842, drew up a notice to architects who were invited to submit plans for a structure to measure 60' by 80' with a basement, spire and a gallery on one end. On behalf of the Church, he offered a premium of $25 for the winning plans. This contest would close on February 22 that year.[45] Henry Dresser won the competition and became the architect and the contractor. On May 23, 1842, the cornerstone was lifted into place, and the new brick building began to rise.[46] A beautiful edifice, it sat on the north portion of this large lot and faced Washington Street. Its dedication took place on November 9, 1843. When the Lincolns began to attend religious services, they did so in this newer house of worship. On March 8, 1843, the trustees of the First Presbyterian Church asked the Sangamon County Commissioners to convey their old building to the Springfield Mechanics' Union. And the following day, the Commissioners duly carried out this request, giving the Mechanics' Union the building and the south 40' off Lot 3 which measured 80' from Third Street eastward.[47] Its south boundary was an alley.

The Springfield Mechanics' Union utilized the old superseded church structure for a school. They fitted it up for classes, but were forced to sell their building at auction on February 10, 1849. We do know that in April of 1852, this building housed the first classes of the new Illinois State University since its own structure was not completed until the fall of 1854. Yet the Preparatory Department of Illinois State University still met in the old Mechanics' Union building in the fall of 1854 when Robert Todd Lincoln entered this institution at the tender age of eleven. Other close chums of Robert's also joined him at this school. Among them were John Milton Hay (1838-1905) who later became Abraham Lincoln's Assistant Secretary; Clinton Levering Conkling (Oct. 16, 1843-Oct. 12, 1920); and DeWitt Wickliffe Smith (Dec. 13, 1844-Jan. 23, 1929). Prior to attending this institution, Robert had gone to an academy located at 7th and Edwards and operated by Abel W. Estabrook. Here, his closest pal was George Clayton Latham (May 16, 1842-Feb. 1, 1921). And before this academy training, Robert had started his education in a little primary "slipper" school taught by an unnamed lady who enforced discipline upon her charges by spanking them with her slipper.

As a child, Robert had a crossed eye and was very shy; some of his unkind fellow students nicknamed him "Cockeye." However, Dr. J. Drake Harper seems to have been the surgeon who straightened his eye by an operation which restored Robert's appearance and sight. At any rate,

Abraham Lincoln testified as to the competence of Dr. Harper in a contemporary newspaper advertisement.

Robert's friendship with Clinton Conkling lasted until the latter died. Their mothers had been members of "the Coterie" that gathered at the Edwards' mansion before they married. Their boys were nearly of the same age and both went off east to college and graduated in 1864; Robert from Harvard and Clinton from Yale. DeWitt Smith became President of the Illinois National Bank and sat for two terms in the Illinois General Assembly but did not seem to keep up his contacts with Robert Lincoln, although he reminisced about Robert in 1926.[48] Robert also saw George Latham from time to time in years that followed; he will be discussed later in this study.

In the early days of 1852, Dr. James Smith conducted "a series of protracted meetings" at the First Presbyterian Church, ably assisted by the Rev. S. J. P. Anderson of the Central Presbyterian Church of St. Louis.[49] Today, such religious conclaves would no doubt be termed revivals. Back in those days, such gatherings might be held both morning and evening for a lengthy period of time.

Since the fall months of 1851, Elizabeth (Gundaker) Dale (Feb. 4, 1823-Dec. 17, 1902), wife of William Malcolm Black, Jr. (Sept. 17, 1821-Jan. 11, 1888)—expecting a child—had been residing in Springfield with her sister-in-law, Mary (Black) Remann (Mar. 5, 1823-Feb. 7, 1888), widow of Henry Christian Remann (born in 1817). Widow Remann resided in a large house at the southeast corner of Eighth and Market (now Capitol), then numbered 33 South Eighth Street. It was a natural living arrangement. Remann had died at midnight, (December 10-11, 1849). He had been very close to his brother-in-law, William M. Black, Jr., who was now away from home looking for a place to establish his business in St. Louis. Previously, the Remann and the Black families had lived and worked in Vandalia. There, both Henry Remann and William Black had served as Masters of Temperance Lodge No. 16, A. F. & A. M. Thus, they had also been Masonic brothers as well as brothers-in-law. In 1847, Henry Remann, who had married Mary Black in Vandalia on April 15, 1844, moved his family to Springfield where he earned a living as a clerk. Here, Remann—a strong Presbyterian—was ordained two years later (January 1, 1849) as an Elder of First Church.

Since Widow Remann resided in the same block as the Lincolns, it was quite normal that she soon became a close friend of Mary Lincoln who also had Presbyterian roots. As an intimate companion of Mary Lincoln's, Mary Remann quickly introduced Elizabeth Black to Lincoln's society-conscience wife. Together, these congenial ladies attended the First Church's revival services with their children, riding there and back in the same carriage.[50] In truth, this "carriage" probably belonged to the Lincolns, because they had owned one of sorts since at least the month of October in 1843.[51] Elizabeth Black, as a temporary inhabitant of Springfield, certainly had none of her own. When Lincoln was away on the circuit, his wife had somebody drive their carriage for her.

Elizabeth gave birth on January 6, 1852, and named the infant Samuel Dale Black. But on the twenty-fourth of March he suddenly died, and Elizabeth earnestly sought even more spiritual consolation. At her invitation, Dr. Smith called and provided useful counsel.[52] Thereafter, both Elizabeth Black and Mary Lincoln decided to add their names, officially, to the membership rolls of First Church.

Upon learning this important news, Rev. Smith advised Mary Lincoln that she should immediately seek her husband's permission. At that time, Abraham lingered at Pekin with the spring session of the Tazewell County Circuit Court.[53] Back came Lawyer Lincoln's written reply, stating that he learned with gladness of her desire to associate formally with the congregation at First Church. Furthermore, "he thought religion was a thing every woman ought to have."[54] Knowing Lincoln's keen sense of humor, one might venture to guess that he took great delight in teasing his dear "Molly" while at the same time giving his serious consent. On the other hand, many men, through the ages, have tended to relegate to their wives the religious duties of the household.

With her loving husband's blessing, Mary Lincoln, on April 13, 1852, presented herself to the Session of First Church where she underwent examination by the Ruling Elders on the subject of "experimental religion."[55] After she had firmly convinced Elders Henry Van Hoff, Joseph K. Lewis and Edmund G. Johns, as well as the Moderator, Dr. James Smith, of her religious experience, she was duly received into the fellowship of the church "on examination." By the use of this exact phrase, it can be proved conclusively that Mary Lincoln had never previously held membership in another church. If so, she would have been received "by letter." At this same Session meeting, the Elders also accepted several of Mary Lincoln's revival companions: Elizabeth Black, Julia E. Jayne and Miss Nancy Sperry. Julie E. (Witherbee) Jayne was the wife of Dr. William Jayne, a local physician educated at Illinois College and Missouri State University. She had married him on October 17,

1850, in Jacksonville, Illinois. Her native state was Vermont where she had been born in 1830. Nancy Sperry was approximately eighteen years of age and the daughter of a cabinetmaker named Peter Sperry.[56] By this date, this church had one hundred and fifty-one communicant members.

Mary could be at ease with her own spiritual conscience, and she probably immediately insisted upon buying a pew. The Lincolns therefore acquired No. 20 in the seventh row from the front of the Presbyterian sanctuary—in the tenth row as counted forward from the rear of the church—on the left-hand side as the worshippers faced the minister. A wooden partition divided each long seat in the middle so that one bench formed two family pews. There were black haircloth cushions on the seats. The Lincolns' pew opened out onto the middle aisle, a very choice and attractive location. In fact, Mary Lincoln described it as "our particular pew to which I was very much attached."

When the Lincolns first began to attend, in about 1850, the congregation numbered about one hundred and twenty-six members who contributed $3,023 in total. Old members of First Church remembered that the Lincolns did not buy their own pew until after Mary Lincoln had formally joined the church in 1852. These reminiscences are correct.[57] Why would the church sell a pew to a non-member?

In Lincoln's day, many congregations raised part of their operating budgets by selling or renting pews. One-third of the pews in First Presbyterian could not be sold. They remained uncommitted as free pews for any who might desire to sit in them but could not afford to purchase one.[58] Exactly what total amount did Father Abraham pay to sit in his own pew? The treasurer's ledger, no longer extant, but supposedly seen by a later minister, disclosed that Lincoln gave $36 for his subscription. That amount would work out perfectly for two-years' taxes, and a pew owner had two years to remit the assessment before he lost his property for back taxes. This matter of pew sales and pew tax proved to be one of the most difficult problems to solve. Fortunately, a deed for a pew in First Church still exists among the museum items in this church. It is reproduced here in its entirety:

Know all Men by these Presents, That we Thomas Mather, Thomas Lewis, Wm. Harrower, John Irwin & John C. Sprigg, Trustees of the First Presbyterian Church and Congregation of Springfield, Illinois, in consideration of the sum of Fifty dollars paid by Goyne A. Sutton, the receipt whereof is hereby acknowledge, do hereby grant, bargain, sell and convey unto the said Sutton, his heirs and assigns, a certain Pew in said Church, numbered Sixty four (64), to have and to hold the same, with the privileges and appurtenances thereof, to the said Sutton, his heirs and assigns forever; and the said Trustees for themselves and their successors in office do hereby covenant with the said Sutton that they are the lawful owners of the said Pew, have good right and authority to sell the same, and will warrant and defend the said Pew, to the said Sutton his heirs and assigns forever against the lawful demand of all persons:

Provided, however, that said Sutton, his heirs or assigns, shall be entitled to hold said Pew, as his own property, only in such manner, and for such uses, as shall be consistent with the usages of said Church, and the worship of God; and that said Pew shall be subject to an annual tax, to be levied by the said Trustees, and their successors in office at their discretion, not exceeding ten per cent on Two hundred dollars, its re-appraised value, and in case said Sutton his heirs or assigns shall fail to pay said Tax for the space of two years, said Pew shall revert to the said Trustees.

Given by us, the Trustees of said Church and Congregation, under our hands and seals this 26th day of April 1849.

Thomas Mather L. S.
Thomas Lewis L. S.
William Harrower L. S.
John Irwin L. S.

As can be seen from this document, the cost of a pew in fee simple, at about the time the Lincolns obtained theirs, was $50. Once the fifty dollars had been paid, the pew holder claimed it as his property. However, if the owner failed for two years running to remit the tax, the seat reverted to the Trustees who might sell it to another party.

SOUTH

					PULPIT						
42	40	38	36	34	AREA		33	35	37	39	41

44	32		31	43
46	30		29	45
48	28		27	47
50	26		25	49
52	24		23	51
54	22		21	53
56	Lincoln 20		19	55
58	18		17	57
60	16		15	59
62	14		13	61
64	12		11	63
66	10		9	65
68	8		7	67
70	6		5	69
72	4		3	71
74	2		1	73

Pew arrangement at the First Presbyterian Church on the corner of Third
and Washington streets when the Lincolns attended there.
Some front pews were later removed.

Although the pew owner paid $50, the trustees claimed the right to re-evaluate it for the purpose of taxation. When Goyne A. Sutton, a carpenter who worked on the Old State House, received the deed to his pew, the contract stipulated that the evaluation was $200 for the purpose of taxation and that the tax would be no more than ten percent of this $200 evaluation. From a minute book of the trustees at this exact time, we learn that the actual rate was then fixed at 9%. Nevertheless, the trustees might raise that percentage when new deeds were drawn for the sales made afterwards. In 1849, Sutton paid $50 for his pew and then was taxed $18 a year to sit there. It seems likely that Lincoln paid a similar amount of yearly tax upon his family's private pew. From time to time, the trustees also might raise the evaluation. Yet they could not change a deed already held by a pew owner. Pew tax, we know was due quarterly.

Thomas Lewis, who served in various capacities in this Church, stated emphatically that Lincoln got his pew for $50 and was scheduled to pay his tax quarterly. He also said that the Lincoln children attended Sunday School in First Church. A few years later, the trustees decreed that the tax was to be raised to 13%. They always needed money to meet their deficit budget.

At first, a collection was taken from the congregation once a month. This was additional money for expenses in addition to pew sales and taxes. When the trustees discovered that they needed an offering more often to pay expenses, they ordered that the plates be passed each Sunday. Non-pew-holders were asked to contribute when they attended.

Based on the Church's needs, Abraham Lincoln's contributions probably varied from year to year. We know for certain that in 1855 he was credited with either twelve or fourteen dollars in one payment to the First Presbyterian Church.[59] On the first day of February in 1860—the tenth anniversary of little Eddie's demise—Lincoln wrote out his personal check on the Springfield Marine Bank to "First Church" for ten dollars.[60] Without further evidence, we must assume that the Lincolns never paid less than $18 in tax plus whatever additional amounts they put in the collection plate on Sundays. Friends have stated that Lincoln contributed "liberally."

There exists one other legal document which can be used to prove that pews were bought and sold as property. In 1848, Pew No. 72 went under the hammer at public auction to settle the estate of James Spence who, in life, had owned it. William Harrower made the successful bid: $5.50.[61] The price seems extremely low, and Harrower already owned a pew. It seems certain that here, a Church Trustee, merely bought the seat back for the Church so that it might be sold legally to another communicant. Perhaps other potential bidders backed off and did not run the price higher out of respect for the Church. This particular pew was not in a prime location, however, being in the next to the last row on the left side of the church and next to the east outside aisle. Of course, it would have been an ideal spot for anybody who consistently arrived late for services.

Harrower (1808-1869), a Scotsman, had arrived in Springfield during 1838. He once toiled as a skilled stone mason on the construction of the State House in the Public Square. He had erected the classical porticos on this beautiful brownish-dolomite-limestone edifice of Greek Revival architecture. His daughter, Agnes, later married Dr. James B. Smith, the physician son of the Rev. Dr. James Smith.[62] But sometime later, William Harrower earned his family's living as a grocer and owned a modest amount of real estate. As has been stated before, he held the position of Trustee in the First Presbyterian Church.[64]

It would appear that the Lincolns contributed generously to the First Presbyterian Church and gave to other worthy causes. John Locke Scripps prepared a campaign biography of Abraham Lincoln with the latter's assistance. After researching the subject of the Candidate's religious affiliations, Scripps announced, "He is a regular attendant upon religious worship, and, though not a communicant, is a pew-holder and liberal supporter of the Presbyterian Church in Springfield, to which Mrs. Lincoln belongs."[65] Note that he said pew-holder and liberal supporter, indicating contributions as well as pew tax.

Not only did Lincoln contribute to his regular place of worship, he also gave freely to other faiths. When the Baptists solicited the citizens of Springfield for funds to erect a "meeting house," Abraham Lincoln dug down into his pockets and donated five dollars, as did his good friend, Edward Dickinson Baker. On a list started October 23, 1855, Lincoln later allowed his name to be added as a subscriber to the building fund for the English Evangelical Lutheran Church which was being constructed on the northwest corner of Sixth and Madison. He generously donated $20, and his account was duly marked "Paid."[66] Page Eaton told a reporter that Lincoln also helped to support the minister of the First Baptist Church even though he did not hold membership under this preacher.[67]

In April of 1855, a pastor arrived in Springfield to fill the pulpit of the First Baptist Church which had been finished in 1850 and stood on the south-west corner of Adams and Seventh Street.[68] This was the very building for which Lincoln had made a contribution toward its construction. This gentle-man, the Rev. Mr. Noyes W. Miner (1818-1893), rented a house "in the same street on a corner [—the northwest—] opposite to the residence of Mr. Lincoln." A Springfield directory confirms the Minister's recollections by record-ing that Miner resided on one corner of Eighth and Jackson.[69] By 1859, this Baptist clergyman had removed to the west side of Seventh Street, between Jackson and Edwards.[70] Quickly, a close friendship developed between the Rev. Miner and Lincoln. Without his asking, Miner pointed out, Abraham Lincoln furnished him with "the free use of his horse and carriage, which for years aided us in our church work."[71]

Mary (Todd) Lincoln confirmed the Rev. Miner's account by identify-ing him as "our clergyman . . . our opposite neighbor, and a friend very much beloved by my husband."[72] When Mary wrote out this statement on Dec. 5, 1881, she stretched the truth somewhat by referring to him as "our clergy-man." Actually, Rev. Miner never served in an official capacity since Mary attended the Presbyterian Church. Nevertheless, Abraham Lincoln some-times, upon occasion, called Mr. Miner his pastor.[73]

It seems safe to assume that Lincoln discovered a common ground with the Rev. Miner. Certainly, Lincoln never forget his early Baptist upbring-ing in Kentucky and Indiana. Miner easily became "a warm personal friend" that often received an invitation to call at the Lincoln home. Lincoln also went into the Miner house where he cuddled the children and spoiled them as he did his own offspring. If the Minister received too many out-of-town guests to accommodate them in his own rented quarters, Abraham Lincoln always vol-unteered the use of a spare bedroom in his own dwelling across the street.[74]

In Springfield, Rev. N. W. Miner stepped forth as a leader in the community. On June 21, 1858, he respectfully petitioned Springfield Lodge No. 4, Ancient, Free & Accepted Masons, for membership. The Brethren of this Lodge elected him on July 19, and he was initiated on August 24. By special dispensation of the Most Worshipful Grand Master, Miner received both the degrees of Fellow Craft and Master Mason on the same day— October 6. Soon he became the Chaplain of his Lodge. Next, when the Knights Templar started a commandery in the city, Rev. and Sir Knight Miner accepted the post of Sword Bearer. Then, at 10 a. m. on October 6, 1859,

Miner was chosen and installed as the Grand Chaplain of the Right Worshipful Grand Lodge of Illinois which convened in the First Presbyterian Church at Springfield.[75] With such a Masonic record, we know the Rev. Mr. Miner had to have been a man of honor who proved to his brothers that he was a truthful person worthy of their trust. For these reasons, the following accounts by Miner should be accepted as factual.

According to the Rev. Miner, he "used to see" Lincoln "at the funerals of this old neighbors, and sometimes at church on the Sabbath, but he was not constant in his attendance at public worship." "At the time Mr. Lincoln was elected President," Miner observed, "I do not think he was what is termed an experimental Christian." By this, the Reverend meant that Lincoln had not professed having a religious experience nor asked for formal church membership. "But," continued Miner, "during my long and intimate acquaintance with him, and the many conversations I had with him from time to time, on numerous subjects, I never heard a word fall from his lips that gave me the remotest idea that his mind was ever tinctured with infidel sentiments; but on the contrary, the more intimate I became acquainted with him, the more deeply was I impressed with the conviction that he believed not only in the overriding Providence of God, but in the Divinity of the Sacred Scriptures, and had a profound reverence for everything true, and noble, and good."[76]

Other reliable witnesses repeat nearly the same story, although not all of them agree as to the frequency of Lincoln's attendance at worship services. Of course, none of them kept a chart of his presence. Their descriptions stemmed from impressions only.

John Todd Stuart proclaimed, when asked, that although "up to that time" Lincoln had not regularly "attended any place of religious worship," after he procured a niche at First Presbyterian he "with his family constantly attended the worship of that church until he went to Washington as President."[77] Robert Todd Lincoln vouched in writing that the scholarly cleric, Dr. James Smith, was his family's pastor and "a very close friend of my father's."[78] Even Beverly P. Herndon, son of William Henry Herndon, so skeptical of Lincoln's religious faith, stated firmly in writing: "I saw Lincoln often, at the 1st Presb[y]terian Church."[79]

The witness who knew best, Rev. Smith, announced proudly that "Mr. Lincoln placed himself and family under my pastoral care, and when at home he was a regular attendant upon my ministry."[80] Lastly—and most important—

Mary Lincoln herself averred strongly that on "Sabbath mornings" her noble husband accompanied her "to hear dear good old Dr[.]Smith" preach.[81]

Once the Lincolns were in his audience, Dr. Smith immediately struck up a social as well as pastoral relationship with Lawyer Lincoln's vivacious wife and restless children. "Scarcely two weeks ever passed," recalled Smith, "during which I did not spend a pleasant evening in the midst of that family circle . . . ."[82]

Again, Mary Lincoln verified Dr. Smith's testimony. "You were so frequently at our house," she reminisced while corresponding with her former Springfield pastor, "making informal calls, meeting a few friends and very frequently large companies . . . ."[83]

A diary kept by a contemporary Christian associate, Elizabeth (Mrs. William M.) Black, substantiates Dr. Smith's and Mary Lincoln's historical claims. When Mrs. Black, a lonely lady, dropped in to visit with Mary Lincoln one Monday evening (May 23, 1852), she discovered Rev. Smith relaxing in the cozy Lincoln parlor. Upon another occasion (March 8, 1852), Elizabeth Black joined Mary Lincoln for a gathering—certainly of a religious nature—at the local Baptist Church. After the meeting she shared a buggy with Mary Lincoln, Mrs. Henry C. Remann, and Dr. James Smith. Elizabeth Black noted in her journal that she "laughed all the way home" at the witty and humorous remarks of Mary Lincoln and Rev. Smith.[84] At this time, Rev. Smith lived in the Manse on Jefferson Street, near Fifth—eight blocks from the Lincoln residence.

After 1852, if the tall barrister happened to be in Springfield instead of on the lengthy law circuit, he could generally be found sitting attentively in his private pew when the 11:00 a.m. Sunday services commenced. William Bishop from Jacksonville once substituted for Dr. Smith who was out of town for some reason. He reported that Mr. Lincoln kept his eyes fixed upon him and "his long legs stretched out in the middle aisle to keep them from . . . being scrounged in the narrow space between the pews." On about the third Sunday of Bishop's supply in First Church's pulpit, Abraham Lincoln came forward and told the young minister, "I can say 'Amen' to all that you have said this morning" about atheism. And if Lincoln chose to return for a Sunday evening worship service, that rite started off at 7:00 p. m.[85]

After years of denial, Billy Herndon finally admitted in writing that "Mr. Lincoln sometimes would go to church as other men do." As he grew more mellow, Herndon divulged that Lincoln "believed in God." He was, Billy conceded, "a deeply and a thoroughly religious man." However, Herndon threw in a caveat on this touchy subject. "I do not say," Billy announced, that Lincoln "was a Christian."[86]

Prayer meetings at the First Presbyterian Church took place on Friday evenings.[87] It is uncertain whether or not Lincoln attended these gatherings, but his pleasingly-plump little spouse did.[88] We know that Abraham sometimes participated actively in affairs held at times other than Sunday morning. Once, after taking a pew there, he addressed the Bible Society of Springfield and proclaimed stoutly that every family in the State of Illinois should have a copy of the Scriptures. This reminiscence is confirmed by Thomas Lewis who vouched that Lincoln occupied the pulpit at the First Presbyterian Church one Sunday evening and spoke on the topic of the Bible.[89] This seems logical since Lincoln had researched the Holy Scriptures thoroughly for his lecture on Discoveries and Inventions which he gave in various cities around Illinois.

After Abraham Lincoln established a meaningful contact with Dr. Smith, the former's religious growth appears to have progressed rapidly. One could argue logically that an ambitious politician or statesman might utter religious platitudes in public to sway voters. Lincoln professed his belief in God as well as in Heaven on January 12, 1851, in a private letter to his stepbrother, little thinking that it would ever be examined by outsiders. He had just learned that his father, Thomas Lincoln, lay seriously ill in Coles County and would in all probability soon die. In reply, he counseled:

> I sincerely hope Father may yet recover his health; but at all events tell him to remember to call upon, and confide in, our great, and good, and merciful Maker; who will not turn away from him in any extremity. He notes the fall of a sparrow, and numbers the hairs of our heads; and He will not forget the dying man, who puts his trust in Him . . . . but that if it be his lot to go now, he will soon have a joyous [meeting] with many loved ones gone before; and where [the rest] of us, through the help of God, hope ere-long [to join] them.[90]

By tradition, Mary Todd's family, for generations, had practiced the Presbyterian faith. Now, she had experienced a religious revival in her life— a rebirth of her very soul. Yet strangely enough, this new moral step occasionally caused Mary to suffer a serious admonition from her honest husband. Whenever she did something not strictly in keeping with the straight-laced religious mores of that era, Father Abraham would quickly chide her by volunteering this free advice: "Mary[,] if I were a church member[,] I would not do so [and so]."[91]

It was not unusual for Abraham Lincoln to take an active part in the extracurricular affairs of the Presbyterian Church, even though he never added his name to the select membership list. On the evening of January 23, 1853, when Dr. James Smith delivered a lecture on temperance, Lincoln was in the audience.[92] And when Rev. Smith found himself confronted with a law suit in Presbytery, the Board of Trustees for First Church, on April 26, 1853, appointed "Abram" Lincoln, Henry Van Hoff and Thomas Lewis as a committee to aid the Minister. The Secretary of the Trustees had difficulty with the spelling of Lincoln's Biblical first name, but at least this church body considered him as part of the congregation by virtue of his holding a pew and attending worship. Lincoln had agreed to speak to the Illinois State Colonization Society on Thursday, January 12, 1854, at 7:00 p.m. in the First Presbyterian Church. However, illness in his family kept him at home, and only O. H. Browning from Quincy gave an address. This organization existed to purchase the freedom of slaves and send them back to Africa as colonists. Dr. Smith took an active part in this group and was elected one of the "managers."[93] Later, as President, Lincoln would suggest this means of dealing with freed blacks.

With all of Lincoln's sincere interests in religious matters, why did he shy away from conversion? After a thorough study of the contemporary sources, this author believes that some answers can, at last, be given. Church members at that period of time often engaged in petty crusades against individuals or groups that were in no way deserving of their vitriolic attacks. For example, at a Session meeting of First Church on February 19, 1855, the sanctimonious Ruling Elders passed a stringent resolution directing the pastor, Dr. Smith, to investigate the rumors then circulating that certain members of the congregation had been observed dancing![94]

Such censure often occurred in the capital city. Governor Joel Aldrich Matteson, a Presbyterian since his youth but a liberal thinker, authorized dancing—after 12 o'clock—at one of his public receptions in Springfield during January of 1856. On the very next Sunday, his minister, the Rev. Albert Hale of the Second Presbyterian Church, preached a scorching sermon against dancing. Matteson expressed his torrid indignation at such humiliating treatment from his own clergyman and for the rest of his life never set foot inside a church of any denomination.[95] Not a whit cowed, he continued to encourage his distinguished guests to dance at his gala parties in his private mansion.

Lincoln certainly would not have seen the unlikely connection between his immortal soul and dancing. What had that to do with reverence toward God, love for fellow humans, belief in God? In fact, Lincoln himself had once acted as one of the managers for a "Cotillion Party" held at the American House in Springfield on December 16, 1839.[96] It is entirely possible that Abraham met Mary Todd for the first time at this very dance. She had not been long in the Capital City when this ball occurred. Following his initial introduction to Mary, Lincoln blurted out, "Miss Todd, I want to dance with you the worst way." Later, when Mary laughingly recounted this amusing episode, she exclaimed, "And he certainly did."[97]

Others agreed with Mary Todd's estimate of Lincoln's ballroom agility. When asked if Lincoln danced, Billy Herndon retorted, "Could a sparrow imitate an eagle[?]" Billy further expressed the facetious thought that "Barnum could make more money on Lincoln's dancing than he could on Gumbo!" "Mr. Lincoln had no ear for music except of the old common kind—" explained Billy, "had no heels for dancing, even our old puncheon floor dances."[98]

Be that as it may, Lincoln relished the conviviality found at such parties, regardless of whether or not he danced well. Being a highly-talented raconteur, he delighted in conversing with the attending couples. Lincoln would never have become a hypocrite by petitioning for church membership while at the same time continuing his attendance at promenades and other innocent forms of social intercourse. Nor would he have welcomed—or tolerated—a prying investigation into his own private social life, even by a distinguished man of the cloth or some officious ecclesiastical committee.

Perhaps this reasoning helps to explain why so many prominent citizens in that uncompromising era waited until their middle years before joining a church. By that time in their lives they had lost a great deal of their former interest in those "sinful" social gatherings where dancing or other "vices" might take place. Growing family responsibilities kept them at home with their children.

As if that were not enough to keep Abraham from joining the church when his wife did, another problem faced him. In those days, the Session examined potential members on their "experimental religion."[99] Through questioning, the Session sought to determine if the candidate had experienced a profound religious encounter. Even as late as the Civil War,

President Lincoln had not solved this matter to his own satisfaction. One day he asked a visitor to the White House, "What constitutes a true religious experience?"[100]

This doctrinal dilemma in his religious contemplation seems to have been one of the rude impediments that wrecked any hope for an easy spiritual conversion. And if Lincoln had not actually experienced such a feeling, he would not have prevaricated in order to become an official communicant. Even Billy Herndon admitted that "what was true, good, and right, and just, [Lincoln] would never surrender; he would die before he would surrender his ideas of these."[101] Mary Lincoln also corroborated Herndon's statement by reporting: "Poor Mr. L[incoln] is almost a monomaniac on the subject of honesty . . . ."[102] Her husband, Mary vouched, "was truth itself . . . ."[103]

Despite his lack of membership, Lawyer Lincoln continued to attend First Church with his understanding wife and family. There, he found an outlet for his religious feelings and expressed them through prayer, quiet meditation, attention to the interesting sermons, etc. All in all, he seems to have been a fatalist.[104] Lincoln probably felt at home with the Presbyterian doctrine of predestination. He had expressed his feeling on this matter to his intimate friend, Joshua Fry Speed, "Whatever he designs, he will do for me yet. 'Stand [ye] still and see the salvation of the Lord' [II Chronicles 20:17] is my text just now."[105] At another time he revealed that he felt a premonition "that the Almighty has sent your present affliction expressly for that object."[106] Lincoln had discovered his correct niche in the church of John Knox.

Whenever the Lincolns occupied Pew No. 20, a young teenager watched them intensely. Known as Elizabeth Jane "Bettie" Stuart (1838-1869), she was the daughter of John Todd Stuart. In 1859 she married Christopher Columbus Brown.[107] The Stuarts sat just two rows behind the Lincolns. Elizabeth Brown recalled that tall man "with a sad face but whose eyes could light up with a merry twinkle." "His black frock coat," she keenly observed, "never seemed exactly new and had a queer fashion of drawing up in the middle of the back, looking as if it were made for some one else."

In complete contrast, however, Lincoln's spouse appeared most "exquisitely gowned." Always carefully aware of the latest fashions, she once arrived at church adorned in an ashes-of-roses silk dress with "satin bayardere stripes spread in rich folds over a voluminous hoopskirt." It had, "Bettie" understood from feminine gossip, been created for Mary by a celebrated dressmaker in St. Louis. Mrs. Lincoln had refused to let a local seamstress, either

Ann or Sophia Van Norstrand of 120 West Jefferson Street, "put the scissors in it." With this noteworthy gown, the proud wife of the successful lawyer wore a black lace shawl, secured at each shoulder with small gold pins. Atop her "smoothly brushed hair" rested a white bonnet decorated with white plumes. A collar of point lace and a pair of white kid gloves completed her ensemble.

"Bettie" remembered one particular Sunday when President-Elect and Mrs. Lincoln appeared in church with guests. "They were rather late and created quite a stir," she recollected, "which had scarcely subsided when a small figure crept furtively in and seated itself close by the President [-Elect]'s side. At the first glance toward the lad—it was Tad—Mary Lincoln grew crimson with mortification, for Master Tad's toilette showed hasty preparation and lack of maternal supervision. All this, however, mattered not to the indulgent Father. He drew the child close to his side, and there in a short time Tad was happily asleep."[108]

Thomas—nicknamed "Tadpole" by his Father and called Tad for short—received the sacrament of holy baptism in the First Presbyterian Church on Wednesday, April 4, 1855, his second birthday.[109] Of the four Lincoln children, only Tad seems to have been baptized in any church. And he was the only one born after Mary became a church member.

On February 14, 1855, the State of Illinois incorporated The Peoria University which was to be governed by the Synod of Illinois for the Presbyterian Church in the United States of America. Among the initial Trustees was James Smith. This institution at Peoria was entitled to establish departments embracing theology, medicine, law, plus the sciences and the arts. It was duly empowered to grant certificates as well as diplomas. On March 9, 1855, the First Presbyterian Church Trustees at Springfield granted Dr. Smith a six-weeks' leave of absence so that he might labor to establish this university as its Financial Agent.

In Springfield, Dr. Smith had once more taken a deep interest in education. Within the first year of his arrival, he established a Female School where young ladies could obtain training in the arts, literature and get a general preparation for higher learning in a Christian atmosphere with some religious instruction. He engaged "a number of competent female teachers" with Miss M. P. Massey as the principal. He promised to visit the school every day and supervise. Later, Dr. Smith sat on the Board of Trustees for Illinois State University and no doubt had gained much useful experience from these administrative duties.[110] When the Synod encouraged Smith to continue with his labors for The Peoria University, Dr. Smith began to rethink his future. It was not a full-time position and probably did not pay much in the way of a salary. So, the Rev. Dr. Smith secured an additional occupation. He obtained employment with the American Sunday School Union as Secretary of Missions for the Northwest which would require him to reside in or around Chicago. This job was to begin on April 1, 1857. But, he resigned from the ministry at First Church on October 19, 1856. Reluctantly, the Trustees accepted his resignation but voted to pay his salary until January 1, 1857. When the Presbytery of Sangamon met on December 17, 1856, it dissolved his pastoral connection with the First Presbyterian Church in Springfield. And that marked his last official duties with First Church. The Presbytery of Chicago received him on September 29, 1857. Next, he appears to have been in Scotland for a couple of years before returning to the United States where he accepted a charge in Belvidere, Illinois, for about a year. Dr. Smith was residing there when the Civil War began, after having preached at special meetings from Chicago to New Orleans as a fund raiser.[111]

Mary Lincoln had a different version of Rev. Smith's change of stations. She asserted that while pastor at the First Presbyterian Church in Springfield, his total pay per year amounted to "some $1600," and he had thought this amount "inadequate" and desired a larger income. When the Session or Trustees failed to increase his emolument, Smith decided to accept a position with The Peoria University and the American Sunday School Union. With sorrow, Mary Lincoln noted his leaving and described Smith as "talented & beloved." She further remarked that her uncle, Dr. John Todd, and some of the other members desired to secure the services of a former Lexington pastor named Brown.[112]

As a result, First Church sent a call to the Rev. Dr. John Howe Brown (1806-1872) on December 24, 1856. He accepted a salary offer of $1350 and, because he was a wealthy man, agreed to pay his own rent. A Mason, a Knight Templar and a worthy preacher "recognized for his great eloquence," Rev. Brown's roots drew direct sustenance from Kentucky soil. He had been born in Greensburg, Green County, Kentucky, and had even been pastor of Mary Lincoln's old church in Lexington for a period of years: 1845-1855. Following his service in the Blue-Grass State, he went on to Jacksonville, Illinois, for fifteen months and then took the pulpit at First Church in Springfield.[113] He preached in the pulpit of First Church on January 11, 1857.[114] Finding the situation to his liking, Dr. Brown accepted the invitation from the Session by means of a letter dated January 13 that year. His first Springfield residence was on the south side of Jackson, near Spring Street. Later, he lived on the southeast corner of 5th and Market (Capitol) and on one corner of Eighth and Jackson.

On the 25th of that same month, Dr. Brown chaired his first Session meeting.[115] His formal installation took place May 3, 1857, with the Rev. J. G. Bergen conducting the ceremonies, assisted by the Rev. Richard V. Dodge (Old School Presbyterian) of Third Church and the Rev. H. R. Lewis of Cass County.[116] Bergen had preached in First Church from 1828 to 1848. Lewis, a Presbyterian minister, was at that time in Virginia Township of Cass County, Illinois.

For the previous year, Dr. Brown and his wife had frequently been in the capital city visiting and buying land. They had numerous relatives already living there, for instance, his nephews, Daniel G. and David A. Brown. These twin sons of his brother, William, at the age of fifteen, had sawed all the lath needed to build the State House on the Public Square.[117]

Dr. Brown, an Old School Presbyterian—as was his predecessor, Dr. James Smith—understood the financial world as well as the intangible one. He owned $40,000 worth of real estate![118] Here was one preacher who could discuss money matters with a board of trustees and talk their language. Such a talent is indeed rare among men of the cloth. On the other hand, Brown could dwell in the ivory tower of scholarship. A gifted man, he even agreed to function as the temporary principal of The Springfield Female Seminary when it opened with four teachers on September 20, 1858. This institution of advanced learning received its sponsorship from the Presbyterian Churches of Springfield, and at that time was conducted on the northwest corner of Market (Capitol) and Seventh, later the exact site of the First Presbyterian Church.[119] This academy also moved about from time to time.

Although Mary Lincoln did not admire him at first, the Rev. Dr. Brown delivered excellent sermons, and the Lincolns continued their worship at First Church. Abraham Lincoln enjoyed listening to a fine speaker. In addition, Dr. Brown was tender, sympathetic, full of human kindness and always prepared to render assistance to those in distress. With his seemingly excellent reputation and his proven intellectual abilities, Rev. Brown might have climbed the ladder to high leadership in the Presbyterian Church, but alas he complained that his constitution had never been very robust, and he seemed to suffer from various illnesses. Perhaps for this reason, he was never driven by religious

The Rev. Dr. John Howe Brown,
taken in Springfield, Illinois, at the National Gallery by G. S. German.
The photo is not dated.

Courtesy of Illinois State Historical Library

Rev. Dr. John Howe Brown (1806-1872) with his second wife, Elizabeth J. (Todd) Grimsley Brown (1825-1895), a cousin of Mary (Todd) Lincoln. They were married on January 29, 1867. This photograph was taken at the Central Photographic Gallery in Lexington, Kentucky, probably while they were on their honeymoon. Mrs. Brown is wearing her "Traveling gown." Elizabeth was perhaps the best liked of the Todd women in Springfield.

ambition to seek larger churches or exercise authority in the General Assembly. But he did sit with Abraham Lincoln as a member of the Board of Trustees for Illinois State University. Back on October 1, 1852, Lincoln had also purchased a scholarship from this college. His son, Robert, of course, used it for his schooling.

A broad smile of approval probably spread across Lawyer Lincoln's craggy countenance on his birthday in 1859 when the Session accepted for membership and communion Jenny Jackson, a "coloured woman," who presented her letter from a church in Laurence, New Jersey. She was single, twenty-two years of age and earned her living as a dressmaker.[120] But on other matters, the Session continued to be extremely narrow-minded. On January 7, 1860, the Elders charged two married ladies of the congregation with the deadly sin of dancing. Both had been observed in their crime while attending a "late party" hosted by Ex-Governor Joel A. Matteson.[121] Lincoln probably wondered in his judicial mind just what the *informers* had been doing at the sinful social gathering. His second thought must have been: "There but for the grace of God . . . and the absence of church membership, go I." Although he certainly puzzled over the ways of his Christian brethren, Lincoln never questioned the supremacy of the Almighty.

Listeners to the public speeches by Lawyer Lincoln in the 1850's would have noted his frequent references to the Holy Scriptures as he re-entered the political arena like a giant crusading gladiator. Sometime after 8 p.m. on the sixteenth of June in 1858, the tall candidate who aspired to replace Stephen A. Douglas in the United States Senate uncoiled to his extreme height of six feet three and three-quarters inches—plus the added elevation of his boot heels—before a large crowd of listeners in the Hall of the House upstairs in the Capitol at Springfield, Illinois, to address the Republican State Convention at its closing forum. In his long, powerful fingers, the former Railsplitter clutched a manuscript which he had carefully prepared after much soul-searching. In the very legislative chamber of the State House where he had formerly debated as a member of the Illinois General Assembly, he uttered four introductory sentences in his high tenor voice, then pronounced the thesis of his shocking oration: "A house divided against itself cannot stand."[122]

All those present, as well as all those who later read this epic discourse, knew—if they conned their Bibles regularly—that Lincoln had extracted his text mainly from St. Mark 3:25 which prophesies: "And if a house be divided against itself, that house cannot stand." Similar statements are also found in St. Matthew 12:25 and St. Luke 11:17. Like the Prophets of ancient Israel, Lincoln had now set forth one of his first amazing political predictions. "I believe," continued Lincoln, "this government cannot endure, permanently half <u>slave</u> and half <u>free</u>." He also quoted from Ecclesiastes 9:4, saying, "But 'a <u>living dog</u> is better than a <u>dead lion</u>.'" "Judge Douglas," reasoned Lincoln, "if not a <u>dead</u> lion <u>for this work</u>, is at least a <u>caged</u> and <u>toothless</u> one."

Still, this was not the first time that Abraham Lincoln had stood boldly before his fellow politicos and referred to the Holy Bible. While a Congressman from the old Seventh District of Illinois, the Hon. A. Lincoln had decried the entry of the United States into the Mexican War. From the marble floor of the House of Representatives in our nation's capitol, he shouted defiantly on January 12, 1848, that "the blood of this war, like the blood of Abel, is crying to Heaven against" the President. He meant, of course, James K. Polk.[123] In this memorable instance, Representative Lincoln paraphrased Genesis 4:10 where the Lord said to Cain, "What hast thou done? the voice of thy brother's blood crieth unto me from the ground."

The Bible was a work much studied by Lincoln. For some months prior to April 6, 1858, Lincoln had been preparing a lecture on Discoveries and Inventions. Since the backbone of his talk dealt with the recordings of these topics in the Bible, he had to have carefully reread the Scriptures with pencil and paper at hand. His professional lecture displayed much careful attention to minute details given in the Bible.

Later, in his race to defeat Senator Douglas, Lincoln addressed a crowd of noisy partisan supporters in Chicago on July 10, 1858. Referring to Douglas, he announced with a smile: "My friend has said to me that I am a poor hand to quote Scripture. I will try it again, however. It is said in one of the admonitions of the Lord, 'As your Father in Heaven is perfect, be ye also perfect.' The Savior, I suppose, did not expect that any human creature could be perfect as the Father in Heaven; but He said, 'As your Father in Heaven is perfect, be ye also perfect.' He set that up as a standard, and he who did most towards reaching that standard, attained the highest degree of moral perfection. So I say in relation to the principle that all men are created equal, let it be as nearly reached as we can."[124]

On this occasion, Lincoln paraphrased Christ's sermon on the mount found in St. Matthew 5:48 which says, "Be ye therefore perfect, even as your Father which is in heaven is perfect." This example proves several points.

First, Lincoln knew the Holy Word so well that he did not seek out certain passages and write them down for his speeches. He simply relied upon his memory of the Lord's words gained from long perusal of the Bible. Second, it mentions the saving power of Jesus Christ. However, Lincoln in this specific instance used the appellation "Savior" instead of calling Him simply Jesus, Christ or Lord as the Bible does in this section.

Abraham Lincoln rarely mentioned the words Jesus Christ. In most of his religious statements he simply referred to God or the Almighty, etc. Could it be that Lincoln was more of a Deist than he was anything else? Yes, he probably was just that. He perhaps reasoned that it was sufficient to call upon the supreme God figure who as the Sovereign Grand Architect had made this entire universe and still ruled it. William H. Herndon, his last law partner, stated emphatically that Lincoln did not "believe that Jesus was God." Billy Herndon proclaimed that Lincoln "was a Theist, somewhat after the order of Theodore Parker."[125]

And in his years as a prairie lawyer, Abraham Lincoln did tend to mention "God," etc., but rarely Jesus Christ. For example, at Kalamazoo, Michigan, on August 27, 1856, Lincoln declared to a gathering of ardent Republicans that "So sure as God lives, the victory shall be yours."[126] Among the fragments of a speech probably composed in 1859, he questioned on paper: "How long, in the government of a God, great enough to make and maintain this Universe, shall there continue knaves to vend, and fools to gulp, so low a piece of [demagoguery] as this[?]"[127] At Clinton, Illinois, on October 14, 1859, Lincoln said, "But I do hope that as there is a just and righteous God in Heaven, our principles will and shall prevail sooner or later."[128]

Such utterances would tend to confirm Herndon's categorization of Lincoln as a Theist. Yet Billy spoke only from his personal observations of Lincoln during his Springfield years. Herndon never witnessed the Sixteenth President who struggled mightily in a crucible of fire during the terrible American Civil War which taxed the very mind, body and soul of Abraham Lincoln. In that frightful struggle of brother against brother and father against son, the immortal Lincoln expanded his spiritual experience with his Maker and drew even closer to his God. His life became almost Christ-like.

Nevertheless, Abraham Lincoln shied away from mentioning Jesus Christ. Ward Hill Lamon, his "particular friend," asserted that Lincoln "never told any one that he accepted Jesus as the Christ, or performed a single one of the acts which necessarily follow upon such a conviction." "Never," avowed Lamon, "in all that time did he let fall from his lips or pen an expression which remotely implied the slightest faith in Jesus as the Son of God and the Saviour of men." When Lincoln called upon God or the Almighty or Divine Providence, explained Lamon, this usage was "not inconsistent with his religious notions."[129] Henry Clay Whitney divulged that Mr. Lincoln was "not a formal or ritualistic Christian."[130] Billy Herndon swore that he "never heard" Lincoln "use the name of . . . Jesus but to confute the idea that he was the Christ."[131]

Later, claims were made that the Rev. Dr. James Smith had "converted" Abraham Lincoln "from 'Unitarian' to 'Trinitarian' belief," but Robert Todd Lincoln informed Billy Herndon in 1866, that he had no knowledge of the matter. In fact, Robert insisted that his father probably did not have "any decided views on the subject as I never heard him speak of it."[132] It is certainly doubtful that Lincoln ever accepted any theological changes in his view of God, alone, as the Supreme Ruler of the Universe.

Sometime during the period that Abraham Lincoln had Billy Herndon as his law partner, he expressed to the younger man that "All that I am, or hope to be, I owe to my angel mother."[133] Here, if Lincoln was making a literal statement, he was referring to Nancy (Hanks) Lincoln. By saying "angel mother," Abraham seems to be saying that he knew that Nancy (Hanks) Lincoln was in Heaven. His stepmother was still alive.

According to Presbytery reports to the General Assembly, the First Presbyterian Church at Springfield had two hundred and one communicant members when the Lincolns left town in 1861. Their church was growing slowly.

References

1   Basler, ed., *The Collected Works*, I, 78; Thomas F. Schwartz, "The Springfield Lyceums and Lincoln's 1838 Speech," *Illinois Historical Journal*, LXXXIII, 48 (Spring, 1990). And women attended these Lyceum meetings, so there was a mixing of the sexes, too, just like in worship services.

2   Joshua F. Speed, *Reminiscences of Abraham Lincoln . . .* (Louisville: John P. Morton & Co., 1884), 32-33.

3   Jas. H. Matheny to J. A. Reed, Springfield, Ill., Dec. 16, 1872, in *Scribner's Monthly*, VI, 337 (July, 1873).

4   John T. Stuart to J. A. Reed, Springfield, Ill., Dec. 17, 1872, in *ibid.*, VI, 336.

5   Basler, ed., *The Collected Works*, I, 272. *Sangamo Journal* (Springfield), Feb. 18, 1842, p. 2, c. 4, Aug. 26, 1842, p. 2, c. 7; Federal Tract Book No 695, p. 530, MS., Illinois State Archives; Thomas P. Reep, *Lincoln at New Salem* (Petersburg: Old Salem League, 1927), 99; Wm. H. Herndon and Jesse William Weik, *Herndon's Lincoln* (Springfield: Herndon's Lincoln Pub. Co., n. d.) I, 140; *Proceedings of the Grand Lodge of Illinois 1840-1850* (Freeport: Journal Print., 1892), 74; *Proceedings of the Grand Lodge of Illinois 1826.*

6   Charles Hamilton and Lloyd Ostendorf, *Lincoln in Photographs* (Dayton: Morningside, 1985), 88.

7   U. S. Census 1850, Springfield, Sangamon Co., Il., p. 75A, ll. 13-14; Matheny Statement, May 3, 1866, MS., Herndon-Weik Coll., Library of Congress; *Illinois State Journal*, July 18, 1882, p. 6, c. 1; Power, *Early Settlers of Sangamon County*, 314-315; Heitman, *Historical Register of the United States Army*, I, 433; research by Tom Lapsley of Portland, Oregon, Apr. 22, 1991; St. Paul's Parish Register, II, 276, MS., St. Paul Cathedral, Springfield, Ill. The Lincoln marriage appears as No. 15 among the marriages. Charles E. Francis, *Francis* (New Haven: Tuttle, Morehouse . . . , 1906). Herndon and Weik, *Herndon's Lincoln*, II, 229n. *Sangamo Journal*, Oct. 28, 1842, p. 2, c. 7 shows the Chatterton partnership just formed the previous day. C. W. Chatterton was another of Lincoln's Masonic friends *Proceedings of the Grand Lodge of Illinois 1840-1850*, 30. For a fine obituary of Simeon Francis and Eliza Francis, see *The Oregonian*, Oct. 26, 28, 1872, May 1, 1893.

8   Robert Stuart Sanders, *History of the Second Presbyterian Church, Lexington, Kentucky* (Lexington: 2nd Presbyterian Church, 1965), 90, 125.

9   Katherine Helm, *The True Story of Mary, Wife of Lincoln* (N. Y.: Harper & Bros., 1928), 29.

10 Under date of Dec. 10, 1863, Lincoln wrote on the bottom of Sayre's letter: "The writer of this, an old man, was a Sunday School teacher of Mrs. L. and she would be glad for him to be obliged. I know no other reason." David A. Sayre to Mrs. Mary Lincoln, Lexington, Ky., Dec. 4, 1863, MS., once owned by King V. Hostick, Springfield, Ill.

David Sayre worked ardently to secure and store guns for the loyal Union militia in Lexington. David A. Sayre to Dr. Lewis A. Sayre, Lexington, Ky., May 14, 1861, cited in William H. Townsend, *Lincoln and His Wife's Home Town* (Indianapolis: Bobbs-Merrill Co., 1929), 316 and n.

11 Sanders, *History of the Second Presbyterian Church*, 74, 137, 155, 138.

12 Dumas Malone, ed., *Dictionary of American Biography* (N. Y.: Charles Scribner's Sons, 1935), VIII, 403.

13 Turner and Turner, eds., *Mary Todd Lincoln*, 706, 709.

14 *Ibid.*, 26.

15 Roger E. Chapin, *Ten Ministers: A History of the First Presbyterian Church of Springfield, Illinois, 1828-1953* (Springfield: First Presbyterian Church, 1953), 72.

16 George N. Black, "Reminiscences of the First Presbyterian Church Sabbath School," in *Seventy-Fifth Anniversary . . . of the First Presbyterian Church* (Springfield: First Presby. Church, 1903), 30; "A Lincoln Nurse" in *Illinois State Journal* (Springfield) Feb. 12, 1895, p. 3, c. 3.

17 Basler, ed., *The Collected Works*, I, 320.

18 St. Paul's Parish Register, II, 106, St. Paul's Cathedral, Springfield, Ill. She was No. 32 among the baptismal records.

19 *Ibid.*, II, 223; Rufus Rockwell Wilson, ed., *Intimate Memories of Lincoln* (Elmira: The Primavera Press, 1945), 423.

20 St. Paul's Parish Register, II, 223.

21 Basler, ed., *The Collected Works*, I, 382.

22 Entry of death in the Levi Owen Todd Bible, formerly owned by Alvin S. Keys of Springfield, Ill. Previously, writers have followed the newspaper obituary which failed to mention whether Robert died before or after midnight. Thus, they used July 16 as the date of death. (Levi was a son of the deceased).

23 Emilie Todd recalled that Lincoln spent much time reading in their library. Helm, *The True Story of Mary*, 101.

24   James Smith's date of birth and the names of his parents are carved upon his tombstone in Glasgow, Scotland. James D. Smith, III, has compiled voluminous notes on Dr. Smith and published some of his findings in an article, "The First Historian of a Frontier Church," *The Cumberland Presbyterian Quill*, Vol. II, No. 1 (Winter, 1985). A very brief story of his life is given in Joseph Wallace, *Past and Present of the City of Springfield . . .* (Chicago: S. J. Clarke Pub. Co., 1904), I, 497-498. Other information can be found in the U. S. Census 1850, Springfield, Sangamon Co., Ill., p. 83A, ll. 18-30. For the start of his career in Springfield, see *Illinois Daily Journal*, Mar. 13, 1849, p. 3, c. 2, Apr. 13, 1849, p. 3, c. 1. Neal M. Gordon, III, has also supplied family research on this subject.

Dr. & Mrs. James Smith's eight children have been difficult to trace. However, a brief outline will be attempted here. Eliza born at Cincinnati in 1820 married a Wallace. Catherine McNabb born in Ohio ca. 1824, married Neal McDougal Gordon. Margaret, born ca. 1826, died in Springfield on August 7, 1851. *Illinois State Journal*, Aug. 8, 1851, p. 3, c. 2. Mary, born in 1830, married Lewis W. Lambkin, Sr., in Springfield on Oct. 2, 1857. *Ibid.*, Oct. 6, 1857, p. 2, c. 3. Ann F., born in 1831, married John Forsythe (of Chicago) on July 11, 1854, in Springfield with the Rev. N. M. Gordon of Ky. officiating. *Ibid.*, July 11, 1854, p. 2, c. 6; Marriage Record, III, 111, MS., Sangamon Co. Clerk's Office, Springfield. Forsythe was a lawyer and practiced with J. Young Scammon, a close friend of A. Lincoln. Helen, born in 1833, married Charles E. Mount (of Springfield) on April 6, 1858, in Chicago at the residence of her sister and brother-in-law, the Forsythes, with the Rev. N. L. Rice officiating. *Illinois State Journal*, Apr. 23, 1858, p. 2, c. 4. Hugh Smith was born in 1838 and became Consul of Dundee, Scotland, but has not been further identified. James B. Smith was born June 3, 1840, in Nashville, Tenn. He became a physician and died in Springfield, Ill., on Dec. 30, 1869. A sketch of his life is included in footnote 11 of Chapter VIII in this volume.

As long as they lived, the Todd family in Lexington cherished this very book which Abraham Lincoln had studied in their library. Townsend, *Lincoln and His Wife's Home Town*, 227n.

Dr. James Smith's politics and views on secessionism are related by Dr. William Bishop in William J. Johnson, *Abraham Lincoln the Christian* (N. Y.: Eaton & Mains, 1913), 46.

Dr. Smith's salary is taken from Minutes of the Board of Trustees, 1829-1866, n. p., MS., Ill. State Hist. Lib.

25   *Illinois Daily Journal* (Springfield), Nov. 19, 1849, p. 2, c. 1.

26   Thomas Lewis to J. A. Reed, Springfield, Ill., Jan. 6, 1873, in *Scribner's Monthly*, VI, 339 (July, 1873).

27 James Smith to W. H. Herndon, East Camno, Scotland, Jan. 24, 1867, in *Chicago Tribune*, Mar. 6, 1867, p. 2., c. 10. Dr. Smith wrote this, publicly, while Tad, Robert and Mary Lincoln were still alive to refute it if untrue.

28 Robert T. Lincoln to Isaac Markens, Manchester, Vt., Nov. 4, 1917, MS., Chicago Historical Society.

29 Illinois State Library Register (1842-1850), I, 1, MS., Illinois State Archives. Even the entry is in Lincoln's hand, but he signed his partner's name since only governmental officials could borrow items.

30 N. W. Edwards to Jas. A. Reed, Springfield, Ill., Dec. 24, 1872, in *Scribner's Monthly*, VI, 338-339 (July, 1873).

31 James Smith to W. H. Herndon, East Camno, Scotland, Jan. 24, 1867, in *Chicago Tribune*, Mar. 6, 1867, p. 2, c. 9.

32 A. Lincoln to John D. Johnston, Springfield, Ill., Feb. 23, 1850, in Basler, ed., *The Collected Works*, II, 77.

33 *Illinois Daily Journal* (Springfield), Feb. 2, 1850, p. 3, c. 1.

34 U. S. Census 1850, Mortality Schedule for Springfield, Sangamon Co., Ill., 787, MS., Illinois State Archives. Today, this sickness would be called tuberculosis.

35 *Illinois Daily Journal*, Feb. 2, 1850, p. 3, c. 1.

36 Harry E. Pratt, "Little Eddie Lincoln—'We Miss Him Very Much,'" *Jour. Ill. State Hist. Soc.*, XLVII, 300-305 (Autumn, 1954); *Illinois Register* (Springfield), Oct. 6, 1843, p. 4, c. 6.

37 James Smith to W. H. Herndon, East Camno, Scotland, Jan. 24, 1867, in *Chicago Tribune*, Mar. 6, 1867, p. 2, c. 9; Turner and Turner, eds., *Mary Todd Lincoln*, 567-568.

38 *Ibid.*

39 First Presbyterian Church Session Minutes, 1828-1862, p. 69, MS., Illinois State Historical Library.

40 *Ibid.*, p. 70.

41 U. S. Census 1850, Springfield, Sangamon Co., Ill., p. 83 A, l. 18; N. L. Rice, *The Old and New Schools* (Cincinnati: John D. Thorpe, 1853).

42 Mary Lincoln wrote that they had occupied their pew "some ten years." Mrs. A. Lincoln to Mrs. Samuel Melvin, Washington, D. C., Apr. 27, 1861, copy in

First Presbyterian Church. Thos. D. Logan to Geo. Pasfield, Springfield, Ill., Oct. 7, 1898, MS., First Presbyterian Church.

43 *Proceedings of the Grand Lodge of Illinois* (Freeport: Journal Print, 1892), 650.

44 It was duly recorded on March 7, 1833. Deed Record, F, 262-264, MS., Recorder's Office, Sangamon Co. Bldg.

45 *Sangamo Journal* (Springfield), Feb. 11, 1842, p. 3, c. 1.

46 *Ibid.*, May 27, 1842, p. 2, c. 3. Dresser had to sue to get his full payment on Aug. 5, 1845. Sangamon Co. Circuit Court Records, I, 55, MS., Sangamon Co. Bldg.

47 Deed Record, U, 204-206, MS., Recorder's Office, Sangamon Co. Bldg.

48 Clinton L. Conkling to Robert T. Lincoln, Springfield, Ill., Oct. 1, 1915, MS., Beckwith Coll., Ill. State Hist. Lib. Among the school teachers were Rev. Francis Springer, the Rev. Ephriam Miller, and a person named Garvey, perhaps William F. Garvey (Aug. 22, 1829-Mar. 16, 1906). *Illinois State Journal*, July 27, 1926, p. 9, c. 5. Although Robert Lincoln wrote the name correctly in his autobiography, housed at the Harvard University Archives, one of his biographers misread the name as "Esterbrook." In 1850, when Robert entered this academy, A. W. Estabrook was 35, a school teacher born in Vermont; his wife, Laura, was 22, born in New York; they had no children at this time. U. S. Census 1850, Springfield, Sangamon Co., Ill., p. 89B, ll. 19-20. It would appear from Robert's own statement that he attended Estabrook's Academy for three years before going to the Mechanics' Union Building for the Preparatory Department of Illinois State University. An original and unidentified newspaper clipping in possession of the author boasts of the surgery performed by Dr. Harper in Springfield.

For information on Smith, see *Portrait Biographical Album of Sangamon County* (Chicago: Chapman Bros., 1891), 515-516 and Death Record No. 3636, Ill. Dept. of Public Health: Vital Records.

49 Lizzie D. Black to Dr. Thomas D. Logan, St. Louis, Mo., Mar. 8, 1909, MS., owned by author.

50 *Ibid.*

51 Earl Schenck Miers, ed., *Lincoln Day by Day* (Washington: Lincoln Sesquicentennial Comm.,1960), I, 212.

52 Black Diary in *Jour. Ill. State Hist.* Soc., XLVIII, 59-64 (Spring, 1955).

53 Miers, ed., *Lincoln Day by Day*, II, 72.

54   Lizzie D. Black to Dr. Thomas D. Logan, St. Louis, Mo., Mar. 8, 1909, MS., owned by the author.

55   First Presbyterian Church Session Minutes, 1828-1862, p. 71, MS., Ill. State Hist. Lib.

56   *Ibid.*, p. 82; Power, *Early Settlers*, 406; U. S. Census 1850 Springfield, Sangamon Co., Ill., p. 73B, l. 2.

57   Mrs. A. Lincoln to Mrs. Samuel Melvin, Washington, D. C., Apr. 27, 1861, Turner and Turner, eds., *Mary Todd Lincoln*, 85-86; annual records collected by the author from various reports kept by the ministers. Thomas D. Logan to Geo. Pasfield, Springfield, Ill., Oct. 7, 1898, MS., First Presbyterian Church.

58   First Presbyterian Church, Minutes of the Board of Trustees, n. p., MS., Ill. State Hist. Lib.

59   *Seventy-Fifth Anniversary of the First Presbyterian Church* (Springfield: Privately printed, 1903), 19; Thomas Lewis, "New Light on Lincoln's Life," *Leslie's Weekly*, LXXXVIII, 134-135 (Feb. 16, 1899); A Lincoln to Joshua F. Amos, June 9, 1856, in Basler ed., *The Collected Works,* II, 343.

Thomas Lewis was born July 9, 1808, on a farm near Baskingridge (Somerset Co.), New Jersey. He was apprenticed to a shoemaker but read law in spare moments. On April 4, 1832, he married Margaret A. Van Norstrand (b. Oct. 4, 1810). On June 9, 1837, Lewis started west with a party of twenty-seven family members. They arrived in Springfield on August 1. Thomas Lewis opened a very successful shoe store which he ran while he studied law in 1841 with Judge Silas W. Robbins, who also had another student, Richard J. Oglesby! Stephen A. Douglas got Lewis the position of Public Administrator which he held for years. Lewis was admitted to the bar, and Lincoln then got him admitted to practice before the U. S. Courts, but he was never a very successful lawyer. He also continued as a merchant on the Square. In the First Presbyterian Church, Lewis served in several positions: Sunday School Superintendent, Treasurer, Trustee, and in 1854 he was ordained an Elder. A wealthy man, he moved to Cairo, Illinois, in 1875 and later went to Kansas City, Missouri, where he died on February 2, 1900. His body was returned by train to Springfield where services were held at the First Presbyterian Church with burial in Oak Ridge Cemetery. John Carroll Power, *History of the Early Settlers of Sangamon County, Illinois* (Springfield: Edwin A. Wilson & Co., 1876), 455; *Illinois State Journal*, Feb. 4, 1900, p. 6., c. 4, Feb. 5, 1900, p. 6, c. 4; Oak Ridge Cemetery Records, MSS., Springfield, Ill.; U. S. Census 1850, Springfield, Sangamon Co., Ill., p. 79A, l. 12.

60   Harry E. Pratt, *The Personal Finances of Abraham Lincoln* (Springfield: Abraham Lincoln Assoc., 1943), photo of check at p. 94.

61   James D. Smith vs. Mary Spence, et al, filed Nov. 28, 1848, MS., in Sangamon Co. Circuit Court Records, IRAD, Illinois State Archives.

62   Power, *History of the Early Settlers of Sangamon County*, 360-361; Auditor's Receipt Book, 1845-1849, MS., Illinois State Archives.

63   U. S. Census 1850, Springfield, Sangamon Co., Ill., p. 115A, ll. 26-32.

64   First Presbyterian Church Session Minutes, 1828-1862, p. 67, Ill. State Hist. Lib.

65   John Locke Scripps, *Life of Abraham Lincoln*, ed. by Roy P. Basler and Lloyd A. Dunlap (Bloomington: Indiana Univ. Press, 1961), 165.

66   "Amounts subscribed for the building of Baptist Meeting house 1848-1850," Springfield Baptist Assoc. Business Papers, 1840-1850, MSS., Ill. State Hist. Lib.; Subscription List, MS., Grace Lutheran Church, courtesy of L. Eugene Rubley.

67   Belvidere (Ill.) *Standard*, Apr. 14, 1868, p. 1.

68   *Buck & Kriegh's City Directory for the year 1859, Springfield, Illinois* (Springfield: B. A. Richards & Co., 1859), 12.

69   *Springfield City Directory, for 1857-'58* (Springfield: S. H. Jameson & Co., 1857), 68.

70   *Buck & Kriegh's City Directory for the year 1859 . . .* , 61.

71   N. W. Miner, "Personal Reminiscences of Abraham Lincoln" written at Trenton, N. J., Oct. 15, 1881, MS., Ill. State Hist. Lib.

72   Turner and Turner, eds., *Mary Todd Lincoln*, 710.

73   Mary Miner Hill, Memoirs, n. d., MS., Ill. State Hist. Lib.

74   N. W. Miner, "Personal Reminiscences of Abraham Lincoln," MS., Ill. State Hist. Lib.

75   *Daily Illinois State Journal*, Dec. 22, 1858, p. 3, c. 1; July 7, 1859, p. 3, c. 2; Oct. 6, 1859, p. 3, c. 1; Oct. 7, 1859, p. 3, cc. 1-2; Membership Record Book, 1849-1861, MS., Masonic Temple, Springfield, Ill.

76   N. W. Miner, "Personal Reminiscences of Abraham Lincoln," MS., Ill. State Hist. Lib.

77   John T. Stuart to J. A. Reed, Springfield, Ill., Dec. 17, 1872, in *Scribner's Monthly*, VI, 336 (July 1873).

78   Robert T. Lincoln to Isaac Markens, Manchester, Vt., Nov. 4, 1917, MS., Chicago Hist. Soc.

79   Beverly P. Herndon to W. E. Barton, Kelvin, Ariz., [1925], MS., once owned by King V. Hostick, Springfield, Ill.

80   Rev. James Smith to W. H. Herndon, East Camno, Scotland, Jan. 24, 1867, in *Chicago Tribune*, Mar. 6, 1867, p. 2, c. 9.

81   Mary Lincoln to John Todd Stuart, Chicago, Dec. 15, 187[3], in Turner and Turner, eds., *Mary Todd Lincoln*, 604.

82   Rev. James Smith to W. H. Herndon, East Camno, Scotland, Jan. 24, 1867, in *Chicago Tribune*, Mar. 6, 1867, p. 2, c. 9.

83   Mary Lincoln to James Smith, Marienbad, Bohemia, June 8, 1870, in Turner and Turner, eds., *Mary Todd Lincoln*, 566.

84   The brief diary of Mrs. William M. Black is published in the *Jour. Ill. State Hist. Soc.*, XLVIII, 63, 61 (Spring, 1955).

85   Rev. Dr. William Bishop's account is reprinted in Johnson, *Abraham Lincoln the Christian*, 43-49; *Illinois Daily Journal*, Mar. 27, 1852, p. 3, c. 1.

86   Wm. H. Herndon to Isaac N. Arnold, Springfield, Ill., Oct. 24, 1883, MS., Chicago Hist. Soc.; Hertz, ed., *The Hidden Lincoln*, 90-91.

87   First Presbyterian Church Session Minutes, 1828-1862, p. 83, Ill. State Hist. Lib.

88   Black Diary, *Jour. Ill. State Hist. Soc.*, XLVIII, 63 (Spring, 1955).

89   Rev. James Smith to W. H. Herndon, East Camno, Scotland, Jan. 24, 1867, in *Chicago Tribune*, Mar. 6, 1867, p. 2, c. 10; Lewis in *Leslie's Weekly*, LXXXVIII, 134-135 (Feb. 16, 1899).

90   Basler, ed., *The Collected Works*, II, 97.

91   Lizzie D. Black to Dr. Thomas D. Logan, St. Louis, Mo., Mar. 8, 1909, MS., owned by the author.

92   Basler, ed., *The Collected Works*, II, 188.

93   First Presbyterian Church Minutes of the Board of Trustees, n. p., MS., Ill. State Hist. Lib.; *Illinois Daily Journal*, Jan. 14, 1854, p. 2, c. 1; Theodore Calvin Pease and James G. Randall, eds., *The Diary of Orville Hickman Browning* (Springfield: Ill. State Hist. Lib., 1925), I, 124.

94   First Presbyterian Church Session Minutes, 1828-1862, p. 123, MS., Ill. State Hist. Lib.

95   James T. Hickey, ed., "An Illinois First Family: The Reminiscences of Clara Matteson Doolittle," *Jour. Ill. State Hist. Soc.*, LXIX, 10 (Feb. 1976).

96   Photo of an original invitation in Carl Sandburg, *Lincoln Collector* (N. Y.: Harcourt, Brace & Co., 1949), 140.

97   Helm, *Mary, Wife of Lincoln*, 74.

98   Wm. H. Herndon to Isaac N. Arnold, Springfield, Ill., Oct. 24, 1883, MS., Chicago Hist. Soc.

99   First Presbyterian Church Session Minutes, 1828-1862, p. 71, MS., Ill. State Hist. Lib.

100   F. B. Carpenter, *Six Months at the White House with Abraham Lincoln* (N. Y.: Hurd & Houghton, 1867), 187.

101   Hertz, ed., *The Hidden Lincoln*, 418.

102   Mrs. A. Lincoln to Abram Wakeman, Soldiers' Home, Sept. 23, [1864], in Turner and Turner, eds., *Mary Todd Lincoln*, 180.

103   Mrs. A. Lincoln to David Davis, Chicago, Ill., Mar. 4, 1867, in *ibid.*, 414.

104   Ward H. Lamon, *The Life of Abraham Lincoln* (Boston: James R. Osgood & Co., 1872), 475.

105   A. Lincoln to Joshua F. Speed, Springfield, Ill., July 4, 1842, in Basler, ed., *The Collected Works*, I, 289.

106   A. Lincoln to Joshua F. Speed, Springfield, Ill., Feb. 3, 1842, in *ibid.*, I, 267.

107   Wayne C. Temple, ed., *Lincoln as Seen by C. C. Brown* (Prairie Village, Kansas: The Crabgrass Press, 1963).

108   Copy of Mrs. C. C. Brown's original recollections, owned by the author.

109   First Presbyterian Church, Register of Baptisms, IV, 80, copy in church.

110   *Illinois Daily Journal*, Aug. 29, 1849, p. 2, c. 4; *Private Laws of the State of Illinois* (Springfield: Lanphier & Walker, 1855), 484-485; *Springfield City Directory . . . for 1855-6* (Springfield: Birchall & Owen, 1855), 60.

111   First Presbyterian Church Session Minutes, 1828-1862, p. 131, MS., Ill. State Hist. Lib.; *Illinois State Journal*, Dec. 25, 1856, p. 3, c. 1.

The Peoria University was not a successful venture, and Dr. Smith certainly was not long connected with it.

112   Mrs. A. Lincoln to Emilie (Todd) Helm, Springfield, Ill., Nov. 23, 1856, in Turner and Turner, eds., *Mary Todd Lincoln*, 47-48.

Dr. John Howe Brown was born in Greensburg, Green County, Kentucky, on March 26, 1806. In Kentucky, he received a classical education at the hands of the Rev. John Howe who was his pastor and the man for whom he was named. Then he studied theology with the Rev. Dr. Thomas Cleland of Mercer County and married his daughter, Miss Clarinda "Clara" Cleland. On September 15, 1828, Brown went to the Presbyterian Church at Richmond, Kentucky, and stayed there until 1845 when he became the minister of the McChord (Second) Presbyterian Church at Lexington, Kentucky, where the Todds worshipped. From 1847 to 1852, he also labored as a trustee of Centre College. After having built a new church building in Lexington, Brown moved to the Presbyterian Church at Jacksonville, Illinois, in 1855. Fifteen months later, he accepted a call from the First Presbyterian Church of Springfield, Illinois, where the Lincolns worshipped. But Dr. Brown resigned in 1864 and began operating a drug store—with his brother, Joel B. Brown—on the southwest corner of the Public Square. From the Manse he moved his place of residence to a house on the corner of Eighth and Jackson, just across from the old Lincoln residence. His wife, Clarinda, moved to a farm owned by her son, Dwight Brown, near Bates in Sangamon County. (It no longer exists but was near New Berlin.) There she died on January 13, 1866, and her remains were brought back to Springfield on the Great Western Railroad where she was buried in Oak Ridge Cemetery after a service in the First Presbyterian Church. She was in her 68th year.

Dr. Brown then took a second wife, on January 29, 1867. This was Elizabeth J. (Todd) Grimsley, a cousin of Mary (Todd) Lincoln's and a great favorite of both Mary and Abraham. She was the daughter of Dr. John Todd and had been born at Edwardsville, Illinois, on January 29, 1825. She first married Harrison J. Grimsley, a Springfield merchant and a Whig, on July 21, 1846. H. J. Grimsley died on January 5, 1865. Dr. Brown supposedly suffered from ill health, but soon began to supply the pulpit of the Fullerton Avenue Church in St. Louis. In 1869, he moved to Chicago as the pastor of the Thirty-First Street Presbyterian Church. When Tad Lincoln died in Room 21 of the Clifton House at Chicago on July 15, 1871, it was Dr. Brown and Robert Lincoln who—among others—escorted the body back to Springfield, Illinois. Mary Lincoln did not make the trip. At 9 a.m. on July 17, Rev. Brown conducted the funeral in the First Presbyterian Church for Tad.

Dr. Brown preached in Chicago until he died rather suddenly just before midnight on February 23, 1872, and his remains were returned to Springfield where a funeral service was conducted in the First Presbyterian Church with burial in Block 7, Lot 187, of Oak Ridge Cemetery, beside his first wife. Dr. Brown was survived by his son, Dwight (also a Mason and Knight Templar like his father) and his wife. Elizabeth J. (Todd) Grimsley Brown did not die until September 23, 1895, at which time she was living at Duluth, Minnesota. Her body was brought back for burial with Dr. Brown in Oak Ridge Cemetery after a service in the First Presbyterian Church. Meanwhile, Dwight Brown—after having been Sheriff of Sangamon County, moved up to Chicago where he established a home at 5548 University Avenue. There he succumbed at the age of eighty-eight on October 14, 1918. His body, likewise, was returned to Springfield for interment at Oak Ridge Cemetery in his own lot that he had purchased back in 1864 and which now contained the bodies of his parents, his stepmother and other members of his family. His parents have matching headstones, but Elizabeth (Todd) Grimsley Brown's grave is unmarked. Yet, she certainly is buried in Grave No. 1 beside Dr. J. H. Brown. *Illinois State Journal*, Jan. 15, 1866, p. 2, c. 5, July 17, 1871, p. 4, c. 2, Feb. 26, 1872, p. 4, cc. 2-3, Sept. 24, 1895, p. 5, c. 6, Sept. 25, 1895, p. 5, c. 6, Sept. 26, 1895, p. 5, c. 5, Oct. 16, 1918, p. 11, c. 3; Marriage Record, IV, 243, MS., Clerk's Office, Sangamon Co. Bldg.; U. S. Census 1860, Springfield, Sangamon Co., Ill., p. 141, ll. 18-20; Cook Co. Death Record No. 28796, MS., Dept. of Public Health: Vital Records, Springfield, Ill.; *Springfield City Directory For 1864* (Springfield: Johnson & Bradford, 1864), 19; Sanders, *History of the Second Presbyterian Church Lexington, Kentucky*, 39-43; Power, *History of the Early Settlers*, 149, 716-717; Oak Ridge Cemetery Records, MSS., Springfield, Ill.

113　Sanders, *History of the Second Presbyterian Church*, 39-43.

114　*Daily Illinois State Journal*, Jan. 10, 1857, p. 3, c. 1.

115　First Presbyterian Church Session Minutes, 1828-1862, p. 133, MS., Ill. State Hist. Lib. Dr. Smith had informed the congregation on October 19, 1856, that he must leave them, and the Presbytery dissolved his connection with First Church on December 17 that year. *Ibid.*, pp. 131-132.

116　*Daily Illinois State Journal*, May 5, 1857, p. 3, c. 1.

117　Turner and Turner, eds., *Mary Todd Lincoln*, 47; Power, *History of the Early Settlers*, 148.

118　U. S. Census 1860, Springfield, Sangamon Co., Ill., p. 141, ll. 18-20; Rev. Brown lived on the southeast corner of 5th and Market (now Capitol).

119　*Daily Illinois State Journal*, Sept. 11, 1858, p. 2, c. 4. *Buck & Kriegh's City Directory For the Year 1859* (Springfield: B. A. Richards, 1859), 31.

120　First Presbyterian Church Session Minutes, 1828-1862, p. 146, MS., Ill. State Hist. Lib.; U. S. Census 1860, Springfield, Sangamon Co., Ill., p. 208, l. 23.

121　First Presbyterian Church Session Minutes, 1828-1862, p. 151.

122　Basler, ed., *The Collected Works*, II, 461.

123   *Ibid.*, I, 439.

124   *Ibid.* II, 501.

125   Hertz, ed., *The Hidden Lincoln*, 408; Herndon, "Lincoln's Characteristics," *Illinois State Journal*, Feb. 14, 1874, p. 2, cc. 3-4. Billy summed up his analysis of Lincoln by explaining, "However, take him all in all, he was as near a perfect man as God generally makes." Herndon proposed that Lincoln's work was "the highest and grandest religion; noble duty nobly done."

126   Basler, ed., *The Collected Works*, II, 366.

127   *Ibid.* III, 399.

128   *Ibid.*, III, 488.

129   Lamon, *The Life of Abraham Lincoln*, 501-502.

130   Whitney, *Life on the Circuit With Lincoln*, 269.

131   *The Index*, I, 5-6 (Apr. 2, 1870).

132   R. T. Lincoln to Wm. H. Herndon, Chicago, Dec. 24, 1866, MS., Letterbooks of R. T. Lincoln, Ill. State Hist. Lib. See also Thomas F. Schwartz, "I have never had any doubt of your good intentions . . . ." *Jour. of the Abraham Lincoln Assoc.*, XIV, No. 1, 39 (Winter, 1993).

133   George Alfred Townsend, *The Real Life of Abraham Lincoln: A Talk With Mr. Herndon* (N. Y.: Bible House, 1867), 6.

For the time prior to Lincoln's taking title to a prestigious pew in the First Presbyterian Church at Springfield, no chronicler has recorded his attendance at devotional meetings conducted in the numerous towns where his law practice led him on that long judicial circuit in Central Illinois. Nevertheless, there still exist various reliable accounts of his out-of-town worship or religious expressions after he formed a close association with the Rev. Dr. James Smith. Such contemporary reports confirm this author's considered contention that a profound spiritual change—among other things—occurred in Lincoln due to the enlightening influence of Dr. Smith, and others. Lincoln was also maturing spiritually from his ever-widening experiences in life.

In order to examine personally some land owned by Norman Buel Judd in Council Bluffs, Iowa, Lincoln undertook a tedious journey out there with Illinois-Secretary-of-State Ozias Mather Hatch (1814-1893) in August of 1859. Hatch was a Presbyterian and attended the same church that the Lincolns did. Ardent followers of the growing Republican Party quickly learned of Lincoln's presence at the Pacific House in their fair city and implored him to address them on the thirteenth. He agreed to do so. The following day being Sunday, Lincoln stayed over in Council Bluffs and worshipped in Concert Hall, the meeting place of the First Presbyterian Church of that place.[1] In all probability, Hatch went with him.

When Senator Stephen A. Douglas made a swing through parts of Ohio to make political speeches, the Republicans sent Abraham Lincoln over there to follow him up with their side of the argument. Lincoln arrived in Dayton, Ohio, shortly before noon on September 17, 1859, and was taken to the Phillips House to freshen up before delivering an address at the Courthouse that afternoon. Sometime during his brief stay in Dayton, Lincoln was introduced to Annie Harries, the daughter of John William Harries, an important citizen of that city and a member of Ohio's General Assembly. A noted brewer, he was, no doubt, a member of the reception committee hastily formed to welcome Lincoln to Dayton. When Miss Harries asked for Lincoln's autograph, the tall Republican from Illinois took a small Bible from her hands and inscribed a telling message in it:

Dayton, Ohio
Sept. 17, 1859

Miss Annie Harries—
Live by the words within these
covers and you will [be] forever happy.

Yours truly, A. Lincoln[2]

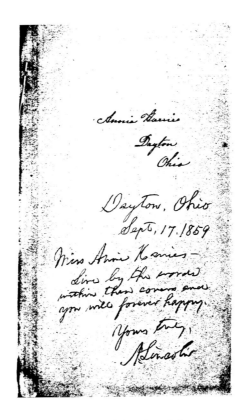

Courtesy of Lloyd Ostendorf

If Abraham Lincoln had a religious creed, it might be summed up in this inscription
which he wrote in the Bible of a young lady in Dayton, Ohio,
on September 17, 1859:
"Live by the words within these covers and you will [be] forever happy."

Original owned by Lloyd Ostendorf, Dayton, Ohio

This is a vital new bit of information concerning Abraham Lincoln's religious credo which has never been previously revealed. It definitely establishes Lincoln's reliance upon the Bible for a basic portion of his philosophy of life before he became President. Perhaps the three most important documents in the development of Lincoln's political thesis were the Bible, the Declaration of Independence and the United States Constitution—not necessarily in that exact order.

At about 2:15 that afternoon Lincoln spoke to approximately two hundred people assembled at the Courthouse and then left at four aboard a train bound for Cincinnati. Reporters summarized his Dayton speech, but his Bible inscription for Ann Harries was quickly forgotten until now.[3] Yet it was one of the most important things that Lincoln did for historians that Saturday in Dayton.

Desiring to introduce himself with great advantage to potential voters in Wisconsin, the ever-hopeful Lincoln accepted a welcomed invitation to deliver a serious agricultural oration to farm folk at the Wisconsin State Fair in Milwaukee on September 30, 1859. He arrived on the 29th and took quarters in the Kirby House. On the following day, the Vice President of the Wisconsin State Fair Association called for Lincoln at his hotel and drove him out to the Cold Spring Fairgrounds, accompanied by the Vice President's ten-year-old son, Darwin D. McCarthy. "Father was a 'dyed-in-the-wool' democrat," explained Darwin, "and tried to hold his ground, but Lincoln was too much for him." "Finally," recalled McCarthy, "Lincoln put his hand on my head and said: 'My little man, I hope you live long enough to see the day you can vote the republican ticket.'" They had a merry ride to the fairgrounds after that with Lincoln telling funny stories and jokes, according to an account by Darwin McCarthy preserved as a clipping from some unidentified local newspaper.

Having traveled many weary miles to fill this engagement for public exposure, Lincoln proceeded to speak in other nearby towns so as to get as much benefit from this expensive excursion as possible. Beloit claimed him first, and then he hurried rapidly on to Janesville for a profitable evening performance. Remaining overnight at the latter place with Mr. and Mrs. W. H. Tallman, the tall Campaigner arose the next morning—October 2—and accompanied this Christian family to the Congregational Church.[4]

Then, early in 1860, Lincoln jolted and bounced those many tiring miles over the rough rails from Springfield to New York City to utter one of the most important political speeches of his entire career. He had been asked to the East for this lecture and jumped at the chance to let the citizens in that area become acquainted with his influential leadership in the Republican Party. As soon as Lincoln arrived in the afternoon hours of February 25, he immediately called upon Henry C. Bowen, the editor of *The Independent*, a religious newspaper published weekly. Since Bowen had been the organizer of the widely-acclaimed Plymouth Church in Brooklyn, Lincoln quite naturally tagged along with Bowen to worship at this red-brick Italianate style church on the following morning. Here, in Pew No. 89, they listened to the preaching of the renowned Henry Ward Beecher (1813-1887).[5] Plymouth Church belonged to the Congregationalists and stood on the west side of Orange Street, between Henry and Hicks streets.

Henry Ward Beecher
(1813-1887)

Several times, Abraham Lincoln heard Henry Ward Beecher preach. Rev. Beecher was a Congregationalist preacher in Brooklyn, New York

Original photograph by Warren of 465 Washington Street, Boston.

When evening came on the following day, February 27, Lincoln presented his polished Cooper Union Address after none other than William Cullen Bryant introduced him to the large, critical audience. This august gathering of strangers caused the Illinois Lawyer to feel most ill at ease, yet he gave a very remarkable performance and departed with great honor to speak before other political groups in New England. While there, he visited his eldest son, Robert, who resided in Exeter, New Hampshire, a student at The Phillips Exeter Academy.

In writing to Mary from Exeter on the 4th of March, Lincoln wryly remarked: "This is Sunday morning and according to Bob's orders, I am to go to church once to-day."[6] Not that Father Abraham needed to be ordered to church on the Sabbath, but he—like most fathers—was certainly trying to reach some rapport with a teen-aged son by allowing Robert to plan their schedule in Exeter. Accordingly, father and son put in their distinguished appearance at the Second Congregational Church and occupied the pew owned by Commodore and Mrs. John Collins Long. This pew still exists, but it is not in the original building. From that illustrious vantage point, father and son gave ear to the Rev. Orpheus T. Lanphear as he imparted the moral message for that happy morning.[7]

In completing his New England campaign circle, Lincoln doubled back to New York City in order to strike out for the far-away town of Springfield, Illinois. Before catching the Erie Railroad cars for home, Lincoln determined to hear the magnificent Rev. Beecher once more. So, on March 11, he joined James A. Briggs, one of those who had arranged his New York speaking appointment at Cooper Union, for another pilgrimage to Plymouth Church. That same Sunday he also heard Edwin H. Chapin preach in the Universalist Church of New York City.[8]

The Republican National Convention had selected Abraham Lincoln as its presidential candidate on May 18, 1860. In the middle of August that year, John Henry Brown paid Springfield a visit to paint a miniature portrait of Lincoln for a Philadelphia client. Not only did Brown pose his illustrious model in various rooms of the State House, but he also observed him in his daily activities. On Sunday, August 26, Brown followed the Lincolns to church. As usual, they worshipped at the First Presbyterian where Artist Brown watched Lincoln intensely with the eyes of a trained painter. Brown noted in his diary that his subject appeared to be "kind and very sociable; immensely popular among the people of Springfield." Even though a few writers had previously described him as homely, Brown declared strongly that he did not agree with such accounts. "There are so many hard lines in his face," explained Brown, "that it becomes a mask of the inner man." "His true character," Painter Brown discovered, "only shines out when in an animated conversation, or when telling an amusing tale, of which he is very fond."[9]

To confer more unobtrusively and meet on neutral ground with Hannibal Hamlin—the man soon to be inaugurated with him as the Vice President of the United States—Lincoln went by rail to Chicago on November

21, 1860, and checked rather calmly into the Tremont House with his wife, Mary. On the following evening, the genial Lincoln escorted Mr. Hamlin to one of the private dining rooms in Tom Andrews' Head Quarters Restaurant at 38 State Street where both enjoyed a confidential talk and the specialty of the house: an "Oysters and Game Supper." A reporter, who found out their secret rendezvous, disclosed that "no man ever enjoyed himself better than did 'old Abe.'" This prying newsman further reported that Andrews' establishment happened to be Mr. Lincoln's favorite eating place whenever he stayed over in the windy city of Chicago.[10]

During a four and a half day visit to Chicago, Lincoln attended to numerous personal chores in addition to his long hours spent with Hamlin discussing vital political matters. One day Lincoln stepped into the shop of the well-known clothier, A. D. Titsworth & Bros. at 113 Lake Street, to be carefully measured for a suit of clothes that he intended to wear at his inauguration on March 4.[11]

When Sunday rolled around on the 25th, the God-fearing President-elect attended public worship services. On this particular occasion, he and Hannibal Hamlin accepted a cordial invitation to be the church guests of the Hon. Isaac Newton Arnold, a Congressman-elect and an old Republican friend of Lincoln's. Arnold escorted his distinguished charges to St. James' Episcopal Church on the corner of Cass and Huron, a new edifice erected in 1857 and staffed by the Rev. Dr. R. H. Clarkson as Rector.[12] A local newspaper announced on Saturday that divine services in this church would take place at 3:00 p. m. on Sunday.[13] Later that same afternoon, Lincoln paid a call, by special invitation, to the Mission Sabbath School where he made a short address to the children who must have been thrilled by such a celebrated public figure.[14] To complete that pleasant day, he dined with Jonathan Young Scammon, a recently-elected Republican House member to the Illinois State Legislature.[15]

Upon arriving back in Springfield by 6:30 p.m. on the evening of November 26, 1860, the Lincolns learned in due course that Governor John Wood had issued a special Thanksgiving Proclamation. Accordingly, the Rev. Dr. Brown at the First Presbyterian Church on the southeast corner of Washington and Third, published a special notice in the press announcing his Thanksgiving service for 11:00 a. m. on Thursday, November 29.[16] Abraham Lincoln, an alert reporter observed, "having special cause to thank his Maker, attended Divine service."[17]

The Lincolns certainly found some of their needed relaxation and comfort on Sundays amidst a spiritual atmosphere. They probably experienced little difference between the erudite sermons of their old pastor, Dr. James Smith, and his successor, Dr. John H. Brown. However, the new minister did introduce one change. He eventually scheduled his Sunday morning worship at 10:30 a. m. instead of 11 and his evening service at 7:30 or 8 instead of 7. On Friday, prayer meeting commenced at 7:30 p. m.[18]

Members of the Methodist Church seemed to have taken a special interest in the politics of Abraham Lincoln. On September 15, 1860, the ministers of the West Wisconsin Conference of Methodist Episcopal Churches made Lincoln a life member of their missionary society. After the certificate was properly lettered, the Rev. Peter S. Mather, of Linden, Iowa County, Wisconsin, the secretary of this Conference, duly forwarded the document to Lincoln on December 5. Although Lincoln did answer the Rev. Mather, we do not know what he told him. The letter is not available to scholars today.[19] We do know Lincoln accepted few memberships with any body, religious or otherwise.

Because of the worsening political situation in the United States after the November elections, President James Buchanan issued a proclamation on December 14, 1860, calling for a national day of "humiliation, fasting and prayer" to be observed across the land on Friday, January 4, 1861.[20] Out in Springfield, Illinois, the local Democratic newspaper ignored the plea, while the Republican organ poked fun at this serious spiritual suggestion of President Buchanan.[21] The latter, of course, accepted a paid notice of an oration and sermon scheduled for this date in the Courthouse. There, J. S. Burt, a graduate of Illinois College and the Chicago Theological Seminary, delivered a discourse in the morning and then preached a religious meditation at 7:00 p. m. concerning the sad plight of the country and pleaded for a religious and political revival.[22]

The most notable public observation of this national fast day in Springfield has escaped the notice of Lincoln scholars. It took place in the First Presbyterian Church where the "most respectable and best people in the city" filled the sanctuary, Rev. Miner reminisced. Folks from all the churches in the capital city attended, and with them in the audience sat President-elect Abraham Lincoln. During the course of their supplications to God, numerous prayers "were offered up for our beloved Country and for the man whom Providence had raised up to guide the Ship of State over a rough and stormy sea!"

At the conclusion of this impressive program, the Rev. Mr. Miner, the Baptist clergyman who lived near the Lincolns, passed down the aisle and discovered Lincoln standing there with his eyes filled to overflowing with tears of gratitude. Taking his good friend Miner by the hand, Lincoln confessed, "This has been a good meeting. I hardly know how it could have been made better. I feel very grateful for the prayers offered for our distracted country and on my behalf, and hope they may be answered."[23]

Indeed, Father Abraham's sensitive feelings often welled up to the surface when deep emotions stirred his very soul. His close acquaintances had learned early that Lincoln possessed a deep sentimental streak that could not easily be contained invisibly within his tall, lanky body.

Taking advantage of a personal invitation from Lincoln, Governor Salmon Portland Chase of Ohio detrained in Springfield later that same day—during the evening hours of January 4, 1861—for a long confidential conversation with the President-elect. Despite these highly-concentrated political conferences, Lincoln's religious pattern changed not a whit. Two days later when the appointed hour for worship arrived, the Lincolns merely took Gov. Chase with them to their regular seat in the First Presbyterian Church. At least two out-of-town witnesses watched this historic event and described the momentous happening by letters which they wrote that very evening to their wives back home.

Edward Needles Kirk happily secured one of the scarce places to sit in the sanctuary prior to the arrival of the dignitaries and watched intensely as "Lincoln & his 'little woman' & Governor Chase of Ohio" made their entrance into First Church for the morning services.[24] Likewise, William H. L. Wallace of Ottawa, Illinois, as a visitor in the city, slipped into this church to catch a glimpse of any distinguished personages that might appear there. Nor did he suffer the slightest disappointment, for Wallace soon noted that Gov. Chase shared Pew No. 20 with Mr. and Mrs. Lincoln. Dr. Brown, "a very able man," observed Wallace, performed in a fine manner and "preached a most excellent sermon."[25] There lay one of the keys to Abraham Lincoln's attendance at the First Presbyterian Church: a most able and interesting minister. He loved a talented, moving speaker and a sincere and learned preacher of the gospel.

Notwithstanding Abraham Lincoln's frequent attendance at religious services, he still clung tenaciously to his belief in fatalism and seemed resigned to his fate—whatever it might be. At times, in fact, he acutely sensed that tragedy would soon befall him. Just after his first election on November

6, 1860, the President-elect reported confidentially to close friends a frightening hallucination.

However, Lincoln never gave serious credence to the practice of Spiritualism, which Mary embraced.[26] She, a Southerner, having been raised with slaves and their beliefs, put a great amount of faith in the séances of the Spiritualists.[27] On numerous occasions, she even participated in them. Despite Abraham's counsel, his wife continued her participation. In speaking of her, Lincoln once uttered that "he had always found it very difficult to make her do what she did not want to."[28]

In the year 1859, Isaac Cogdal—who had known Lincoln since approximately 1834—happened to be in the Lincoln and Herndon law office in Springfield when the two old friends got into a mild discussion concerning religion. Lincoln declared that "he could not believe in the endless punishment of any one of the human race." In other words, Lincoln did not believe in Hell. To this remark Cogdal replied that Lincoln would make a good Universalist. Naturally, the shrewd Lincoln did not comment further on this delicate point. Billy Herndon was present at this chance encounter and vouched, in writing, for the correctness of Cogdal's memory. Herndon first interviewed Cogdal in either 1866 or 1867, and Cogdal later wrote out an independent account of this discussion with Abraham Lincoln.[29]

References

1   Miers, ed., *Lincoln Day by Day*, II, 258; *Illinois State Journal*, Mar. 14, 1893, p. 4, c. 4.

2   Original Bible in the Lincoln collection of Dr. Lloyd Ostendorf, Dayton, Ohio.

3   Lloyd Ostendorf, *Mr. Lincoln Came to Dayton* (Dayton: The Otterbein Press, 1959).

4   Miers, ed., *Lincoln Day by Day*, II, 262.

5   Andrew A. Freeman, *Abraham Lincoln Goes to New York* (N. Y.: Coward McCann, 1960), 13-58. This sermon reproduced in Edgar DeWitt Jones, *Lincoln and the Preachers* (N. Y.: Harper & Bros., 1948), 183-203.

6   Basler, ed., *The Collected Works of Abraham Lincoln, Supplement* (Westport: Greenwood Press, 1974), 49.

7   Elwin L. Page, *Abraham Lincoln in New Hampshire* (Boston: Houghton Mifflin Co., 1929), 111-112.

8   Miers, ed., *Lincoln Day by Day*, II, 275.

9   J. H. Brown Journal, MS., The Lincoln Museum, Fort Wayne, Ind.

10   *Chicago Daily Journal*, Nov. 23, 1860, p. 3, c. 2.

11   *Chicago Daily Tribune*, Nov. 24, 1860, p. 4, c. 6. Titsworth eventually completed the costly suit. "We had the pleasure yesterday," February 7, 1861, reported a local editor in Springfield, Illinois, "of inspecting the magnificent suit which has been in course of preparation for Mr. Lincoln, since his visit to Chicago. It is manufactured by A. D. Titsworth & Bro., merchant tailors of Chicago, and consists of a dress coat, pants, vest and cravat. The coat is of the best cloth that could be bought in the country, and made up with a taste and in a style that cannot be surpassed in any country. The pants are of the best and finest black cashmere. The vest is made of the finest grenadier silk, and lined with buff goods of the same kind. The whole are presented to Mr. Lincoln, with the following inscription: 'To Hon. Abraham Lincoln, from A. D. Titsworth, Chicago, Illinois,' which is beautifully worked on the inside of the coat collar." *Illinois State Journal* (Springfield), Feb. 8, 1861, p. 3, c. 6.

12   *Chicago City Directory, 1860-61* (Chicago: D. B. Cooke & Co., 1860), 309; Appendix, 16.

13   *Chicago Daily Tribune*, Nov. 24, 1860, p. 1, c. 6.

14   *Chicago Daily Journal*, Nov. 26, 1860, p. 2, c. 2.

15   N. Y. *Herald*, Nov. 26, 1860, p. 4, c. 6; *Illinois State Journal*, Nov. 7, 1860, p. 2, c. 4.

16   *Illinois State Journal*, Nov. 29, 1860, p. 3, c. 2.

17   *New York Daily Tribune*, Dec. 1, 1860, p. 6, c. 6.

18   *Illinois State Journal*, Dec. 1, 1860, p. 3, c. 2; *Williams' Springfield Directory . . . for 1860-61* (Springfield: Johnson & Bradford, 1860), 20.

19   R. T. L. Coll., Ser. 1, No. 4829, MSS., The Library of Congress.

20   N. Y. *Herald*, Jan. 4, 1861, p. 5, c. 5.

21   *Illinois State Journal*, Dec. 29, 1860, p. 3, c. 2.

22   *Ibid.*, Jan. 4, 1861, p. 3, c. 1.

23   N. W. Miner, "Personal Recollections of Abraham Lincoln," MS., Ill. State Hist. Lib.

24   Edward Needles Kirk to his wife, Springfield, Ill., Jan. 6, 1861, MS., Ill. State Hist. Lib.

25   Wm. H. L. Wallace to his wife, Ann, Springfield, Ill., Jan. 6, 1861, Wallace Dickey Papers, MSS., Ill. State Hist. Lib.

26   John G. Nicolay and John Hay, *Abraham Lincoln: A History* (N. Y.: The Century Co., 1890), X, 346.

27   Pease and Randall, eds., *The Diary of Orville Hickman Browning*, I, 608; Mrs. Nettie Colburn Maynard, *Was Abraham Lincoln a Spiritualist?* (Chicago: The Progressive Thinker Pub. House, 1917), 36-37.

28   Basler, ed., *The Collected Works*, IV, 218.

29   On the margin of Isaac Cogdal's remarks, Herndon wrote: "This is true," and in another place, "This is correct." See the Herndon-Weik Collection at The Library of Congress. Cogdal later repeated his comments in a letter to B.F. Irwin on April 10, 1874. This missive was published in the *Illinois State Journal*, May 16, 1874, p.2, c. 4. Benjamin F. Irwin was born in Sangamon County, Illinois, on May 18, 1822. At the time of this letter, Irwin lived at Pleasant Plains, Ill. Since April 14, 1869, Irwin had been either a Justice of the Peace or a Police Magistrate in Pleasant Plains, Cartwright Township, Sangamon County. He was still in office at the time Cogdal wrote him in 1874. Since Cogdal practiced law at this time, he must have known Irwin quite well. Justices of the Peace, 1865-73, p. 338, 339, *ibid.*, 1873-89, p. 176, MSS., Illinois State Archives; Power, *Early Settlers of Sangamon County, Illinois*, 404.

Dr. samuel Houston Melvin

Drawing of Dr. Samuel Houston Melvin by Lloyd Ostendorf
from a drawing by F. Day published in the *Oakland Tribune*,
Feb. 11, 1898, p. 1, c. 3.

Chapter Five–Second Chronicles

In ending his address at Cooper Institute in New York City on February 27, 1860, Lincoln implored his listeners: "Let us have faith that right makes might, and in that faith, let us, to the end, dare to do our duty as we understand it."[1] This seems to be an imploring of his audience to put their faith in some power that rules the universe. It gives one the feeling that Lincoln intended a religious meaning to be attached to his closing statement.

Then on May 18, 1860, the delegates to the National Republican Nominating Convention in Chicago selected Lincoln as their candidate for President. Suddenly, the mantle of leadership was clapped over Lincoln's strong shoulders. And he was an imposing figure, too. Glee clubs noted his unusual stature and sang about Lincoln as being "in height somewhat less than a steeple."[2] Lincoln gladly accepted his role like Moses of Biblical times. The old "Railsplitter" put his large hand into the even larger hand of God and accepted his heavy responsibilities. To Joshua R. Giddings he wrote on May 21: "May the Almighty grant that the cause of truth, justice, and humanity, shall in no way suffer at my hands."[3] Two days later, he dispatched a letter to George Ashmun, President of the Republican National Convention, saying, "Imploring the assistance of Divine Providence, and with due regard to the views and feelings of all who were represented in the convention . . . I am most happy to co-operate for the practical success of the principles declared by the convention."[4] He would do his duty as God gave him to see that duty and as God gave him strength to do it.

Without much reasonable doubt, Lincoln certainly acquired the words "Divine Providence" from the Declaration of Independence. In the last sentence of this immortal document are these brave words: "with a firm reliance on the protection of divine Providence, we mutually pledge to each other our Lives, our Fortunes and our sacred Honor." Again and again, Abraham Lincoln read and studied the Declaration of Independence. He stated this publicly when he spoke at Independence Hall in Philadelphia on February 22, 1861. "I have never had a feeling politically," revealed Lincoln, "that did not spring from the sentiments embodied in the Declaration of Independence." He, like the Founding Fathers, accepted the guidance of God in the affairs of man.

Switching to the New Testament (Matthew 26: 69-74), for a text on June 5, Lincoln declared to Senator Lyman Trumbull, "Remembering that Peter denied his Lord with an oath, after most solemnly protesting that he never would, I will not swear I will make no committals; but I do think I will not."[5] And it appears that Lincoln carried a volume of Scriptures with him during the campaign months that he spent in the Governor's Chambers at the State House in Springfield. Governor John Wood had offered Lincoln these handsome quarters shortly after the latter had been nominated for the Presidency, and Lincoln remained there for seven months.[6] Newton Bateman, the Superintendent of Public Instruction, occupied an office right next to Lincoln's borrowed rooms and stated that he saw Lincoln quite often during this critical period of time. Once he observed Lincoln drawing a "pocket New Testament" from his coat. Lincoln then exclaimed, "I know there is a God."[7] This volume might have been just the Psalms, etc., and not the entire New Testament.

William Reid, the United States Vice Consul at Dundee, Scotland, testified on March 4, 1874, that, "I am proud to think that I have in my possession—as a reward [f]or a few insignificant services done by me on account of Mrs. Lincoln—the great and martyred President's psalm book, which he used while at the White House . . . ."[8] Yet this was perhaps not the book which Bateman witnessed in Lincoln's possession back in 1860. Reid's treasured gift was *The Book of Psalms: Translated out of the Original Hebrew* (N. Y.: American Bible Society, 1857), a volume of two hundred and twelve pages, leather-bound and measuring 9 1/4" by 6". If Bateman actually meant that Lincoln had the book in his pocket, then perhaps he referred to a miniature volume called *The Believer's Daily Treasure* (London: The Religious Tract Society, 1852). On this volume's inside cover is the name "A. Lincoln."[9] Yet Lincoln rarely signed his name in his personal books. In any event, Lincoln often quoted the Bible in these difficult days before the election.

While declining to repeat his stand on slavery at the request of William S. Speer, Lincoln remarked on October 23, 1860, "If they hear not Moses and the prophets, neither will they be persuaded though one rose from the dead."[10] Here, he quoted from Luke 16:31. Once more, Lincoln seems to be thinking of prophets and his own role in the scheme of things to come.

November 6, 1860, election day, dawned clear and bright in Springfield, Illinois. Early risers discovered some ice and frost on the ground. All through the remainder of the day, heavy clothing felt very comforting to the chilly local inhabitants, but no rain fell.[11] Throughout most of that day, Abraham Lincoln remained in his usual quarters in the Governor's Chambers at the State House. Quietly he observed the proceedings of the local folks from a window overlooking the Courthouse.[12] Polls in Springfield opened at 8:00 a. m. and closed at 6:00 p.m.[13] Lincoln had informed the press corps on the previous day that he intended to give Richard Yates a vote for Governor.[14] Although he had said that he would wait until 5:00 p. m. to cast his ballot, he found a lull in the line at the Courthouse about 3:00 p. m. He walked over there and proceeded up to the court room on the second floor where he cut his own name from the top of the Republican ballot and deposited the ballot in the box. He did not vote for himself. In all, Lincoln was absent about five minutes before he returned from his polling place to the State House.[15]

On election night, Lincoln sat for a time in the "social circle" at the Chenery House on the northeast corner of Fourth and Washington. That hostelry was considered a Republican hangout. However, he spent most of the night in the telegraph office.[16] Before the sun rose on the following morning, Lincoln learned that he had been elected President of the United States. Now, the burden upon him was even greater. He would need every bit of faith he could muster to face this most difficult challenge. And his physical, mental and moral strengths would be stretched to their very limits.

On the day following Lincoln's election, he experienced a most chilling vision which caused him some soul-searing anguish and once more gave him evidence that some higher power was revealing the future to him. Lincoln recalled to his confidant, Noah Brooks, that on that day he "was well tired out, and went home to rest, throwing myself down on a lounge in my chamber. Opposite where I lay was a bureau with a swinging glass upon it, and looking in that glass i saw myself reflected nearly at full length; but my face, I noticed, had two separate and distinct images, the tip of the nose of one being about three inches from the tip of the other. I was a little bothered, perhaps startled, and got up and looked in the glass, but the illusion vanished. On lying down again, I saw it a second time, plainer, if possible, than before; and then I noticed that one of the faces was a little paler—say five shades—than the other. I got up, and the thing melted away, and I went off, and in the excitement of the hour forgot all about it—nearly, but not quite, for the thing would once in a while come up, and give me a little pang as if something uncomfortable had happened. When I went home again that night I told my wife about it, and a few days afterward I made the experiment again, when sure enough! the thing came again but I never succeeded in bringing the ghost back after that, though I once tried very industriously to show it to my wife, who was somewhat worried about it. She thought it was a 'sign' that I was to be elected to a second term of office, and that the paleness of one of the faces was an omen that I should not see life through the last term." Both Mary Lincoln and John Hay confirmed what the President had told Brooks on November 9, 1864.[17] This happening reveals that Mary Lincoln also believed that supernatural signs or illusions foretold the future.

When Henry J. Raymond, editor of the New York *Times*, asked the President-elect for a political statement about his coming administration, Lincoln replied with a paraphrase of Matthew 12:38-39 by saying, "They seek a sign, and no sign shall be given them."[18] Later, on December 18, 1860, Lincoln again corresponded with Raymond about a false story being circulated by William C. Smedes who was a correspondent of the *Times*: "What a very mad-man your correspondent, Smedes[,] is," exclaimed an angry Lincoln. Mr. Smedes, Lincoln declared, "seems sensitive on the questions of morals and christianity." "What does he think of a man who makes charges against another which he does not know to be true," questioned Lincoln, "and could easily learn to be false?"[19] Here were some of the things which troubled honest Abraham Lincoln about followers of Christ, many of whom he found to be extremely untruthful. How could such folks continue to represent themselves as Christians? Would Christ have born false witness?

Again paraphrasing the Bible, Lincoln took a text from Proverbs 25:11 when early in January of 1861, he compared Liberty and the U. S. Constitution to an apple of gold surrounded by a picture of silver.[20]

In the hustle and bustle of preparing for their removal to the White House, the Lincolns neglected to take steps which would enable them to retain their pew at the First Presbyterian Church until they came back to Springfield. Since Mary Lincoln was the actual member of this institution, it seems certain that the President-elect left the matter entirely to her. At any rate, it was Mary who wrote to Sarah Amanda (Slemmons) Melvin from Washington on April 27, 1861, and confessed that she "had intended requesting Mr. Melvin to have given me a promise, that on our return to S[pringfield] we would be able to secure <u>our particular pew</u>, to which I was very much attached, and which we occupied some ten years." "I hope," pleaded Mary, "that he will be able to do so."[21] It is obvious that Mary Lincoln did not intend to pay an annual tax upon a pew they could not occupy for at least four years, and perhaps—with good fortune—a longer period. And if the levy was not paid for two years, the pew could actually be sold for back taxes just as could any piece of real estate.

Mary Lincoln had indeed sent her plea to the right source, but no previous author has thoroughly researched the Melvins in order to explain their intimate connection to the Lincolns and the First Presbyterian Church. The Melvins deserve a prominent mention in the history of the Lincolns. Samuel Houston Melvin was born on April 22, 1829, in Florence, Washington County, Pennsylvania, the son of James and Matilda (McMillan) Melvin. James had been born in Cecil County, Maryland, in 1804, the son of William and Margaret (McCaig) Melvin, both natives of Ireland who had come across the Atlantic to Maryland. About 1812, the Melvins settled in Washington County, Pennsylvania. James Melvin was a teacher. In 1834, he took his family to Steubenville, Ohio, where he acted as County Auditor and a Justice of the Peace.

At Steubenville, young Samuel H. Melvin studied medicine under Dr. James Sinclair and graduated from the Medical Hall Institute in that city at the age of twenty-three with the degree of Doctor of Medicine. He immediately began practicing his profession. The following year, on August 9, 1853, he married Sarah Amanda Slemmons of Cadiz, Ohio. She had been born in that town on March 30, 1834, the daughter of Samuel and Susanna (Osborn) Slemmons. She and her family were Presbyterians; her father was an Elder as was her grandfather. After her marriage to Dr. Melvin, both husband and wife joined the Presbyterian Church.

After about fifteen months of practicing medicine, Dr. Melvin joined Dr. Thomas S. Hening in operating a wholesale drug business in Steubenville, Ohio. In July of 1859, Dr. Melvin and his partner moved to Springfield, Illinois, where on the 22nd, Melvin purchased the drugstore of J. B. Fosselman, located on the northwest corner of Fifth and Washington. Dr. Melvin announced that he was an experienced pharmacist and would compound prescriptions either day or night for his customers.[22] He also dealt in wholesale and retail drugs, paints, oils, perfumes, and surgical and dental instruments. The Melvins took up residence on the northeast corner of Eighth and Market (now Capitol) just one block north of the Lincolns' home.[23]

Soon, the Melvins and the Lincolns became fast friends. It has been said that Lincoln and Melvin often played checkers in Dr. Melvin's drugstore, and that Mary Lincoln and her children often called upon Sarah Melvin and her growing family: Samuel Slemmons Melvin, born in 1854; James Breed Melvin, born about 1856; Charles Stuart Melvin, born about 1857; and William Patterson Melvin, born about 1859. In early 1861, Sarah Melvin gave birth to a daughter whom they named Mary Lincoln Melvin, after their good friend and neighbor. From the White House, Mary Lincoln acknowledged the event and presented a bonnet cap to her namesake.[24]

Dr. Melvin had become a man of means. He owned real estate and had $7,000 in his personal estate by 1860. He could afford to keep a domestic servant in his home, an Irish girl of eighteen named Mary Marra. By 1870, the Melvins employed two domestics, Mary Marra and Bridget Dolan. Dr. Melvin's worth had also increased. By 1870, he owned $40,000 in real estate and had $50,000 in his personal estate.[25]

Because of his education, his personality and his abilities, Dr. Melvin quickly became a leader in the Springfield community. On November 12, 1859, Dr. and Mrs. Melvin joined the First Presbyterian Church by certificate from a previous church membership in Ohio. As fellow parishioners, they would see the Lincolns even more frequently. Recognizing Melvin's leadership qualities, First Church elected him a Trustee on January 16, 1860. By the twenty-ninth of the same month, he had been chosen as Treasurer of the Board of Trustees.[26] Since the Trustees had charge of pew sales and taxes, it was only natural that Mary Lincoln would have asked Sarah Melvin to inform her husband that they wanted their old pew back when they returned to Springfield.

The Melvins played another role in the Lincolns' lives. Previous writers have failed to discover that Lincoln sought Dr. Melvin's expertise for some of his medicinal needs. It is true that from February 15, 1855, until December 23, 1860, Abraham Lincoln patronized the Corneau & Diller Drugstore.[27] After that time, however, he seems to have taken his business to Dr. Melvin, who now owned one of the largest pharmaceutical businesses in all of central Illinois, was skilled in his profession, and was also a very strong Republican.

One of the items which Lincoln sought constantly from Dr. Melvin was laxative pills. John Todd Stuart and Billy Herndon eventually revealed that Lincoln was often constipated, explaining that Mr. Lincoln's bowels moved slowly.[28] When Lincoln departed for Washington, he enjoyed good health.[29] Nevertheless, he requested that Dr. Melvin continue to supply him with his "pills." On April 3, 1861, Dr. Melvin informed the President by letter that he was sending five boxes of the pills which Lincoln had requested of him. Four boxes, Melvin explained, had been compounded by P. C. Canedy who kept a shop on the west side of the Public Square. Melvin, himself, had prepared the fifth box from one of his own formulas. In closing his missive, Dr. Melvin asked to be remembered to Mrs. Lincoln and Mrs. Grimsley.[30]

It would appear that one box contained a month's supply of pills. We know President Lincoln quit taking the laxative pills about five months after he arrived in Washington. Evidently he exhausted his supply from Dr. Melvin, and was determined to stop relying on laxatives, or perhaps somebody saw to it that his diet was improved. President Lincoln later divulged simply that his "pills" had "made him cross," and he had abandoned them.[31] However, Lincoln must have appreciated the services of Dr. Melvin. He offered an official position with the government if the druggist so desired. Melvin declined. His own enterprises were more profitable.

Contact with the Melvins did not end there. Through much personal sacrifice and monetary aid, Dr. Melvin assisted sanitary and hospital associations during the Civil War. After Springfield established a Home for the Friendless, Dr. Melvin became its President and promptly wrote to President Lincoln for his endorsement of the project.[32]

Dr. Melvin spent much of his time with financial institutions. When the First National Bank was chartered, the stockholders elected him a Director on December 12, 1863.[33] After the Civil War, his influence continued. On February 28, 1867, the Springfield Savings Bank was incorporated with Dr. Melvin again as one of the Directors.[34] At the organizational meeting, he was chosen President and held his post until 1874.

All through the dark days of the Civil War, Dr. Melvin tenaciously supported and labored for the Republican Party. He was chosen as a delegate to the Illinois State Republican Convention.[35] When the Convention convened on May 25, 1864, in the Hall of the House of Representatives in the Illinois State House, he won election from District 8 as a member of the State Central Committee, although he did not serve as a delegate to the national convention at Baltimore.[36] For the election of 1864, there was a name change; the Republicans had become the Union Party. And because the State of Illinois had been assigned a draft quota which proved to be grossly in error, Dr. Melvin was one of those who journeyed to Washington to lay their case before Lincoln. Although a member of the Union State Central Committee, Dr. Melvin signed the petition as a Commissioner of the State Union League

Association. President Lincoln met with these gentlemen on September 16, 1864, endorsed their petition and directed them to see James B. Fry, the Provost Marshal General.[37] The conscription quota for Illinois was greatly reduced, and only 3,538 men were drafted as a result of this appeal to President Lincoln for a correct computation. Illinois had been asked to produce 29,797 drafted men. As it was, Illinois had been extremely patriotic; sending 259,092 men to fight for the Union. Its total population in 1860 was but 1,711,951.

And Melvin's association continued. Of the eleven people selected to escort the remains of President Lincoln from Washington to Springfield, Dr. Melvin was one of them. He joined such men as John Todd Stuart, Jesse K. Dubois, Shelby M. Cullom, and John Williams—all old friends of Lincoln.[38] Melvin also sat on a special committee in charge of the music and the requiem in Springfield for the assassinated President.[39] And perhaps most important of all, Dr. Melvin became a Director of the National Lincoln Monument Association. At its first meeting in the State Library of the State House, Melvin acted as the Secretary *pro tem.*[40]

When the Springfield Board of Trade was organized in 1869, Dr. Melvin became its first President. That same year, on April 19, the Illinois General Assembly amended the act which had previously incorporated the Gilman, Clinton & Springfield Railroad Company in 1867.[41] Dr. Melvin reorganized this company which quickly constructed one hundred and ten miles of track to connect Springfield with the Illinois Central Railroad, furnishing Springfield with two lines to Chicago. In 1870, Melvin became President of the Springfield & St. Louis Railroad Company and later of the Keokuk & Kansas City Railroad. However, the Panic of 1873 ruined Dr. Melvin's financial holdings. Nevertheless, his Springfield Savings Bank protected the accounts of its depositors, and they did not lose any of their money. The Chicago Fire of 1871 had also seriously crippled Dr. Melvin's investments there.

When his wife became ill in 1875, Dr. Melvin took his family to California and settled at St. Helena in Napa County. There, he operated a stock ranch in partnership with General G. B. Rutherford. Upon the death of his partner in 1876, he went into the fruit canning business and a general commission business in San Francisco until 1885. He also established the Clinton Pharmacy in East Oakland, California. In 1888, he was defeated for the office of mayor by just seventy-three votes. But the following year, he became President of the California College of Pharmacy in the University of

California. In 1891, the Governor appointed Melvin a Director of the California State Board of Pharmacy. Later, he became President of this Board. He also served on the board of the Free Library.

During the early hours of February 11, 1898, Dr. Melvin died in his sleep at his residence in the Clinton House on Sixth Avenue near East Twelfth Street in East Oakland, California. Brights disease had finally killed this old friend of Lincoln's. Although Dr. Melvin had once been an Elder in the Presbyterian Church, upon coming to East Oakland, he and his wife joined the First Congregational Church and then transferred to the Pilgrim Congregational Church; he rose to the position of Deacon there. He was also a Mason, belonging to the Brooklyn Lodge. His Masonic brothers, as well as hundreds of mourners, attended his funeral services at the Pilgrim Congregational Church on Sunday afternoon, February 13.[42] Sarah Melvin survived her husband, dying on the morning of May 11, 1900. Her obituary truthfully declared that she and her husband had been "near neighbors and intimate friends of Abraham Lincoln and his family." When she died, Sarah's faithful companion, Mary Marra, was still with her—after nearly forty-four years of service.[43]

When Sarah Melvin showed her husband Mary Lincoln's letter, Dr. Melvin probably did little about the matter since the Lincolns had two years to pay their pew tax before any action would be taken by the Trustees. Very fortuitously, before the time expired, the problem was solved without causing Dr. Melvin any difficulty. On August 9, 1862, Benjamin Stephenson Edwards and his wife, Helen Kissam (Dodge) Edwards, joined the First Presbyterian Church. They transferred their letter of membership from the Second Presbyterian Church which then stood on the northwest corner of Fourth Street and Monroe. They had probably originally joined the Second Presbyterian because it sat just opposite their first home in Springfield. Three days after their arrival, the Edwardses had purchased a new residence for $6,500 which stood on Lot No. 1 of the Washington Iles Addition to the Town of Springfield, being nicely located on the southwest corner of Monroe and Fourth. This lot measured 80 feet by 157 feet, and the Edwardses secured it from Robert and Clara C. Irwin.[44] But bitter political feelings later developed against the Edwardses in their church, and they determined to leave on June 22, 1862, and worship with the congregation of the First Presbyterian Church. Since they were in-laws of the Lincolns, the Edwardses merely occupied the famous pew "previously owned by Mr. Lincoln."[45] In all probability, they simply paid the annual pew tax so as to secure and retain the pew for the Lincolns, who actually held title, until Abraham and Mary would return to Springfield and reclaim it.

Governor Ninian Edwards (1775-1833) married Elvira Lane, and they had three sons: Ninian Wirt Edwards (1809-1889); Albert Gallatin Edwards (1812-1892); and Benjamin Stephenson Edwards (1818-1886). Benjamin, their youngest son, was born at Edwardsville, Illinois, on June 3, 1818, and was named for Benjamin Stephenson of Edwardsville who sat in Congress from 1814-1816. All the Edwards children bore the names of prominent polit-ical figures of that day.

Although A. G. Edwards went to the United States Military Academy at West Point,[46] Benjamin entered Yale where he graduated in 1838. Then he enrolled in Yale's Law School for a year's study. While in college, he met Helen Kissam Dodge who was taking courses at a ladies school in New Haven, Connecticut. She had been born in Kaskaskia, Illinois, on November 14, 1819, the daughter of Colonel Henry Augustus and Jane (Dey Varrick) Dodge. Helen and Benjamin were married on August 13, 1839. They then determined to return to Illinois where Benjamin would enter the legal field. On January 4, 1840, they arrived in Springfield by stagecoach and immediately proceeded to their temporary living quarters with Ninian Wirt Edwards and his wife, Elizabeth (Todd) Edwards. Upon opening the door just off Second Street and across from Jackson, the young couple was greeted by Mary Todd, who, as a sister to Elizabeth, was also staying with the Edwardses—until she could find a husband. "I was attracted to her at once," recalled Helen (Dodge) Edwards. "This bond of friendship was continued to the end of her life," Helen testified.[47] The young Edwardses remained friends with Mary and witnessed her marriage to Abraham Lincoln on November 4, 1842. Mary and Abraham's son, Robert Todd Lincoln, continued this friendship with Benjamin and Helen and sometimes visited them on trips back to Springfield.[48]

Although Helen Edwards had been raised in the Dutch Reformed Church on Broadway in New York City, she and her husband quickly joined the Second Presbyterian Church, just across the street from their Springfield home. Benjamin then read law a short time with Stephen Trigg Logan before being admitted to the bar on February 11, 1840.[49] At this time, Benjamin Edwards espoused the Whig Party and associated with men like Edward Dickinson Baker and Abraham Lincoln. When the Republican Party was born, Edwards joined. If he had not later switched political parties, Benjamin S.

Edwards would no doubt still be remembered today as one of Lincoln's closest friends. As it is, he has been largely ignored, and no competent short study of his life has been made. It seems appropriate to present a brief outline of his career.

Benjamin Edwards associated with some of the best legal minds in Springfield. License in hand, he had formed a law partnership with E. D. Baker by March 5, 1840.[50] But this firm was dissolved on February 18, 1841.[51] Edwards then joined forces with Justin Butterfield, Jr., at the end of June in 1842.[52] Butterfield & Edwards' most famous case was as defense lawyers for the Mormon Prophet, Joseph Smith, when he was tried in Federal Court in Springfield on January 2, 1843.[53] The partnership of Butterfield & Edwards ended by November of 1843, and Edwards then began to practice law with John Todd Stuart.[54] He remained with Stuart until the latter died.

An examination of the deed records in Sangamon County reveals that all three sons of Governor Ninian Edwards speculated rather heavily in real estate. They had certainly inherited quite a bit of wealth from their father. To cite but two examples from the voluminous record: in 1842, B. S. Edwards, together with William Dormady, commenced erecting a store building on the north side of the Public Square in Springfield.[55] Then, on June 26, 1843, Benjamin and Helen Edwards purchased the grand home of Dr. Thomas & Ann Houghan for $4,000 and moved directly into it. Built in 1833, the house stood in an impressive grove of walnut trees on fifteen acres of land.[56] As the town of Springfield expanded north toward them, this location was identified as being north of Union Street and just off of Fourth. A shrewd investment, it cost them much less than they had paid for their first residence near the center of the original town of Springfield. In coming years, they enlarged this house into a magnificent showplace where members of Springfield's society often gathered to enjoy the hospitality of the Edwardses. After their deaths, an heir donated this building to the Springfield Art Association, and it still serves the community as Edwards Place.

The Edwardses raised three daughters. Helen M. married Moses Condell. Alice E. married Benjamin Hamilton Ferguson. Mary S. married James Henry Raymond. Benjamin Edwards supported his family well with his law practice and his investments. He frequently was associated with Abraham Lincoln in giving legal opinions and sometimes even practiced law together with him on the same cases. At least once they sat in the same audience. On the evening of January 23, 1853, they all listened to Dr. James Smith speak on the subject of temperance.[57] Thus, Benjamin made the acquaintance of this minister from the First Presbyterian Church. When the Springfield Gas Light Company was chartered on February 27, 1854, B. S. Edwards was one of the directors of this corporation.[58] It was no doubt a profitable enterprise.

B. S. Edwards actively supported the new Republican party until their delegates met in Springfield on September 25, 1856, and nominated John Wood for Lieutenant Governor. Although Edwards addressed this gathering in the State House, he was greatly disappointed in not being chosen for the second spot on the State Republican ticket. Up to this time, he had been anti-slavery, anti-Nebraska and in favor of prohibition, but this slight by the Republicans caused him to leave the party a year later.[59] His brother, Ninian Wirt Edwards, had already deserted the Whig Party after his 1851-52 term in the Illinois General Assembly and in 1854 was appointed by the Democratic Governor, Joel Aldrich Matteson, as Superintendent of Public Instruction. This move greatly mortified his brother-in-law, Abraham Lincoln. Of course, old Governor Ninian Edwards had been a Democrat.

Benjamin Edwards quickly placed himself in the camp of Senator Stephen A. Douglas which made him less anti-slavery. When the "Little Giant" came to Springfield aboard his private campaign train on the rainy morning of July 17, 1858, Douglas proceeded to Edwards' Grove where B. S. Edwards welcomed his personal hero with a rousing speech. Several thousand people braved the muddy conditions to catch a glimpse of Douglas and hear his political rhetoric.[60] But when the Civil War came, Edwards, as the leader of the Springfield Democrats, spoke out for the Union cause and helped to raise troops to support President Lincoln. This political stance, however, did not make him an abolitionist.

Further exercising his political ambitions, Ben Edwards won election on November 5, 1861, as a delegate to the Illinois State Constitutional Convention due to convene on January 7 the following year. He led the polling for the two seats from the 26th District (Sangamon County). He and James D. Smith easily beat out old Peter Cartwright who also aspired to help formulate a new constitution. Democrats controlled the convention, and they drafted a document which greatly favored their political party. Republicans were outraged, and the 1862 Constitution went down to defeat at the polls. Since there were so many Republicans in the Second Presbyterian Church, the Edwardses found themselves to be persona non gratae. They switched to the First Presbyterian Church which was more favorable to their views.[61]

Seeking yet another political office, Ben Edwards ran for Congress against Republican Shelby M. Cullom on November 3, 1868, but lost 22,193 to 19,309.[62] Edwards would try politics once more.

On March 11, 1869, the Illinois General Assembly created a new judicial circuit, the 30th, which comprised Sangamon County, alone. This act decreed that an election for this judgeship of this circuit should be held on April 6 of that year.[63] Being the only candidate from either party, he was assured of election, receiving 830 votes.[64] Three days after the election, he was sworn into office and filed his oath with the Governor.[65] Then, just over a year later, May 14, 1870, Benjamin Stephenson Edwards informed Governor John M. Palmer that he was resigning on June 1.[66] His explanation was that he preferred, "the excitement and emoluments of private practice to the dignity and scant salary attaching to the bench."[67] On July 2 of that year, a special election was held, and John A. McClernand, another Democrat, succeeded Edwards. McClernand was duly commissioned on July 12 and sworn in two days later.[68] This short stint as a circuit judge seems to have cured Edwards of any desire for further political office.

Benjamin S. Edwards died in his majestic home on February 4, 1886, being at the time President of the Illinois State Bar Association. Two days later, his funeral was conducted in the First Presbyterian Church, by then located at the northwest corner of Seventh and Capitol.[69] His wife, Helen, lived on until March 18, 1909, when she, too, succumbed at the family residence. Two days afterward, the Rev. T. D. Logan of the First Presbyterian Church presided over her funeral services in the deceased's home, and her body was interred in Oak Ridge with her husband's.[70] It had been her daughters, no doubt, who presented to the First Presbyterian Church an artistic stained glass window in loving memory of their father, Benjamin Stephenson Edwards. This gorgeous window still can be observed in the south wall of the sanctuary at Seventh and Capitol.

Without evidence to the contrary, it should be assumed that the Benjamin Edwardses and their three daughters occupied the Lincoln family pew in the First Presbyterian Church at Third and Washington until the building was sold to another denomination in 1871. This transfer came about in an interesting way, and the brief history of it must be told.

As in most organizations, dissension and ambition soon caused divisions in the First Presbyterian Church. One group of members split off in 1835, becoming the Second Presbyterian Church (now called Westminster).

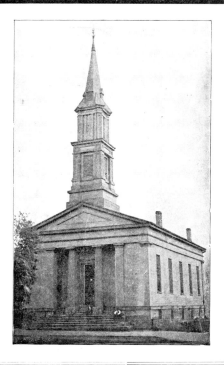

Lincoln Centennial Religious Services

Friday, Feb. 12, '09=At 10:30 A. M.

At St. John's Evangelical Lutheran
Church Formerly the 1st Presbyterian
Church of Springfield, Illinois
Abraham Lincoln's Church 1849=1861

The old First Presbyterian Church building, where the Lincolns had
attended, as it appeared in 1909 when centennial services were held there.
At that time, the structure was owned by
the St. John's Evangelical Lutheran congregation.

In 1849, another cluster left to form the Third Presbyterian Church. It has been stated that the First Presbyterian never wholeheartedly supported abolition, and this fact assisted in the splitting of the original congregation. If so, this explains further why Ben Edwards and his family switched churches in 1862. He must not have favored the abolition of slavery but did advocate the preservation of the Union. Therefore, he would have felt much more comfortable in the First Presbyterian than in the Second.

The Third Presbyterian Church determined to construct a grand edifice. From Susan M. Slater, the Trustees on July 15, 1865, acquired for $5,000, Lots 9 and 12 in Block 1 of the E. Iles Addition, except for 18 feet off the west end of these lots.[71] This land lies on the northwest corner of Seventh and Capitol. The church officials engaged L. D. Cleveland as their architect who designed the edifice to be constructed of brick and in the Romanesque Style. Work on the building started in February of 1866, with the cornerstone being laid on June 25 that same year. After an expenditure of $69,108.09, the structure was completed. Its north spire stretched 106 feet into the air, and the south spire rose to a height of 177 feet. On Easter Sunday, April 12, 1868, this new house of worship was dedicated. However, the Third Presbyterians could not meet their mortgage payments and simply went broke.

Since the congregation of the First Presbyterians Church contained numerous affluent parishioners, its Trustees offered to purchase this regal property for $20,000 and assume the remaining mortgage. They insisted upon getting all the furniture as well as the new pipe organ which had already been installed. Trustees of the Third gave the Trustees of the First the deed to this land and structure on November 28, 1871.[72] Now, the First Presbyterian Church owned two sanctuaries. Accordingly, they sold their old building to the Trustees of the St. John's Evangelical Lutheran Church on December 2, 1871, for $8,000, reserving the bell from the tower since the ladies of the church had once labored so diligently to purchase it.[73] Yet, the Lincoln pew was not reserved and went with the rest of the church furniture to the Lutherans. First Church evidently did not prize this pew or pay particular attention to it at this time. But in 1898, Dr. George Pasfield installed a silver plaque upon the arm of the Lincoln pew. After corresponding with Dr. Thomas D. Logan, then a pastor of the First Presbyterian Church, he decided that he should inscribe these words on it: "A. LINCOLN Family Pew 1852-1861."[74] Evidently, Dr. Pasfield took the beginning date from the time that

Mary Lincoln formally joined. Dr. Logan had acquired this knowledge by questioning those members who had actually worshipped with the Lincolns.

When the centennial of Abraham Lincoln's birth drew near, the entire country began to seek out Lincoln stories and Lincoln associations with every community where the great man had been. Accordingly, at 10:30 a. m. on Friday, February 12, 1909, Dr. Thomas D. Logan was granted permission to hold a special program in the old church building, by now commonly called St. John's German Evangelical Lutheran Church. A large bouquet of flowers was arranged upon a small table which had stood in the building when the Lincolns worshipped there, and the ancient pulpit was located and brought out to occupy its old familiar position. The venerable Lincoln pew was draped with the National Colors, and a United States Flag was positioned at each end of it.

Termed the "Lincoln Centennial Religious Services," Dr. Logan preached on the topic "Lincoln as a Worshiper." During the course of his oration, he called particular attention to the Lincoln pew. "The sacred edifice was thronged, while countless others sought in vain to gain an entrance," observed one local paper. Those who had witnessed the Lincolns in this church could see very little change since then in this time-honored building. When the congregation joined the choir in singing the "Battle Hymn of the Republic," the aged walls and rafters fairly shook with the reverberating sounds. It was a thrilling experience for those who could gain admission to the sanctuary.[75] These fortunate few must have felt that they indeed were on holy ground. For, the immortal Abraham Lincoln had trod those floorboards, and his voice had echoed off those very walls.

This centennial celebration kindled a renewed interest in the Lincoln pew. Since 1907, the First Presbyterian Church had had a Finance Committee, consisting of George B. Hemenway, Col. Charles F. Mills and Samuel J. Willett. These men frequently debated the subject of how they might regain possession of the Lincoln pew and remove it to their church building on Seventh and Capitol. By March 5, 1912, the St. John's German Lutherans had paid off their mortgage and were ready to sell their church property for commercial development.[76] They were constructing a new church at the southeast corner of College and Monroe. Immediately, the Finance Committee of First Church asked its Secretary, Mr. Willett, a merchant tailor at 315 East Monroe, to make contact with the authorities of St. John's. But first, Willett went to John Whitfield Bunn (June 21, 1831-June 7,

1920), President of the Marine Bank and a member of the church, and asked him if he would pay for the pew if it could be obtained. John Bunn, a single man, a philanthropist and a brother of Jacob Bunn, told him to go ahead and find out the asking price for the pew. Willett proceeded to approach the officers of St. John's.

John H. Requarth, Treasurer of St. John's, informed Willett that an unnamed party in Philadelphia had made an overture of $1,000 for it. Willett promptly declared that First Church would not give such a huge amount, whereupon Requarth dropped the price to $500. After further dickering, Willett offered $250, and this bid was accepted, Requarth remarking that he would much rather the Lincoln pew remain in Springfield than be shipped to Philadelphia. When Bunn was told of the bargain made, he wrote out a check to Willett and handed it to him. Willett immediately departed, endorsed the check and gave the draft to Requarth. This transaction took place on March 29, 1912.

When Willett called to pick up the pew, he discovered that it was indeed already crated and ready for shipment to Philadelphia. However, the Lutherans had saved only that half of the double pew which had accommodated the Lincolns, Pew No. 20. They had thrown out the left hand portion (No. 56), since it was not the seat of the Lincolns. Willett complained that he needed another end to make the pew usable and suitable for display. Upon hearing this reasonable request, Willett's guide took him to the rear of the building where workers had piled up some of the remaining pews. He selected another half (No. 15) in good condition, knowing full well that it was not the original companion to the Lincoln side of the long bench, but, not being able to find the correct one, he took heart in the fact that he had at least gained possession of the precious bench of the Lincolns. Pushing his luck once more, Willett asked for the cushions which had once adorned the ancient pew. The custodian led him to a shed on the rear of the lot where the discarded pillows had been stashed. Once more, Willett selected two which were the best available but not the ones used by the Lincolns. Those original ones of Lincoln's era had been of black hair-cloth and, because of wear, had been replaced in 1890. The Lincoln pew had actually been used after the First Family left Springfield in 1861.

Because the old pew sales and tax books could not be discovered—this practice of selling pews had been stopped in 1909—Willett questioned various members of First Church to corroborate his own research. Among the most reliable of the witnesses was Alice E. (Edwards) Ferguson (August 11, 1844-March 2, 1921), the wife of Benjamin Hamilton Ferguson and the daughter of B. S. and Helen Edwards. She had, of course, sat in this very pew with her parents. Alice declared it to be the Lincoln seat beyond a shadow of a doubt; so did the others who had seen the Lincolns sitting in it and knew it well. They remembered the number as well as the location when shown the seating chart acquired by Willett. By the following Sunday, March 31, 1912, Willett had the famous bench sitting at the front of First Church—in a corner. At this time, the other pews were situated in three distinct sections with two wide center aisles and two very narrow side aisles.[77] The Lincoln pew was much longer than any of those already in place.

Since Ex-President Theodore Roosevelt was scheduled to speak in the Illinois State Armory on the evening of April 6, 1912, Willett, on behalf of the Session, sent a telegraphic message to him, inviting the famous Colonel of the Rough Riders "to attend Easter service in the First Presbyterian Church, the congregation of which Lincoln was a member while living in Springfield, and to occupy the old Lincoln pew." Col. Roosevelt was a prominent Mason and a great admirer of Abraham Lincoln. His special railroad car, named the "Pilgrim," rolled into Springfield on the tracks of the Chicago, Alton & St. Louis during the evening of April 6. He was due to speak at 8:00 p. m., but his train was one hour and forty minutes late, and he did not mount the stage until 9:40. There, he spoke for fifty minutes, often quoting President Lincoln and castigating Senator William Lorimer. When he concluded his remarks, his party took up quarters in fifteen rooms at the New Leland Hotel. The old Colonel of Spanish-American-War fame had addressed 6,000 people in the Armory and must have been tired when he finally reached his rooms in the Executive Mansion after a very long day of travel and waiting.

Nevertheless, when Colonel Roosevelt arose on the following morning, Easter Sunday, April 7, he was determined to attend worship services at the First Presbyterian Church. At 10:45, the program commenced with Roosevelt sitting in the celebrated Lincoln pew which had been moved back several rows from the front of the sanctuary. Rev. Thomas D. Logan preached on the topic, "Some Men Will Say How." It was a signal honor for First Church to have Roosevelt in the congregation. Rev. Logan also baptized sixteen young people and served communion. It must have been inspirational for Roosevelt, too. He was actually occupying the bench where the immortal Lincoln had listened to sermons prior to his presidency.

At the conclusion of the services, President Roosevelt had lunch in the Executive Mansion with Governor Charles S. Deneen, a Republican. Next, he visited Lincoln's Tomb in Oak Ridge Cemetery to pay his respect to the martyred President, and then toured the Lincoln Home at Eighth and Jackson. Presbyterians would long remember the visit of Theodore Roosevelt to pay homage to Abraham Lincoln.[78] Every seat in the First Church had been filled; chairs had even been placed in the aisles and in front of the platform. It was most fitting that somebody who revered Abraham Lincoln as much as Theodore Roosevelt did, should be the first to occupy the Lincoln pew after its transfer from the old site of the First Presbyterian Church to the new one at Seventh and Capitol. Strange as it might seem, though, Robert T. Lincoln strongly disagreed with Teddy Roosevelt in 1912 and supported William Howard Taft for President. He also objected to Roosevelt's comparing his ideals to President Lincoln's.

After the Easter service, Willett asked David A. DeVares, an Elder of the church and a general contractor, builder, and real estate agent, to shorten the two pews, join them together properly and varnish them with expert care. When completed, he had the Lincoln pew set in front of the center section of seats, right in front of the pulpit.

After Easter Sunday, Willett made one more trip to see John W. Bunn. This church official now wanted permission to have a silver plate inscribed to the effect that Bunn had purchased the Lincoln pew for the First Church. At first, Bunn declined vociferously, saying he wanted to remain anonymous. But Willett persisted and reminded Bunn that he had been a political ally of Abraham Lincoln and it would mean so much to future generations if they knew who had saved the pew. At last John Bunn relented and authorized Willett to have the plate prepared. Carl H. Klaholdt, of J. C. Klaholdt Company at 514 East Adams, engraved it, and Willett attached it to the end of the famous pew under the number 20 while the Rev. Logan observed this operation with watchful eyes. Bunn insisted upon paying for the identification plaque which cost $21.00. It read:

This Pew occupied during his residence in Springfield by
A. LINCOLN. Presented by his Personal Friend JOHN W. BUNN
to the First Presbyterian Church April 14th 1912.

That was the date which had been chosen for the formal dedication of the pew.

At 3:00 p. m. on that April 14, an ecumenical religious service began in the First Presbyterian Church in memory of the martyred Abraham Lincoln. With John W. Bunn seated on the platform, eight Protestant ministers spoke. They eulogized Lincoln, their theme being the religious Lincoln. In commemorating his tragic assassination, attention was also called to the precious pew sitting just below the platform. It was publicly dedicated at this union meeting of preachers and listeners.[79]

After the church's interior was remodeled in 1941, the seating arrangement was changed completely. Now, there were only two sections of new seats with one center aisle. Therefore, the Lincoln pew was shifted to the right-hand side of the sanctuary, as viewed by the congregation looking to the front of the building, and placed in the very first row. It remains there, with a cord across its front so that it can be occupied mostly upon special occasions by certain fortunate dignitaries who visit First Church. Presidents and Governors, as well as others of lesser note, have had the privilege of sitting in it since 1912, including this author.

References

1   Basler, ed., *The Collected Works*, III, 550.

2   New-York *Tribune*, Nov. 10, 1860, p. 6, c. 2.

3   Basler, ed., *The Collected Works*, IV, 51.

4   *Ibid.*, IV, 52.

5   *Ibid.*, IV, 71.

6   Sunderine (Wilson) Temple and Wayne C. Temple, *Illinois' Fifth Capitol* (Springfield: Phillips Bros. Printers, 1988), 159-168.

7   J. B. McClure, ed., *Anecdotes of Abraham Lincoln* (Chicago: Rhodes & McClure, 1879), 80.

8   William Reid in *Illinois State Journal*, May 16, 1874, p. 2, cc. 5-6.

9   Carl Sandburg wrote an introduction for a reprint of this tiny volume, and it was duly released as *Lincoln's Devotional* (Great Neck, N. Y.: Channel Press, 1957).

10 Basler, ed., *The Collected Works*, IV, 130.

11 David Davis to his wife, Danville, Ill., Nov. 11, 1860, MS., Davis Papers, Ill. State Hist. Lib.; Pease and Randall, eds., *The Diary of Orville Hickman Browning*, I, 434; *Chicago Daily Tribune*, Nov. 7, 1860, p. 1, c. 5.

12 New-York *Tribune*, Nov. 10, 1860, p. 6, c. 1.

13 *Illinois State Journal*, Nov. 6, 1860, p. 3, c. 2.

14 New-York *Tribune*, Nov. 10, 1860, p. 6, c. 1. On November 14, 1885, Billy Herndon claimed that he was the one who had persuaded Lincoln on election day to at least vote for the Republican state candidates, but Lincoln had already informed the press, while at the Post Office on the previous day, that he would vote. Hertz, ed., *The Hidden Lincoln*, 102-103. Here is another case of Herndon aggrandizing himself.

15 New-York *Tribune*, Nov. 7, 1860, p. 5, c. 4.

16 Chicago *Daily Tribune*, Nov. 10, 1860, p. 1, c. 2.

17 Noah Brooks, *Washington in Lincoln's Time* (N. Y.: The Century Co., 1895), 220-222; Lamon, *The Life of Abraham Lincoln*, 476-477.

18   Basler, ed., *The Collected Works*, IV, 146.

19   *Ibid.*, IV, 156.

20   *Ibid.*, IV, 169.

21   Turner and Turner, eds., *Mary Todd Lincoln*, 85-86.

22   *Illinois State Journal*, July 22, 1859, p. 2, c. 3.

23   *Williams' Springfield City Directory For 1860-61* (Springfield: Johnson & Bradford, 1860), 111.

24   U. S. Census 1860, Springfield, Sangamon Co., Ill., p. 149, ll. 38-40, p. 150, ll. 1-4; U. S. Census 1870, Springfield, Sangamon Co., Ill, p. 186, ll. 19-28; Turner and Turner, eds., *Mary Todd Lincoln*, 85-86. Mary Lincoln Melvin married A. A. Dewing of San Francisco.

25   *Ibid.*

26   Session Minutes of the First Presbyterian Church, 1828-1862, I, 151, MS., Ill. State Hist. Lib.; Board of Trustees Minutes, 1829-1866, n. p., *ibid.* Dr. Thos. S. Hening became an Elder on Feb. 8, 1861.

27   Pratt, *The Personal Finances of Abraham Lincoln*, 151-153.

28   Hertz, ed., *The Hidden Lincoln,* 64; Milton H. Shutes, *Lincoln's Emotional Life* (Philadelphia: Dorrance & Co., 1957), 104; Justin G. Turner, ed., "Lincoln and the Lost Ledger," *Lincoln Herald*, LXIII, 114 (Fall, 1961).

29   Hertz, ed., *The Hidden Lincoln*, 412.

30   S. H. Melvin to A. Lincoln, Springfield, Ill., Apr. 3, 1861, MS., Ser. I, No. 8729, R. T. L. Coll., The Library of Congress; *Williams' Springfield Directory For 1860-61*, 65.

31   Shutes, *Lincoln's Emotional Life*, 104.

32   S. H. Melvin to A. Lincoln, Springfield, Ill., Dec. 14, 1863, MS., Ser. I, No. 28671-2, R. T. L. Coll., The Library of Congress.

33   *Illinois State Journal*, Dec. 15, 1863, p. 3, c. 4.

34   *Private Laws of the State of Illinois Passed by the Twenty-fifth General Assembly* (Springfield: Baker, Bailhache & Co., 1867), I, 62-65. In addition to Melvin, the other incorporators were: John A. Chestnut, Benjamin F. Fox, Rufus S. Lord, William M. Springer, Charles A. Helm, Edward L. Baker, John S. Bradford and R. P. Able.

35   *Illinois State Journal*, May 16, 1864, p. 3, c. 4.

36   *Ibid.*, May 26, 1864, p. 2, c. 5.

37   *The War of the Rebellion: Official Records* (Washington: Govt. Printing Office, 1900), Ser. III, Vol. IV, pp. 700-702.

38   *Illinois State Journal*, Apr. 19, 1865, p. 2, c. 3.

39   *Ibid.*, Apr. 21, 1865, p. 2, c. 2.

40   *Ibid.*, May 19, 1865, p. 2, c. 3.

41   *Private Laws of the State of Illinois Passed by the Twenty-Sixth General Assembly* (Springfield: Illinois Journal Printing Office, 1869), III, 295.

42   Unless otherwise identified in the footnotes above, information on Dr. Melvin has been taken from *The Bay of San Francisco: A History* (Chicago: The Lewis Pub. Co., 1892), II, 293-295; *Oakland Tribune*, Feb. 11, 1898, p. 1, cc. 3-4, Feb. 14, 1898, p. 2, c. 3; *San Francisco Call*, Feb. 12, 1898, p. 11, cc. 4-5.

43   *San Francisco Call*, May 12, 1900, p. 11, c. 3.

44   Session Minutes of the First Presbyterian Church, I, 168-169, MS., Ill. State Hist. Lib.; Deed Record, P, 443-444, MS., Recorder's Office, Sangamon Co. Bldg., Springfield.

45   Reminiscences of Mrs. B. S. Edwards dictated to her daughter, Mary (Edwards) Raymond, MS., Sangamon Valley Collection, Springfield Public Library.

46   Albert Gallatin Edwards was born at Elkton, Kentucky, on October 15, 1812, being named for the famous Albert Gallatin. He graduated from the U. S. Military Academy at West Point on July 4, 1832, with the rank of Brevet Third Lieutenant. Having arrived in the West too late for participation in the Black Hawk War with the Mounted Rangers, young Edwards was assigned to the First Dragoons and became a Brevet Second Lieutenant at Jefferson Barracks, near St. Louis, on August 14, 1833. Col. Henry Dodge commanded this unit. There, he married Louise Cabanne on April 28, 1835, and quickly resigned from the Army on May 2. He joined a wholesale commission business headed by William L. Ewing. His wife died in 1841. Edwards then joined the Second Presbyterian Church in St. Louis and became an Elder. Later, he married Mary Ewing Jencks and moved to Kirkwood where he constructed a fine home. Being Pro-Union, A. G. Edwards accepted a Brigadier General's commission in the Missouri State Militia from the Loyal Union Governor Hamilton R. Gamble. But the Governor also named him a Missouri Bank Examiner, thus keeping him away from combat. President Lincoln gave

Edwards a commission on April 9, 1865, as Assistant Secretary of the Treasury for the Sub-Treasury Bank at St. Louis. This important position he held until March of 1887. The next month, with his son, Benjamin Franklin Edwards, he started the brokerage firm named A. G. Edwards & Son, their headquarters being in St. Louis. After a full life with much honor coming to him, General Edwards died on April 20, 1892, at his home in Kirkwood. Janice K. Broderick, "A. G. Edwards & Sons: Celebrating 100 Years of Brokerage History," *Gateway Heritage*, VII 1-41 (Spring, 1987); Francis B. Heitman, *Historical Register and Dictionary of the United States Army* (Washington: Govt. Printing Office, 1903), I, 398; *Illinois State Register*, Apr. 23, 1892, p. 5, c. 2. Some sources carry an incorrect date for his death. This author has relied upon a contemporary obituary published in Springfield, Ill.

47   Reminiscences of Mrs. B. S. Edwards.

48   *Illinois State Register*, Mar. 19, 1909, p. 12, c. 1.

49   *Ibid.*; Roll of Attorneys, MSS., Clerk's Office, Illinois Supreme Court Bldg., Springfield.

50   *Sangamo Journal*, Mar. 6, 1840, p. 3, c. 3.

51   *Ibid.*, Feb. 26, 1841, p. 3, c. 5.

52   *Ibid.*, July 1, 1842, p. 3, c. 1.

53   *Ibid.*, Jan. 12, 1843, p. 3, c. 2.

54   *Ibid.*, Nov. 9, 1843, p. 3, c. 5.

55   *Ibid.*, June 3, 1842, p. 3, c. 3.

56   Its legal description is the Southeast part of the West Half of the Northwest Quarter of Section 27 in Township 16 North, Range 5 West of the Third Principal Meridian. The deed was notarized the same day as the transfer and recorded the following day. Deed Records, U, 342-343, MS., Recorder's Office, Sangamon Co. Bldg., Springfield, Ill.; *Illinois State Register*, Mar. 19, 1909, p. 12, c. 1.

57   Basler, ed., *The Collected Works*, II, 188.

58   *Laws of the State of Illinois Passed by the Eighteenth General Assembly . . . Second Session* (Springfield: Lanphier & Walker, 1854), 189.

59   *Illinois State Journal*, Sept. 27, 1858, p. 2, c. 2.

60   *Illinois State Register*, July 19, 1858, p. 2, c. 2.

61   Election Returns 1850-1862, p. 314, MS., Illinois State Archives; Mercy
        Conkling to Clinton Conkling, Springfield, Ill., June 23, [1862], Conkling
        Papers, Ill. State Hist. Lib.

62   Election Returns 1862-1873, p. 202, MS., Illinois State Archives.

63   *Public Laws of the State of Illinois. . . Twenty-Sixth General Assembly*
        (Springfield: Illinois Journal Printing Office, 1869), 90-91.

64   *Illinois Daily State Journal*, Apr. 7, 1869, p. 3, c. 2. The election returns were
        never recorded at the state level.

65   Executive File; Executive Record, XII, 102, MSS., Illinois State Archives.

66   Executive File, MS., Illinois State Archives.

67   Newton Bateman and Paul Selby, eds., *Historical Encyclopedia of Illinois and
        History of Sangamon County* (Chicago: Munsell Pub., Co., 1912), I, 153; II,
        1200.

68   Executive Record, XII, 152; Executive File, MSS., Illinois State Archives.

69   *Illinois State Journal*, Feb. 5, 1886, p. 4, c. 4.

70   *Illinois State Register*, Mar. 19, 1909, p. 12, c. 1.

71   Deed Record, XXV, 102-103, MS., Recorder's Office, Sangamon Co. Bldg.

72   *Ibid.*, XLV, 262.

73   *Ibid.,* XLV, 13. The legal description of the old building site was Lot 3 in Block
        15 of Old Town Plat, except 40 feet off the south side of the lot where the first
        structure stood and had been given to the Mechanics' Union for its school.
        For the story of the church bell, see Temple and Temple, *Illinois' Fifth Capitol*,
        116-117. For the facts on the new First Presbyterian Church, see the *Illinois
        Daily State Journal*, Apr. 13, 1868, p. 4, cc. 4-5.

74   Thomas D. Logan to Dr. George Pasfield, Springfield, Ill., Oct. 7, 1898, MS.,
        First Presbyterian Church.

75   Program of this service in author's collection; *The Springfield Record*, Feb.
        12, 1909; *The Springfield News*, Feb. 12, 1909, p. 6, cc. 1-6 has the entire
        sermon while p. 2, c. 6 has the story; *Illinois State Journal*, Feb. 13, 1909, p.
        12, c. 1.

76   Deed Record, CCXVIII, 154 and Mortgage Record, CCXX, 553, MSS.,
        Recorder's Office, Sangamon Co. Bldg.

77   Photo of the sanctuary in *Seventy-Fifth Anniversary of First Presbyterian Church* (Springfield: n. p., 1903), 26.

78   *Illinois State Journal*, Mar. 29, 1912, p. 2, c. 1, Apr. 6, 1912, p. 2, c. 1, Apr. 7, 1912, p. 1, cc. 6-7, p. 9, c. 3, Apr. 8, 1912, p. 2, cc. 1-2, p. 12, c. 2.

79   *Ibid*, Apr. 13, 1912, p. 5, c. 5, Apr. 15, 1912, p. 3, cc. 1-2. The history of the Lincoln pew was related by Samuel J. Willett and John H. Requarth in a notarized statement dated February 12, 1931, and filed with the official papers of the First Presbyterian Church, now housed at the Illinois State Historical Library.

Chapter Six—Exodus

In preparing to take his leave from Springfield, Illinois, Abraham Lincoln seated himself at his desk on January 29, 1861, and wrote out a notice for his favorite newspaper, the *Illinois State Journal*. It duly appeared the following day on page 3 in column 7:

> AT PRIVATE SALE—THE FURNITU[R]E consisting of Parlor and Chamber Sets, Carpets, Sofas, Chairs, Wardrobes, Bureaus, Be[d]steads, Stoves, China, Queensware, Glass, etc., etc., at the residence, on the corner of Eighth and Jackson streets, is offered at private sale, without re[s]erve. For particulars apply on the premises at once.   jan. 29 dtf.

Among those who took advantage of this offering of Lincoln furniture was their druggist and friend, Dr. Samuel H. Melvin. He purchased six chairs, one spring mattress, 1 wardrobe, 1 whatnot, 1 stand, 9 1/2 yards of stair carpet and 4 comforters for a total price of $82.25. He paid Lincoln on February 9.

On February 8, Lincoln rented the family residence to Lucian Tilton, President of the Great Western Railroad, for $350 per year. By the next evening, the Lincolns had taken up temporary quarters in the Chenery House, a favorite hostelry for Republicans. Shortly afterward, Lincoln paid a visit, for the last time, to his old law office on the west side of the Square. There, he told Billy Herndon just to let their old signboard hang at the foot of the stairway leading to their upstairs office. "If I live I'm coming back some time, and then we'll go right on practicing law as if nothing had ever happened." Note again, the President-elect's deep streak of fatalism and sense of impending death when he remarked to Bill, "If I live . . . ."[1]

At 7:30 a. m. on February 11, the President-elect left his hotel and rode in a carriage to the Great Western Railroad Depot located on the southwest corner of Tenth and Monroe. Into the waiting room of the depot he trudged and stood where his friends could pass "by him and take his hand for the last time."[2] "I was surrounded by a large concourse of my fellow citizens," recalled Lincoln later in the day, "almost all of whom I could recognize."[3] A great crowd had assembled in the station and all along each side of the tracks. One reporter estimated that "over a thousand persons of all classes" were present that morning. Another declared that it was not a partisan gathering since there was no distinction of party.[4] In all of Springfield, there were less than ten thousand inhabitants at this time.[5]

During the previous day, rain had fallen upon Springfield, and the streets were muddy. One witness noted that it was very warm for that time of year.[6] The morning of February 11 turned out to be a gloomy, "unpleasant[,] cloudy[,] rainy day."[7] At precisely five minutes before 8:00 a. m., Lincoln slowly made his way from the waiting room to the Presidential Special which stood nearby on the iron rails.[8] Just at that moment, Mary Lincoln's carriage drew up at the depot, and Thomas D. Jones, a noted sculptor from Cincinnati, offered her his arm and held an umbrella over her as they inched their way to the front of the assemblage.[9] There, Lincoln said good bye to his wife, who would take a later train, and proceeded to the rear platform of the last car in the Presidential Special where he removed his hat and asked for silence so that he might be heard.[10] By that time, it was raining very fast, yet each gentleman took off his hat, as Lincoln had done. Most listeners bent slightly forward to catch his every word.[11] While he had been in the waiting room, Lincoln's "face was pale, and quivered with emotion so deep as to render him almost unable to utter a single word."[12] Now, on the observation platform of the train, this great man was "affected to tears." "His own breast heaved with emotion and he could scarcely command his feelings sufficiently to commence."[13] Deep beneath his rugged exterior lay a soft, sentimental nature.

In competition with the hissing of the Rogers locomotive, named the "Wiley," which tarried there motionless with its baggage, smoking and three passenger cars, an emotional Lincoln began to speak.[14] Since an eyewitness recorded that the members of the Illinois General Assembly were present,[15] it must be assumed that none other than Robert Roberts Hitt took down Lincoln's parting words in shorthand. He had captured the Lincoln-Douglas debates in 1858, and the Senate hired him the next year to make a shorthand record of their proceedings.[16] The following version of Lincoln's Farewell Address has been quoted here as it appeared in the *Illinois State Journal* on the day after Lincoln's departure from town. Certainly, it is much more accurate than the version compiled by Lincoln shortly after the event.

Hitt probably sold or gave a copy of his transcript to the local press for its use. And Billy Herndon always declared that this particular text was the most accurate of them all.[17]

Friends,

No one who has never been placed in a like position, can understand my feelings at this hour, nor the oppressive sadness I feel at this parting. For more than a quarter of a century I have lived among you, and during all that time I have received nothing but kindness at your hands. Here I have lived from my youth until now I am an old man. Here the most sacred ties of earth were assumed; here all my children were born; and here one of them lies buried. To you, dear friends, I owe all that I have, all that I am.

All the strange, chequered past seems to crowd now upon my mind. To-day I leave you; I go to assume a task more difficult than that which devolved upon General Washington. Unless the great God who assisted him, shall be with and aid me, I must fail. But if the same omniscient mind, and Almighty arm that directed and protected him, shall guide and support me, I shall not fail, I shall succeed. Let us all pray that the God of our fathers may not forsake us now. To him I commend you all—permit me to ask that with equal security and faith, you all will invoke His wisdom and guidance for me. With these few words I must leave you—for how long I know not. Friends, one and all, I must now bid you an affectionate farewell.[18]

When the President-elect exclaimed "With the earnestness of a sudden inspiration of feeling" that with God's help he would not fail, "there was an uncontrollable burst of applause."[19] Toward the end of his brief remarks, both Lincoln and his rain-soaked audience were moved to tears.[20] There Lincoln stood like a towering prophet, giving a benediction to his deferential followers, friends and townsfolk. A noticeable religious message ran throughout his parting remarks to the assembled throng. A close ally testified that this same highly religious feeling remained within Lincoln's mind until the end of his life.[21] Back on July 6, 1852, when he had given his eulogy on Henry Clay, Lincoln had stated that our Nation must "strive to deserve, as far as mortals may, the continued care of Divine Providence, trusting that, in future emergencies, He will not fail to provide us the instruments of safety and security."[22] Now, Abraham Lincoln thought of himself as that instrument of God given to the populace in a time of grave danger. And he fully recognized and accepted this leadership role as an instrument of the Almighty.

Within a few minutes, Lincoln would commence to write down what he thought he had said or what he wished he had said. But the motion of the swaying railroad car forced him to hand the paper and pencil to Nicolay, his private secretary. After a moment of careful reflection, Lincoln continued to record his remarks by dictating: "I now leave, not knowing when, or whether ever, I may return . . . ."[23] That was not in his original speech, but it well exhibited his fatalistic feelings about himself.

After his 1858 campaign against Douglas, Lincoln had told Herndon that "I feel as if I should meet with some terrible end."[24] Lincoln once more had caught a mystic glimpse of the dark future as he took his leave from Springfield. His life would indeed end in tragedy, and he never would return, alive, to Springfield.

With a great billowing cloud of escaping steam, the special train clattered away from the station at exactly 8:00 a. m. As Lincoln took his last look at his old neighbors and friend, they—in turn—uttered an audible "good bye & God speed."[25] They, too, felt the extreme sadness of the parting. Not so Robert T. Lincoln. He spent most of his time in the smoking car, "the gayest of the gay." Robert certainly foresaw no revelation of the terrible events which would unfold later for him and his family. Unlike his abstemious father, Robert enjoyed smoking. This habit would later get him into trouble at Harvard. As a college student, Robert also enjoyed drinking whiskey with close friends.[26]

Although President-elect Lincoln carried a new overcoat with him—the gift of Isaac Fenno of Boston, Massachusetts—by February 13 he was suffering from a cold.[27] His hatless exposure to the rain in Springfield probably hastened the onset of this malady. But he continued on his way despite every obstacle which attempted to thwart his inauguration. He appeared to be a man on a holy mission, so to speak.

For several weeks prior to his departure from Springfield, Lincoln had carefully prepared written addresses for some of the major cities where his train would stop on its circuitous journey to Washington.[28] Nevertheless, he soon discovered he was expected to say something to the assembled onlookers wherever his train merely paused for water, wood, etc., in smaller communities. These brief impromptu messages he delivered extemporaneously, and in many of them his religious feelings shone through. While stopped at Danville, Illinois, he told the crowd that "if he had any blessing to dispense, he would certainly dispense the largest and roundest to his good old friends of Vermilion county."[29] In making such a good-natured remark, Lincoln sounded somewhat like an itinerant preacher on circuit.

At Lafayette, Indiana, the President-elect observed that the people around his car were strangers to him. "Still," he declared, "we are bound together, I trust in christianity, civilization and patriotism . . . ."[30] It was not often that Lincoln mentioned Christianity, and when he did he generally used a small "c" for this noun. In addressing listeners at Indianapolis on February 11, Lincoln told them: "When the people rise in masses in behalf of the Union and the liberties of their country, truly may it be said, 'The gates of hell shall not prevail against them.'" Here, he quoted Matthew 16:18. Once more he reiterated his theory that he was "but an accidental instrument" of God, "temporary, and to serve but for a limited time . . . ."[31] At the Bates House in that city, Lincoln reminded his audience that "Solomon has said, that there is a time to keep silence."[32] Those who knew their Bible would have recognized that message as coming from Ecclesiastes 3:7. The harried Lincoln was telling his listeners that he was not going to reveal any of his plans for dealing with the coming fury until his inauguration.

"I have been selected to fill an important office for a brief period," explained Lincoln on his birthday to a group at Lawrenceburg, Indiana, "and am now, in your eyes, invested with an influence which will soon pass away; but should my administration prove to be a very wicked one, or what is more probable, a very foolish one, if you, the PEOPLE, are but true to yourselves and to the Constitution, there is but little harm I can do. Thank God!"[33] In this instance, his reference to God was probably intended to be a rather humorous remark. However, at Cincinnati that same day, he became more serious and related that he trusted the good sense of the American people, "on all sides of all rivers in America," and he knew, "under the Providence of God, who has never deserted us," that all Americans would "again be brethren, forgetting all parties—ignoring all parties." Furthermore, he invited oppressed foreigners to come to this country and "bid them all God speed."[34]

In explaining to the Legislature at Columbus, Ohio, on February 13 that his task was even greater than Washington's had been, Lincoln felt that he could not "but turn and look for support without which it will be impossible for me to perform that great task." "I turn, then," continued Lincoln, "and look to the American people and to that God who has never forsaken them."[35] On the following day at Steubenville, he prophesied that he would not be successful in his quest "unless sustained by the great body of the people, and by the Divine Power, without whose aid we can do nothing."[36]

Even though Lincoln had for years become very used to speaking out in the open air and had never experienced any difficulties even during the long Lincoln-Douglas Debates, the cold which he had contracted took its toll this time. At Hudson, Ohio, on February 15, Lincoln told an audience at the station, "You see by my voice that I am quite hoarse."[37] By the 16th, he admitted that he had lost his voice and could not make a speech but that his intentions were good.[38] With rest, he recovered; his physical constitution was very strong.

At 4:30 p. m. on February 16, 1861, Lincoln's train arrived in Buffalo, New York. He was immediately taken to the American House where he spoke from the balcony, saying, "I am sure I bring a heart true to the work. For the ability to perform it, I must trust in that Supreme Being who has never forsaken this favored land, through the instrumentality of this great and intelligent people. Without that assistance I shall surely fail. With it I cannot fail."[39] On the next morning, Sunday, at 10:00 a. m., Ex-President Millard Fillmore and A. M. Clapp called for Abraham Lincoln at his hotel with a carriage. But Mary Lincoln declined to go with them to church services. She remained in her quarters while Fillmore and Lincoln heard the Rev. Dr. George W. Hosmer preach in the First Unitarian Church on the corner of Eagle and Franklin streets. Lincoln appeared "pale and worn;" his vocal pitch seemed unusually low because of his cold, but he spoke with a steady voice. After church service, the President-elect returned to the hotel where the little party picked up Mary Lincoln for lunch at Fillmore's house. After dinner with Fillmore's family, Lincoln went to a religious service conducted by Father John Beason, identified as an Indian preacher, but he did not reside in Buffalo.[40]

At Syracuse, New York, Abraham Lincoln declined to mount the platform especially erected for him but did make a few remarks to the gathered throng, saying: "I wish you a long life and prosperity individually, and pray that with the perpetuity of those institutions under which we have all so long lived and prospered, our happiness may be secured, our future made brilliant, and the glorious destiny of our country established forever."[41]

Upon arrival at Albany, New York, the Presidential suite had rooms at the Delavan House which they reached on the afternoon of February 18.

Thurlow Weed was present at this hostelry. That afternoon, Lincoln addressed the New York State Legislature. "I still have confidence that the Almighty, the Maker of the Universe will, through the instrumentality of this great and intelligent people," declared Lincoln, "bring us through this as He has through all the other difficulties of our country." "Relying on this," vouched Lincoln, "I again thank you for this generous reception."[42]

At the Astor House in New York City on February 19, Lincoln was taken to its Reception Room where the political giants, Daniel Webster and Henry Clay, had once been received. He spent some minutes explaining why he was not going to make a speech to them or disclose his public policies, but he never mentioned God or introduced any religious sentiments.[43]

To the Mayor of Newark, New Jersey, Abraham Lincoln said on February 21 that "With my own ability I cannot succeed, without the sustenance of Divine Providence, and of this great, free, happy, and intelligent people. Without these I cannot hope to succeed; with them I cannot fail."[44] Later, he spoke before the New Jersey State Senate. He told the members that he, as a small boy, had gotten hold of a little book by Parson Mason Locke Weems (1759-1825) on the life of George Washington. This clergyman's biographical study greatly influenced him, admitted Lincoln. When he continued, Lincoln explained that he would "be most happy indeed if I shall be an humble instrument in the hands of the Almighty, and of this, his almost chosen people . . . ."[45] Here, he certainly was pointing out that the American people were almost the chosen nation, although from Biblical times the Jews had long claimed this honor. In speaking to the House of Representatives across the hall, Lincoln uttered no religious platitudes.

On February 21, Lincoln replied to Mayor Alexander Henry of Philadelphia and expressed a wish that he might remain there long enough to "listen to those breathings rising within the consecrated walls" of Independence Hall "where the Constitution of the United States, and, I will add, the Declaration of American Independence were originally framed." He hoped that he would never do anything "inconsistent with the teachings of those holy and most sacred walls." By these references, President-elect Lincoln placed Liberty and the Constitution on a level with religion. "I have never asked anything," continued Lincoln, "that does not breathe from those walls. All my political warfare has been in favor of the teachings coming forth from that sacred hall." In ending his brief remarks, Lincoln quoted from Psalms 137:5-6, saying, "May my right hand forget its cunning and my tongue cleave to the roof of my mouth, if ever I prove false to those teachings."[46]

On the following day, Lincoln was welcomed to Independence Hall by Theodore L. Guyler, President of the Select Council of Philadelphia. "I am filled with deep emotion at finding myself standing here in the place where were collected together the wisdom, the patriotism, the devotion to principle, from which sprang the institutions under which we live," divulged Lincoln in reply. In a prophetic statement, Lincoln told his listeners that if he could not save the Nation without giving up Liberty, he "would rather be assassinated on this spot than to surrender it." Lincoln had not prepared this speech but rather spoke off-the-cuff. Nevertheless, he testified that he had "said nothing but what I am willing to live by, and, in the pleasure of Almighty God, die by."[47]

Contrary to what some writers have stated, this was not the first time Abraham Lincoln had seen Independence Hall. On June 7, 1848, the National Nominating Convention of the Whig Party convened their meeting in the Museum Building on the northeast corner of Ninth and Sansom streets in Philadelphia. Among those attending was Congressman A. Lincoln. Two days later, the attendees adjourned to Independence Square for a ratification meeting. Independence Hall, of course, is on this square, and Lincoln certainly went along. He had come to sample the political events of this convention and did not leave until the tenth.

When Lincoln raised the Flag over Independence Hall on February 22, 1861, he read from a prepared address. He stated that when the Flag had originally been raised there, it had but thirteen stars. "I wish to call your attention to the fact," Lincoln continued, "that, under the blessing of God, each additional star added to that flag has given additional prosperity and happiness to this country . . . ." In recalling this event later that day to the Pennsylvania General Assembly at Harrisburg, Lincoln told the members that when he pulled the Flag to the top of the pole and then yanked a special cord which released the folded Ensign so that it "flaunted gloriously to the wind without an accident" and whipped proudly in the bright sunshine, he took that as an omen that success would crown his political efforts, too. Here, once more, Lincoln demonstrated his belief in omens and showed a part of his superstitious nature which had played a part throughout his entire life. And yet his prediction of coming success based upon this happening pleased the legislators no end; they gave him much loud applause.[48]

Lincoln seemed to entertain his listeners wherever he went; he said just the right things to them. For instance, at Leaman Place on February 22, the assembled group called vociferously for Mary Lincoln to appear before them. Upon bringing her out, Lincoln declared the he was giving them "the long and short of it." The listeners roared their approval.[49] They had just heard an original Lincoln joke for which he had already become famous.

In recognizing the welcome of Governor Andrew G. Curtin at Harrisburg, Pennsylvania, Lincoln said he felt the great weight of the responsibilities resting upon himself. Yet he knew "that, under God, in the strength of the arms and wisdom of the heads of these masses, after all," he would find the necessary support. An immense amount of cheering followed this remark.[50]

Because Allan Pinkerton concluded after his detective work that Abraham Lincoln's life would be in grave danger if he passed through Baltimore with public fanfare, it was determined to terminate Lincoln's public appearances after Harrisburg. Therefore, Lincoln, with Ward Hill Lamon and Pinkerton (using the alias "E. J. Allen of N. Y.") secretly returned to Philadelphia on February 22 and during the night made their way unannounced to Baltimore and on into Washington which was reached at 6:00 a. m. on the following morning.

Upon his covert arrival in Washington, Lincoln simply rode to Willard's Hotel in a carriage. W. H. Seward had been notified of this change in the schedule and before 6:00 a. m. had arrived at Willard's to await the President-elect's appearance. Swiftly, the hotel clerk assigned Lincoln to Parlor No. 6 with its several adjoining rooms. Not until 4:00 p. m. that day did Mary Lincoln, with the three Lincoln sons and the rest of the Illinois party, steam into Washington at the scheduled hour and check into Willard's. Among those actually signing the register were R. T. Lincoln, Lockwood Todd, Dr. W. S. Wallace, J. G. Nicolay, J. M. Hay, N. B. Judd, David Davis, Col. E. V. Sumner, Capt. J. Pope, Capt. G. Hazzard & lady, and Col. E. E. Ellsworth.[51]

It had been a most arduous excursion from Springfield to Washington, but evidently Abraham Lincoln wanted this campaign-like trip for several reasons. Although he did not wish to reveal any details or plans for his coming governmental actions, he did want the people of the North to catch a glimpse of him and realize that he was not the ogre so often depicted in the hostile press. He also intended to reemphasize his determination to preserve the Union but with a strict observance of Liberty and the United States Constitution. By personally talking to thousands of people—and through the media of the press, to thousands more, both North and South—Lincoln desired to ask the electorate for their support in his future difficult endeavors. He wanted the public to feel they were a vital part of his administration about to commence.

Throughout this lengthy journey, Lincoln often announced that he was an instrument of God, selected to lead this Nation towards a peaceful solution to its divisive problems. He constantly spoke of his belief in the Almighty God and how this Heavenly Father would stand by him in his time of need. Thus, it was quite natural that the people began to call him Father Abraham, their earthly leader, just as God the Father was their spiritual leader. By his numerous religious references and his several quotations from the Bible, his listening and reading audiences realized that Lincoln was not an agnostic as was sometimes hinted in whispered conversations. His very conduct was most reassuring to them that here was an honest man, a God-fearing man, who would never desert them or take advantage of their trust. In that era, most citizens attended some church and expected their elected leaders to do likewise. Even if they did not hold membership in a particular denomination, a majority of the public recognized a Sovereign Being. And Lincoln was truly a person who believed in a God, even though he seems at this time to have had reservations about the divinity of Christ. Lincoln's actions during this trip convinced numerous religious leaders of the North that they should support Lincoln's government. By his many references to Liberty, many liberal ministers no doubt thought that he stood solidly for freedom of the slaves. And yet he did not say so in so many words. He merely pleaded for unity and fairness while he sought to preserve the Union.

All in all, Abraham Lincoln's lengthy and circuitous tour of the Northern States has to be termed a brilliant exercise of statesmanship. When he asked the common men and women to pray for him, Lincoln made them a supportive element in his determined effort to preserve the Republic established by the Founding Fathers. That was Lincoln's sacred promise to himself and to the citizens of this Country. If God would stand by him, he would stand by God as His instrument to maintain the Federal Government for the good of all.

References

1   Basler, ed., *The Collected Works*, IV, 189; Wayne C. Temple, *By Square and Compasses: The Building of Lincoln's Home and Its Saga* (Bloomington: The Ashlar Press, 1984), 67; Henry Villard, *Lincoln on the Eve of '61* (N. Y. : Alfred A. Knopf, 1941), 69; Pease and Randall, eds., *The Diary of Orville Hickman Browning*, I, 453; William H. Herndon and Jess William Weik, *Herndon's Lincoln* (Springfield: The Herndon's Lincoln Pub. Co., n. d.), III, 484.

2   New-York *Tribune*, Feb. 12, 1861, p. 5, c. 3.

3   Basler, ed., *The Collected Works*, IV, 192.

4   *New York Herald*, Feb. 12, 1861, p. 4, c. 6; *Illinois State Journal*, Feb. 12, 1861, p. 2, c. 3.

5   Temple and Temple, *Illinois' Fifth Capitol*, 328.

6   Pease and Randall, eds., *The Diary of Orville Hickman Browning*, I, 453.

7   Feb. 11, 1861, entry in the Journal of Henry C. Latham, MS., Latham Papers, Ill. State Hist. Lib.

8   *Illinois State Journal*, Feb. 12, 1861, p. 2, c. 3.

9   T. D. Jones to Wm. Linn McMillen, Springfield, Ill., Feb. 11, 1861, MS., Lincoln Coll., Indiana Univ. Lib., Bloomington; T. D. Jones, "Recollections of Mr. Lincoln," *Cincinnati Commercial*, Oct. 18, 1871, p. 4, c. 6.

10   *New York Herald*, Feb. 12, 1861, p. 4, c. 6.

11   *Illinois State Journal*, Feb. 12, 1861, p. 2, c. 3.

12   *New York Herald*, Feb. 12, 1861, p. 4, c. 6.

13   James C. Conkling to Clinton L. Conkling, Springfield, Ill., Feb. 12, 1861, in Harry E. Pratt, ed., *Concerning Mr. Lincoln* (Springfield: The Abraham Lincoln Assoc., 1944), 50; entry of Feb. 11, 1861, in Journal of Henry C. Latham, MS., Latham Papers, Ill. State Hist. Lib.

14   *Illinois State Register*, Feb. 12, 1861, p. 3, c. 3; Villard, *Lincoln on the Eve of '61*, 74, 80; *Chicago Daily Tribune*, Feb. 11, 1861, p. 1, c. 3.

15   N. W. Miner, "Personal Recollections of Abraham Lincoln," MS., Ill. State Hist. Lib. Miner was a Chaplain to the Senate and knew this body very well.

16   Temple and Temple, *Illinois' Fifth Capitol*, 145 ff.

17   Basler, ed., *The Collected Works*, IV, 190-191.

18   *Ibid.*

19   *Illinois State Journal*, Feb. 12, 1861, p. 2, c. 3.

20   *New York Herald*, Feb. 12, 1861, p. 4, c. 6.

21   Isaac N. Arnold, *The Life of Abraham Lincoln* (Chicago: A. C. McClurg & Co., 1901), 183.

22   Basler, ed., *The Collected Works*, II, 132.

23   *Ibid.*, IV, 190-191.

24   Hertz, ed., *The Hidden Lincoln*, 103.

25   Entry of Feb. 11, 1861, in Journal of Henry C. Latham, MS., Latham Papers, Ill. State Hist. Lib.

26   *New York Herald*, Feb. 12, 1861, p. 5, c. 1; Harold Holzer, *Dear Mr. Lincoln: Letters to the President* (Reading, Mass.: Addison-Wesley Pub. Co., 1993), 314-315; Frank J. Williams, "Robert Todd Lincoln and John Hay, Fellow Travelers," *Lincoln Herald*, XCVI, 4 (Spring, 1994).

27   *New-York Tribune*, Feb. 23, 1861, p. 5, c. 2; Basler, ed., *The Collected Works*, IV, 179; Villard, *Lincoln on the Eve of '61*, 81.

28   T. D. Jones, "Recollections of Mr. Lincoln," *Cincinnati Commercial*, Oct. 18, 1871, p. 4, cc. 5-6.

29   Basler, ed., *The Collected Works*, IV, 191-192.

30   *Ibid.*, IV, 192.

31   *Ibid.*, IV, 193-194.

32   *Ibid.*, IV, 195.

33   *Ibid.*, IV, 197.

34   *Ibid.*, IV, 198-199, 203.

35   *Ibid.*, IV, 204.

36   *Ibid.*, IV, 207.

37   *Ibid.*, IV, 218.

38   *Ibid.*

39   *Ibid.*, IV, 220-221.

40   *New York Herald*, Feb. 18, 1861, p. 4, cc. 1-6; *Buffalo Daily Courier*, Feb. 18, 1861, p. 3, cc. 1-3; *Buffalo Commercial Advertiser*, Feb. 19, 1861, p. 1, cc. 1-2.

41   Basler, ed., *The Collected Works*, IV, 222.

42   *Ibid.*, IV, 226.

43   *Ibid.*, IV, 230-231.

44   *Ibid.*, IV, 234.

45   *Ibid.*, IV, 235-236.

46   *Ibid.*, IV, 239.

47   *Ibid.*, IV, 240-241.

48   *Ibid.*, IV, 241, 244-245.

49   *Ibid.*, IV, 242.

50   *Ibid.*, IV, 243.

51   N. W. Miner, "Personal Recollections of Abraham Lincoln," Trenton, N. J., Oct. 15, 1881, MS., Ill. State Hist. Lib.; Arnold, *The Life of Abraham Lincoln*, 186. It is extremely doubtful that anybody met Lincoln at the station. Pinkerton evidently only notified Seward who stationed himself at the hotel. Washington *Evening Star*, Feb. 23, 1861, p. 2, c. 1; Feb. 25, 1861, p. 4, c. 1.

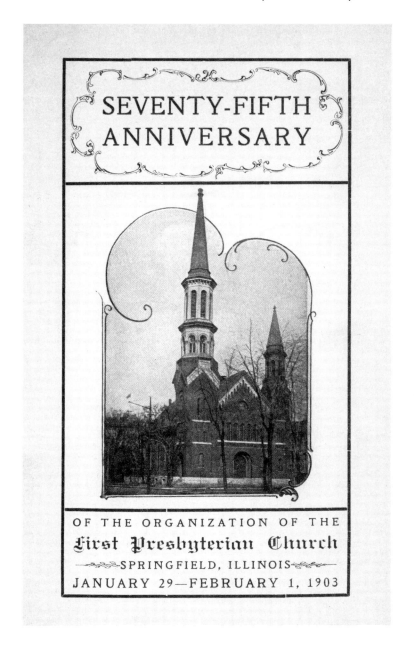

In 1882, the First Presbyterian Church appeared as it does in this picture.
The steeples have been greatly altered in more recent years.

Even though the First Family had not been many hours in Washington, D. C., the President and Mrs. Lincoln agreed to attend separate church services on Sunday, February 24, 1861. Senator William Henry Seward called for Lincoln at Willard's Hotel, and together they walked from the 14th Street entrance to St. John's Episcopal Church on Lafayette Square, opposite the White House. This edifice had been designed by the noted architect Benjamin Henry Latrobe and was shaped like a Latin Cross. Built of brick, it was covered with stucco. President-elect Lincoln sat "at the head of Mr. Seward's pew" which was located near the altar and then enumerated as No. 1. While the pew still exists, it has been identified as No. 65 since 1883. At this 11:00 o'clock service, the Rev. Dr. Smith Pyne preached. He may have recognized Lincoln. Certainly, he asked a special blessing for the incoming administration.

Lincoln appeared in "plain black clothes," and the ladies present who spotted him declared that his black hair and whiskers were well trimmed. They found him to be a completely different man from the pictures and drawings they had previously seen of him. In fact, some of these insisted he was "almost good-looking." An observant New York correspondent for the *Herald* reported that Abraham Lincoln "read the service with the regular worshippers."[1]

Seward and Lincoln were close political allies, and Seward was about to become Secretary of State in the new administration. However, there were noticeable differences between them. Seward smoked and swore like a trooper.[2] Lincoln did neither. Later, the President would make a joke concerning Seward's profanity. On April 9, 1863, while the President was reviewing the Army of the Potomac, he and Noah Brooks, a close friend, were riding in an old ambulance pulled by six mules over a very rough corduroy road. As the vehicle jolted up and down over this temporary roadway, the military driver "occasionally let fly a volley of suppressed oaths." After awhile, Lincoln leaned forward and tapped the soldier on the shoulder. "Excuse me, my friend, are you an Episcopalian?" questioned the Commander-in-Chief.

"No, Mr. President; I am a Methodist," replied the mule skinner.

"Well," explained Lincoln, "I thought you must be an Episcopalian, because you swear just like Governor Seward, who is a churchwarden."[3]

Mary Lincoln did not accompany her distinguished husband and Seward to St. John's Church on February 24. Instead, she went to morning services that day with Senator Edward Dickinson Baker and his family.[4] Baker had been baptized into the Disciples of Christ Church, better known as the Christian Church, after his marriage, but he never seemed to be a serious follower of this denomination.

The Christian Church, in those days, had but few members in Washington, and they met in various homes or other locations since they had no building of their own. When Senator Baker escorted Mary Lincoln to church, the Disciples of Christ probably assembled for services in Temperance Hall at 914 E Street, N. W., which they rented for $5.50 per month. However, it seems doubtful that Senator Baker took her there. Instead, he probably drove Mary Lincoln to hear the minister at the First Presbyterian Church on 4 1/2 Street, between C and Louisiana Avenue. Baker must have attended this church upon occasion, because its minister preached his funeral service later that year. This was Dr. Byron Sunderland. It is possible that the minister of this church and the Elders observed Mary Lincoln there on that Sunday and for this reason quickly invited the Lincolns to take a pew in their congregation's sanctuary.[5]

Not only were the Lincolns old and dear friends of Baker, but Baker also served with Senator Solomon Foot of Vermont and Senator James Alfred Pearce of Maryland on the Committee of Arrangements for the Inauguration of the President on March 4.[6] Here was a fine chance for Baker to quiz Mary Lincoln about her desires for this important social and political event. She could quickly inform Baker exactly what her husband liked to eat, etc. No doubt they discussed this coming affair to some extent.

Soon after Abraham Lincoln arrived in Washington, Congressman Henry Laurens Dawes and Judge Horatio Nelson Taft met him. According to his daughter, Taft remarked: "Lincoln was the man sent by Divine Providence to serve the country in the dark hours before us."[7] Later, Lincoln's own secretary, John Hay, wrote, "I believe the hand of God placed him where he is."[8] The President accepted their prognoses and expressed his own feeling that he, indeed, was the instrument of God.[9]

To the Committee of Congress, which reported to him the results of the Electoral College count of the votes for President, Lincoln replied on

February 26, 1861, saying he would meet the national perils "with a firm reliance on the strength of our free government, and the ultimate loyalty of the people to the just principles upon which it is founded, and above all an unspoken faith in the Supreme Ruler of nations . . . ."[10] Here, once more, he publicly expressed his belief in God. But he as yet had not encountered a "religious experience" so necessary in that day to join the ranks of most Christian denominations.

As Washington prepared for the inauguration ceremonies, the city officials discovered that Pennsylvania Avenue gave the appearance of "a heap of dust." It probably would have to be watered down for carriages to negotiate this broad thoroughfare in comfort and dignity.[11] Meanwhile, some members of the Todd clan began arriving in the Nation's Capital to witness the coming events of state.[12]

On Sunday, March 3, 1861, President-elect Lincoln remained in his quarters at Willard's, working on his inaugural address and contemplating Cabinet appointments. He did not attend any church services. Despite the many distractions, Lincoln managed to revise and complete his address. But not until the very morning of March 4, did he indite the last paragraph of this important message. Upon concluding the closing remarks, he read them to his family and then asked them to leave the room and allow him to be alone for awhile. Mary Lincoln recalled that she could clearly hear her husband praying aloud to God and asking for His divine aid. Like the prophet Daniel, he was talking to the Heavenly Father while surrounded by a host of enemies. Washington's old families mainly favored the South unless they were Northerners living there temporarily as governmental officials.

Shortly afterwards, Senator Douglas came to Willard's and asked to ride with Lincoln to the Capitol.[13] Mary Lincoln, with her several relatives, had already left long before the formal procession commenced. Earlier that morning there had been a slight rainfall which had laid the dust.[14]

When Lincoln and Douglas reached the speaking platform at the Capitol, the President-elect could find no safe spot to deposit his tall hat. A contemporary newspaper and several witnesses reported that, without hesitation, Senator Douglas took it himself, saying, "Permit me, Sir," and gallantly held it while Lincoln read his entire inaugural address.[15]

But first, William Thomas Carroll, Clerk of the United States Supreme Court, brought forth a Bible so that the President-elect might take his oath of office. He held it while Chief Justice Roger Brooke Taney administered the oath to Lincoln who stood with his hand upon the sacred volume and repeated the words. Perhaps the new President felt somewhat uncomfortable facing Taney who had written the majority opinion in 1857 that Dred Scott was not a citizen and that the Missouri Compromise was completely unconstitutional. After that date, Lincoln had openly and strongly criticized Taney for the Supreme Court's stand upon this politically volatile issue.

Lincoln, nevertheless, took his Presidential oath seriously and publicly affirmed his religious belief in Heaven and the justice of God. In addressing the South, President Lincoln would say a few minutes later in his Inaugural Address, "In your hands, my dissatisfied fellow countrymen, and not in mine, is the momentous issue of civil war. The government will not assail you. You can have no conflict, without being yourselves the aggressors. You have no oath registered in Heaven to destroy the government, while I shall have the most solemn one to 'preserve, protect and defend' it."

This Bible which was utilized in President Lincoln's First Inauguration is now kept in the Rare Book and Special Collections Division of The Library of Congress. It is one of the many Lincoln treasures owned by this institution.

At the proper moment, after the oath ceremony, Senator E. D. Baker of Oregon arose and stepped to the front of the dais where he simply announced, "Fellow Citizens, Abraham Lincoln, President of the United States, will now proceed to deliver his inaugural address."[16] An early Illinois Whig friend and ally of Lincoln's, Baker had made a trip back to Springfield from Washington, D. C., on December 24, 1860, to renew his close association with the President-elect and no doubt had asked during that visit to introduce Lincoln at the coming March 4th inauguration, although he was not a Senator from Illinois at that time.[17]

As Lincoln drew toward the end of his address, he declared: "If the Almighty Ruler of nations, with his eternal truth and justice, be on your side of the North, or on yours of the South, that truth, and that justice, will surely prevail, by the judgment of this great tribunal, the American people." "Intelligence, patriotism, Christianity, and a firm reliance on Him, who has never yet forsaken this favored land, are still competent to adjust, in the best way, all our present difficulty," Lincoln told his audience. In closing, Lincoln stated, "The mystic cords of memory, stre[t]ching from every battle-field, and patriot grave, to every living heart and hearthstone, all over this broad land, will yet swell the chorus of the Union, when again touched, as surely they will be, by the better angels of our nature."[18] That poetic finale read like a sermon from Father Abraham to the Nation.

At the Inaugural Ball that evening, Mary Lincoln came into the hall on the arm of Senator Douglas. "She wore a rich watered silk, an elegant point lace cape, deeply bordered, with camellias in her hair, and pearl ornaments," reported a journalist.[19] And she danced a quadrille with her partner, Stephen A. Douglas.[20] Dancing was one of the several things that Presbyterian Church members did not do. A foreign visitor to Washington during the Civil War would note in his diary: "Presbyterian maids and matrons neither dance nor attend the theatre."[21] Of course, Mary Lincoln did both despite her church membership. Later that year, she was observed at the Mansion House in Long Branch, New Jersey, participating in a grand ball—without her husband. Beyond all comparison, Mary Lincoln was the most elegantly dressed lady present. She had on "an elegant robe of white grenadine, with a long flowing train, the bottom of the skirt puffed with quillings of white satin, and the arms and shoulders uncovered, save with an elegant point lace shawl." In addition, she wore a necklace and bracelets of pearls and carried a pearl fan. Her headdress was wreathed with wild white roses.[22] If the President had been with her when she dressed, he would no doubt have remarked about her bare arms and shoulders, as he did on numerous occasions, mostly in jest, of course. Except for the period when she was in mourning for her son, Willie, Mary Lincoln continued to attend dances and fancy balls.[23]

In participating as she did, Mary Lincoln was defying the strict teachings of the Presbyterian Church in these matters. However, she did accept Christ as her Saviour—declaring it on paper—writing: "our only refuge in our distress, is in the Saviour, who suffered & died for us."[24] On the other hand, Mary could be irreverent in her references. Her personal seamstress and companion revealed that Mary's favorite expression was "God, no!"[25]

Quickly, President Lincoln attempted to establish a routine for his administration. Ordinarily, Cabinet meetings were scheduled for Tuesday and Friday, although an emergency might cause conferences with his Cabinet on other days. Infrequently, he even summoned these officials on Sunday.[26] "The President respected the sanctity of the Sabbath and disapproved of unnecessary work upon that day," recalled General Herman Haupt, Chief of the U. S. Military Railroads.[27] However, Lincoln often labored on Sundays even if he did not ask his staff or Cabinet to do so. He was known upon occasion to summon a person to his office on Sunday morning, "if [the person is] not going to church." James Matlock Scovel, a journalist, revealed that Lincoln frequently spent the hours of ten to noon with either Secretary Seward or a personal barber.[28]

Close friends sometimes criticized the Lincolns for not being observant enough of Sundays. Orville Hickman Browning gratuitously told the President that he did not think that Sunday was a good time for a dinner party.[29] At another time, "an eminent theologian" presented himself at the White House, claiming to be the representative for a group of clergymen who objected to having battles fought on Sundays.[30] Fortunately, we have the answer President Lincoln gave to another person on this very subject. Said Lincoln, "I sincerely wish war was an easier and pleasanter business than it is; but it does not admit of holy-days."[31] Even one of Lincoln's house guests, a cousin of Mary Lincoln, infringed upon the secular activities of the First Family. After lunch on Sunday, March 10, 1861, William Wallace "Willie" Lincoln wandered into the Red Room of the White House and commenced to play some popular airs upon the piano. Whereupon Elizabeth J. (Todd) Grimsley, a most religious lady who later took a preacher for her second husband, remonstrated with Willie and sternly cautioned him to remember the Sabbath and keep it holy. While she remained in the White House, poor Willie could not even play the piano on Sundays[32]—a considerable change for a child who had been given virtually free reign back in Springfield, Illinois.

Although the Lincoln family did not conduct devotions in the Executive Mansion, both the President and Mary observed some religious customs and attended church rather regularly.[33] One officer thought Abraham Lincoln's faith was more like that of an Old Testament prophet than that of an ordinary American of the Nineteenth Century.[34] Indeed, the President seems to have enjoyed the rare gift of clairvoyance, too. He once remarked to John Hay, "I believe I feel trouble in the air before it comes."[35] As President, he still dreamed dreams and believed in them to a large extent.[36] He was blessed with an uncanny sixth sense.

It has been said that of all the books Lincoln read, two of them impressed him greatly: the Bible and writings of William Shakespeare.[37] He simply loved the drama of the Bard from Stratford Upon the Avon. His favorite plays were *King Lear*, *Richard III*, *Henry VIII*, *Hamlet*, and, above all, *Macbeth*. The latter was "wonderful," declared Lincoln.[38] While President,

Lincoln studied the Bible and gave the appearance of enjoying it for its literary style as well as its religious instruction. As he had grown older, Lincoln had gradually lost his initial skepticism toward the Bible. He once explained to Chittenden, his Register of the Treasury, that the Bible should be judged fairly, just like a person in court. "If we had a witness on the stand whose general story we knew was true," explained Lincoln, "we would believe him when he asserted facts of which we had no other evidence." "I decided a long time ago," admitted Lincoln, "that it was less difficult to believe that the Bible was what it claimed to be than to disbelieve it." "It is a good book for us to obey," he conceded. Among the many important parts of the Bible, Lincoln mentioned the Ten Commandments and the Golden Rule. Lincoln acknowledged that "No man was ever the worse for living according to the directions of the Bible."[39]

A copy of the Bible "commonly lay on his desk." And he knew its contents extremely well. When a group of dissatisfied Republicans gathered at Cleveland, Ohio, on May 31, 1864, to pick John C. Frémont for their Presidential candidate, a warm political friend informed the President that only about four hundred persons attended this opposition convention. Immediately, Lincoln picked up his Bible and turned to I Samuel 22:2 and read: "And every one that was in distress, and every one that was in debt, and every one that was discontented, gathered themselves unto him; and he became a captain over them; and there were with him about four hundred men."[40] Lincoln readily remembered, as he often did, passages from the Bible.

Lincoln also kept a Bible on a small stand at one end of his sofa. During the dark and terrible days of early 1863, the tired and dejected President would collapse on this couch and exclaim that everything everywhere was dark, very dark. Then he would take up this Bible and con it until his face would lighten up and his expression would undergo a complete change. Upon one such occasion after Lincoln left, a White House witness examined the sacred pages to learn what the great man had been perusing; it was Job.[41] For some of his important messages to Congress, President Lincoln would search out particular sentiments from the Bible and incorporate them into his writings. If he could not remember the exact wording or citation, he would rely upon an index complied by Alexander Cruden (1701-1770), a Scotsman born in Aberdeen. In the Library, Lincoln kept this book which was entitled *A Complete Concordance to the Holy Scriptures of the Old and New Testament . . . .* It had appeared in many editions.[42]

Just two days after his inauguration, the First Presbyterian Church of Washington sent an invitation to the new President. "In the name of the First Presbyterian Church . . . (Rev. [Byron] Sunderland D. D.) we have the honor to inform you that a Pew in this church has been placed at the disposal of yourself and family, should it be your pleasure to attend public worship with us," explained the Temporal Committee which included W. Gunton, Z. D. Gilman, A. W. Russell, N. W. Galt and Y. E. Page.[43] Probably, these men had already learned that the Lincolns had a pew in a Presbyterian Church during their Springfield years and sought the prestige of numbering the President among their attendees. And they perhaps witnessed Mary Lincoln in their church on February 24.

Lincoln did not accept this cordial offer from the First Presbyterian Church. On the very next Sunday, March 10, 1861, the Lincoln Family and their house guests attended the New York Avenue Presbyterian Church where Dr. Phineas Densmore Gurley (1816-1868) preached.[44] His father had been raised as a Quaker. This church stood at the intersection of New York Avenue, Thirteenth and H streets, just three blocks from the White House. Gurley had previously preached in Dayton, Ohio, and had attended Union College and Princeton Theological Seminary. In 1858, he had been elected Chaplain of the U. S. Senate. Dr. Gurley, a member of the Old School Presbyterians who had previously been at the F Street Church, was known to preach a fine service and make a grand appearance.[45] Gurley's merged congregation worshipped in a brand new structure which had just been dedicated on October 14, 1860, but the history of this flock went back many years.

In 1807, a group of Presbyterians had constructed an edifice on F Street near the corner of Fourteenth, and they became known as the F Street Church. The Second Presbyterian Church was born in 1819, and its building was constructed soon thereafter on New York Avenue. Then on September 25, 1859, the two congregations formally merged, with the F Street property being sold to the Willards. Since the lot owned by the Second Presbyterian was more centrally located, the combined congregations determined to tear down this old building, erect a new church on New York Avenue, and call themselves by the Avenue's name. Among the Presidents who had worshipped on this site were John Quincy Adams, Andrew Jackson and James Buchanan.[46] Lincoln did not immediately decide upon a church home. He wished to ponder the question further and perhaps determined to let Mary make the final decision. Despite her irreverent behavior, she was the avowed Presbyterian.

Brevet Lieutenant General Winfield Scott, General-in-Chief of the Army since July 5, 1841, invited President Lincoln to attend church with him on March 17, 1861. Scott, a Freemason and a devoted Episcopalian, took the President to St. John's Episcopal Church, opposite the White House at the corner of H Street North and Sixteenth Street West, where the latter had been with Seward on February 24. The Rev. Smith Pyne again preached with Lincoln in the audience. Once more, the President heard a distinguished preacher, but he made no commitment to rent a pew. General Scott retired from the Army on November 1, 1861, and died on May 29, 1866.[47]

Lincoln even consulted with friends and the members of his Cabinet before selecting a house of worship. "I wish to find a church," Lincoln declared, "whose clergyman holds himself aloof from politics."[48] In the past, he had suffered somewhat from preachers. One, Peter Cartwright, had even run against him twice for public office. During the 1860 canvas for President, Abraham Lincoln had compiled a list of Springfield ministers and how they voted or said they were going to vote. Out of twenty-three, only three voiced any support for Lincoln![49] Elizabeth J. (Todd) Grimsley later revealed that while President Lincoln occupied the White House, he had been troubled by many arrogant preachers. She thought there had been two exceptions: Bishop Matthew Simpson of the Methodist Episcopal Church and Archbishop John Joseph Hughes, a Roman Catholic from New York. After the Mason and Slidell debacle, Archbishop Hughes was persuaded by the State Department and Secretary Seward to undertake an unofficial mission to Europe and pour oil upon the troubled waters. He was gone for eight months and did much good for the Lincoln Administration.[50] As it turned out, even Dr. Gurley would also take advantage of his friendship with Lincoln to lobby the President on behalf of disloyal ministers, convicted criminals or other malefactors.[51]

Contemporary observers came to the conclusion that Abraham Lincoln was a sincere man when it came to being truly religious.[52] Sometimes his expressions along this line turned out to be very amusing. At a reception in the Blue Room of the White House one night, an old man from Buffalo, New York, shook Lincoln's hand and asserted, "Up our way, we believe in God and Abraham Lincoln." As the President kindly urged the old gentleman on down the reception line, he answered, "My friend, you are more than half right."[53]

While Lincoln pondered his choice of a church, he continued to sample the sermons of Dr. Gurley. The President had certain criteria by which he judged a preacher. One item in that list stands out starkly. "The fact is," confessed Lincoln, "I don't like to hear cut and dried sermons. No—when I hear a man preach, I like to see him act as if he were fighting bees!"[54] Whether or not the Rev Dr. Gurley possessed this talent, we do not know. But he did preach with a great amount of eloquence.[55]

Another factor which interested Mr. Lincoln was the musical portion of a church program. He appreciated musical selections which were rendered well by talented musicians.[56] These qualities Lincoln found at the New York Avenue Presbyterian Church since the minister there took an active interest in the music selected, played and sung in his services. In college, Gurley had performed on the flute and been a member of the choir. He fostered tuneful melodies in his church, such as "Rock of Ages."[57] Most Presbyterian hymnals do not contain an abundance of tuneful numbers.

When Father Abraham or his wife finally decided to attend the New York Avenue Presbyterian Church, the minister was notified of this decision, and one of the gentlemen who passed the plate—certainly one of the Deacons—took the plat of the pew arrangement over to the White House for the President and Mrs. Lincoln's inspection and selection.[58] By chance or by choice, the Lincolns picked B-14, the vacant pew previously held by President James Buchanan. It was in the seventh row from the front and on the right hand of the center aisle. Although Buchanan had been a Mason for many, many years, he had never formally joined a church, but he did attend and did rent a pew at the New York Avenue Presbyterian Church. He once said "I hope I am a Christian;" yet, he confessed that he had never had a "religious experience." After he left the White House, however, Buchanan did join the Presbyterian Church on September 23, 1865, at Lancaster, Pennsylvania, his home and the location of his Masonic Lodge, Number 43.[59]

Like Buchanan, President Lincoln had not as yet felt a "religious experience" nor did he join, but he did rent a pew for $50 per year, payable quarterly in the amount of $12.50. From the fact that Lincoln remitted $4.17 to the church on June 30, 1861, it can be stated for certain that he legally made his contract for the pew June 1. A contemporary newspaper corroborates this calculation that the Lincolns began renting a pew on June 1.[60] President Lincoln submitted his payments quite regularly until the last quarter of 1864 when the Board of Trustees voted to tender the pew to the

Lincolns free of charge.[61] Other Presidents have regularly occupied this historic pew since the Lincolns left: McKinley, Taft and Eisenhower. Woodrow Wilson also accepted this seat and sat in it for the first time on March 9, 1913.[62] This original pew still exists, although it now reposes in a new sanctuary on the same site.

Lincoln's attendance is well documented. His two secretaries vouched that "the President and his family habitually attended worship."[63] Another witness described Lincoln's attendance as frequent.[64] Nevertheless, Mary Lincoln never added her name to the membership roster in Washington. Instead, her letter remained with the First Presbyterian Church back in Springfield.[65]

Abraham Lincoln's great height was more in the length of his legs than in his torso. Because there was insufficient space between the seats at the New York Avenue Presbyterian Church, Lincoln discovered that it was not easy for him to sit down without bumping his knees. "Owing to [the pew's] construction," recalled one witness, "President Lincoln seemed to be always ill at ease, finding much apparent difficulty in accommodating his tall frame to its meager proportions." "He generally managed to fit himself to it, however," continued this observer, "before the sermon commenced upon which he was ever an attentive and most respectful listener."[66]

Dr. William Henry Roberts went to Washington in the fall of 1863 and became a member of Lincoln's church. He sat not far from the Lincolns and detected that the President was "an earnest and devout worshipper." Roberts, who later became the Stated Clerk of the General Assembly of the Presbyterian Church, testified: "When the time for the long prayer came, according to immemorial usage in many Presbyterian congregations," testified Roberts, "a number of the men stood up for prayer, and among those upright figures I noticed in particular that of the President of the United States."[67] In addition to Lincoln's observance of a custom which he had learned years before in Springfield, the tall President probably found welcomed relief in standing after sitting in a tight pew.

Another member told of a ruse often practiced by another pew holder. This schemer would direct "the old colored sexton" at the rear of the church to seat others in his own pew until it was entirely filled. Thereupon the plotter would wander down the aisle hopelessly trying to find a place to sit. With a pitiful expression upon his face, he would survey the parishioners to see which one might invite him to sit with them. When he reached Lincoln's pew, the President's lengthy arm would automatically reach out and sweep him into his pew and seat him beside himself. Never did Lincoln appear to realize what was happening, but the congregation always smiled knowingly at the antics of this devious man.[68]

Not only did Abraham Lincoln participate in the Sunday services at the New York Avenue Presbyterian Church, but he also upon occasion attended the weekly prayer meetings held in the basement on Thursday evenings, said Sidney I. McCleary Lauck in an affidavit. "It having become known that he was an attendant at the prayer meeting," revealed Dr. Roberts, "many persons would gather in or near the church at the close of the service in order to have access to him for various purposes." Desiring to put a stop to these unwelcomed interruptions, Dr. Gurley proposed that Mr. Lincoln sit in the pastor's study, also in the basement, "the door of which opened upon the lecture room, and there Mr. Lincoln would take a silent part in the service." The President confided to Dr. Gurley that "he had received great comfort from the meetings" and appreciated the prayers especially. The Rev. Gurley found that Lincoln had a "deeply religious character." The invaluable settee upon which Lincoln sat for these prayer meetings is also well preserved and venerated in the current church building.[69]

In addition to paying pew rent, members also deposited money in the collection plate when it was passed. One Deacon who officiated in taking up the offering saw President Lincoln make liberal deposits in the plate. Said this church officer, one "morning there was some kind of extra collection taken, some appeal had been made from the pulpit for a charity, and as usual I handed the plate into Mr. Lincoln's pew. Mrs. Lincoln, as was her custom, contributed, and the President also placed a sum on the plate. I started to the next pew in front when a long arm reached out and drew me back, and the President leaned over and whispered: 'I want to contribute more than that; come to the White House in the morning.' I obeyed the request, and received a check upon which was written a goodly amount."[70] At other times, Lincoln also made out checks to his church in Washington. On June 25, 1863, he wrote one, numbered 43, for $25 and payable to "Rev. Dr. Gurley (for church)."[71] As in the past, Abraham Lincoln continued to be a generous giver to religious causes.

Quite naturally, the Lincolns enrolled Willie and Tad in Sunday School at the New York Avenue Presbyterian Church. Willie relished the teaching and loved this religious experience, but Tad went merely to be with his more studious brother. They entered Miss Mattie Waller's class, but when she suddenly died on November 22, 1861, a Miss Dunham took over their group as teacher. In addition, Willie participated in the Youth's Missionary Society which collected money to sponsor a native missionary in China.[72]

Within a short time, however, Tad rebelled at going to Sunday School, whereupon President Lincoln explained quietly that "Every educated person should know something about the Bible and the Bible stories, Tad." Although Thomas attended Sunday School upon occasion after that, he often went to church instead with Julia Taft and her younger brothers who were about the same age as the Lincoln boys. Julia was just sixteen but already dating some of the youthful Union officers. The Tafts attended the Fourth Presbyterian Church, New School, located on Ninth Street between G and H streets where the Rev. Dr. John C. Smith preached. Tad especially thought this church much more entertaining since a great many members of this congregation sympathized with the South. Whenever the pastor would pray for the President of the United States, those who disagreed with him would immediately take their noisy departure from the sanctuary, stomping out and banging not only their pew doors but also the outside door.

After several weeks of this outrageous behavior, a stern-looking Lieutenant appeared there one Sunday with a file of soldiers under his command. This no-nonsense military officer marched to the front of the sanctuary, did an about-face, and announced in a loud voice that "It is the order of the Provost Marshal that any one disturbing this service or leaving it before it is out will be arrested and taken to the guardhouse." This startling demonstration of power completely quieted the Secessionists. Tad, however, defiantly proclaimed that "If I was Secesh, I wouldn't let him stop me banging pew doors." Willie reminded him that the army men would then put him under arrest. To this Tad replied, "Well, I guess Pa could get me out."

Generally, Tad would seat himself on the floor within the pew and play with whatever he chanced to have in his pockets. He rarely paid much attention to the sermon or the other devotions. On one occasion, Julia's escort, a callow officer not much older than she, gave his pocketknife to Tad, believing that he did not have the strength to open it. Somehow Tad managed to pull out the blade and cut himself. This accident forced Julia to bind up his finger with her very best embroidered handkerchief. Angrily, she hissed to him, "I will never take you to church again, Thomas Lincoln."[73]

Even though the White House sat just three blocks from the New York Avenue Presbyterian Church, the Lincolns went there by carriage on

Sundays. There were three carriages at the Executive Mansion for their use, and Mary Lincoln had her own vehicle and horses.[74] Frequently, the Lincolns would invite their friend, Orville Hickman Browning, to ride home with them after service for lunch. If the President had stayed at the White House to work, Mary Lincoln often took her own carriage and picked up Browning on her way to church. If Robert T. Lincoln happened to be in Washington, he and his mother would attend church together. And if Browning happened to be in the congregation that morning, they would take him to his own home.[75]

Sometimes President Lincoln walked the short distance to the church for prayer meetings in the evening, however. It, no doubt, was relaxing for the mentally-tired executive to amble over instead of ride. Then, too, it made his visits more confidential. One evening after a light snow had fallen, two boys at the church, Will Gurley and John D. McChesney, determined to find out who it was that sat alone in the study instead of the meeting room for the prayer service. So, they followed Lincoln's footprints back to the White House and discovered it was the President himself. When Lincoln arrived home, he turned about and said to the young detectives, "Thanks for the escort, boys."[76]

Dr. Gurley became a frequent visitor to the Executive Mansion and won the admiration of both Abraham and Mary Lincoln. The latter would sometimes forward choice items to the minister and his family. Once she sent raisins and figs from Smyrna; at another time, flowers; and on November 25, 1864, a prized turkey for Thanksgiving.[77]

References

1   Washington *Evening Star*, Feb. 25, 1861, p. 3, cc. 1-2; N. Y. *Herald*, Feb. 25, 1861, p. 1, c. 4; Robert Zinsmeister, Jr., "The Forgotten Pew," *Lincoln Herald*, LXXVII,114-120 (Summer, 1975).

2   *New York Herald*, Dec. 19, 1861, p. 7, c. 1.

3   Brooks, *Washington in Lincoln's Time*, 50-51.

4   New York *Tribune*, Feb. 25, 1861, p. 5, c. 3.

5   Harry C. Blair and Rebecca Tarshis, *Lincoln's Constant Ally: The Life of Colonel Edward D. Baker* (Portland: Oregon Hist. Soc., 1960), 8; Hilda E. Koontz, *A History of the National City Christian Church* (Washington: The church, 1981), 1-5.

6   *Daily National Intelligencer*, Feb. 25, 1861, p. 1, c. 1.

7   Julia Taft Bayne, *Tad Lincoln's Father* (Boston: Little, Brown & Co., 1931), 77-78.

8   Tyler Dennett, ed., *Lincoln . . . in the Diaries and Letters of John Hay* (N. Y.: Dodd, Mead & Co., 1939), 76.

9   Lucius E. Chittenden, *Recollections of President Lincoln and His Administration* (N. Y.: Harper & Bros., 1891), 448.

10   Basler, ed., *The Collected Works*, IV, 246.

11   *Daily National Intelligencer*, Mar. 2, 1861, p. 1, c. 6.

12   *Washington Evening Star*, Mar. 4, 1861, p. 2, c. 2.

13   Mary Lincoln related this happening to her old friend, Rev. N. W. Miner from Springfield, who later entered it in his "Personal Recollections of Abraham Lincoln," MS., Ill. State Hist. Lib.; Washington *Evening Star*, Mar. 4, 1861, p. 3, c. 1.

14   *New York Herald*, Mar. 5, 1861, p. 1, c. 1; Washington *Evening Star*, Mar. 4, 1861, p. 3, c. 1.

15   *Cincinnati Daily Commercial*, Mar. 11, 1861, p. 2, c. 3. See also Rev. Miner's account, told him by Lincoln himself, as well as Arnold, *The Life of Abraham Lincoln*, 189-190, a Congressman who was present, and Wayne Andrews, ed., *The Autobiography of Carl Schurz* (N. Y.: Charles Scriber's Sons, 1961), 169, another man who sat on the platform with Lincoln. In recalling this event, the *Daily National Intelligencer*, Mar. 7, 1865, p. 2, c. 4, stated that Lincoln

had read his address in a "clear, loud, and distinct voice" while Judge Douglas held his hat.

16   *Cincinnati Daily Commercial*, Mar. 6, 1861, p. 3, c. 4.

17   *Illinois State Journal*, Dec. 25, 1860, p. 2, c. 1.

18   Basler, ed., *The Collected Works*, IV, 270-271.

19   *Frank Leslie's Illustrated Newspaper*, XI, 285 (Mar. 23, 1861).

20   *Harper's Weekly*, V, 167 (Mar. 16, 1861).

21   Marquis Adolphe de Chambrun, *Impressions of Lincoln and the Civil War* (N. Y.: Random House, 1952), 88.

22   *New York Herald*, Aug. 24, 1861, p. 8, cc. 3-4.

23   *Ibid.*, Mar. 8, 1865, p. 5, c. 2.

24   Turner and Turner, eds., *Mary Todd Lincoln*, 444.

25   Elizabeth Keckley, *Behind the Scenes* (N. Y.: G. W. Carleton & Co., 1868), 150, 101.

26   David Donald, ed., *Inside Lincoln's Cabinet . . . Salmon P. Chase* (N. Y.: Longmans, Green & Co., 1954), 104-105. This occurred on August 3, 1862.

27   *Reminiscences of General Herman Haupt* (Milwaukee: Wright & Joys Co., 1901), 298.

28   Basler, ed., *The Collected Works*, VI, 53; Rufus Rockwell Wilson, ed., *Intimate Memories of Lincoln* (Elmira: The Primavera Press, 1945), 520.

29   Pease and Randall, eds., *The Diary of Orville Hickman Browning*, I, 592.

30   William O. Stoddard, *Lincoln's Third Secretary* (N. Y.: Exposition Press, 1955), 93.

31   Basler, ed., *The Collected Works*, V, 452.

32   Elizabeth Todd Grimsley, "Six Months in the White House," *Jour. Ill. State Hist. Soc.*, XIX, 49 (Oct., 1926-Jan., 1927).

33   Bayne, *Tad Lincoln's Father*, 183.

34   John Eaton, *Grant, Lincoln and the Freedmen* (N. Y.: Longmans, Green & Co., 1907), 313. Eaton was a Ph.D. and a General.

35   Dennett, ed., *Diaries of John Hay*, 92.

36   Basler, ed., *The Collected Works*, VI, 256.

37   de Chambrun, *Impressions of Lincoln*, 101.

38   Basler, ed., *The Collected Works*, VI, 392.

39   Bayne, *Tad Lincoln's Father*, 183-184; Chittenden, *Recollections of President Lincoln*, 449-450.

40   John G. Nicolay and John Hay, *Abraham Lincoln: A History* (N. Y.: The Century Co., 1890), IX, 40.

41   Keckley, *Behind the Scenes*, 118-119.

42   Alexander Williamson, "Reminiscences of Lincoln," Washington (D. C.) *Sunday Chronicle*, Mar. 7, 1869, p. 4. See also Temple, *Alexander Williamson—Tutor to the Lincoln Boys* (Madison: Lincoln Fellowship of Wisconsin, 1971).

43   Robert Todd Lincoln Coll., No. 7831-2, MS., The Library of Congress.

44   Grimsley, "Six Months in the White House," *Jour. Ill. State Hist.* Soc., XIX, 49.

45   Howard K. Beale, ed., *The Diary of Edward Bates 1859-1866* (Washington: U. S. Govt. Print. Office, 1933), 176.

46   Frank E. Edgington, *A History of The New York Avenue Presbyterian Church* (Washington: N. Y. Ave. Presby. Church, 1961), 19, 43, 51-54.

47   *New York Herald*, Mar. 18, 1861, p. 1, c., 2; Gilbert H. Hill, "Brother Winfield Scott," *Knight Templar*, XXII, 7 (Mar., 1976).

48   *The Washington (D. C.) Post*, Mar. 12, 1893, p. 2, c. 7.

49   J. B. McClure, ed., *Anecdotes of Abraham Lincoln* (Chicago: Rhodes & McClure, 1879), 80.

50   Grimsley, "Six Months in the White House," *Jour. Ill. State Hist.* Soc., XIX, 60.

51   Basler, ed., *The Collected Works*, VI, 378, VIII, 291; Basler, ed., *The Collected Works Supplement 1832-1865* (Westport: Greenwood Press, 1974), 262.

52   Carpenter, *Six Months at the White House*, 185-186.

53   John Hay, "Life in the White House in the Time of Lincoln," *The Century*

Magazine, XLI, 35 (Nov., 1890).

54   Leonard W. Volk, *The Lincoln Life-Mask and How It Was Made* (Separate reprint made in 1915).

55   de Chambrun, *Impressions of Lincoln*, 114.

56   Mary Miner Hill Memoirs, MS., Ill. State Hist. Lib. She was the daughter of Rev. N. W. Miner mentioned previously.

57   Kenneth A. Bernard, *Lincoln and the Music of the Civil War* (Caldwell: Caxton Printers, Ltd., 1966), 156-157.

58   *Washington Post*, Mar. 12, 1893, p. 2, c. 7.

59   Philip Shriver Klein, *President James Buchanan* (Univ. Park: Penn. State Univ. Press, 1962), 349, 427.

60   *The Sun* (Baltimore), June 6, 1861, p. 1, c. 7.

61   "Ledger—Pew Rental," 84, MS., N. Y. Ave. Presbyterian Church Archives, Washington, D. C.

62   *Illinois State Register*, Mar. 9, 1913, p. 2, cc. 3-4.

63   Nicolay and Hay, *Abraham Lincoln: A History*, X, 318.

64   David Homer Bates, *Lincoln in the Telegraph Office* (N. Y.: The Century Co., 1907), 215.

65   Membership List in rear of Session Minutes, 1828-1862, MS., Ill. State Hist. Lib.

66   *Washington Post*, Mar. 12, 1893, p. 2, c. 7.

67   Wm. Henry Roberts, "Foreword," in William J. Johnson, *Abraham Lincoln the Christian* (N. Y.: Eaton & Mains, 1913), 13.

68   *Washington Post*, Mar. 12, 1893, p. 2, cc. 7-8.

69   Edgington, *A History of the New York Avenue Presbyterian Church*, 244-245; Johnson, *Abraham Lincoln the Christian*, 13-14.

70   *Washington Post*, Mar. 12, 1893, p. 2, c. 7. This was probably Nov. 24, 1864, a Thanksgiving Day service on a Thursday.

71   Photo of original in Edgington, *A History of The New York Avenue Presbyterian Church*, 237.

72   Grimsley in *Jour. Ill. State Hist. Soc.*, XIX, 49; Records of Sunday School, MSS., N. Y. Avenue Presbyterian Church.

73   Bayne, *Tad Lincoln's Father*, 184, 29-31.

74   Turner and Turner, eds., *Mary Todd Lincoln*, 95; Dennett, ed., *Diaries and Letters of John Hay*, 40.

75   Pease and Randall, eds., *Diary of Orville Hickman Browning*, I, 488, 517, 546, 553, 548, 595, 610, 654, 657.

76   Edgington, *A History of The New York Avenue Presbyterian Church*, 243.

77   *Ibid.*, 239; Turner and Turner, eds., *Mary Todd Lincoln*, 126, 177.

DR. AND MRS. PHINEAS D. GURLEY
Washington, D. C. 1864

Drawing by Lloyd Ostendorf.

Dr. and Mrs. Phineas D. Gurley
Washington, D. C. 1864.

Chapter Eight–Proverbs

Few people today realize how often Mary Lincoln took her leave from Washington to relax and partake of her favorite pastime: sight-seeing. Nor would she merely excuse herself for a few days. She often remained away from the White House and her besieged husband for weeks at a time. Sometimes he pleaded with her by telegram to return home, generally to no avail until she was completely ready to reappear back in Washington. Was Mary Lincoln finally getting even with her husband who as a circuit-riding lawyer spent months away from home while she attempted to raise their sons in his absence?

Mary Lincoln had not been long in the Executive Mansion until she escaped from her duties, taking Elizabeth Grimsley and a few friends for an excursion to Philadelphia, New York City and other points to the north. She arrived by train in New York at 6:30 p.m. on May 11, 1861. There, she took up a suite of apartments in the Metropolitan Hotel. Reporters found her to be in the very best of health and full of spirit. She informed them that she relished the opportunity to relax in New York for a couple of weeks. She also intended to do some extensive shopping and then visit her son up at Harvard.

Following her arrival in New York City, the First Lady determined on May 12 to sit in the sanctuary of the Plymouth Church over in Brooklyn and hear the noted Rev. Henry Ward Beecher preach. President Lincoln had no doubt informed her about this famous minister, since he himself had heard him sermonize on February 26 and March 11, 1860. It was, as previously mentioned, a Congregationalist Church. Quite naturally, Mary's entrance created a great sensation among the worshippers. "The attention of the congregation was about equally divided between listening to the sermon and gazing at the unexpected distinguished visitors, and at the close a tremendous rush for the door took place to catch a glimpse of Mrs. Lincoln's pleasant face as she left the church," reported a journalist who was present.[1] Beecher's fame would turn into infamy and notoriety when he was sued in 1874 for adultery.

While Mary Lincoln sojourned in cooler cities to the north, President Lincoln attended a wedding at Trinity Episcopal Church located on the corner of Third and C streets, Northwest. He appeared there at 9 a. m. on May 16, 1861, to witness the marriage of 1st Lt. Lorenzo Thomas, Jr., to Miss M. G.

Bradley. The Rev. Dr. Clement M. Butler performed the ceremony which Lincoln attended out of respect for the groom's father, Brig. Gen. Lorenzo Thomas, Sr., the Adjutant General of the Army (1861 to 1869). After the nuptials were completed, the President congratulated the happy pair and returned to his arduous labors.[2]

By May 23, Mary Lincoln had returned to Washington, and on the following day a telegram was received at the War Department announcing the death of Colonel E. Elmer Ellsworth (April 11, 1837-May 24, 1861). When Gustavus V. Fox, the Assistant Secretary of the Navy, delivered this message in person to the President, Lincoln became completely unnerved. He strode to the window and gazed sadly out toward the Potomac where Ellsworth had fallen. Soon thereafter, Senator Henry Wilson of Massachusetts and a reporter for the *New York Herald* called upon Lincoln and found him much distraught. "Excuse me but I cannot talk," explained the President with tears streaming down his face. "I will make no apology, gentlemen, for my weakness;" sobbed Lincoln, "but I knew Ellsworth well, and held him in great regard."

Ellsworth had accompanied the Lincolns as their military escort from Springfield to Washington and then raised the 11th New York Volunteers, a Zouave regiment of firemen. So eager was Colonel Ellsworth to get into action that he had departed from New York with his men in a rather irregular manner without having them first sworn into Federal service and without the final approval of the New York State Adjutant General.

On the evening of May 24, both President and Mrs. Lincoln visited the Navy Yard to view the lacerated corpse of the gallant little Colonel who had been killed by a shotgun blast fired by the proprietor of the Marshall House in Alexandria, Virginia, after Ellsworth had torn down a Confederate flag from the roof of this hostelry. Since Ellsworth had been such a personal friend of the President and his family and a special "pet," the Commander-in-Chief ordered the body removed to the East Room of the White House where a funeral service would be held on May 25.

Both the President and his wife sat through this solemn burial rite of the Episcopal Church which lasted from 8:00 a. m. until 11:00 a. m. The Rev. Dr. Smith Pyne of St. John's took charge of the service with assistance from the Rev. Dr. Clement M. Butler of Trinity, Dr. Joshua Morsell of Christ Church (located near the Navy Yard), and a Chaplain from one of the Zouave regiments. When the funeral had concluded, President Lincoln stepped into his carriage and—surrounded by his personal mounted guard—rode in the cortège to the rail station from whence the body would be returned to Mechanicville, New York, on the Hudson River. Later that day, the tearful Commander-in-Chief wrote out a message of condolence for the parents of Colonel Ellsworth, saying, "May God give you that consolation which is beyond all earthly power."[3]

Like Lincoln, Ellsworth had not been a church member, although he believed in God and intended to become a Mason when he had saved enough money for the initiation fee.[4] Since Lt. Gen. Winfield Scott, the General-in-Chief, attended the funeral and had taken part in the arrangements, it was probably he who asked his own minister, Dr. Pyne, to conduct the funeral services for Col. Ellsworth, the first Union officer killed in the Civil War.

Lincoln had known Ellsworth "less than two years" at the time of his death.[5] The Colonel had only resided in Springfield for "several months" during 1860-61. But in this "brief residence," Ellsworth made the acquaintance of Abraham Lincoln and was invited by him to read law as a student in the office of Lincoln & Herndon, a rare honor, indeed, since the senior partner rarely offered to teach an apprentice, especially as he was seeking the Presidency.[6] No doubt it was also Lincoln who got Ellsworth a job at the State House as a clerk in the office of the State Auditor, Jesse K. Dubois.[7] This clerkship gave Ellsworth a modest living; however, he was only a nominal student of Lincoln's. He studied but little law since his spare moments were mostly taken up with military thoughts and activities. Lincoln remarked, "That young man has a real genius for war!"[8]

Since September 1, 1859, Ellsworth had been the Paymaster General of the Illinois State Militia, a non-salaried position with the rank of Colonel. Prior to that, he had served as the Senior Major of the First Independent Regiment of Utah Volunteers, having been commissioned in that rank on April 6, 1858.[9] This unusual regimental name came about because of Brigham Young's refusal to obey Federal statutes in 1857. As a result, President James Buchanan ordered Federal troops dispatched into Utah Territory to subdue the Mormons. Colonel Albert Sidney Johnston finally led his regulars into Salt Lake City on June 26, 1858, and the troubles ceased immediately. However, from the name of Ellsworth's Illinois State Militia unit, it is evident that patriotic men in Illinois had enlisted in this particular regiment in case the President of the United States might need volunteers to assist Col.

Johnston and his soldiers from Fort Leavenworth, Kansas, on the so-called Mormon Expedition. Needless to recount, the Illinois men never were sent to Utah Territory.

But Ellsworth's deepest interest lay with a company of boys, many of whom were too young to join the official Militia. He gathered them together as a competitive drill team and became their titular "Captain." On May 31, 1859, he signed a bond for $1,200 so that Governor Wm. H. Bissell could issue his group the necessary arms and equipment. These striplings were called "Cadets" and as such were somehow allowed to attach themselves to the 60th Regiment in the 2nd Brigade of the 6th Division within the regular Militia maintained at Chicago. The actual status of Ellsworth's "Cadets" has long been unknown until recently when the Abraham Lincoln Book Shop acquired a legal document signed by Ellsworth and others in order that they might draw military accouterments from the State of Illinois. Many previous authors have assumed that Ellsworth's "Cadets" were a full-fledged unit of the State Militia, but they were not, and Ellsworth's only commission at that time was for Major in another unit.

When civil war seemed to be imminent, Ellsworth began to re-write the Militia law for the State of Illinois. Even though Ellsworth never learned much law from Lincoln, he became like a son to him. Ellsworth wrote and made numerous campaign speeches for Lincoln in 1860. Understandably, President Lincoln shed many bitter tears when Col. Ellsworth fell before the deadly double-barreled gun of James W. Jackson, the civilian proprietor of the Marshall House and a radical Confederate sympathizer.

When Senator Stephen A. Douglas died in Chicago on June 3, 1861, President Lincoln followed the traditional religious marks of respect by ordering the Executive Mansion in Washington and other governmental buildings there to be draped in mourning on the day of the funeral in Chicago, June 7. In honor of Douglas' memory, Lincoln also refused to receive visitors on that day.[10] Despite their many political differences, Lincoln and Douglas had remained personal friends.

Early in June of 1861, the Rev. Dr. James Smith, formerly the Presbyterian pastor of the Lincolns at Springfield, showed up in Washington and was immediately invited to take up temporary living quarters at the White House. Back on February 8, John Forsythe, who had married Dr. Smith's daughter, Ann F., on July 11, 1854, came down to Springfield and handed President-elect Lincoln a letter before the

Photo by Roger D. Hunt

Tombstone of Dr. James Smith
Lincoln's old pastor is buried in Old Calton Graveyard in Glasgow, Scotland.
His headstone reads:

REV^{d.} JAMES SMITH, D. D.
SON OF PETER & MARGARET SMITH.
WAS BORN AT GLASGOW, MAY 11th A. D. 1798.
A MINISTER OF THE GOSPEL FOR FORTY YEARS
IN THE
UNITED STATES OF AMERICA:
IN HIS DECLINING YEARS HE WAS APPOINTED
U. S. CONSUL AT DUNDEE
BY ABRAHAM LINCOLN,
WHOSE PASTOR HE HAD BEEN,
AND WHERE HE DEPARTED THIS LIFE
JULY 3rd A. D. 1871.
A SINNER SAVED BY GRACE

Drawing by Lloyd Ostendorf

Abraham Lincoln discusses religion with the Rev. Dr. James Smith in front of the First Presbyterian Church on the southeast corner of Third and Washington in Springfield, Illinois.

"Railsplitter" left town for Washington, D. C. Forsythe informed Lincoln that Dr. Smith was advanced in age and desired to return once more to his native land, "Old Scotia." He was poor in this world's goods, explained Forsythe, and needed an income to support himself and "the old lady" in Scotland. Since Dr. Smith had been Lincoln's "personal and political friend," Forsythe reasoned that Lincoln should appoint Smith Consul to Glasgow where the old minister had been born.

At this time, Dr. Smith resided at Belvidere in Boone County, Illinois. From there he had addressed another letter to President Lincoln on March 9, 1861, saying that both Mr. Jonathan Young Scammon and Mr. Forsythe, law partners in the Chicago firm of Scammon & Forsythe, had recommended him for a Consulship in Scotland. Dr. Smith revealed that he indeed did desire to return to Scotland and would take his son, James B., with him. This young man was studying for the ministry, Dr. Smith informed Lincoln. Of course, Smith remarked that he would also accept the position of Consul to Dundee if Glasgow was already filled. On that same day, Dr. Smith also indited a missive to Mary Lincoln, citing her "long tried friendship" for him and pleading with her to remind the President that he had told Mr. Forsythe, in person, that "he would not forget" to appoint his old pastor to a place in Scotland. Mrs. Smith was, he confided, very unwell and had been sick all winter.[11]

The Rev. Dr. Smith had certainly come to Washington in June on a political mission as well as a social one. Both Mary Lincoln and Elizabeth Grimsley lobbied the President to appoint Smith to some post. They reminded him that Dr. Smith was an "ardent Republican."[12] The President probably excused himself by stating that the Republican Party already thought that he had given too many political plums to his Illinois friends. There remained one other avenue for solving this problem. Lincoln agreed to appoint Dr. Smith's other son, Hugh Smith, about twenty-two years of age, since he was a resident of Kentucky. The good Doctor could return to Scotland and live with him. On June 10, President Lincoln wrote to Secretary Seward and asked him to "Please send me quietly, a comm[ission] for Hugh Smith of Ky. as consul to Dundee." Aberdeen also lay in this jurisdiction. Two days later a commission was duly "sent up."[13] With this delicate matter amiably settled, the Lincolns invited guests to the White House on the evening of June 10 to converse with their much-respected houseguest, Dr. Smith. The First Family asked a number of Army chaplains to the Executive Mansion, and all present enjoyed the little party in honor of Rev. Smith.[14]

In due course, Consul Hugh Smith entered upon his duties at Dundee on September 2, 1861. Unfortunately, he became ill and reported to the State Department on May 27, 1862, that he was forced to return to the United States and that his father would act in his stead. Yet such a delegation of authority was not sanctioned by the State Department in Washington. On August 4, 1862, Washington officials informed Hugh Smith that unless he returned to his post, it would be declared vacant and another man selected to fill it. No reply to this letter was returned from Scotland. Congressman-elect Archibald McAllister (1813-1883) from Pennsylvania, a Democrat, wrote from Blair County on October 29, 1862, and proposed to Secretary Seward that the Hon. L. W. Hall, formerly the Speaker of the Pennsylvania State Senate, be appointed to a position in Europe. On November 28, Hall was duly appointed to replace Hugh Smith.

Dr. Smith, who had been acting illegally as Vice Consul, received notice from Washington on December 19, 1862, telling him that another man had been named Consul to Dundee and ordering him to turn over the office to Hall. Smith immediately wrote to his son-in-law, John Forsythe in Chicago, who—in turn—informed Senator O. H. Browning by a letter written on January 6, 1863, what had happened. Immediately upon its receipt, Senator Browning rushed over to see President Lincoln who turned the Forsythe letter over and penned a note to Seward, saying, "Dr. Smith, mentioned within, is an intimate personal friend of mine; and I have unconsciously superseded him, if at all. Sec. of State please inform me how it is." He dated it January 9. Five days later, President Lincoln wrote: "As I understand the Consulate at Dundee has not been accepted by Mr. Hall, and as I was [u]nconscious, in appointing Mr. Hall, (if I did it) that I was interfering with my old friend, Dr. Smith, I will be obliged if the Sec. of State will send me a nomination for Rev. James Smith, of Ills. for that Consulate." Evidently, some strong arm twisting took place during that hiatus of five days. Certainly Lincoln never intended for Seward to replace Rev. Smith, a Republican, with Hall, a Democrat. The United States Senate confirmed Dr. James Smith, and the official records list him as taking the position as of February 24, 1863. The new Consul declared that he was an American citizen and claimed Illinois as his residence.[15]

After President Lincoln's assassination in 1865, Robert T. Lincoln personally secured the pledge of each incoming administration that it would not remove Dr. Smith from his political post at Dundee.[16] In July and August of 1869, Mary Lincoln and Tad toured Scotland after having confirmed the fact their "old & dear friend, Dr. Smith" still lived there. He came down from Scotland by steamer and met them in London where he showed them the sights for five days before escorting them back to Scotland for several weeks of touring. He even loaned Mary money when she ran short.[17] Not surprising. There were some Todds in Dr. Smith's ancestry.

Having been in ill health for several years, Dr. Smith unfortunately contracted typhoid fever on October 16, 1870. He seems to have never recovered completely. He was last confined to his bed at his residence on June 22, 1871. There he died on the night of July 3 from, according to his surgeon, hepatic disease—liver problems—and dropsy—an abnormal collection of fluids.

At first, local colleagues intended to have only private obsequies, but Provost Magistrate Yeaman "felt that the character and talents of the late Doctor, and the respect entertained for the nation he so worthily represented, demanded some distinct recognition, if there was no decided objection to this on the part of friends." When no disapproval was raised, a public funeral procession was immediately planned and a formal program printed. After a memorial observance was conducted in his residence at 81 Murrygate in Dundee, the solemn cortège fell into formation shortly after 12 o'clock on July 10. Leading the procession was a detachment of police, followed by the town officers in costume carrying their halberds. Next came the hearse-and-four with the body of Dr. Smith. After it marched the chief mourners, the magistrates, the town council, the chamber of commerce members, a number of public bodies and other civilians. Guarding the rear of the column, which trooped along four deep, was another detachment of police. There was also a military escort which filed along on either side of the column. It was composed of elements from Her Majesty's 90th Regiment and the Warship *Brilliant*. At least 200 merchants from Dundee took part in the ceremonial death march. Even the mayor was present.

This solemn and impressive pageant of mourners moved up Murrygate, across High Street, along Nethergate and down Union Street to that railway station where the trains ran to Perth for additional connections. Dundee's bells pealed, and flags were lowered to half-mast while the cortège proceeded to the Perth Station where the train departed with the casket at 1:00 p. m. Later that day, Dr. Smith was buried in his father's lot at Old Calton Churchyard in Glasgow. His wife, Elizabeth, had returned to the United States in 1867. She died on July 21, 1872, in Woodford County, Kentucky, but her remains were sent back to Springfield, Illinois. Upon arrival there on July 24, a funeral service was held over her body at the home of Mrs. Rev. Dr. John H. Brown with interment at Oak Ridge Cemetery in Block 10 on a lot owned by Jacob Bunn. With his usual kindness and generosity, Bunn had befriended this widow of a former minister of the First Presbyterian Church where the Bunn family worshipped and contributed lavishly to its upkeep. Often the Bunn family kept their good works secret and contributed anonymously when special projects were in need of a financial sponsor.[18]

Upon examining Dr. Smith's will, it was discovered that he had left a most valuable gold-headed walking cane to the Hon. John Bright, Member of Parliament. Mary Lincoln had sent Smith this walking stick on April 27, 1868, while she was contemplating her first visit to Europe. It had previously belonged to her martyred husband and bore the following inscription on its staff: "J. A. M'Clernand to Hon. A. Lincoln—June 1857." In June of that year, Lincoln and John Alexander McClernand had been appointed defense attorneys by the United States District Court at Springfield. Perhaps McClernand presented the cane to Lincoln at that time. Mary Lincoln later prepared a gold ferule for this cane which read: "Presented to the Rev. Jas. Smith, D. D., late pastor of First Presbyterian Church, Springfield, Ill., by the family of the late President Lincoln, in memoriam of the high esteem in which he was held by him and them as their pastor and dear friend—27th April 1868."[19]

Evidently, Mary Lincoln had asked Dr. Smith to pass the cane along to John Bright when his estate was settled after his death. Dr. Smith's bequest stated: "I give, devise, and bequeath unto John Bright, Esq., member of the British House of Commons, and to his heirs, the gold-mounted staff or cane which belonged to the deceased President Lincoln of the United States, and presented to me by the deceased's widow and family as a mark of the President's respect, which staff is to be kept and used as an heirloom in the family of the said John Bright, as a token of the esteem which the late President felt for him because of his unwearied zeal and defense of the United States in suppressing the civil rebellion of the Southern States." A vast majority of English editors, and the British public in general, strongly disliked Abraham Lincoln,[20] but John Bright had been one of the few exceptions.

John Bright (1811-1889) was of Quaker descent—like Lincoln—and a reformer who first took a seat at the House of Commons in 1843. When the Civil War came in America, Bright supported the North and spoke in defense of President Lincoln's actions. Both Lincoln and Bright admired each other greatly, although they never met. They carried on a correspondence through Secretary of State Seward. A bust of John Bright stood in the State Department, a gift from some friend in England. After Lincoln's death, this statue was transferred to a prominent place in the White House. President Lincoln kept a clipping from one of Bright's speeches in his pocket; it was found there when the contents of his wallet were examined after his assassination. The President also displayed a large photograph of this British statesman over a mantel in the anteroom next to his office in the Executive Mansion. In turn, Bright had a photograph of Abraham Lincoln in his quarters. After Lincoln's death, Mary Lincoln presented this picture of Bright to Senator Charles Sumner on May 14, 1865. No doubt Bright greatly cherished the Lincoln cane when if finally came into his possession.[21] Mary Lincoln had known of her late husband's fondness for Bright and thought he should have a memento of the Sixteenth President who so admired this Britisher.

Lincoln was curious and tolerant of the religious differences in people. While President and Mary Lincoln, together with Elizabeth Grimsley and Schulyer Colfax, were inspecting the camp of the Garibaldi Regiment on the afternoon of June 25, 1861, they were invited to attend a funeral being held there for a Private of that unit. It proved to be a most impressive ceremony, conducted according to the custom observed in Hungary.[22] That was certainly the first such Hungarian religious service ever witnessed by the Lincolns.

The words and actions of others did play a part in Lincoln's public communication. Religious or spiritual references, for instance, did not always originate with Lincoln, but were approved by him or altered by him to more closely reflect his beliefs. When Queen Victoria lost her mother, the Duchess of Kent, President Lincoln sent this monarch an official message, saying, "I tender to you my sincere condolence, with that of the whole American people, in this great bereavement, and pray God to have Your Majesty and your whole Royal Family constantly under [H]is gracious protection and care." Secretary of State Seward probably composed the letter, but Lincoln approved and signed it together with Seward.[23]

President Lincoln referenced a higher being when he gave his blessing to Isabel II of Spain on August 17, 1861. "May God have Your Majesty always in His safe and holy keeping!" exclaimed Lincoln to the Queen.[24]

In making a reply to the Tycoon of Japan, Lincoln ended his remarks by saying, "Wishing abundant prosperity and length of years to the great State over which you preside, I pray God to have Your Majesty always in His safe and holy keeping."[25] Secretary Seward once more had his hand in this matter, but its tone is clearly Lincoln's. As an interesting aside, it must be noted that John Hay, the President's assistant secretary, began referring to Lincoln as "the Tycoon" quite early in the President's first term.[26]

On June 29, 1861, President Lincoln responded to an invitation to raise the flag at an impressive ceremony. A huge tent had been erected upon the south lawn of the White House for the occasion. He complied with this request after a suitable military parade. The Rev. Smith Pyne of St. John's Episcopal Church presided, reading an appropriate prayer and reciting the Lord's Prayer in the President's presence.[27]

Another time, having called a special session of Congress on July 4, 1861, the President explained some previous action, asked for approval of his present actions, and ended his message with: "And having thus chosen our course, without guile, and with pure purpose, let us renew our trust in the justness of God, and go forward without fear, and with manly hearts." In making his final revision, Lincoln struck out "in the justness of" and merely said "our trust in God."[28] Clearly, Lincoln was unashamed of his belief in God, and openly exhibited it to all those in Congress as well as the whole nation.

When a joint committee of Congress suggested there should be "a day of Public humiliation, prayer and fasting," President Lincoln hastened on August 12, 1861, to issue a proclamation for such a day to be observed on September 26 that year. The proclamation is a masterpiece and deserves to be read in full:

> And whereas it is fit and becoming in all people, at all times, to acknowledge and revere the Supreme Government of God; to bow in humble submission to his chastisements; to confess and deplore their sins and transgressions in the full conviction that the fear of the Lord is the beginning of wisdom; and to pray, with all fervency and contrition, for the pardon of their past offenses, and for a blessing upon their present and prospective action:

> And whereas, when our own beloved Country, once, by the blessing of God, united, prosperous and happy, is now affiliated with faction and civil war, it is peculiarly fit for us to recognize the hand of God in this terrible visitation, and in sorrowful remembrance of our own faults and crimes as a nation and as individuals, to humble ourselves before Him, and to pray for His mercy,—to pray that we may be spare

further punishment, though most justly deserved; that our arms may be blessed and made effectual for the re-establishment of law, order and peace, throughout the wide extent of our Country; and that the inestimable boon of civil and religious liberty, earned under His guidance and blessing, by the labors and sufferings of our fathers, may be restored in all is original excellence:—

Therefore, I, Abraham Lincoln, President of the Untied States, do appoint the last Thursday in September next, as a day of humiliation, prayer and fasting for all the people of the nation. And I do earnestly recommend to all the People, and especially to all ministers and teachers of religion of all denominations, and to all heads of families, to observe and keep that day according to their several creeds and modes of worship, in all humility and with all religious solemnity, to the end that the united prayer of the nation may ascend to the Throne of Grace and bring down plentiful blessings upon our Country.[29]

The hand of Secretary Seward probably added "the fear of the Lord . . . ," but these magnificent words ring out like a miniature sermon which might have been delivered by a prophet from the Old Testament—reflecting the President's view of himself as an instrument of God.

Lincoln sought out spiritual comfort for himself and others. On Sunday, August 25, 1861, the Commander-in-Chief, with Secretaries Seward and Welles, paid a visit to the Army of the Potomac and attended church services at the camp of the 2nd New Hampshire Regiment after which he reviewed General Joseph Hooker's brigade and Colonel E. D. Baker's California regiment.[30] Even in the field, the President exhibited his desire to participate in divine worship if possible. It seems to have given him solace and the strength to continue his arduous duties steering the ship of state.

After having been solicited by "Christian Ministers, and other pious people," President Lincoln determined to appoint chaplains who would care for the spiritual needs of those soldiers confined to Army hospitals. By September 25, 1861, he had begun to act upon this request, but Lincoln realized that there was no law which would allow him to commission such officers not serving with regiments. So he asked for volunteers and promised to pay them just as if they were ministering to troops in the field.[31] Among those ministers whom Lincoln invited to serve were the Reverends G. G. Goss, John G.

Butler, Henry Hopkins, F. M. Magrath, F. E. Boyle, John C. Smith and William Y. Brown.[32]

Never a bigot, the President had quickly contacted Archbishop John J. Hughes and implored him to nominate Roman Catholic priests for such hospital duties. He reminded the Archbishop that "chaplains are more needed, perhaps in the hospitals, than with the healthy soldiers in the field."[33]

Although Abraham Lincoln had never officially joined any denomination, he seems to have respected all religions which acknowledged the supremacy of one true God, the Father of all mankind. In explaining why he had never cast his lot with the Know-Nothing Party, Lincoln cited the Declaration of Independence which stated that all men are created equal. He pointed out that the creed of the Know-Nothings was "all men are created equal, except negroes, and foreigners, and catholics."[34]

Quite naturally, it was soon brought to the President's attention that there were no Jewish chaplains in the Army. The Rev. Dr. Arnold Fischel of New York had an interview with Lincoln on December 11, 1861, and urged him to appoint Jewish Rabbis for every military district. At that time, such appointments were not allowed by statute. President Lincoln assured Dr. Fischel that he would point out this glaring omission to Congress and felt certain that the exclusion was altogether unintentional on the part of the legislative branch.[35] Three days later, Lincoln wrote to Dr. Fischel and explained that he would "try to have a new law broad enough to cover what is desired by you in behalf of the Israelites." Jewish chaplains were admitted to the service when the law was changed on March 12, 1862.[36]

From at least the 1850's, Lincoln had established many close friendships with Jews, some of whom aided him and the Republican Party. One of these, Abraham Jonas, practiced law in Quincy and had become the first Grand Master of Masons in Illinois when the Grand Lodge was reorganized in 1840. In addressing him, Lincoln once wrote, "Your friend as ever."[37] When Lincoln experienced great pain due to corns on his feet, he allowed Dr. Isachar Zacharie, a noted chiropodist, to operate and remove them. Then, he wrote out a beautiful testimonial for the good Doctor on September 22, 1862.[38] They became warm friends. After General U. S. Grant issued an order expelling all Jews from his department, President Lincoln immediately ordered General H. W. Halleck to revoke this mandate, saying that no officer could proscribe an entire religious sect. Many Jews, Lincoln pointed out, soldiered bravely in the Union Army. He would only allow Grant to expel traitors or unwanted peddlers.[39]

Rabbi Isaac M. Wise related that Abraham Lincoln once told him that he was "bone from our bone and flesh from our flesh."[40] Here, the President was paraphrasing Ephesians 5:30 which states: "For we are members of his body, of his flesh, and of his bones." In this, Lincoln meant to imply that we are all brothers in God's sight. Rabbi Sabato Morais remarked that Lincoln's breast "was ever kindled with that divine spark."[41] Rabbi Samuel Myer Isaacs vouched that the fallen President had been "so good, so religious a being." This Rabbi declared that Lincoln was "the especial object of Divine love."[42] Philip J. Joachimsen of New Orleans said that Lincoln had been "favored of God." "And we, as Jews," Joachimsen continued, "had a distinct ground to love, respect and esteem him." "I know," asserted this Rabbi, "that he, in his high position, appreciated those of our creed who had come forward to sustain him. His mind was not subject to the vulgar clamor against Jews . . . ."[43]

Because Abraham Lincoln constantly implored the mercy of the Almighty God without mentioning Jesus Christ, unless quoting some of His words from the New Testament, those of the Jewish faith could relate very closely to Lincoln. Like the majority of Jews, Lincoln seems to have recognized Christ as a prophet but certainly not the messiah or Saviour or God's son as claimed by most Christian churches. As far as is known, President Lincoln did not pray to Jesus Christ or the Virgin Mary but rather to God himself. It seems safe to say that Abraham Lincoln accepted those parts of various religions which appeared to him to be true and faithful to God's divine will and not to those which merely suited some men's purposes. For one example of Lincoln's tolerance of even foreign religions, he expressed this thought to Padischah Abd ul Aziz Kahan, ruler of the Ottoman Empire: "And so I recommend Your Majesty to the protection of the Almighty."[44] When reading the term "Almighty," this Muslim could readily associate it with his own Supreme Being, Allah.

General Edward Dickinson Baker, born in London on February 24, 1811, met his untimely death at Ball's Bluff while leading his troops in an ill-advised skirmish with the Confederates on October 21, 1861. His body was terribly riddled by at least six balls and perhaps as many as eight.[45] Immediately upon learning of his old friend's demise at the hands of the enemy, President Lincoln expressed a wish that a solemn state funeral could be held at the White House—like Colonel Ellsworth's. But Mary Lincoln was refurbishing the East Wing of the Executive Mansion, and therefore it was "not in a fit condition for such a ceremony."[46] Instead, the fallen

General's lacerated remains were conducted to the private residence of General James Watson Webb, No. 363, at the corner of 14th and H streets.[47]

Webb, a close friend of Baker's, had been born in Claverack, New York, on February 8, 1802, the son of General Samuel Blachley and Catherine (Hogeboom) Webb. In his youth, he had soldiered in the Regular Army, leaving the service with only the rank of 1st Lt. However, this journalist and diplomat was later named a General at the time he became Minister to Austria, evidently to give him more standing and prestige with this foreign power. He died on June 7, 1884.

During the morning hours of October 24, a huge crowd of mourners assembled in Gen. Webb's mansion for Baker's funeral service. Among those present were President and Mrs. Lincoln as well as Cabinet members: Seward, Chase, Cameron, Welles, Smith and Bates. The Rev. Dr. Byron Sunderland from the First Presbyterian Church on 4 1/2 Street gave the sermon and the prayer. Upon the conclusion of these obsequies at noon, President Lincoln joined the somber procession which escorted Baker's body to the Congressional Burying Ground for temporary interment.[48] Eventually, Baker was entombed at Lone Mountain Cemetery near San Francisco on December 11, 1861, by a Universalist minister, Thomas Starr King (1824-1864). Baker had not been strongly attached to any one church; however, he probably had his closest contacts with the Presbyterians while in Washington, D. C., as a Senator. On the same day that Baker's reburial took place in far-off California, President Lincoln sat beside Vice President Hannibal Hamlin in the Senate Chamber and listened to a eulogy upon the life of the late Senator Baker.[49] As reported, Lincoln attended at least one Presbyterian burial service and sometimes moved in these same Presbyterian circles at Washington.

As soon as President Lincoln learned that the authorities of the municipal governments of Washington and Georgetown had proclaimed November 28, 1861, as a day of thanksgiving, he ordered the Federal offices closed, "in order that the officers of the government may partake in the ceremonies."[50] Without doubt, many of these observances were religious in nature. After giving thanks to his Maker, Lincoln ate a Thanksgiving dinner at the White House where Joshua Fry Speed and his lady from Kentucky were among the chosen few to enjoy a special meal with the First Family.[51] Speed had shared his Springfield room with Lincoln when the latter first moved into town from New Salem, and they became intimate friends for life.

In his first Annual Message to Congress on December 3, 1861, the President began his report by saying that "In the midst of unprecedented political troubles, we have cause of great gratitude to God for unusual good health, and most abundant harvests." In the same religious mood, Lincoln closed his lengthy remarks by stating that "With a reliance on Providence, all the more firm and earnest, let us proceed in the great task which events have devolved upon us."[52] Most certainly his august audience noted these particular words of praise to God. In the case of this President, the statements were sincere and earnest, without doubt. Quite often Lincoln expressed his belief that he was indeed an Instrument of Providence.

In the midst of a war which was going badly for the Union, there occurred one happy event in December 1861 which perhaps was the most important social event in Washington that month. On the evening of the tenth at the palatial residence of her parents on the corner of 18th and F streets, Sally V. Carroll became the wife of Captain Charles Griffin, an artillery officer in the Regular Army. Griffin had been born December 18, 1825, at Granville, Ohio. He graduated from West Point in 1847, served in the Mexican War and taught at his Alma Mater prior to the Civil War.[53] His bride was the daughter of William Thomas Carroll (May 2, 1802-July 13, 1863) who was the son of Major Charles & Ann (Sprigg) Carroll of "Belle Vue" Estate at Hagerstown, Maryland. With his parents he had moved to the District of Columbia in 1811. This family was on intimate terms with President James and Dolley Madison. William studied law, and in 1827, Henry Clay—a close friend—got him appointed as the Chief Clerk of the Supreme Court of the United States. About three years later, Wm. Thomas Carroll married Sarah "Sally" Sprigg (March 27, 1812-February 11, 1893) and became an Episcopalian, the church of his wife. Prior to his marriage, he had followed the teachings of the Roman Catholic Church as did most of the other Carrolls and Spriggs. Sarah was the daughter of Governor Samuel and Violetta (Lansdale) Sprigg of Maryland. Samuel served as Governor of that State from 1819 to 1822. A Democrat, Gov. Sprigg was descended from Thomas Sprigg who had come to Maryland in 1661. Mrs. William Thomas Carroll eventually inherited the grand mansion of her father, the Governor, who had removed to Washington, D. C., and purchased the property at 18th and F.[54] The Spriggs and the Carrolls were all intermarried and prominent families in Maryland as well as the District of Columbia.

Since William Thomas Carroll was a noted and active member of St. John's Episcopal Church in Washington, he naturally arranged for Dr. Smith

Pyne to officiate at this marriage of his daughter on the night of December 10, 1861.[55] And among the distinguished witnesses to this wedding, and the gala party which followed it, were President Abraham and Mary Lincoln.[56] As they listened to the words of this Episcopal wedding service, they had to have been reminded of their own marriage which likewise was performed by an Episcopal priest back in Springfield, Illinois. In all, Abraham Lincoln experienced the Episcopal nuptials ceremony at least four times in his life.

Why did a busy President of the United States take time from his many other duties to attend the wedding of Sally V. Carroll? Of course, Wm. Thos. Carroll was a very important governmental official, earning approximately $20,000 a year in fees. However, his friendship with Lincoln went back a long way. Among Carroll's relatives was Daniel whose farm had become a part of Washington, he being one of the commissioners to locate the new District of Columbia. He lived from 1730 to 1796 and was elected as a Federalist to the First Congress. When Lincoln went to Washington as a Representative in 1847, he selected quarters in Carroll Row with Mrs. Anna G. Sprigg who kept a boardinghouse on land once owned by Charles Carroll, father of William Thomas Carroll. She was the widow of Benjamin Sprigg who had been a clerk in the House of Representatives prior to his death in November of 1833. It seems quite natural that Congressman Lincoln was eventually introduced to William Thomas Carroll at an early date during his stay in Washington since the Carrolls and Spriggs were all interconnected. This boardinghouse stood just opposite the Capitol on the east side of First Street, the fourth house from A Street. President Lincoln remembered Mrs. Sprigg with fondness and saw to it that she received a political plum in 1864 when he appointed her to a clerkship in the Loan Branch of the Treasury Department.[57]

Abraham Lincoln had another important connection with Carroll. On March 7, 1849, Congressman Lincoln appeared in the Supreme Court of the United States to obtain a license for practicing law before it. With the Hon. Roger B. Taney presiding as Chief Justice and Associate Justices John McLean, Peter V. Daniel, Samuel Nelson, Levi Woodbury and Robert C. Grier present, the Supreme Court opened that day with Robert Wallace as Marshal and William Thomas Carroll as Clerk. Rep. Sidney Lawrence, a Democrat from New York State, but not standing for reelection, made the motion and the Court "ordered that Abraham Lincoln Esquire of Illinois be admitted to practice as an Attorney and Counselor of this Court and he was sworn accordingly."[58] To be admitted, a lawyer had to have practiced for at least three years in his own state's supreme court and possess a good reputation, both professionally and privately. It would seem that Lincoln never forgot the early kindnesses of Clerk Carroll who also filed Lincoln's Supreme Court case of William Lewis v. Thomas Lewis for him that same year. On March 4, 1861, Carroll held the Bible for Lincoln at his inauguration, and in 1862, Carroll would once more render a most-appreciated favor to the Lincolns.

Another relative also had a brief association with President Lincoln. Anna Ella Carroll (1815-1894) submitted strategic plans to the Commander-in-Chief on November 30, 1861. The President probably examined her scheme for winning the war more out of courtesy than need. She would later claim that she had won the war for the Union, etc.

Unfortunately, Mary Lincoln's violent temper and unreasonable jeal-ousy would greatly embarrass Sally V. (Carroll) Griffin on March 25, 1865, during a Presidential review of the Army of the Potomac. By this date, her husband was now General Griffin, and Sally had obtained the personal per-mission of the President to remain with her husband at the front. When Mary Lincoln learned this fact, she threw a tantrum and screamed, "Do you know that I never allow the President to see any woman alone?" This most public outburst of vituperation, which went on and on, greatly shocked all the officers who heard her as well as Mrs. U. S. Grant. It also brought tears to the eyes of Sally Griffin who counted the President as one of her personal friends of long standing. Although he tried, Lincoln could not mollify his raging wife, and Mrs. Grant and others determined then and there never again to be caught in Mary Lincoln's presence if they could avoid it. On the following day when the Army of the James was reviewed, Mary Lincoln once more flew into a rage when she learned that Mrs. Ord, wife of the commander of this army, had rid-den her horse beside the President in the review. In a huff, Mary returned to Washington without the President.[59]

The Young Men's Christian Association held a convention after the war started and selected George H. Stuart to be chairman of The Christian Commission which was to render physical and spiritual aid to soldiers and sailors serving the Union. On December 11, 1861, Chairman Stuart submit-ted a plan to President Lincoln for such religious work. Upon the following day, the President replied to him by letter saying, "Your christian and benev-olent undertaking for the benefit of the soldiers, is too obviously proper, and praise-worthy, to admit any difference of opinion. I sincerely hope your plan may be as successful in execution, as it is just and generous in conception."[60] Note that Lincoln did not capitalize the word "christian." In speaking about this charitable organization, Lincoln remarked, "Nothing is better for the soldiers than to be followed with Christian influences."[61] The President believed the teachings of the New Testament furnished men and women with a code of behavior which helped sustain them in times of great stress. Lincoln also appreciated the efforts of The United States Sanitary Commission, started in June of 1861 with the Rev. H. W. Bellows as its principal figure. He was a Unitarian, and thus the organization exhibited many traits of that particular church.

When dealing with those servicemen who had fallen afoul of the military justice system, Lincoln tended to pardon all who had been sentenced to death. In justifying his actions to a person who had criticized his tender heart, the President replied, "If God wanted me to see it, he would let me know it, and until he does, I shall go on pardoning and being cruel [to the military courts] to the end."[62] Here, again, the Commander-in-Chief exhibited his sincere belief that he was actually God's instrument, having a special relationship with the Almighty who revealed His wishes to him exactly like He did to the prophets of old.

However, the President could be completely unmerciful for some crimes. Captain Nathaniel Gordon of Maine had been condemned to death for slave trading. When he appealed to Lincoln for a pardon, the President wrote this to him on February 4, 1862: "In granting this respite, it becomes my painful duty to admonish the prisoner that, relinquishing all expectation of pardon by Human Authority, he refer himself alone to the mercy of the common God and Father of all men." Upon the expiration of this brief postponement of his sentence, Captain Gordon was hanged.[63] Indeed, Lincoln could be most unforgiving when slavery was involved. He felt slavery was a crime against God's intentions as well as the principles laid down by the Founding Fathers in the Declaration of Independence when they declared that all men were created equal. In addition to expressing his views on justice in this particular case, Lincoln also revealed his conception that there was but one God no matter what various religions might call Him. This was the central theme of Lincoln's religious creed. One cannot emphasize this point too often when attempting to explain Lincoln's theology.

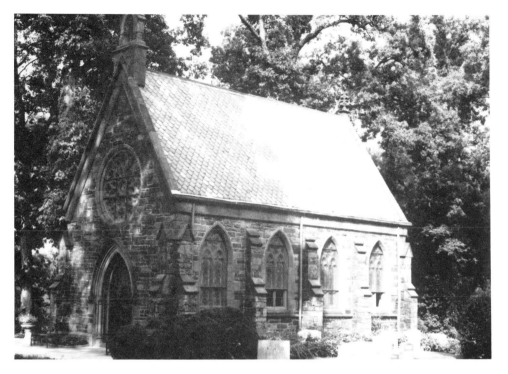

Photo by Roger D. Hunt.

In this Gothic Chapel at Oak Hill Cemetery at Georgetown, a brief service was held
over Willie Lincoln's body. It was later placed in
William Thomas Carroll's vault nearby.

Photo by Roger D. Hunt

William Thomas Carroll allowed President Lincoln to place Willie Lincoln's body in his own vault at Oak Hill Cemetery in Georgetown. Here, it remained until 1865 when it was returned to Springfield, Illinois.

References

1   N. Y. *Herald*, May 12, 1861, p. 1, c. 5, May 13, 1861, p. 5, c. 5; N. Y. *Tribune*, May 13, 1861, p. 5, c. 5.

2   Washington Evening *Star*, May 16, 1861, p. 3, c. 1; N. Y. *Tribune*, May 17, 1861, p. 5, c. 2.

3   N. Y. *Herald*, May 25, 1861, p. 1, c. 5, May 26, 1861, p. 4, c. 6, p. 1, c. 1; *Evening Star*, May 25, 1861, p. 3, cc. 1-2; *The War of the Rebellion: Official Records* (Washington: Govt. Printing Office, 1899), Ser. III, Vol. I, p. 189; Basler, ed., *The Collected Works*, IV, 386.

       Pvt. Francis Edwin Brownell, Co. A, 11th New York Infantry, was escorting Col. Ellsworth and immediately killed James W. Jackson when he murdered Ellsworth. This was the first deed in the Civil War which merited the Medal of Honor from Congress, and it was finally issued to him on January 26, 1877. President Lincoln had promoted him to 2nd Lt. and then 1st Lt. for his bravery. Brownell retired on Nov. 4, 1863, and died Mar. 15, 1894. *The Congressional Medal of.Honor* (Forest Ranch: Sharp & Dunnigan, 1984), 731.

4   Ruth Painter Randall, *Colonel Elmer Ellsworth* (Boston: Little, Brown & Co., 1960), 201-202.

5   Basler, ed., *The Collected Works*, IV, 385.

6   *Illinois State Journal*, May 27, 1861, p. 3, c. 3, May 28, 1861, p. 1, c. 2.

7   Randall, *Colonel Elmer Ellsworth*, 200. He was working for Dubois by November 17, 1860.

8   Herndon and Weik, *Herndon's Lincoln*, II, 319.

9   Executive Record, VII, 597, 319, MS., Illinois State Archives.

10   Wayne C. Temple, *Stephen A. Douglas: Freemason* (Bloomington: The Masonic Book Club, 1982), 52-58; N. Y. *Herald*, June 8, 1861, p. 1, cc. 1-2.

11   *The Sun* (Baltimore), June 12, 1861, p. 4, c. 3; Letters of Application and Recommendation During the Administration of A. Lincoln, Record Group 59, MSS., The National Archives; Marriage Record, III, 111, MS., Clerk's Office, Sangamon Co. Bldg., Springfield, Ill.

       James B. Smith had been born in Nashville, Tennessee, on June 3, 1840. Although he commenced the study of religion, he switched to medicine, choosing Dr. Rufus A. Lord of Springfield as his preceptor. Later, on October 12, 1864, he married Agnes Harrower, daughter of Wm. and Janette

Blacklock Harrower, members of the First Presbyterian Church of Springfield. He finally graduated in 1865 from the Cincinnati Medical College and began to practice in Cerro Gordo and Dawson, Ill. Dr. James B. Smith died in the American House at Springfield about 7:00 p. m. on December 30, 1869, from an overdose of morphine. He was buried in Block 12, Lot 16 at Oak Ridge Cemetery next to the Harrowers. Power, *Early Settlers*, 360-361; *Springfield City Directory 1863*, 124; *Illinois State Journal*, Dec. 31, 1869, p. 3, c. 2; Oak Ridge Cemetery Records, MSS., Springfield, Ill.

12   Grimsley, *Jour. Ill. State Hist. Soc.*, XIX, 64.

13   Basler, ed., *The Collected Works Supplement*, 77; Record Group 59, MSS., The National Archives.

14   *The Sun* (Baltimore), June 12, 1861, p. 4, c. 3.

15   Record Group 59, MSS., The National Archives.

16   Paul M. Angle, ed., *A Portrait of Abraham Lincoln in Letters by His Oldest Son* (Chicago: The Chicago Hist. Soc., 1968), 47-48.

17   Turner and Turner, eds., *Mary Todd Lincoln*, 512, 514, 602-603.

18   Dr. Matthew Nimmo to U. S. State Dept., 130 Nethergate, Dundee, Scotland, June 22, July 5, 1871; *The Dundee* (Scotland) *Advertiser*, July 11, 1871, MSS., Record Group 59, The National Archives, Washington, D. C. The Consul Office had clipped articles from the Dundee newspaper and sent them back to the State Dept. as well as the correspondence of Dr. Nimmo.

        Dr. Smith's tombstone gives the exact date of his birth. Roger D. Hunt of Rockville, Md., has visited this site and photographed the stone. This old cemetery is no longer used for burials.

        The account of Mrs. James Smith's death is in the *Illinois State Journal*, July 24, 1872, p. 4, c. 4. Her burial record is at Oak Ridge Cemetery.

19   Clipping from *The Dundee* (Scotland) *Advertiser*, July 11, 1871, MS., in State Dept. Record Group 59, The National Archives.

20   *Ibid.*; Thomas Keiser, "Lincoln, the Abused President: Lincoln as Seen in the North, the South, and in England," *Papers From the Third Annual Lincoln Colloquium October 15, 1988*, 10-14.

21   Donald B. Cole and John J. McDonough, eds., *Benjamin Brown French: A Yankee's Journal* (Hanover: Univ. Press of New England, 1989), 510.

        The contents of Abraham Lincoln's pockets are now housed within a glass case in the Great Hall of The Library of Congress. Mary said her late husband "prized" Bright's likeness very much. Turner and Turner, eds., *Mary Todd Lincoln*, 228; J. G. Randall, *Lincoln the Liberal Statesman* (N. Y. : Dodd, Mead & Co., 1947) contains a whole chapter (VI) entitled "Lincoln and John Bright." This particular cane is mentioned but no source is cited by Randall.

22 N. Y. *Herald*, June 26, 1861, p. 1, c. 3.

23 Basler, ed., *The Collected Works*, IV, 417.

24 *Ibid.*, IV, 490.

25 *Ibid.*, IV, 468.

26 Dennett, ed., *Diaries and Letters of John Hay*, 5.

27 Cole and McDonough, eds., *Benjamin Brown French*, 361-362.

28 Basler, ed., *The Collected Works*, IV, 441.

29 Basler, ed., *The Collected Works*, IV, 482-483.

30 *New-York Times*, Aug. 26, 1861, p. 1, c. 2.

31 Basler, ed., *The Collected Works*, V, 8-9.

32 *Ibid.*, V, 53-54.

33 *Ibid.*, IV, 559.

34 *Ibid.*, II, 323.

35 N. Y. *Herald*, Dec. 13, 1861, p. 3, c. 3.

36 Basler, ed., *The Collected Works*, V, 69.

37 *Ibid.*, II, 380.

38 *Ibid.*, V, 436.

39 *The War of the Rebellion: Official Records* (Washington: Govt. Printing Office, 1889), Ser. 1, XXIV, Pt. 1, p. 9.

40 Emanuel Hertz, ed., *Abraham Lincoln: The Tribute of the Synagogue* (N. Y.: Bloch Pub. Co., 1927), 98.

41 *Ibid.*, 9.

42 *Ibid.*, 74.

43   *Ibid.*, 31.

44   Basler, ed., *The Collected Works*, IV, 546.

45   Washington *Evening Star*, Oct. 23, 1861, p. 2, c. 2.

46   *N. Y. Herald*, Oct. 23, 1861, p. 1, c. 3.

47   Washington *Evening Star*, Oct. 23, 1861, p. 2, c. 2.

48   *Ibid.*, Oct. 24, 1861, p. 3, c. 6: *N. Y. Herald*, Oct. 25, 1861, p. 8, c. 2.

49   Washington *Evening Star*, Dec. 12, 1861, p. 2, cc. 1, 3.

50   Basler, ed., *The Collected Works*, V, 32.

51   N. Y. *Herald*, Nov. 29, 1861, p. 4, c. 6.

52   Basler, ed., *The Collected Works*, V, 35, 53.

53   He became a Major General of Volunteers on Apr. 2, 1865, and after the war served as a Colonel of the 35th Regiment of Regulars. He died in Galveston, Texas, on Sept. 15, 1867, and was buried in Oak Hill Cemetery, Georgetown, D. C. His widow married Count Esterhazy of Austria.

54   Robert F. McNamara, "In Search of the Carrolls of Belle Vue," *Maryland Hist. Mag.*, LXXX, 99-113 (Spring, 1985); when Wm. T. Carroll died, he left two sons, Col. Sprigg Carroll and Capt. Chas. Carroll. Washington *Evening Star*, July 15, 1863, p. 3, c. 2. Although her marriage license merely listed her name as Sally V. Carroll, the "V" probably stood for Violetta, her grandmother's name. Marriage License, MS., The Superior Court of the District of Columbia, courtesy of Georgia M. Dudley, Deputy Clerk.

55   Alexander B. Hagner, "History and Reminiscences of St. John's Church, Washington, D. C.," *Records of the Columbia Hist. Soc.*, XII, 96 (1909); Records of Marriages, MSS., St. John's Church, Washington, D. C., courtesy of James C. Holmes, confirm that Dr. Pyne did indeed marry this couple. Prior to June 1, 1870, the District of Columbia did not require that clergymen return a copy of the marriage license after they had solemnized the nuptials of a couple. Thus, the license for the Carroll-Griffin marriage does not contain the name of the minister, but fortunately St. John's Church has preserved this vital information.

56   N. Y. *Herald*, Dec. 11, 1861, p. 1, c. 4; New-York *Tribune*, Dec. 12, 1861, p. 5, c. 1. In these years, the address for the Carrolls was 174 F Street, North. *Boyd's Washington and Georgetown Directory 1862* (Washington: Thomas Hutchinson, 1862), 56; Pease and Randall, eds., *Diary of Orville Hickman Browning*, I, 513.

57   Mathilde D. Williams, "Why Willie Lincoln Was Temporarily Placed in the Carroll Vault, Oak Hill Cemetery, Georgetown, D. C.," MS., Peabody Room, District of Columbia Public Library; Basler, ed., *The Collected Works*, IV, 391n, VII, 454n; Paul Findley, *A. Lincoln: The Crucible of Congress* (N. Y.: Crown Pub., 1979), 85.

58   Minutes of the Supreme Court of the United States, M, 5961-5962, MS., Library, Supreme Court, Washington, D. C., courtesy of Anne R. Ashmore.

59   Adam Badeau, *Grant In Peace* (Hartford: S. S. Scranton & Co., 1887), 357.

60   Basler, ed., *The Collected Works*, V, 67.

61   Rev. R. H. Neale in *Sermons . . . on the Death of Abraham Lincoln* (Boston: J. E. Tilton & Co., 1865), 166.

62   Chittenden, *Recollections of President Lincoln*, 445.

63   Basler, ed., *The Collected Works*, V, 128-129.

Courtesy of Lloyd Ostendorf

This stern-looking cleric is Methodist Episcopal Bishop Matthew Simpson.

Chapter Nine—The Book of Job

When Mary Lincoln first took possession of the White House on March 4, 1861, she thought it to be in a most deplorable condition. Paint was peeling from the outside as well as the inside; wallpaper was faded; carpets were worn out; and the furniture was very shabby. Congress agreed with her assessment of the Executive Mansion and appropriated $20,000 to refurbish it. With her usual exuberance in buying and disregard of public moneys, Mary plunged into a widely-publicized spending spree in various cities, purchasing china, goldware, silverware, drapes, furniture, glassware, wallpaper, mirrors, etc. Upon receiving all the bills, she discovered to her chagrin that she had overspent the appropriation by $6,700. The President became furious when informed on December 14; he declared that he would pay the overrun out of his own pocket. Calling his wife's expensive acquisitions "flub dubs," he reminded her that soldiers even lacked blankets while she had wasted Federal funds on a "damned old house" that "was furnished well enough" when they arrived—"better than any house they ever lived in." Mary Lincoln readily admitted that she and her honest husband were of "opposite natures." She loved to impress people; her mate could have cared less. Fortunately for the reputation of his administration, Congress made additional appropriations which were buried in a future budget.[1]

After the last contractor had finished his labors, Mary Lincoln could boast that "Our home is very beautiful[;] the grounds around us are enchanting." The world, she thought, smiled at her and paid due homage.[2] But the coming season would be the winter of their discontent. To show off her remodeling as well as her social skills, Mrs. President Lincoln—as she preferred being called—planned a grand ball at the White House for February 5, 1862. One observer on the scene declared that Mrs. Lincoln had indeed put her foot in it. Those who did not receive an invitation were furious. One correspondent termed the party a social blunder. Plebeians were excluded from the festivities, said some of the newspapermen. Others piously denounced Mary Lincoln for giving a ball while she herself held membership in a church which discountenanced dancing. Some faulted the First Lady for making merry while the country was impoverished, distracted and in mourning because of the war. A few pointed out that fancy balls had not been conducted in the White House since the Tyler administration. Despite these many criticisms, most Washingtonians predicted it would be the "most magnificent affair ever witnessed in America." All the local gossip centered around this coming party.[3]

Shortly after 9:00 p. m., President and Mrs. Lincoln took up their station near the center of the East Room and began receiving the long line of invitees who were dressed in their finest clothes. Lincoln, however, appeared in a plain suit of black and "wore a bland and pleased expression" upon his rugged and lined face. Mary, on the other hand, "was dressed in a magnificent white satin robe, with a black flounce half a yard wide, looped with black and white bows, a low corsage trimmed with black lace, and a bouquet of crape myrtle on her bosom." Upon her head she wore a wreath of black and white flowers with some crape myrtle on the right side. Her jewelry consisted of necklace, earrings, brooch, and bracelets fashioned from pearls. Her dress, simple yet elegant, had been designed in half mourning style out of courtesy and respect to Queen Victoria of England who had lost her eldest son, a recent visitor to the Executive Mansion in Washington. Caterers served dinner at 11:30, and the merry making was still going on at 2:00 a. m. when the correspondents rushed out to file their stories. Ironically, there was no dancing at this "ball."[4]

Despite the gaiety exhibited by those present at this dinner-reception greatly enhanced by the melodious music of the Marine Band, Mary Lincoln could not concentrate her thoughts completely upon the guests who swirled around her that evening in the East Room, the State Dining Room, the Red Parlor, the Blue Room and the Green Parlor. Upstairs in the family quarters, Willie Lincoln lay dangerously ill. Several times Mary left the celebrants to check on the condition of this favorite son, just eleven years of age.[5] He was an extremely bright young man. His tutor, Alexander Williamson, reported that William Wallace Lincoln "had only to con over once or twice a page of his speller and definer, and the impression became so fixed that he went though without hesitation or blundering, and his other studies in proportion."[6] Like his brilliant father, Willie could even write poetry, and he divulged to his tutor that he wanted to become either a school teacher or preacher. Yet, like most children his age, he was full of pranks. Standing in an anteroom of the executive office in the White House was a marble bust of John Forsythe, the former Secretary of State from 1834 to 1841. Its easy accessibility proved too tempting for Willie to resist. He had taken a pencil and drawn a beard and goatee on the face of this statue! Nor had the Executive Mansion cleaning staff removed Willie's handiwork; there it stood eleven days after the little chap's death.[7]

Mary Lincoln's seamstress explained that Willie had been given a pony which he insisted upon riding every day in good weather or bad, but he caught a severe cold which turned into a fever.[8] After that night of February 5, his devoted mother did not leave his bedside. By February 8, the press disclosed that Willie suffered from "bilious fever." At times the fever abated, but Willie did not improve to any large extent. As a result, the usual Saturday receptions and Tuesday levees were canceled until further notice.[9] On February 12, the reporters were informed that Willie was "out of danger."[10] However, within a day or two, the public learned that now both Willie and Tad were sick. In fact, there were serious apprehensions "as to the recovery of the youngest" son, Tad. A deep gloom descended upon the entire White House.[11] This was not a new experience for the President and Mrs. Lincoln. There was strong evidence that three of the Lincoln children were tubercular. On February 1, 1850, Edward Baker Lincoln—not yet four years of age—died of chronic consumption—now known as tuberculosis.[12] Early in 1859, Mary Lincoln announced that Tad was quite sick and that the doctor had diagnosed his illness as "lung fever."[13] Willie had been severely ill with similar symptoms in 1860.[14] Only the eldest, Robert, usually enjoyed good health.

On February 16, an announcement stated that the Lincoln children had improved to the point that their recovery was expected soon.[15] The next day's medical bulletin told the anxious public that little Willie had been declared "past all hope of recovery," and the Monday Cabinet meeting in the White House was canceled that day as well as the levee scheduled to be held in the Red Parlor or the Blue Room that night.[16] Dr. Robert King Stone, Professor of Medicine and Ophthalmology at Columbia Medical College (now George Washington University), served as the Lincoln Family physician and in collaboration with Dr. Neal Hall was treating both Willie and Tad in this crisis.[17] A most distinguished physician, Dr. Stone had received his A. B. degree from Princeton and his M. D. from the University of Pennsylvania. After these diplomas, he took further post-graduate work in Edinburgh, Paris, and Vienna. These two doctors declared that Willie suffered from an "intermittent fever" which "assumed a typhoid character." They reported that at times Willie's mind wandered, too, as would have been natural with high fever. His exact illness will probably never be known. The family minister, Dr. P. D. Gurley, later asserted that Willie had died as a result of varioloid, a form of smallpox. Since the words varioloid and smallpox created panic when spoken in those times, Dr. Gurley said Willie's disease had been concealed from the public, and the funeral service was very private.[18]

On February 18, Edward Bates, the Attorney General, noted in his diary that Willie was then thought to be "in extremis" with the President "nearly worn out, with grief and watching."[19] Next day a local correspondent for a New York paper reported that the White House was "overspread with the gloom of the expected death of the President's second son." There was no hope for Willie's recovery. Both Lincoln and his wife were overwhelmed with their grief.[20] Finally, at approximately 5:00 p. m. on February 20, Willie, "the pride and pet of the household," succumbed. It was given out that pneumonia had killed him. Of course, many ailments terminate with pneumonia or a filling of the lungs with fluid. He had perhaps suffered from multiple diseases at the same time. Such a sad event further plunged the Executive Mansion into the deepest of grief. The only good news was that young Tad was said to be recovering.[21]

After the angel of death had removed little Willie from him, the President walked up and down his private office muttering, "This is the hardest trial of my life! Why is it? Why is it?" Somebody in his presence remarked that citizens all over the North were praying for him. Upon hearing this, Lincoln exclaimed, "I am glad to hear that. I want them to pray for me. I need their prayers."[22] Another close colleague recounted that the President believed "in the efficacy of prayer" and had a desire "to be in accord with the Providential plan."[23] But there was no consoling Mary Lincoln. She took to her bed immediately. Trying to cope with this difficult situation, President Lincoln sent his carriage to bring Senator and Mrs. Orville Hickman Browning over to the White House as companions for his inconsolable wife.[24] Mary was still on good terms with the Brownings and knew them quite well. They often attended church with the Lincolns in Washington and were also Presbyterians. Back in Springfield, Browning had been one of the few invited to partake of a family meal in the Lincolns' home.

Orville Hickman Browning had been born in Cynthiana, Harrison County, Kentucky, on February 10, 1806. He attended Augusta College and then studied law until he was admitted to the bar in 1831, at which time he moved up to Quincy, Illinois, on the Mississippi River. During the following year, he soldiered as a Private in the Black Hawk War, as did A. Lincoln. Browning served in the Illinois General Assembly at the same time that Lincoln sat there, and they became warm friends.

Eliza Caldwell had been born October 23, 1807, near Richmond, Kentucky. She was a tall and rather portly woman—never considered beautiful, even in her youth. She enjoyed her bourbon and smoked a pipe. On February 25, 1836, at Richmond, Madison County, Kentucky, Browning was married to Eliza H. Caldwell, daughter of Robert and Frances Irvine Caldwell, by the Rev. Dr. John H. Brown, the same Presbyterian minister who later filled the pulpit of the First Presbyterian Church in Springfield while the Lincolns attended there.[25]

Orville assisted in organizing the Republican Party in Illinois. Later, when Senator Stephen A. Douglas died, Governor Richard Yates appointed Browning to succeed him on June 26, 1861.[26] He remained in the U. S. Senate until January 12, 1863, and in 1866, President Andrew Johnson named him Secretary of the Interior. Orville died on August 10, 1881, and Eliza succumbed on January 23, 1885. Both were interred in Woodland Cemetery at Quincy, Illinois.[27]

President Lincoln asked Senator Browning to take charge of the funeral arrangements for little Willie. Browning agreed to make some of the preparations, but in turn, asked B. B. French, Commissioner of Public Buildings, to oversee the arrangements in the White House for the obsequies there.[28] On February 21, the small body was embalmed by Dr. Charles B. Brown and Dr. John Alexander, assisted by Dr. Charles A. Wood in the presence of the Lincoln family physicians, Dr. Robert King Stone and Dr. Neal Hall. Watching the whole procedure were Senator Browning and Isaac Newton, Lincoln's Commissioner of Agriculture. The embalmers utilized the Sagnet of Paris method, and the results proved to be entirely satisfactory to Browning and the others. Frank T. Sands acted as the undertaker.

Tad Lincoln still remained very ill in his room upstairs in the White House.[29] On the following day, Julia (Coalter) Bates, wife of Lincoln's Attorney General, spent the day nursing Tad and taking care of him while the funeral preparations continued.[30] Elizabeth Keckley, seamstress to Mary Lincoln, washed the body and helped dress Willie in a plain brown suit of clothes. On his left breast they laid the greenish-yellow flowers of the mignonette.[31] When properly encased in a metallic coffin, the remains were placed in the Green Room of the White House. Here the body would remain; the funeral service would take place in the great East Room without the casket being there.[32] Upon being shown the corpse, Abraham Lincoln, testifying to his belief in Heaven, exclaimed with tears in his eyes, "My poor boy[;] he was too good for this earth. God has called him home. I know that he is much better off in heaven, but then we loved him so. It is hard, hard to have him die!"[33] This statement is a further example that Lincoln believed in Heaven.

Assuming the Lincolns would eventually return the body of Willie to Illinois, William Thomas Carroll, Clerk of the Supreme Court of the United States, volunteered to allow the President to entomb the body, on a temporary basis, in his own vault. On Sunday afternoon, February 23, Senator Browning took the President's personal carriage and drove over to Georgetown with William Carroll to examine the proffered vault. Browning knew Carroll very well. He had attended the wedding of Carroll's daughter, Sally, on December 10, 1861, and Browning had also pleaded many cases before the Supreme Court.[34] Upon examining the beautiful upground tomb, Browning pronounced the arrangements most satisfactory and returned to the White House.

The early morning fog and clouds were driven away on February 24 by a tremendous wind storm which unroofed houses, blew down churches and caused much havoc. This violent wind swept in from the northwest like a tornado. Even the skylights in The Library of Congress were demolished, and waves from the Potomac washed over the Long Bridge.[35]

Nature seemed to be duplicating the devastation which was being experienced by the First Family on the day of Willie's funeral. Mary Lincoln, still inconsolable, refused to leave her bedchamber to attend the burial services downstairs.[36] That morning, friends of the family called to pay their respects and view for the last time the remains reposing in the solemn Green Room. They noted that Willie was attired in the usual type of clothing worn for everyday. It consisted of pants, jacket, white stockings and low-cut shoes. The white shirt collar was turned down over the jacket, and the cuffs were turned back over the sleeves. A sheet of white crepe covered the sides of the metallic coffin which gave the appearance of being rosewood. On the lid was a square silver plate with his name and the dates of Willie's life. All the mirrors in the public areas of the Executive Mansion had been draped in mourning.[37]

Promptly at 2:00 p. m. that day, President Lincoln and Robert T. Lincoln took their places in a circle formed within the East Room. Tad had remained in his sick bed and was not present. Among the one hundred mourners, the press noted the entire Cabinet, the Congressional members from Illinois and General George Brinton McClellan, who sat beside Secretary Stanton. Lincoln's pastor, the Rev. Dr. Phineas Densmore Gurley, from the

New York Avenue Presbyterian Church, had been asked to officiate. At the proper moment, he arose and delivered the following oration:

Sad and solemn is the occasion that brings us here to-day. A dark shadow of affliction has suddenly fallen upon this habitation, and upon the hearts of its inmates. The news thereof has already gone forth to the extremities of the country.

The Nation has heard it with deep and tender emotions. The eye of the Nation is moistened with tears, as it turns to-day to the Presidential Mansion; the heart of the Nation sympathizes with its Chief Magistrate, while to the unprecedented weight of civil care which presses upon him is added the burden of this great domestic sorrow; and the prayer of the Nation ascends to Heaven on his behalf, and on behalf of his weeping family, that God's grace may be sufficient for them, and that in this hour of sore bereavement and trial, they may have the presence and succor of Him, who has said, "Come unto me all ye that labor and are heavy laden, and I will give you rest."

Oh, that they may all be enabled to lay their heads upon His infinite bosom, and find, as many other smitten once have found, that He is their truest refuge and strength; a very present help in trouble.

The beloved youth, whose death we now and here lament, was a child of bright intelligence and of peculiar promise. He possessed many excellent qualities of mind and heart, which greatly endeared him, not only to the family circle of which he was a member, but to his youthful companions, and to all his acquaintances and friends.

His mind was active, inquisitive, and conscientious; his disposition was amiable and affectionate; his impulses were kind and generous; and his words and manners were gentle and attractive. It is easy to see how a child, thus endowed, would, in the course of eleven years, entwine himself round the hearts of those who knew him best; nor can we wonder that the grief of his affectionate mother to-day is like that of Rachel weeping for her children, and refusing to be comforted because they were not.

His sickness was an attack of fever, threatening from the beginning, and painfully productive of mental wandering and delirium. All that the tenderest parental care and watching, and the most assiduous and skillful medical treatment could do, was done; and though at times, even in the latest stages of the disease, his symptoms were regarded as favorable, and inspired a faint and wavering hope that he was not beyond recovery, still the insidious malady, day after day, pursued its course unchecked, and on Thursday last, at the hour of five in the afternoon, the silver cord was loosed, the golden bowl was broken, and the emancipated spirit returned to God, who gave it.

That departure was a sore bereavement to the parents and brothers; but while they weep, they also rejoice in the confidence that their loss is the unspeakable and eternal gain of the departed; for they believe, as well they may, that he has gone to Him who said: "Suffer the little children to come unto me, and forbid them not, for of such is the kingdom of heaven;" and that now, with kindred spirits, and with a departed brother, who he never saw on earth, he beholds the glory and sings the praises of the Redeemer. Blessed be God.

> "There is a world above
> Where sorrow is unknown;
> A long eternity of love,
> Formed for the good alone;
> And faith beholds the dying here
> Translated to that glorious sphere."

It is well for us, and very comforting, on such an occasion as this, to get a clear and a scriptural view of the providence of God. His kingdom ruleth over all. All those events which in anywise affect our condition and happiness are in his hands, and at his disposal. Disease and death are his messengers; they go forth at his bidding, and their fearful work is limited or extended, according to the good pleasure of His will.

Nor a sparrow falls to the ground without His direction; much less any one of the human family, for we are of more value than many sparrows.

We may be sure,—therefore, bereaved parents, and all the children of sorrow may be sure,—that their affliction has not come forth of the dust, nor has their trouble sprung out of the ground.

It is the well-ordered procedure of their Father and their God. A mysterious dealing they may consider it, but still it is His dealing; and while they mourn He is saying to them, as the Lord Jesus once said to his Disciples when they were perplexed by his conduct, "What I do ye know not now, but ye shall know hereafter." What we need in the hour of trial, and what we should seek by earnest prayer, is confidence in Him who sees the end from the beginning and doeth all thing well.

Only let us bow in His presence with an humble and teachable spirit; only let us be still and know that He is God; only let us acknowledge His hand, and hear His voice, and inquire after His will, and seek His holy spirit as our counselor and guide, and all, in the end, will be well. In His light shall we see light; by His grace our sorrows will be sanctified—they will be made a blessing to our souls—and by and by we shall have occasion to say, with blended gratitude and rejoicing, "It is good for us that we have been afflicted."

> "Heaven but tries our virtues by affliction;
> And oft the cloud which wraps the present hour
> Serves but to brighten all our future days."[38]

After Dr. Gurley's sermon, the Rev. Dr. John C. Smith, pastor of the 4th Presbyterian Church where the Lincoln children sometimes attended, gave a prayer. At the conclusion of these ceremonies, nearly all of those present joined the funeral procession which would escort the body over to Georgetown. Six young pallbearers placed the casket in the hearse and proceeded with it to Oak Hill Cemetery. Upon arrival there, the coffin was borne into the Gothic Chapel which stood upon the grounds of Oak Hill. Here, several verses from the Scriptures were read, and the mourners then took their departure, leaving the body to be transferred into Carroll's family vault at a later time. Riding with President Lincoln in his private carriage were Robert Lincoln as well as Illinois Senators Lyman Trumbull and O. H. Browning.

After relaxing over tea, Browning returned to the White House that evening and sat up with Tad until 2:00 a. m. Mrs. Browning and their ward, Emma Lord, were at the bedside, too. They all remained at the Mansion to sleep until breakfast was served to them next morning. In the evening hours of February 25, Senator Browning took the President's carriage and picked up Elizabeth (Todd) Edwards at the train station. She had arrived from Springfield, Illinois, to take care of her sister, Mary Lincoln. Elizabeth was one of the few people who could handle the sorrowing and erratic First Lady. Although the Brownings had spent many long hours at the Executive Mansion, they continued to stay there a few days more.[39]

Dr. Gurley's words certainly gave some comfort to President Lincoln when he said, ". . . the prayer of the Nation ascends to Heaven on his behalf, and on the behalf of his weeping family, that God's grace may be sufficient for them, and that in his hour of sore bereavement and trial, they may have the presence and succor of Him, who has said, 'Come unto me all ye that labor and are heavy laden, and I will give you rest.'" And by the 26th of February, Tad Lincoln was rapidly recovering. In appreciation of his services, the First Family presented Dr. Gurley with an ebony cane whose head was six inches long and full of small gold roses. It was inscribed: "Rev. P. D. Gurley, D. D., from Mr. and Mrs. Abraham Lincoln, 1862."[40]

Mary Lincoln, however, continued to suffer from illness and defective mental health and did not venture out until sometime after March 20. Her usual receptions at the White House remained canceled.[41] Yet, she did see Dr. Gurley sometime after the funeral. She placed five dollars into his hand and related that Willie's last wish was that his savings should be given to the Sunday School Mission Program. Willie had been "a constant attendant at the Sabbath-school" and manifested a deep interest in this institution.[42] Mary Lincoln revealed that this five dollars was the exact amount discovered in Willie's possession when he died.[43] Tears must have accompanied the money as Mary relayed this story to her pastor. At the annual meeting of the church, James V. A. Shields, Superintendent of the Sunday School, included this tale in his report which as dated April 10, 1862.[44] Mary Lincoln never completely recovered from the tragedies which befell her during the Civil War. A Cook County Court found her legally insane on May 19, 1875, and she never regained her complete sanity even though the same court, in June of 1876, restored her legal status and released her from confinement on June 15, 1876.[45]

Mary was not the only Lincoln to undergo mental agonies. Abraham Lincoln sometimes suffered severe mental depression and often became melancholy. On the fatal first day of January in 1841, he had broken his engagement to Mary Ann Todd and immediately lapsed into a deep depression. He remarked that "If what I feel were equally distributed to the whole human family, there would not be one cheerful face on the earth." "I must die or be better," he reasoned on January 23 of that year.[46] He recovered in due course and eventually married Mary Todd. But Lincoln would not often let himself become incapacitated as Mary did. Instead, he told funny stories, joked with his colleagues and found a vent for his depression. In 1862, the responsibility of being President of the Union and prosecuting the war would not allow Lincoln to give up, go to bed and neglect his duties. Yet he probably felt as deeply hurt and as much grief as Mary did when Willie was taken from their midst and placed in a cold tomb. President Lincoln utilized other ways to compensate for his loss, consciously or unconsciously.

The sorrowing Commander-in-Chief once asked a Union Army officer, "Do you ever find yourself taking with the dead?" Before the soldier could reply, Lincoln continued, "Since Willie's death, I catch myself every day involuntarily talking with him, as if he were with me."[47] With his favorite son gone forever, Lincoln now "kept Tad with him almost constantly." He became almost like another older brother to Thomas, joining in his boyish games and plots. Perhaps Tad helped fill the awful longing for Willie.[48]

Religion appears to have become much more important to Abraham Lincoln following Willie's death. Dr. Gurley often came to the White House to talk with the Lincolns and to comfort them.[49] Another famous divine happened to be in Washington shortly after Willie died. This was the Rev. Dr. Francis Vinton (Aug. 29, 1809-Sept. 29, 1872). He had been born in Providence, Rhode Island. After graduating from West Point, he enrolled in law courses at Harvard, while still in the army, and was admitted to the bar in 1834. Then he resigned from the service two years later and studied theology, being ordained in 1838. His wife was a daughter of Commodore Oliver Hazard Perry. Vinton was a most highly educated and accomplished man in all three fields and became a most eloquent preacher at Trinity Episcopal Church on Broadway in New York City. His parents were David and Mary (Atwell) Vinton. His father earned his living as a goldsmith and a merchant. At the urging of Mary Lincoln and her sister Elizabeth (Todd) Edwards, who had become an Episcopalian after her marriage to Ninian Wirt Edwards, Dr. Vinton paid a call to the White House and attempted to comfort the President. He told the sad Chief Executive that Willie was alive in Paradise. That statement seemed to give some solace to Lincoln.[50] Rev. Vinton loaned copies of his sermons on death to the Lincolns, probably in manuscript form since there is no record that they were printed. Both Mary and the President seemed to have read these discourses before Mary returned them to the author with a kind letter on April 13, 1862.[51]

With the death of Willie, President Lincoln admitted that the "blow overwhelmed me."[52] To another witness, Lincoln declared that "When my [Willie] died, the severest trial of my life, I was not a Christian."[53] Yet one of these men thought that the President felt a religious experience as a result of his son's passing beyond the pale. When asked if he now was a Christian, the President replied, "I hope I am a Christian."[54] From this noncommittal reply, F. B. Carpenter jumped to the conclusion that the President had at last become a Christian and accepted Jesus Christ as his personal Saviour. But Lincoln made no such profession of faith to Carpenter. This artist, like many others of that era and later, failed to recognize that Lincoln could accept God as Sovereign Grand Architect of the Universe without acknowledging Christ as the Saviour of the faithful. He, like many others, also attempted to make Lincoln a Christian so that the latter's high reputation would not be tarnished because he was not a formal member of a Christian denomination.

In speaking to Billy Herndon about Lincoln's religious beliefs, Mary (Todd) Lincoln, on September 5, 1866, explained that she "thought" her husband had a religious experience following Willie's demise. But she quickly admitted that Lincoln had never joined a church and thus "he was not a technical Christian." Nevertheless, Mary declared, "he was a religious man always."[55] As time passed, however, she, too, felt a need to gather Father Abraham into the folds of the Christian religion. With exaggeration, Mary Lincoln wrote to Dr. James Smith on June 8, 1870, and declared that when Willie "was called away from us, to his Heavenly Home, with God's chastising hand upon us" Mr. Lincoln "turned his heart to Christ."[56] However, a reading of President Lincoln's letters and speeches does not confirm Mary Lincoln's later assertions on this important matter.

President Lincoln's old Baptist friend, the Rev. Noyes W. Miner, paid a visit to the White House in April of 1862 and made some notes after his conversations with his old Springfield neighbor. Lincoln freely admitted to Miner that "If I were not sustained by the prayers of God's people, I could not endure this constant pressure." "It has pleased Almighty God to place me in my present position," Lincoln continued, "and looking up to Him for wisdom and divine guidance I must work my destiny as best I can." Lincoln did not say he'd had a change of heart or mention Christ to Noyes. Instead, he spoke of God. In looking back on that conversation, Rev. Miner said years later, "If Mr. Lincoln was not a Christian, he was acting like one."[57] Lincoln did follow the moral teachings of the Bible which he read so very often.

In sending a message of consolation to Fanny McCullough of Bloomington, Illinois, after her father had died, President Lincoln clearly expressed his understanding of the sorrow at the death of a loved one. On December 23, 1862, he penned these words to Fanny: "In this old world of ours, sorrow comes to all; and, to the young, it comes with bitterest agony, because it takes them unawares. The older have learned to expect it. I am anxious to afford some alleviation of your present distress. Perfect relief is not possible, except with time. . . .I have had experience enough to know what I say; and you need only to believe it, to feel better at once."[58]

So this is how Father Abraham solved his bitter sadness over the loss of his dear Willie. He kept extremely busy and let time heal his wounds to some extent.

On the other hand, Mary Lincoln was ill prepared "to pass through the fiery furnace of affliction." Because of her disposition and her seemingly inherited mental difficulties, she found it impossible to cope with the trying situation caused by Willie's passing. "I had become so wrapped up in the world," she admitted, "so devoted to our own political advancement that I thought of little else besides." "Our Heavenly Father sees fit, oftentimes to visit us, at such times for our worldliness[;] how small & insignificant all worldly honors are, when we are <u>thus</u> so severely tried," Mary explained to a friend. Here, she was stating some of her religious philosophy a couple of years after the event. "The fairest, are most frequently taken, from a world of trial, for some wise purpose, which we cannot understand," she commented. As a result, Mary felt that "everything appears a mockery, the idolized one, is not with us," she agonized; "he has fulfilled his mission and we are left desolate."[59]

Willie's death probably put a severe strain upon Mary Lincoln's religious beliefs. "How often, I feel rebellious, and almost believe that our Heavenly Father, has forsaken us, in removing, so lovely a child from us!" Mary asserted. "Yet I know," she continued, "a great sin, is committed when we feel thus." She realized at times, too, that she was in danger of losing her sanity. "I have sometimes feared," she revealed, "that the <u>deep</u> <u>waters</u>, through which we have passed would overwhelm me."[60] Yet she retained her strong belief in Heaven. Once she related to an acquaintance that her deceased children were far happier in Heaven than they had been on earth. Mary surmised that Willie had now joined Eddie in Heaven.[61]

Like all frail mortals, Mary Lincoln did not always emulate the teachings of her church. She could be very vindictive upon occasion. "I understand that you <u>forgive</u> <u>me</u>, for all <u>past</u> <u>offenses</u>," she told Simon Cameron with vituperation, "Yet I am not Christian enough, to feel the same towards <u>you</u>."[62] Such rash comments both spoken and written, never won many true friends for Mary Lincoln. Thus, when she suffered personal tragedy, few people felt obligated to comfort her or commiserate with her unless there might be personal gain for themselves. As long as she remained the First Lady, however, there was always some sycophant to flatter her.

At one time, Mary Lincoln expounded upon religion and concluded that "Heaven is just."[63] At least by April 13, 1862, she and the President had reappeared for worship services in their accustomed place in the New York Avenue Presbyterian Church. An old friend from Springfield attended Dr. Gurley's church that morning and took a seat just behind the President and Mary Lincoln. This observer noted that Lincoln "evidently got very tired," and Mrs. Lincoln "was so hid behind her immense black veil, and very deep black flounces, that one could scarcely tell she was there."[64] Mary remained in mourning dress for a lengthy period of time after this observance. But as always, she demanded the very best in mourning bonnets and veils. To Ruth Harris, her milliner in New York City, Mary Lincoln demanded that these items must be exceedingly plain, rich, "very best material & genteel . . . ." Even in sorrow, she was concerned with fashion.[65] And nothing Harris later sent Mary Lincoln satisfied her. The product was never fine enough and at the same time, cheap enough. She was a most difficult customer to please.

Because of his official position, sadness was never far removed from President Lincoln's daily routine. As if Willie's death had not been tragic enough for the President, a respected friend died not long afterward. Brigadier General Frederick West Lander (born Dec. 17, 1821) succumbed at Camp Chase on March 2, 1862. This native of Massachusetts was about to be given a new and important military command when he passed away. By train, under the watchful eyes of a loyal honor guard, his discolored corpse was returned to Washington, arriving early on the morning of March 5. It was borne with dignity to 410 Seventh Street where Doctors Brown and Alexander embalmed it with great difficulty because of the delay in receiving it from the front. At 9:00 a. m. on the following morning, the General's body was transported to the private residence of Secretary Salmon Portland Chase on the corner of E and 6th. Shortly before noon, the doors were thrown open for those who wished to pay their respects and view, for the last time, the remains of this important officer. Among those appearing was President Lincoln and his Cabinet members. When this tearful ceremony ended, Lincoln joined the funeral procession which escorted the fallen General to the Church of the Epiphany on G Street, between 13th and 14th. This was an Episcopal Church, and Bishop Thomas March Clark (1812-1903) of Rhode Island, celebrated the burial rites with the assistance of the Rev. Dr. Charles H. Hall, pastor of this local congregation. The tired Chief Executive sat through this lengthy ritual and perhaps was again reminded of his dear departed son, Willie. But Mary Lincoln was spared such taxing and deadly functions, and her husband suffered alone with his grief and sorrow.[66] Once more, Abraham Lincoln had witnessed an Episcopal Church function. He was becoming more familiar with this denomination.

During the evening hours of July 10, 1862, death again visited the official family of President Lincoln. James Hutchison Stanton, nine-month-old son of Secretary of War Edwin McMasters and Ellen M. (Hutchison) Stanton, died at the rural home of his parents, Glen Ellen Farm, near Georgetown. The funeral was scheduled for Sunday, July 13, at 10:00 a. m. in the Stanton residence.[67] Although the President determined that he would attend the burial service, his wife was once more absent from the White House and could not lend her much-needed presence and comfort to the beleaguered Commander-in-Chief. She had arrived at the Metropolitan Hotel in New York City on July 9 and did not leave for Washington until July 17.[68] The President, however, was accustomed—even in his Springfield days—to personally pay his respects and tender his sincere condolences to old family friends who had lost a loved one.[69] He continued this visitation policy as President.

In the absence of his sojourning wife, the President invited William Henry Seward, Frederick William Seward and Gideon Welles to join him in his private carriage for the gloomy ride out to the Stanton country residence. During this trip, Lincoln mentioned for the first time that he was thinking of issuing a proclamation of emancipation to free the slaves.[70]

Secretary Stanton had attended Kenyon College, an Episcopal institution in Ohio, and both he and his second wife had pews in an Episcopal Church when they first met. Yet Mr. Stanton was not baptized into this denomination until just a year before he died, proving once more that many adults in that century did not rush into official church membership. After the funeral, little James H. Stanton was interred in the Georgetown Cemetery where his illustrious father would later join him in 1869.[71]

With the weighty cares of the Nation upon his shoulders and because of the personal tragedies which had befallen him, President Lincoln appeared greatly altered from the "happy-faced Springfield lawyer of 1856," reported Noah Brooks when, after a long hiatus, he once more caught a glimpse of Lincoln at the New York Avenue Presbyterian Church on November 30, 1862. Mary Lincoln, Brooks noted, was still wearing her mourning clothes. The President, he discovered, attended this church when the press of business did not preclude it. Brooks observed with sadness that Lincoln's hair was now grizzled, his "gait more stooping, his countenance sallow, and there is a sunken, deathly look about the large cavernous eyes, which is saddening to those who see there the marks of care and anxiety, such as no President of the United States has ever before known." From his seat in the gallery, Brooks pensively watched the President as he moved down the church aisle, "Recognizing, with a cheerful nod, his friends on either side, his homely face lighted with a smile." His fellow parishioners, in turn, looked with commiserating admiration upon the tall, mournful figure of Abraham Lincoln as he passed by them. "May God bless him," exclaimed Noah Brooks.[72]

President Lincoln found solace and succor through prayer and supplications to the Almighty, sometimes invoking God's aid by attending church. However, Mary not only went to regular worship services, but also drifted into Spiritualism and séances. Noah Brooks thought the black seamstress, Elizabeth Keckley, had introduced Mary Lincoln to mediums and their dark trade.[73] Some friend, on May 21, 1862, even presented the President with a volume on Spiritualism entitled *Further Communication from the World of Spirits*, yet there is no evidence that Lincoln took time to read it. This book shows no wear at all, and Lincoln cannot be listed as a follower of this occult practice.[74]

Spiritualism is the belief that deceased persons can communicate with the living by rappings, etc. John D. Fox of Hydesville, New York, had three daughters who are said to have originated this theory and practice in 1846. It spread rather rapidly with mediums claiming to be able to interpret noises and happenings. Because of the many uncertainties and untimely deaths occasioned by the Civil War, mediums and clairvoyants openly advertised in the newspapers of Washington, D. C., to gain paying clients. The District of Columbia evidently was a fertile ground for these practitioners. A "Mrs. Acken" plied her nefarious trade right in the Delevan House at 9th and Pennsylvania Avenue.[75] Others conducted their séances in the privacy of their own homes or in the dwellings of their followers. Little cells of these believers flourished in the Capital City. Many of the Spiritualists that Mary Lincoln became acquainted with had regular occupations and only acted as mediums in spare moments. Some, of course, wanted her to obtain Federal jobs for them. One of these cult members known to Mary Lincoln was a former Unitarian minister, John Pierpont, who was then a clerk in the Treasury Department.[76]

Only a few of these Spiritualists that had contact with Mary Lincoln can be identified today. Henrietta (Sturdevant) Colburn (1841-1892), called "Nettie," was one of them, a trance-medium. Born in Bolton, Connecticut, she later moved to Hartford and began lecturing around the New England States before going to Washington in an attempt to aid her brother who was in the service and ill. She was accompanied by Parthenia R. Hannum of South Adams, Massachusetts, who acted as "Nettie's" controlling spirit and was nicknamed "Parnie." "Nettie" Colburn later married William Porter Maynard, the postmaster of White Plains, New York, and Parthenia Hannum married E. R. Colburn, an uncle of "Nettie's." The two women arrived in Washington during November of 1862 with a letter of introduction to Thomas Gales Foster, a prominent speaker on the subject of Spiritualism. He lived at 466 Twelfth Street and had recently been made a clerk in the War Department. Previously, he had sold tobacco. In a year or two, he moved to 450 Sixth Street, close to Secretary S. P. Chase.[77] In order to assist "Nettie," Foster took her to see John Tucker who acted as General Transport Agent for the War Department. He issued her the necessary travel passes which enabled her to visit this sick brother. It is not known whether or not Tucker was a Spiritualist, but he was most friendly with Foster.

Foster then introduced "Nettie" to Cranstoun Laurie, the Chief Clerk of the Post Office in Washington. He was a Spiritualist and resided at 21 First Street in Georgetown.[78] Both Mr. and Mrs. Laurie, as well as their daughter,

Belle Miller, were Spiritualists. Belle specialized in making a piano move! Mary Lincoln may already have met the Lauries before "Nettie" came to town with "Parnie."

Another person who aided and abetted Mary Lincoln's attendance at "Circles" or séances had easy access to the White House because he was a trusted government official. This was Isaac Newton (March 31, 1800-June 19, 1867). He had been born in Burlington County, New Jersey, of Quaker stock and was a farmer. About 5' 6" tall and rather heavyset, he could manage an office, but never was known for having a great mind. His speech was folksy, and he had no education beyond the common school. In 1861, Lincoln had approved of his appointment as Chief Clerk in the Bureau of Agriculture within the Patent Office. During the following year, Lincoln named him Commissioner of Agriculture, but it was not on the Cabinet level as it is today. His home was at 401 C Street. Newton became a close friend of the Lincolns. It appears that old Isaac Newton was always a rather strange man. John Hay visited him on February 13, 1867, and heard Newton relate one of his strange visions. It seems that Abraham Lincoln had called upon him in person from Heaven and informed the old man that he was going to stay all night with him. Newton discovered, however, that his bed was too short for tall Lincoln. With such vivid dreams, old Isaac Newton was a perfect candidate for Spiritualism and its practitioners.[79]

On December 31, 1862, Mary Lincoln took Isaac Newton in her personal carriage to Georgetown where they intended to celebrate New Year's Eve with a circle at the Cranstoun Lauries. Somebody suggested that "Nettie" Colburn and her control figure, "Parnie" Hannum, be fetched for a séance. Fitting action to words, Mary Lincoln sent Laurie with her driver and carriage to bring these girls back to Georgetown. They both were staying at the residence of Thomas Gales Foster. Back they all rode to 21 First Street in Georgetown. There, "Nettie" discovered that none other than Mary Lincoln awaited her. Among those present were Newton, John Pierpont and the Hon. Daniel Eton Somes (1815-1888), a former member of Congress from Maine who was practicing patent law in Washington. He was not a Spiritualist but only an interested observer. Mary Lincoln had gone to watch Belle (Laurie) Miller. When Mary learned that "Nettie" was a trance medium, she asked to have her come and exhibit her talents.

For an hour, "Nettie" performed in a trance and made startling revelations to Mary Lincoln. She talked of Willie Lincoln and other matters. Upon the conclusion of this exhibition, Mary Lincoln exclaimed that "This young lady must not leave Washington." However, "Nettie" coyly informed the President's wife that she lived by speaking and had no other job and must return to her lecturing. Thereupon, Mary Lincoln turned to Isaac Newton and begged him to hire not only "Nettie" but also "Parnie." Thus it came about that "Nettie" Colburn and "Parnie" Hannum received jobs in the agricultural division, working from 9 to 12 and 1 to 3 sewing up little bags which contained one gill of seeds. For this labor, each earned one dollar per day, a very nice salary in those days. Mary Lincoln later tried to obtain even better positions for them in the Treasury Department.

With a secure income and free lodgings with Anna M. Cosby, in a brick mansion on Capitol Hill, "Nettie" and her friend could hold séances for the benefit of Mary Lincoln.[80] Once, she even performed in the august Red Parlor of the White House together with her friends, the Lauries, and their daughter, Belle Miller. President Lincoln stumbled onto them there and watched with his usual curiosity. At another time, he accompanied Mary Lincoln out to the Georgetown home of the Lauries to observe the action of these Spiritualists. But there is no indication that Lincoln ever believed in Spiritualism. He seemed simply to consider it a form of curiosity or entertainment, or perhaps he wished to protect his gullible wife. Lincoln expressly told Dr. Gurley that he was not interested in Spiritualism.[81]

Another trickster who won Mary Lincoln's support and attention was Charles J. Colchester. He held séances for Mary at both the White House and the Soldiers' Home where the Lincolns resided in the summer months. President Lincoln seems to have greatly mistrusted the man who sometimes referred to himself as "Lord Colchester." President Lincoln even sought the advice of Dr. Joseph Henry (1797-1878), the Secretary of the Smithsonian Institution, on the matter.

Lincoln's contact with Dr. Henry had developed over a period of years. Dr. Henry was considered one of the greatest scientists of his time. He had come to Washington from Princeton, and although he had been appointed to the Smithsonian on December 3, 1846, the edifice was still being constructed while Lincoln was in Congress. During Lincoln's presidency, Henry attended the same church the Lincolns did, and would eventually serve as an Elder in the New York Avenue Presbyterian Church (1874 to 1878). Because both Dr. Henry and the President had scientific minds and great curiosity, Dr. Henry was sometimes invited to visit the White House where he conversed with the President on a variety of subjects. On March 3, 1863, President Lincoln signed a bill which established the National Academy of Sciences. He had, undoubtedly, consulted with Dr. Henry before approving this measure.

Lincoln also asked Dr. Henry's opinion regarding Colchester's séances. Dr. Henry invited Colchester to demonstrate his abilities in Henry's office at the Smithsonian. This astute scientist heard the sounds and determined that they came from Colchester's person, but he could not ascertain how Colchester produced them without examining the medium's body. Dr. Henry informed Lincoln that he believed Colchester was a fake, but admitted that he did not discover how the strange noises had been produced. At a later date, completely by chance, Dr. Henry met a man who had actually manufactured an electrical device for Colchester to use during the séances. Colchester wore the mechanism upon his arm under his coat and operated it by contracting and relaxing his muscles. Nevertheless, Colchester continued to prey upon the First Lady's credulity. He still came to the White House and held séances where he gave out supernatural messages to Mary Lincoln. In return for these performances, he began to demand favors, such as railroad passes. Noah Brooks attended one of these circle meetings and exposed Colchester by grabbing his arm and calling for a cohort to strike a light. There was Colchester beating a drum and making mysterious noises and sounds. Brooks, a Congregationalist and a very close friend of the Lincolns, informed Colchester that he was not welcome in the Executive Mansion any more. Although he did not bother Mary Lincoln in the future, Colchester evidently did not leave Washington as Brooks had warned him to do.[82]

It would appear that Mary Lincoln's mental state continued to be a source of concern. Certainly, her reliance on Spiritualism continued. In November of 1863, her half-sister, Emilie (Todd) Helm, stopped at the White House for a short visit. One night Mary divulged to Emilie that Willie "comes to me every night, and stands at the foot of my bed with the same sweet, adorable smile he has always had; he does not always come alone; little Eddie is sometimes with him . . . ." Such a revelation greatly shocked Emilie; it frightened her because she could see that Mary had become so nervous and unstable that the supernatural was ruling her life.[83]

On February 20, 1864, Mary Lincoln even invited General Daniel Edgar Sickles (1825-1914), to spend "an hour's pleasant past time" with the medium, Thomas Gales Foster.[84] At the urging of his friend Sam Ward, Dr. Joseph Henry had also attended a séance at Foster's home. Dr. Henry found nothing supernatural about the exhibition, but he formed a very low opinion of Foster.[85] Mary Lincoln, however, continued attending Foster's gatherings.

Even after President Lincoln's assassination, female Spiritualists, probably "Nettie" and "Parnie," persisted in coming into the White House where "They poured into [the widow's] ears pretended messages from her dead husband." These women nearly drove Mary Lincoln completely crazy. Finally, Robert Todd Lincoln ordered them out of the Executive Mansion.[86] Unlike his permissive father, Robert would not tolerate such harmful shenanigans.

On November 15, 1867, Mary Lincoln revealed to Elizabeth Keckley that she felt Abraham Lincoln's "watchful, loving eyes" watching over her.[87] Taking advantage of Mary's belief, one Spiritualist even faked a photograph of the deceased President standing behind Mary with his hands upon her shoulders.[88] As late as 1872, Mary Lincoln was still patronizing Spiritualists, one of whom showed her a shadowy figure of her deceased son, Tad, who had died on July 15, 1871, in Chicago.[89] During her period of insanity in 1875, Mary Lincoln disclosed that an Indian spirit was removing wires from her eyes, etc. It seems reasonable to suppose that this hallucination came about because of her previous exposure to "Nettie" and "Parnie." These two women frequently conjured up a spirit who purported to be an Indian maiden called "Pinkie."[90] It would appear that Mary Lincoln had been permanently scarred by her association with Spiritualists.

This "spirit photograph" of Mary (Todd) Lincoln was taken by William H. Mumler and stamped "Specialty by Mumler, 170 West Springfield St., Boston, Mass." Mary had secretly visited Boston in 1872 and had been photographed by this fraud. It depicts a ghostly shadow of Abraham Lincoln with his hands upon his widow's shoulders. Mary denied she believed in Spiritualism, saying, "I am not EITHER a spiritualist—but I sincerely believe—our loved ones, who have only, 'gone before' are permitted to watch over those who were dearer to them than life."
Turner and Turner, eds., *Mary Todd Lincoln*, 525.

For more information on Mary and Spiritualism, see Kristine Adams Wendt, "Mary Todd Lincoln: 'Great Sorrows' and the Healing Waters of Waukesha," *The Lincoln Ledger*, Vol. I, No. 3 (May, 1993).

References

1   Cole and McDonough, eds., *Benjamin Brown French Journal*, 382; Turner and Turner, eds., *Mary Todd Lincoln*, 88-89, 200; Harry E. Pratt and Ernest E. East, *Mrs. Lincoln Refurbishes The White House* (Harrogate: Lincoln Memorial Univ., 1945). B. B. French was the Commissioner of Public Buildings and handled this matter in the course of his duties.

2   Turner and Turner, eds., *Mary Todd Lincoln*, 128.

3   Simeon Whiteley to his wife, Washington, D. C., Feb. 5, 1862, MS., Ill. State Hist. Library.

4   N. Y. *Herald*, Feb. 6, 1862, p. 5, cc. 4-5; Washington *Evening Star*, Mar. 6, 1862, p. 1, c. 2.

5   Keckley, *Behind the Scenes*, 98-100.

6   *New York World*, Mar. 8, 1862, p. 7, c. 1 (weekly edition).

7   Washington *Evening Star*, Feb. 21, 1862, p. 2, c. 1; *Lincoln Herald*, XCIV, 158 (Winter, 1992).

8   Keckley, *Behind the Scenes*, 98.

9   N. Y. *Herald*, Feb. 10, 1862, p. 5, c. 3.

10   *Ibid.*, Feb. 13, 1862, p. 5, c. 1.

11   *Ibid.*, Feb. 16, 1862, p. 5, c. 2.

12   U. S. Census 1850, Mortality Schedule, Springfield, Sangamon Co., Ill., p. 787, l. 23, MS., Illinois State Archives.

13   Mary Lincoln to O. M. Hatch, Springfield, Ill., Feb. 28, 1859, MS., Richard & Madelyn Hatch Morris, Springfield, Ill.

14   Turner and Turner, eds., *Mary Todd Lincoln*, 128.

15   N. Y. *Herald*, Feb. 17, 1862, p. 5, c. 1.

16   *Ibid.*, Feb. 19, 1862, p. 1, c. 3. Mary Lincoln favored the Blue Room.

17   Dr. R. K. Stone testified under oath that he "was the family physician" of the Lincolns. Ben Pittman, *The Assassination of President Lincoln and the Trial of the Conspirators* (N. Y.: Moore, Welstach & Baldwin, 1865), 81. Dr. Stone is also identified as their physician in the news releases during the Lincoln sons' illness.

18   Washington *Evening Star*, Feb. 21, 1862, p. 2, c. 1; Ervin Chapman, *Latest Light on Lincoln* (N. Y.: Fleming H. Revell Co., 1917), 505.

19   Howard K. Beale, ed., *The Diary of Edward Bates 1859-1866* (Washington: U. S. Govt. Printing Office, 1933), 233.

20   N. Y. *Herald*, Feb. 20, 1862, p. 1, c. 4.

21   *Ibid.*, Feb. 21, 1862, p. 4, c. 6.

22   Stoddard, *Lincoln's Third Secretary*, 148-149.

23   Eaton, *Grant, Lincoln and the Freedmen*, 313.

24   Pease and Randall, eds., *Diary of Browning*, I, 530-531.

25   Marriage Register, I, 209, MS., Clerk's Office, Madison Co. Courthouse, Richmond, Ky.

26   Executive Record, VIII, 290, MS., Illinois State Archives; death record for Mrs. Browning, Courthouse, Adams Co., Quincy, Ill.

27   Wm. H. Collins and Cicero F. Perry, *Past and Present of the City of Quincy and Adams County, Illinois* (Chicago: S. J. Clarke Pub. Co., 1905), 390; *Genealogies of Kentucky Families A-M* (Baltimore: Genealogical Pub. Co., 1981), 570; Maurice G. Baxter, *Orville H. Browning: Lincoln's Friend and Critic* (Bloomington: Indiana Univ. Press, 1957), 12-13.

28   Washington *Evening Star*, Feb. 22, 1862, p. 3, c. 1; Cole and McDonough, eds., *Benjamin Brown French Journal*, 389.

29   *Ibid.*; N. Y. *Herald*, Feb. 22, 1862, p. 4, c. 5.

30   Beale, ed., *Diary of Edward Bates*, 236.

31   Keckley, *Behind the Scenes*, 103; N. Y. *Herald*, Feb. 24, 1862, p. 5, c. 2.

32   N. Y. *Herald*, Feb 26, 1862, p. 10, cc. 3-4.

33   Keckley, *Behind the Scenes*, 103.

34   Pease and Randall, eds., *Diary of Browning*, I, 530-531, 513; David M. Silver, *Lincoln's Supreme Court* (Urbana: Univ. of Illinois Press, 1957), 103.

35   Washington *Evening Star*, Feb. 24, 1862, p. 3, c. 5.

36   Keckley, *Behind the Scenes*, 104-105, 109. Nathaniel Parker Willis declared that Willie had been his father's favorite son.

37   Washington *Evening Star*, Feb. 24, 1862, p. 3, c. 5.

38   Printed oration in the collection of the Illinois State Historical Library.

39   N. Y. *Herald*, Feb. 25, 1862, p. 4, c. 6; Feb. 26, 1862, p. 10, cc. 3-4; Pease and Randall, eds., *Diary of Browning*, I, 531.

40   N. Y. *Herald*, Feb. 27, 1862, p. 1, c. 1; Chapman, *Latest Light on Lincoln*, 505.

41   N. Y. *Herald*, Mar. 21, 1862, p. 5, cc. 1-2.

42   *New York World*, Mar. 8, 1862, p. 7, c. 1 (weekly edition); *Frank Leslie's Illustrated Newspaper*, XIII, 263 (Mar. 15, 1862).

43   Records of the Sunday School, MSS., N. Y. Ave. Presbyterian Church, Washington, D. C.

44   *Ibid.*

45   Mark E. Neely, Jr. and R. Gerald McMurtry, *The Insanity File: The Case of Mary Todd Lincoln* (Carbondale: Southern Ill. Univ. Press, 1986).

46   Basler, ed., *The Collected Works*, I, 229.

47   Bishop Matthew Simpson heard this account and included it in a sermon printed in *Voices from the Pulpit* (N. Y.: Tibbals & Whiting, 1865), 406.

48   Wm. H. Crook, *Through Five Administrations* (N. Y. : Harper & Bros., 1910), 18.

49   *Ibid.*, 29.

50   McClure, ed., *Anecdotes of Abraham Lincoln*, 107.

51   Turner and Turner, eds., *Mary Todd Lincoln,* 125.

52   Carpenter, *Six Months at the White House,* 187-188.

53   Sermon of the Rev. Mr. Isaac E. Carey at the First Presbyterian Church on the southeast corner of Walnut and Stephenson streets in Freeport, Illinois, on Nov. 24, 1864, and printed in the *Freeport Weekly Journal,* Dec. 7, 1864, p. 1, c. 3. Note that this interview was reported prior to Abraham Lincoln's assassination.

54   Carpenter, *Six Months at the White House*, 187.

55   Wm. H. Herndon interview with Mrs. Abraham Lincoln, Springfield, Ill., Sept. 5, 1866, MS., Herndon-Weik Coll., Group IV, No. 1561, The Library of Congress.

56   Turner and Turner, eds., *Mary Todd Lincoln,* 568.

57   Noyes W. Miner, "Personal Recollections of Abraham Lincoln," 41, 44, 45, MS., Ill. State Hist. Lib.

58   Basler, ed., *The Collected Works,* VI, 16-17.

59   Turner and Turner, *Mary Todd Lincoln,* 189, 128.

60   *Ibid.,* 131, 189.

61   *Ibid., 147,* 189.

62   *Ibid.,* 83.

63   *Ibid.,* 111.

64   Mrs. Mary (Logan) Hay to Milton Hay, her husband, Washington, D. C., Apr. 13, 1862, MS., Stuart-Hay Papers, Ill. State Hist. Lib.

65   Turner and Turner, eds., *Mary Todd Lincoln,* 125, 127.

66   Washington *Evening Star,* Mar. 5, 1862, p. 2, c. 1; Mar. 6, 1862, p. 3, c. 6. This newspaper misspelled the Bishop's name as "Park." He started his career as a Presbyterian minister.

67   *Ibid.,* July 11, 1862, p. 3, c. 3. This newspaper listed the deceased as "Lewis H. Stanton" instead of the correct name. Lewis was another Stanton son.

68   N. Y. *Herald,* July 10, 1862, p. 4, c. 6; July 18, 1862, p. 4, c. 4.

69   N. W. Miner, "Personal Recollections of Abraham Lincoln," 9-10, MS., Ill. State Hist. Lib.

70   Howard K. Beale, ed., *Diary of Gideon Welles* (N. Y.: W. W. Norton & Co.,1960), I, 70.

71   Benjamin P. Thomas and Harold M. Hyman, *Stanton* (N. Y.: Alfred A. Knopf, 1962).

72   "Castine," Washington, D. C., Dec. 4, 1862, in *Sacramento Daily Union,* Dec. 30, 1862, p. 1. "Castine" was the pen name of Noah Brooks.

73   Brooks, *Washington in Lincoln's Time,* 64.

74   Jay Monaghan, "Was Abraham Lincoln Really a Spiritualist?" *Jour. Ill. State Hist. Soc.,* XXXIV, 209-232 (June, 1941).

75   Washington *Evening Star*, Apr. 2, 1862, p. 2, c. 6.

76   Nettie Colburn Maynard, *Was Abraham Lincoln a Spiritualist?* (Chicago: The Progressive Thinker, 1917), 37.

77   Turner and Turner, eds., *Mary Todd Lincoln*, 168.

78   *Hutchinson's Washington Directory 1863*, 231.

79   *Ibid.*, 155; Washington *Evening Star*, June 20, 1867, p. 2, c. 2, p. 3, c. 2; Beale, ed., *Diary of Edward Bates*, 222n, 267; Pease and Randall, eds., *Browning Diary*, I, 591, II, 100; Dennett, ed., *Diaries of John Hay*, 274.

80   Pease and Randall, eds., *Diary of Browning*, I, 608; Maynard, *Was Abraham Lincoln a Spiritualist?*, 22, 36-38, 46; Turner and Turner, eds., *Mary Todd Lincoln*, 150. Mary Lincoln confided in Browning about this venture, but he was certainly not a Spiritualist. On June 5, 1855, he had gone to see a female Spiritualist at Warsaw, Illinois. "Her talk," he recorded, "was intolerable twaddle, incomprehensible nonsense. Soon got tired & left." *Browning Diary*, I, 186.

81   Maynard, *Was Abraham Lincoln a Spiritualist?*, 40, 48; Chapman, *Latest Light on Lincoln*, 506.

82   Thomas Coulson, *Joseph Henry: His Life and Work* (Princeton: Princeton Univ. Press, 1950), 308-309; Brooks, *Washington in Lincoln's Time*, 64-66. For a discussion of Lincoln's scientific mind, see Wayne C. Temple, *Lincoln's Connections with the Illinois & Michigan Canal, His Return from Congress in '48, and His Invention* (Springfield: Illinois Bell, 1986).

83   Helm, *Mary, Wife of Lincoln*, 226-227.

84   Turner and Turner, eds., *Mary Todd Lincoln*, 168.

85   Coulson, *Joseph Henry*, 309.

86   Crook, *Through Five Administrations*, 69-70.

87   Turner and Turner, eds., *Mary Todd Lincoln*, 454.

88   Lloyd Ostendorf, *The Photographs of Mary Todd Lincoln* (Springfield: Ill. State Hist. Soc., 1969), 59.

89   Lillian Kruegar, "Mary Todd Lincoln Summers in Wisconsin," *Jour. Ill. State Hist. Soc.*, XXXIV, 249-253 (June, 1941).

90   Neely and McMurtry, *The Insanity File*, 11; Maynard, *Was Abraham Lincoln a Spiritualist?*, 78.

Chapter Ten—Leviticus

President Lincoln had little time to grieve. A heavy work schedule may have helped take his mind off his personal grief after the death of Willie. On March 6, 1862, despite the trauma of his personal life, the President asked Congress for a joint resolution which would offer to pay the States that freed their slaves. Note the Chief Executive's reference to his God in this message. Said Lincoln:

> While it is true that the adoption of the proposed resolution would be merely initiatory, and not within itself a practical measure, it is recommended in the hope that it would soon lead to important practical results. In full view of my great responsibility to my God, and to my country, I earnestly beg the attention of Congress and the people to the subject.[1]

Despite the fact that Major General George Brinton McClellan proved to be a disappointment to Lincoln—he never pushed the Peninsular Campaign with vigor—in the Western Theater, the Union forces gained steady victories. On February 6, Fort Henry fell to the North, and Fort Donelson followed suit on the 16th of that same month. Union troops occupied Nashville, Tennessee, on February 25, and Pea Ridge, Arkansas, proved to be a Northern victory during March 6-8. The iron warship *U. S. S. Monitor* drove off the Confederate ironclad *Merrimack* on March 9. That was one of the few Federal triumphs in the Eastern Theater of operations. On April 7, Major General Ulysses Simpson Grant managed to salvage his reputation at Shiloh, and on that same day, Island No. 10 in the Mississippi River surrendered to the Union forces.

Grateful for these scattered military successes, President Lincoln issued a Proclamation of Thanksgiving for Victories on April 10, 1862: "It has pleased Almighty God to vouchsafe signal victories to the land and naval forces engaged in suppressing an internal rebellion," declared Lincoln, "and at the same time to avert from our country the dangers of foreign intervention and invasion. It is therefore recommended to the People of the United States that, at their next weekly assemblages in their accustomed places of public worship which shall occur after notice of this proclamation shall have been received, they especially acknowledge and render thanks to our Heavenly Father for these inestimable blessings . . . ." He further asked the public to "reverently invoke the Divine Guidance" for their governmental leaders.[2] This message to the people of the North certainly demonstrates once again President Lincoln's great belief in God and His divine intervention in the affairs of mankind.

Among those religious leaders who heeded the President's proclamation for thanksgiving was the Rabbi Sabato Marais with the Hope of Israel Congregation in Philadelphia. A copy of his sermon and prayer were forwarded to Lincoln by Abraham Hart, President of this synagogue. Accordingly, Lincoln thanked him heartily for his "kindness and confidence."[3] Those of the Jewish faith generally gave Abraham Lincoln their firm support in his war efforts to save the Union.

At 11:00 a. m. on May 13, 1862, a committee from the General Synod of the Evangelical Lutheran Church came to the President and presented resolutions which had been passed by their Synod on the preservation of the Republic. The Rev. Prof. L. Sternberg and the Rev. Dr. H. N. Pohlman addressed the Chief Executive. When they concluded, Lincoln replied to them, saying he appreciated their loyal support and sympathy and added: "You all may recollect," the President continued, "that in taking up the sword thus forced into our hands this Government appealed to the prayers of the pious and the good, and declared that it placed its whole dependence upon the favor of God. I now humbly and reverently, in your presence, reiterate the acknowledgment of that dependence, not doubting that, if it shall please the Divine Being who determines the destinies of nations that this shall remain a united people, they will, humbly seeking the Divine guidance, make their prolonged national existence a source of new benefits to themselves and their successors, and to all classes and conditions of mankind."[4] Whenever possible, President Lincoln acknowledged the various religious denominations which lent encouragement to his administration.

Later that same day, the Twelfth Infantry Regiment of Indiana Volunteers came to the White House and passed in review. They had enlisted for one year only and were about to be discharged on May 16 to return home. Colonel William H. Link complimented the President for the manner in which he had performed his duties in the difficulties that then surrounded the Nation. In making his reply, the Chief Magistrate declared: "For the part that you and the brave army of which you are a part have, under Providence, performed in this great struggle, I tender more thanks—greatest thanks that can be possibly due—and especially to this regiment, which has been the subject of good report. The thanks of the Nation will follow you, and may God's blessing rest upon you now and forever."[5] This blessing from the Commander-in-Chief was similar to a benediction which might have been spoken by a minister. Lincoln thought of himself as both a political and spiritual leader.

It being the season for conventions, three representatives from the East Baltimore Conference of the Methodist Episcopal Church called upon the President about May 15, 1862, and presented him with copies of the resolutions passed by their Conference. Lincoln thanked them for the "kind words of approval" contained in the resolutions and preamble. He noted that this religious group was a numerous body of "intelligent Christian people" without any suspicion of having sinister motives. Their supportive words gave encouragement to the President in his difficult political endeavors. "By the help of all-wise Providence," explained Lincoln, "I shall endeavor to do my duty; and I shall expect the continuance of your prayers for a right solution of our national difficulties, and the restoration of our country to peace and prosperity."[6] Here, Lincoln used the word "Providence" instead of "God," as he often did.

A delegation of Progressive Friends saw the President on June 20, 1862, and urged him to emancipate the slaves. Lincoln revealed that "He had sometime thought that perhaps he might be an instrument in God's hands of accomplishing a great work and he certainly was not unwilling to be" such an instrument. However, the President reminded these Quakers that God's intentions might be different than theirs. He promised, nevertheless, that he would earnestly endeavor "to do his duty in the place to which he had been called" and would put his "firm reliance upon the Divine arm" and seek "light from above" to accomplish his tasks.[7] Even though the President had already privately determined to free the slaves, he was not about to let his secret resolution leak out before he was entirely ready to issue his proclamation. Two days prior to the visit of these Quakers, Lincoln had read his Emancipation Proclamation to Vice President Hannibal Hamlin. But the President apparently felt the time was not right for its release to the public.

Another religious body appeared before President Lincoln on July 17, 1862. This time a committee from the Reformed Presbyterian Synod presented him with their resolutions concerning the evils of slavery. Lincoln informed these men that he would proceed with caution in regard to emancipation. He ended by saying, "Feeling deeply my responsibility to my country and to that God to whom we all owe allegiance, I assure you I will try to do my best, and so may God help me."[8] He continued his non-committal attitude on this touchy matter until completely ready to announce his proclamation. At times he even played the devil's advocate to see how his listeners reacted.

In reply to Reverdy Johnson, who had been appointed as a special agent of the State Department to investigate affairs in Louisiana, the President declared, on July 26, 1862, that Louisiana residents had little to complain about. It was their fault, said Lincoln, that he had been forced to send an army to their state and occupy it. Now, the Union men there surmised that the President would free their slaves. Lincoln doubted the sincerity of friends who would hold his hands while his enemies stabbed him. "I am a patient man—always willing to forgive on the Christian terms of repentance;" explained the President, "and also to give ample time for repentance." "Still," continued Lincoln, "I must save this government if possible. What I cannot do, of course[,] I will not do; but it may as well be understood, once for all, that I shall not surrender this game leaving any available card unplayed."[9] In this statement, the religious Lincoln openly accepted some of Christ's philosophy which he sincerely admired and studied. Yet the harried Commander-in-Chief did not mention the divinity of Jesus Christ or equate him as an equal of God, the Supreme Being.

When Count Agenor-Etienne de Gasparin wrote to President Lincoln on July 18, 1862, he informed Lincoln that many friends in Europe prayed for him. The Count then predicted that if the United States ever became indifferent to slavery or, on the other hand, became carried away in favor of the extreme abolitionists, then enemies in Europe would certainly intervene on behalf of the Confederate States. To this Lincoln replied on August 4 that he was pleased his course of action so far had not lost him friends in Europe. "I can only say," Lincoln advised him, "that I have acted upon my best convictions without selfishness or malice, and that by the help of God, I shall continue to do so."[10] Here is another example of the President's reliance upon God and His assistance.

As a young man, Abraham Lincoln had been a champion wrestler; now, as President of the United States, he was engaged in another wrestling match where the stakes were much higher. This time he wrestled against his own conscience as well as the proponents and opponents of slavery. If he sought guidance from his Bible, Lincoln may have consulted Ephesians 6:12 which states: "For we wrestle not against flesh and blood, but against principalities, against power, against the rulers of the darkness of this world, against spiritual wickedness in high places."

Lincoln also struggled to save the Union when there were far too few Northern victories on the battlefields. After the Federal forces were again defeated at Bull Run on August 30, 1862, President Lincoln's spirits dipped very low. Once more he sought to learn God's plan for him. He sat down at his desk in the White House the first week in September and penned what he termed "Meditation on the Divine Will." It is most doubtful Lincoln ever meant it to be made public. In it, he attempted to reason in his own mind what God's will was in the matter of the Civil War. Perhaps he committed his innermost thoughts to paper in order to study them more completely. It is well-known Lincoln generally read outloud, saying when he both saw and heard the information, it was easier for him to remember it.

"The will of God prevails," admitted President Lincoln. "In great contests each party claims to act in accordance with the will of God. Both <u>may</u> be, and one <u>must</u> be wrong. God can not be <u>for</u>, and <u>against</u> the same thing at the same time. In the present civil war it is quite possible that God's purpose is something different from the purpose of either party—and yet the human instrumentalities, working just as they do, are of the best adaptation to effect His purpose. I am almost ready to say this is probably true—that God wills this contest, and wills that it shall not end yet. By his mere quiet power, on the minds of the now contestants, He could have either <u>saved</u> or <u>destroyed</u> the Union without a human contest. Yet the contest began. And having begun He could give the final victory to either side any day. Yet the contest proceeds."[11] He seems to have been analyzing the situation to be sure he was on God's side in the struggle between North and South. In seeking a sign, he was acting like a prophet from the Old Testament.

On September 7, 1862, Christians of many denominations held a meeting in Bryan Hall at Chicago and adopted a memorial to President Lincoln favoring a national emancipation of the slaves. Rev. William W. Patton and Rev. John Dempster presented it to Lincoln in person. Lincoln replied to this petition on September 13 in a religious vein. In addition, he again questioned the efficacy of a proclamation of emancipation, although privately he had decided to issue one when the time was right. Here, again, Lincoln was testing the waters and waiting. He said:

The subject presented in the memorial is one upon which I have thought much for weeks past, and I may even say for months. I am approached with the most opposite opinions and advice, and that by religious men, who are equally certain that they represent the Divine will. I am sure that either the one or the other class is mistaken in that belief, and perhaps in some respects both. I hope it will not be irreverent for me to say that if it is probable that God would reveal his will to others, on a point so connected with my duty it might be supposed he would reveal it directly to me; for, unless I am more deceived in myself than I often am, it is my earnest desire to know the will of Providence in this matter. And if I can learn what it is I will do it! These are not, however, the days of miracles, and I suppose it will be granted that I am not to expect a direct revelation. I must study the plain physical facts of the case, ascertain what is possible and learn what appears to be wise and right. The subject is difficult, and good men do not agree. For instance, the other day four gentlemen of standing and intelligence [naming one or two of the number] from New York called, as a delegation, on business connected with the war; but, before leaving, two of them earnestly beset me to proclaim general emancipation, upon which the other two at once attacked them! You know, also, that the last session of Congress had a decided majority of anti-slavery men, yet they could not unite on this policy. And the same is true of the religious people. Why, the rebel soldiers are praying with a great deal more earnestness, I fear, than our own troops, and expecting God to favor their side; for one of our soldiers, who had been taken prisoner, told Senator Wilson, a few days since, that he met with nothing so discouraging as the evident sincerity of those he was among in their prayers. But we will talk over the merits of the case.

What good would a proclamation of emancipation from me do, especially as we are now situated? I do not want to issue a document that the whole world will see must necessarily be inoperative, like the Pope's bull against the comet! Would my word free the slaves, when I cannot even enforce the Constitution in the rebel States? Is there a single court, or magistrate, or individual that would be influenced by it there? And what reason is there to think it would have any greater effect upon the slaves than the late law of Congress, which I approved, and which offers protection and freedom to the slaves of rebel masters who come within our lines? Yet I cannot learn that the law has caused a single slave to come over to us. And suppose they could be induced by a proclamation of freedom from me to throw themselves upon us, what should we do with them? How can we feed and care for such a multitude? General Butler wrote me a few days since that he was issuing more rations to the slaves who have rushed to him than to all the white troops under his command. They eat, and that is all, though it is true Gen. Butler is feeding the whites also by the thousand; for it nearly amounts to a famine there. If, now, the pressure of the war should call off our forces from New Orleans to defend some other point, what is to prevent the masters from reducing the blacks to slavery again; for I am told that whenever the rebels take any black prisoners, free or slave, they immediately auction them off! They did so with those they took from a boat that was aground in the Tennessee river a few days ago. And then I am very ungenerously attacked for it! For instance, when, after the late battles at near Bull Run, an expedition went out from Washington under a flag of truce to bury the dead and bring in the wounded, and the rebels seized the blacks who went along to help and sent them into slavery, Horace Greeley said in his paper that the Government would probably do nothing about it. What could I do? [Here your delegation suggested that this was a gross outrage on a flag of truce, which covers and protects all over which it waves, and that whatever he could do if white men had been similarly detained he could do in this case.]

Now, then, tell me, if you please, what possible result of good would follow the issuing of such a proclamation as you desire? Understand, I raise no objections against it on legal or constitutional grounds; for, as commander-in-chief of the army and navy, in time of war, I suppose I have a right to take any measure which may best subdue the enemy. Nor do I urge objections of a moral nature, in view of possible consequences of insurrection and massacre at the South. I view the matter as a practical war measure, to be decided upon according to the advantages or disadvantages it may offer to the suppression of the rebellion.[12]

After waiting several months for a significant Union victory in battle, President Lincoln finally decided the engagement at Antietam on September

17, 1862, had been somewhat of a triumph for the North. At least, the Confederate forces had been forced to retreat. At a special meeting of his Cabinet on September 22, Lincoln revealed that "he had made a vow, a covenant, that if God gave us the victory in the approaching battle, he would consider it an indication of Divine Will, and that it was his duty to move forward in the cause of emancipation." After reading the document carefully, Secretary Chase—a devout Episcopalian—remarked that he thought the Emancipation Proclamation ought "to make some reference to Deity." Somewhat stunned, the President replied, "I overlooked it. Some reference to Deity must be inserted." Lincoln then proceeded to request that Chase revise the wording. When Chase finished his assignment, the last full paragraph read: "And upon this act, sincerely believed to be an act of justice, warranted by the Constitution, upon military necessity, I invoke the considerate judgment of mankind, and the gracious favor of Almighty God."[13]

Secretary Chase confirmed Secretary Welles' account of this Cabinet meeting and noted in his diary that Lincoln had told them that "When the rebel army was at Frederick, I determined, as soon as it should be driven out of Maryland, to issue a Proclamation of Emancipation such as I thought most likely to be useful." "I said nothing to any one;" revealed Lincoln, "but I made the promise to myself, and (hesitating a little)—to my Maker. The rebel army is now driven out, and I am going to fulfill that promise."

On that same day, September 22, when the President's mind was full of thoughts on the Emancipation Proclamation, a Catholic nun, Sister Mary Carroll, obtained an interview with Lincoln. She came to plead the cause of Father Joseph B. O'Hagan, the Chaplain of the Excelsior Brigade's Fourth Regiment. So that he would not forget the facts, the Commander-in-Chief wrote a memo to himself. "She says," Lincoln noted, "that nearly all the Catholics of his regt. are now in hospital, and that the Catholic chaplains already appointed can not possibly attend all the Catholic soldiers in hospital." As a result, Father O'Hagan wished to be named a hospital chaplain.[14]

Few people today realize how much President Lincoln relied upon God in making his important decisions. Once he related to a friend, "That the Almighty does make use of human agencies, and directly intervenes in human affairs, is" he said, "one of the plainest statement of the Bible. I have had so many evidences of [H]is direction, so many instances when I have been controlled by some other power than my own will, that I cannot doubt that this power comes from above. I frequently see my way clear to a decision when I am conscious that I have no sufficient facts upon which to found it. But I cannot recall one instance in which I have followed my own judgment, founded upon such a decision, where the results were unsatisfactory; whereas, in almost every instance where I have yielded to the views of others, I have had occasion to regret it. I am satisfied that when the Almighty wants me to do or not to do a particular thing, [H]e finds a way of letting me know it. I am confident that it is [H]is design to restore the Union. He will do it in [H]is own good time. We should obey and not oppose [H]is will."[15]

In acknowledging a serenade given him at the White House on September 24, 1862, Lincoln said of his Emancipation Proclamation, "I can only trust in God I have made no mistake."[16] Shortly after the Proclamation was issued, the Rev. Cornelius Van Santvoord visited the President. He was the Chaplain of the 80th New York Infantry Regiment and a close friend of Dr. Gurley. Lincoln told him, "God helping me, I trust to prove true to a principle which I feel to be right."[17]

S. Peck from the Baptist Home Mission Society wrote to President Lincoln on September 26, 1862, and indicated that there were several religious denominations at Port Royal in South Carolina about to come into conflict over their jurisdiction among the freedmen of that area. Three days later, Lincoln called this matter to the attention of Edwin M. Stanton, saying, "I should think each church should minister according to it's [sic] own rules, without interference by others differing from them; and if there still be difficulties about places of worship, a real christian charity, and forbearance on the part of all might obviate it."[18] Note the President's reference to "real christian charity," with a small "c." He probably shook his head and puzzled how those who professed to be religious leaders could act so badly toward one another. In this war, churchmen sometimes caused Lincoln some of his most difficult problems—the hardest to solve without losing the support of the various denominations.

Since it was the Union victory of Antietam which permitted the President to finally issue his preliminary Emancipation Proclamation, Lincoln determined to visit the battlefield and also thank the officers and men in the Army of the Potomac. Accordingly, he left Washington on October 1 with a small party of guests, bound first for Harper's Ferry. Among his invited friends were U. S. Marshal Ward Hill Lamon, Ozias Mather Hatch, Major General John Alexander McClernand, and Joseph C. G. Kennedy, the Superintendent of the U. S. Census. They toured the camp of the Army of the Potomac before departing for Frederick, Maryland, where Lincoln praised the citizens as well as the brave soldiers who had defended this city from a Confederate army. After this sentimental tour, the Commander-in-Chief left Frederick on a special train and arrived back in Washington at approximately 10:00 p. m. on October 4. Immediately, Lincoln held a conference with Secretary of War Stanton before retiring for the night. The next morning, Sunday, October 5, he called a special meeting with a few of his Cabinet to discuss the embarrassing situation caused by General McClellan's not having followed up his initial success after merely repelling the forces of General Robert E. Lee. This strategy session certainly interfered somewhat with any church plans which these Cabinet members may have had, but the President desired the earliest possible opinion from these particular department heads.[19] He might have explained to them, "I sincerely wish war was an easier and pleasanter business than it is; but it does not admit of holy-days."[20] All members were not present. Chase remained at home nursing a sore foot,[21] and Secretary Welles was ill.[22]

Down at Antietam, President Lincoln had become very weary, sad and melancholy. He seemed extremely disheartened over the turn of events.[23] He found it difficult to shake off his disappointment after returning to the White House. Seeking solace from the Almighty, Lincoln closed his Sunday morning Cabinet meeting on Oct. 5 and proceeded over to attend services at the New York Avenue Presbyterian Church. There, he was closely observed by one member who described the extreme sadness etched deeply upon Lincoln's face. This observer thought that the pathos exhibited by Lincoln was Christ-like. He had so many wearisome burdens to bear for his people in this time of crisis.[24]

During the forenoon of October 27, 1862, Eliza P. Gurney, widow of Joseph J. Gurney, and a group of her Quaker friends, obtained an interview with the President. Eliza was an English Quaker, a writer on religious matters and a philanthropist. She ended the audience by kneeling and praying for God to guide Abraham Lincoln. The President replied that he was pleased to have this interview and to know that he had the sympathy and prayers of this denomination. "In the very responsible position in which I happen to be placed," explained Lincoln, "being a humble instrument in the hands of our Heavenly Father, as I am, and as we all are, to work out [H]is great purposes, I have desired that all my works and acts may be according to [H]is will, and that it might be so, I have sought [H]is aid—but if after endeavoring to do my best in the light which [H]e affords me, I find my efforts fail, I must believe that for some purpose unknown to me, He wills it otherwise." If the war continued, Lincoln thought that God, "permits it for some wise purpose of [H]is own, mysterious and unknown to us; and though with our limited understandings we may not be able to comprehend it, yet we cannot but believe, that [H]e who made the world still governs it."[25] Yet again, President Lincoln proclaimed himself an instrument of God and placed the outcome of the war in His hands completely. Nevertheless, Lincoln declared that he was doing his very best to determine what God willed him to do.

After a body of gentlemen from New York City requested that the Sabbath be better observed in the Army and Navy, President Lincoln as Commander-in-Chief issued the following order on November 15, 1862, and signed his full name to it—as he did for official documents:

> Executive Mansion, Washington, November 15, 1862. The President, Commander-in-Chief of the Army and Navy, desires and enjoins the orderly observance of the Sabbath by the officers and men in military and naval service. The importance for man and beast of the prescribed weekly rest, the sacred rights of Christian soldiers and sailors, a becoming deference to the best sentiment of a Christian people, and a due regard for the Divine will, demand that Sunday labor in the Army and Navy be reduced to the measure of strict necessity.
>
> The discipline and character of the national forces should not suffer, nor the cause they defend be imperiled, by the profanation of the day or name of the Most High. "At this time of public distress"—adopting the words of Washington in 1776—"men may find enough to do in the service of God and their Country without abandoning themselves to vice and immorality." The first General Order issued by the Father of his Country after the Declaration of Independence, indicates the spirit in which our institutions were founded and should ever be defended: "The General hopes and trusts that every officer and man will endeavor to live and act as becomes a Christian soldier defending the dearest rights and liberties of his country."
>
> Abraham Lincoln[26]

Before he or his staff promulgated this order, they must have done a bit of research to discover the words of General George Washington on this very subject. However, it would have been more acceptable if the belea-guered Civil War President had signed an order including both "Christian and Jewish soldiers and sailors" instead of merely citing the Christian ones. This certainly was a slip of somebody's mind, because Father Abraham well knew that quite a few men of the Jewish faith were fighting in the ranks of the Union forces. Nevertheless, this message did set a moral tone for the armed forces to follow. Minorities tended to be largely unnoticed by the Government at this time, and yet it was Lincoln who had asked for Jewish chaplains to be assigned to military units. Perhaps the writer neglected to mention the Jews because George Washington had not included them in his original sugges-tions which were utilized as the basic theme for this Civil War order. Thus, they were omitted in the press of more important labors being done that day. Lincoln would have regretted their omission in his order if he had discovered the error in time. It is quite probable that these words were ghostwritten for him since no manuscript of this directive has been found in Lincoln's own hand. It is most unlikely that Lincoln would knowingly have slighted any rec-ognized religious faith held by defenders of the Union.

In giving his annual message to Congress on December 1, 1862, the President summarized the events which had occurred since the members' last session. It, too, had a religious flavor. "And while it has not pleased the Almighty to bless us with a return of peace," lamented Lincoln, "we can but press on, guided by the best light He gives us, trusting that in His own good time, and wise way, all will yet be well." He ended by saying, "The way is plain, peaceful, generous, just—a way which, if followed, the world will forev-er applaud, and God must forever bless."[27]

Ministers in territory held by the Union Army sometimes caused President Lincoln difficult problems when they espoused Rebel sympathies. Major General Samuel R. Curtis attempted to support one of his subordinate officers who was facing disloyal activities from the Rev. Dr. Samuel B. McPheeters of the Pine Street Presbyterian Church in St. Louis. Naturally, this divine rushed to Washington and pleaded his case with Secretary Bates and then with the President. As a result, Lincoln suspended the order clos-ing the church, etc. He instructed General Curtis that the "U. S. government must not, as by this order, undertake to run the churches." The President agreed that when an individual became dangerous to the Union cause, "he must be checked; but let the churches, as such[,] take care of themselves. It will not do for the U. S. to appoint Trustees, Supervisors, or other agents for the churches."[28] Although the President meant well, his actions did not sit well with the military commanders who were on the scene and subject to the harassment of enemy clerics. Yet Lincoln seems to have held most theologians in high regard unless they proved completely unbearable by their overt actions.

To a Religious Society of Friends in the State of Iowa which had approved of the President's Emancipation Proclamation, Lincoln replied on January 5, 1863: "It is most cheering and encouraging for me to know that in the efforts which I have made and am making for the restoration of a righteous peace in our country, I am upheld and sustained by the good wishes and prayers of God's people. No one is more deeply than myself aware that without His favor our highest wisdom is but as foolishness and that our most strenuous efforts would avail nothing in the shadow of his displeasure. I am conscious of no desire for my country's welfare, that is not in consonance with His will, and of no plan upon which we may not ask His blessing. It seems to me that if there be one subject upon which all good men may unitedly agree, it is imploring the gracious favor of the God of Nations upon the struggles our people are making for the preservation of their precious birthright of civil and religious liberty."[29] It would seem the Quakers, in general, stood behind the President in his efforts to free the slaves even if they did not believe in war.

In writing to Green Adams in Kentucky, Lincoln ended his letter of January 7, 1863, with a benediction, as he sometimes did. "So far as I can see," Lincoln pronounced, "Kentucky's sons in the field, are acting loyally and bravely, God bless them!"[30]

Among the several ministers whom President Lincoln delighted in hearing was Bishop Matthew Simpson (June 21, 1811-June 18, 1884). He had been born in Cadiz, Ohio, and studied at Madison College at Uniontown, Pennsylvania, a school which later became merged with Allegheny College. He entered the ministry of the Methodist Episcopal Church and served as President of Asbury College (now De Pauw), in Greencastle, Indiana. He became a Bishop of the Methodist Church in 1852, his station being at Philadelphia. However, he traveled far and wide, speaking being his great strength and attraction. In due course he met Abraham Lincoln. They became friends despite the Bishop's constant carping. Evidently, Bishop Simpson found favor with Lincoln because of his strong support of the Union cause, his animated style of eloquent preaching and his important church position. Simpson often asked for political favors, just like any politician would. He was quick to solicit positions for fellow Methodists, naturally, and even influenced the appointment of a Cabinet member, Senator James Harlan of Iowa, a strong Methodist. President Lincoln appointed Harlan Secretary of the Interior on March 9, 1865, but Harlan did not take office until after Lincoln was killed. Mary Lincoln termed Simpson "that great and noble man." Robert T. Lincoln escorted Senator Harlan's daughter to the Second Inauguration, and Bishop Simpson later married Robert and Mary Eunice Harlan on September 24, 1868. She, like her father, was evidently at this time a Methodist.[31] She would later join the church of the Lincolns, the Presbyterian, and years later, another denomination.

Bishop Simpson had been invited to preach on Sunday, January 18, 1863, at the Foundry Methodist Church on the corner of G and 14th in Washington when the annual missionary collection would be taken up.[32] It would seem that Simpson's coming appearance caused President Lincoln to gather a group of colleagues and attend this service with them. Chase, Seward and Stanton of the Cabinet were present as well as Senator James Harlan of Iowa, Senator Henry S. Lane of Indiana, and the Hon. Joseph A. Wright, later Minister to Prussia. Other notables were present but not listed by the press.

Dr. Simpson preached an "elegant and interesting sermon" concerning the missionary cause. It was delivered in a very happy style to an audience where there was standing room only after the pews were completely filled. In concluding, Simpson paid tribute "to the glorious stars and stripes of our country." His stirring words brought tears to the eyes of both Lincoln and Stanton. The Bishop appealed for money to support the missionary efforts of the Methodist Church. A large amount was subscribed. Suddenly, somebody in the sanctuary proposed that this assembly make President Lincoln a Life Director of the Missionary Society. Such a membership cost $150. Fitting action to words, the plates were passed, and $160 was collected. Even Lincoln himself—greatly startled by this turn of events—contributed to the fund. Today, there is a Lincoln window in this Washington church.

In due course, the President received an engraved certificate denoting his Life Directorship. It was signed by E. S. Janes, President, and David Terry, Secretary of this Society, and read:

This Certifies
That His Excellency, Abraham Lincoln, Pres't of the U. S. A.
is constituted a Life Director of the Missionary Society
of the Methodist Episcopal Church
by the payment of One Hundred and Fifty Dollars

This document, engraved on parchment and framed in gilt and walnut, was soon afterwards displayed in the White House. Bishop Simpson must have later observed this Life Membership diploma hanging there, because he was quite often in the White House as President Lincoln's guest.[33]

A few writers have cited this certificate to prove that Abraham Lincoln was a member of the Methodist Episcopal Church. But this Life Directorship was for a missionary society and not the Methodist Church itself. Nevertheless, it does depict Abraham Lincoln's intense interest in the labors of this organization on behalf of the downtrodden and poor. He accepted memberships in very few organizations, indeed.

For a number of years, Lincoln had closely followed the vicissitudes of the various religious denominations when the subject of slavery began to split their membership. At Alton, Illinois, on October 15, 1858, Debater Lincoln had pointed to the Methodist Church and asked, "What divided the great Methodist Church into two parts, North and South?" Well did President Lincoln understand the difficulties which faced this particular denomination because of the slavery issue. He also was cognizant of the troubles which had begun in the 1850's in his wife's denomination. In that same debate with Senator Douglas, he questioned his audience, "What has raised this constant disturbance in every Presbyterian General Assembly that meets?"[34] And eventually, most of the churches had taken sides; denominations split into those favoring the North and those supporting the South. President Lincoln greatly appreciated the Methodist Church in the North because its members largely supported him. A great number of Methodists had joined the Union Army.

In replying to the Rev. Alexander Reed, General Superintendent of the U. S. Christian Commission, on February 22, 1863, President Lincoln declined the honor of acting as presiding officer for their meeting in the Hall of the House of Representatives in Washington, scheduled for that very day. He gracefully declined to take the gavel but approved of the gathering. "Whatever shall be sincerely, and in God's name devised for the good of the soldier and seaman, in their hard spheres of duty, can scarcely fail to be blest," declared Lincoln. "And whatever shall tend to turn our thoughts from the unreasoning, and uncharitable passions, prejudices, and jealousies incident to a great national trouble, such as ours, and to fix them upon the vast and long-enduring consequences, for weal, or for woe, which are to result from the struggle; and especially, to strengthen our reliance on the Supreme

Being, for the final triumph of the right, can not but be well for us all," Lincoln avowed. It so happened that George Washington's birthday fell that year on Sunday. President Lincoln noted this fact and asserted that "the highest interests of this life, and of that to come, is most propitious for the meeting proposed."[35] Here, again, Abraham Lincoln proclaimed his belief in Heaven, and for this reason alone the above communication is very important in an analysis of his faith. It also indicates the high regard in which the President was held by clergymen, such as the Rev. Reed. They recognized him as a truly religious man and accepted him as if he were a Christian.

George Whipple, Corresponding Secretary of the American Missionary Association at 61 John Street in New York City, informed President Lincoln on March 5, 1863, that their missionaries in Siam (now Thailand) sent him their very best wishes and their prayers. They wanted the President "endowed with wisdom from on high, and sustained by the power of the Almighty" so that he might crush the rebellion.[36] Clearly, this particular group of churchmen favored the North and especially Abraham Lincoln.

Because Lincoln placed his faith in one omnipotent God and largely ignored lesser deities, such as Jesus Christ, he was able to appreciate the religion of the American Indian. On March 27, 1863, a large assemblage of Indians crowded into the East Room of the Executive Mansion where they were greeted by Lincoln in person. Among the tribes represented were the Cheyenne, Iowa, Arapahoe, Comanche, Apache and Caddo. President Lincoln shook the hand of every chief and then spoke to them at some length. Since they had asked Lincoln for advice, he stated that he did not know, "Whether, in the providence of the Great Spirit, who is the great Father of us all, it is best for you to maintain the habits and customs of your race, or adopt a new mode of life." His honesty and his reference to the "Great Spirit" pleased these Indians and brought forth from them frequent applause and oral approbation. They could relate to Father Abraham, a humble leader of a great nation.[37] Even though as Captain Abraham Lincoln of the Illinois Volunteers he had fought against Indians in 1832,[38] the President exhibited no animosity towards these native Americans and treated them with respect and consideration.

With the war going badly for the Northern armies and few victories to celebrate, Senator James Harlan of Iowa sponsored a Senate Resolution which was adopted on March 3, 1863. It requested that the Commander-in-Chief proclaim a special day for "national prayer and humiliation." The

President issued his proclamation on March 30. It is a very religious document and deserves to be quoted in full, although other governmental officials may have assisted in its preparations.

A Proclamation

Whereas, the Senate of the United States, devoutly recognizing the Supreme Authority and just Government of Almighty God, in all the affairs of men and of nations, has, by a resolution, requested the President to designate and set apart a day for National prayer and humiliation:

And whereas it is the duty of nations as well as of men, to own their dependence upon the overruling power of God, to confess their sins and transgressions, in humble sorrow, yet with assured hope that genuine repentance will lead to mercy and pardon; and to recognize the sublime truth, announced in the Holy Scriptures and proven by all history, that those nations only are blessed whose God is the Lord:

And, insomuch as we know that, by His divine law, nations like individuals are subjected to punishments and chastisements in this world, may we not justly fear that the awful calamity of civil war, which now desolates the land, may be but a punishment, inflicted upon us, for our presumptuous sins, to the needful end of our national reformation as a whole People? We have been the recipients of the choicest bounties of Heaven. We have been preserved, these many years, in peace and prosperity. We have grown in numbers, wealth and power, as no other nation has ever grown. But we have forgotten God. We have forgotten the gracious hand which preserved us in peace, and multiplied and enriched and strengthened us; and we have vainly imagined, in the deceitfulness of our hearts, that all these blessings were produced by some superior wisdom and virtue of our own. Intoxicated with unbroken success, we have become too self-sufficient to feel the necessity of redeeming and preserving grace, too proud to pray to the God that made us!

It behooves us then, to humble ourselves before the offended Power, to confess our national sins, and to pray for clemency and forgiveness.

Now, therefore, in compliance with the request, and fully concurring in the views of the Senate, I do, by this my proclamation, designate and set apart Thursday, the 30th of April, 1863, as a day of national humiliation, fasting and prayer. And I do hereby request all the People to abstain, on that day, from their ordinary secular pursuits, and to unite, at their several places of public worship and their respective homes, in keeping the day holy to the Lord, and devoted to the humble discharge of the religious duties proper to that solemn occasion.

All this being done, in sincerity and truth, let us then rest humbly in the hope authorized by the Divine teachings, that the united cry of the Nation will be heard on high, and answered with blessings, no less than the pardon of our national sins, and the restoration of our now divided and suffering Country, to its former happy condition of unity and peace.

In witness whereof, I have hereunto set my hand and caused the seal of the United States to be affixed.

Done at the City of Washington, this thirtieth day of March, in the year of our Lord one thousand eight hundred and sixty-three, and of the Independence of the United States the eighty seventh.

[L. S.]   By the President: Abraham Lincoln
                          William H. Seward, Secretary of State[39]

This signed document is not in Lincoln's hand. Secretary Seward may have composed much of it, especially the references to the Lord.

In no uncertain terms, this proclamation parallels the dependence of President Lincoln upon God's will. It implores His succor so that the cruel war might come to a close and union be restored as quickly as possible. It is the document of an extremely devout believer in the Heavenly Father.

During Lincoln's lengthy search for a competent general to lead the Army of the Potomac, he was forced on January 25, 1863, to replace the inept Major General Ambrose E. Burnside with Joseph Hooker. To encourage General Hooker later that year, May 6, President Lincoln dispatched him a message which ended with another of the Commander-in-Chief's well-known benedictions: "And now, God bless you, and all with you."[40] Truly, Lincoln managed his high office in a manner not unlike a prophet of the Old Testament, constantly reminding his flock of God's presence in all the affairs of the world and invoking His blessings upon the faithful. Yet—unlike powerful lay or religious leaders, past and present—President Lincoln displayed an inordinate quantity of modesty. Once, when George B. McClellan failed to keep an important appointment with the President and others present berated this overt lack of respect, Lincoln retorted, "Never mind; I will hold McClellan's horse if he will only bring us success."[41]

The Reverend J. C. Richmond from the St. Elizabeth Hospital in Washington brought a group of recuperating veterans to see the President on May 22, 1863. As their chaplain, Rev. Richmond made a brief speech on behalf of his charges and declared that he was running the devil out of the Capital City. Many of these wounded soldiers were amputees and thus called themselves "The One-Legged Brigade." Although their tragic appearance certainly stirred a sympathetic chord in the President's being, Lincoln relieved the tension of the sad moment by replying with a few sprightly observations upon the Chaplain's boastful claims. Sprinkling his humor with religious connotations, Lincoln asked the Chaplain to inform him when he could present the devil "at the White House on his stumps, and therefore somewhat incapable of further rebellion against constituted and divine authority." In like vein, the Chaplain replied that "he would send him word when the funeral of that arch rebel and great secessionist was to take place."[42] Again, the President had adroitly combined tales of the Bible with the current political situation in the United States. Very cleverly, the President had employed a mirthful anecdote to cut through the tension of the moment and to point out the sinfulness of the rebellion against the legally elected President, duly inaugurated in Washington, D. C., who was trying to restore law and order as well as reunite the Union. Well did Lincoln know his remarks would be published by the press for the public to read.

After resolutions were passed by the Presbyterian General Assembly on May 27, 1863, John A. Foote of Cleveland, Ohio, presented them to President Lincoln on June 2. The Presbyterians had voted to support the Lincoln Administration; for this, the President was extremely grateful. In acknowledging these resolutions, Lincoln divulged that he had received similar testimonies from a number of Christian denominations. All of them, said Lincoln, claimed to be loyal, in some degree or other. That pleased the

President. From the very beginning of the war, Lincoln explained, "the issues of our great struggle depended on the Divine interposition and favor. If we had that, all would be well." "Relying, as I do, upon the Almighty Power, and encouraged as I am by these resolutions which you have just read, with the support which I receive from Christian men," promised Lincoln, "I shall not hesitate to use all the means at my control to secure the termination of this rebellion, and will hope for success."[43] Here, once more, the President expounded on his dependence upon the Divine will for success. It was never far from his mind.

As the Civil War raged on, Lincoln suffered greatly from the actions of his incompetent military officers. General Hooker could not defeat Lee at Chancellorsville, May 1-5, 1863. Brazenly bold, General Robert E. Lee now decided to actually invade the North! Just before the battle of Gettysburg started on July 1, Lincoln replaced Hooker with a little-known but distinguished leader from West Point, General George Gordon Meade. What commenced as an incidental brushing together of the two armies, turned out to be the greatest battle of the entire bloody war.

On July 2, Major General Daniel Edgar Sickles of New York, commanding the Third Corps of the Union forces, lost his right leg in the battle. After his limb was amputated just above the knee joint, General Sickles was transported directly to Washington, where he arrived on Sunday, July 5. He took up residence in a private dwelling located on F Street, across from the Ebbitt House. There, shortly after 3:00 p. m. on that same day, Lt. Col. James Fowler Rusling, a member of Sickle's staff, called to find how his chief was faring. He found him lying upon a hospital stretcher on the first floor of the house. Within a few minutes, none other than Abraham Lincoln—accompanied by Tad—appeared and was ushered into the front room where Sickles rested, calmly smoking a cigar while he combated the intense pain in what remained of his right leg. Years later, Sickles would be awarded the Medal of Honor for his heroic actions at Gettysburg.

After inquiring about Sickles' wound, the President questioned him concerning the fighting at Gettysburg which had ended in victory for the Union on July 3. After answering all of President Lincoln's military inquiries, General Sickles asked his Commander-in-Chief what he thought about Gettysburg. And here occurred a priceless private recitation of Lincoln's great belief that he was an instrument of God, acting in a holy cause. In answer to Sickles' query, "What was your opinion of things while we were campaigning and fighting up there?" Lincoln said calmly, "O, I didn't think much about it. I was not much concerned about you!" Sickles expressed amazement, telling the President that he had heard that Washington residents were greatly excited and fearful of the outcome. Lincoln admitted that many were scared the city might be captured and that some of the Cabinet even ordered a gunboat to escape from the Capital City. But Lincoln related that he told his Cabinet, "No, gentlemen, we are all right and we are going to win at Gettysburg." "No, General Sickles, I had no fear of Gettysburg!" When Sickles asked the President how he knew they would beat Lee, Lincoln divulged the answer but warned Sickles and Rusling not to repeat the story because "People might laugh if it got out, you know."

"But the fact is," confessed Lincoln, "in the very pinch of the campaign there, I went to my room one day and got down on my knees, and prayed Almighty God for victory at Gettysburg. I told Him that this was His country, and the war was His war, but that we really couldn't stand another Fredericksburg or Chancellorsville. And then and there I made a solemn vow with my Maker, that if He would stand by you boys at Gettysburg, I would stand by him." "And after thus wrestling with the Almighty in prayer, I don't know how it was, and it is not for me to explain," continued Lincoln, "but, somehow or other, a sweet comfort crept into my soul, that God Almighty had taken the whole business there into His own hands, and we were bound to win at Gettysburg!" "And He <u>did</u> stand by you boys at Gettysburg," exclaimed Lincoln, "and now I will <u>stand</u> <u>by</u> <u>Him</u>."

Lt. Col. Rusling thought Abraham Lincoln looked just like Moses must have when he came down from Mt. Sinai. He thought Lincoln solemn and very impressive as he related this tale to the two officers sitting there with him in a sick room at Washington.

After a little pause, General Sickles said, "Well, Mr. President, what are you thinking about Vicksburg, nowadays? How are things getting along down there?" Gravely, President Lincoln answered, "O, I don't quite know Grant is still pegging away down there. As we used to say out in Illinois, I think he 'will make a spoon or spoil a horn' before he gets through. Some of our folks think him slow and want me to remove him. But, to tell the truth, I kind of like U. S. Grant. He doesn't worry and bother me. He isn't shrieking for reinforcements all the time. He takes what troops we can safely give him, considering our big job in this war—and does the best he can with what he has got, and doesn't grumble and scold all the while. Yes, I confess, I like General

Grant—U. S. Grant—'Uncle Sam Grant!' [dwelling humorously on this last name]. There is a great deal to him, first and last. And, Heaven helping me, unless something happens more than I see now, I mean to stand by Grant a good while yet."

To this, General Sickles asked, "So, then, you have no fears about Vicksburg either, Mr. President?" "Well, no; I can't say that I have," replied Lincoln, soberly; "the fact is—but don't say anything about this either just now—I have been praying to Almighty God for Vicksburg also. I have wrestled with Him, and told Him how much we need the Mississippi, and how it ought to flow unvexed to the sea, and how the great valley ought to be forever free, and I reckon He understands the whole business down there, 'from A to Izzard.'" "Now," said Lincoln, "it is kind of borne in on me that somehow or other we are going to win at Vicksburg too. I can't tell how soon. But I believe we will." Such a victory would "be in line with God's laws besides," declared Lincoln.

Although the President did not know it at that time, Vicksburg had already surrendered to Grant on July 4. However, the telegraph did not get the message to Washington, D. C., until July 7. How prophetic Lincoln had been, and how steadfastly he had believed in the efficacy of prayer during these two momentous turning points in the long Civil War.

As President Lincoln prepared to take his leave, he shook General Sickles' hand and declared, "General, you will get well." In reply, Sickles expressed grave doubts and confided to the President that his physicians gave him but little hope for recovery. Brushing aside Sickles' pessimistic prognosis for an uncertain future, Lincoln exclaimed, "I am a prophet to-day general, and I say that you will get well, and that we will have glorious news from Vicksburg." Once again President Lincoln had proclaimed himself a prophet. General Sickles corroborated Colonel Rusling's account of this interview which the latter had written down at the time.[44]

Although this report could not have been word for word as Lincoln spoke to Sickles at the time, Rusling's careful attention to this momentous event in his life appears to be very accurate. The language attributed to Lincoln is certainly in keeping with his patterns of speech, even to the allusion of wrestling with God. He often used this expression, and in his youth, Lincoln had been a noted wrestler. Such accounts as this one show vividly the mystical relationship which Abraham Lincoln claimed he had with God.

Upon learning that Vicksburg had finally fallen to the force of Union arms, a large group of Washington citizens assembled on the evening of July

7 at the residence of the President, who, at the time, was sojourning at the Soldier's home because it was much cooler there. These jubilant townsmen were accompanied by a band, and all wanted to celebrate with Lincoln on this joyous happening. After expressing his gladness at seeing his well-wishers, Lincoln remarked, "I will not say I thank you for this call, but I do most sincerely thank Almighty God for the occasion on which you have called." Turning the conversation to politics, the President recalled that eighty-seven years ago a group of American representatives had assembled and declared as a self-evident truth that "all men are created equal." "That began our independence," said Lincoln, and since that first Fourth of July, several "peculiar recognitions" had taken place upon that very date. Both Thomas Jefferson and John Adams had died on July 4, 1826, Lincoln pointed out to his audience. Furthermore, James Monroe had also succumbed on July 4, 1831. Now, said Lincoln, two great victories have taken place on July 4: Gettysburg and Vicksburg. "The cohorts of those who opposed the declaration that all men are created equal, 'turned tail' and run," exclaimed the President. "Gentlemen," Lincoln told his listeners, "this is a glorious theme, and the occasion for a speech, but I am not prepared to make one worthy of the occasion." So, he called for the music to begin.[45] Abraham Lincoln knew the history of his country and used it to elucidate his firm belief in freedom. As Lincoln had told Congress on December 1, 1862, "we cannot escape history."[46] Yet, Lincoln began this impromptu address to the crowd assembled about him on July 7 by thanking "Almighty God" for providing the occasion for their rejoicing that evening. Again, Lincoln referred only to God.

As soon as Lincoln could find time in his hectic schedule, he composed a formal Proclamation of Thanksgiving on July 15, 1863. Quite naturally, as was his habit, the President began by saying, "It has pleased Almighty God to hearken to the supplications and prayers of an afflicted people, and to vouchsafe to the army and the navy on the United States victories on land and on the sea so signal and so effective as to furnish reasonable grounds for augmented confidence that the Union of these States will be maintained, their constitution persevered, and the peace and prosperity permanently restored." Therefore, Lincoln announced that he had set apart Thursday, August 6, as a day of National Thanksgiving, Praise and Prayer. He invited "the People of the United States to assemble on that occasion in their customary places of worship, and in the forms approved by their own consciences, render the homage due to the Divine Majesty, for the wonderful things [H]e has done in the Nation's behalf, and invoke the influence of His Holy Spirit to subdue the anger, which has produced, and so long sustained a needless and cruel rebellion, to change the hearts of the insurgents, to guide the counsels of the Government with wisdom adequate to so great a national emergency, and to visit with tender care and consolation throughout the length and breadth of our land all those who, through the vicissitudes of marches, voyages, battles and sieges, have been brought to suffer in mind, body or estate, and finally to lead the whole nation, through the paths of repentance and submission to the Divine Will, back to the perfect enjoyment of Union and fraternal peace."[47]

Although President Lincoln deeply regretted that General Meade had not followed up his victory at Gettysburg and pursued the wily Lee until the latter surrendered, he gradually began to feel more sanguine about the Union victory at Gettysburg. By Sunday, July 19, 1863, Lincoln was in an effervescent frame of mind, and his spirits soared in a more hopeful mood. He sat down at his desk and composed a whimsical piece of doggerel. Lincoln had not written poetry—that we know of—since 1858, and his earlier verses had been mostly in the melancholy style of William Knox or Robert Burns. But now he poked fun at Robert E. Lee and dashed off a piece, pretending that it had been composed by the defeated Confederate General Lee:

Verses on Lee's Invasion of the North
Gen. Lee[']s invasion of the North written by himself—

In eighteen sixty three, with pomp,
and mighty swell,
Me and Jeff's Confederacy, went
forth to sack Phil-del,
The Yankees they got arter us, and
giv us particular hell,
And we skedaddled back again,
and didn't sack Phil-del.

President Lincoln does not seem to have been in church on this day that he dashed off these rhymes for the amusement of himself and John Hay. Nevertheless, he remembered his own proclamation for observing a day of thanksgiving and the next month asked Hay to accompany him on August 6 to hear Dr. Byron Sunderland at the First Presbyterian Church on 4 1/2 Street, between C and Louisiana Avenue. Upon arriving at their destination, they learned that this gifted theologian was away from his pulpit, so the President and Hay continued on to the New York Avenue Presbyterian Church were they heard Dr. Gurley preach. Hay thought Gurley gave an unusually strong prayer and message in favor of the Union. Perhaps, he surmised, the recent Union military successes had greatly strengthened Dr. Gurley's support of the Government at Washington.[48]

Without doubt, many citizens of Washington anxiously waited to see if the President had attended a place of worship on this national day of thanksgiving. Those who did were not disappointed. The religious Abraham Lincoln had once more joined them in thanking his Maker for the bounty bestowed upon them all.

Although Abraham Lincoln had once stated publicly that he was "not, nor ever have been in favor of bringing about in any way the social and political equality of the white and black races,"[49] he always treated the blacks with respect and understanding. And of course, slavery was anathema to him. When on August 21, 1863, a committee of Negro Baptist ministers representing the American Baptist Missionary Convention, which was then meeting at the First Colored Baptist Church, called upon the President with a request, Lincoln listened politely to them and granted their wishes with a military order. "To-day I am called upon by a committee of colored ministers of the Gospel, who express a wish to go within our military lines and minister to their brethren there," explained the Commander-in-Chief. "The object is a worthy one," declared Lincoln, "and I shall be glad for all facilities to be afforded them which may not be inconsistent with or a hindrance to our military operations."[50] Lincoln could well have ignored the request, since members of their race had little political power, but the President showed little prejudice against them where religion was concerned. We must always judge Abraham Lincoln by the standards of his era; in his time, he was a radical when he so early advocated freeing the slaves. Most of the men who enlisted in the Federal armed forces did so to preserve the Union—not to free the Negroes.

Upon being asked to address a gathering of unconditional Union men at Springfield, Illinois, on September 3, 1863, President Lincoln composed a long message for the occasion on August 26, and sent it off to James C. Conkling, explaining that he could not personally leave Washington at that time. During this mass meeting at the Springfield fairgrounds, Lincoln's letter was read to the crowd. It was published widely in the press and thus influenced national opinion. In ending his communication, Lincoln stated that peace did not appear so distant as it had previously. Yet, he cautioned, "Let us not be over-sanguine of a speedy final triumph. Let us be quite sober. Let us diligently apply the means, never doubting that a just God, in his own good time, will give us the rightful result."[51] Here, again, Lincoln publicly expressed his belief that God was the final arbiter in all matters. It was He who would end the war.

On October 3, 1863, President Lincoln issued a Proclamation for Thanksgiving to be observed on the last Thursday of November, the 26th. He pointed out that we are prone to forget from whom our bounties come. Every heart, he thought, should be softened and sensible "to the ever watchful providence of Almighty God." "No human counsel hath devised nor hath any mortal hand worked out these great things," Lincoln proclaimed. "They are the gracious gifts of the Most High God, who, while dealing with us in anger for our sins, hath nevertheless remembered mercy," the President pointed out. These Godly blessings "should be solemnly, reverently and gratefully acknowledged as with one heart and one voice by the whole American People," Lincoln declared. At this Thanksgiving Day, the public should praise the beneficent Father who dwelt in Heaven. Also, the loyal citizens of the Union should offer their ascription to Him for deliverances and blessings and ask His tender care for widows, orphans, mourners or sufferers. They should "feverently implore the interposition of the Almighty Hand to heal the wounds of the nation and to restore it as soon as may be consistent with the Divine purposes to the full enjoyment of peace, harmony, tranquillity and Union."[52] With his devout religious suggestions, the President had practically outlined suitable prayers for the ministers to employ when they spoke to their congregations. Certainly these recommendations were eloquent. They read like words in a sermon.

Charles Daniel Drake (1811-1892), and a delegation from Missouri, called upon Lincoln on September 30, 1863, and complained about General John McAllister Schofield's administration of affairs in their home state, among other things. To restrain spies for the Confederacy and prevent trade with the enemy, a system of levies upon known Rebels was being employed. In commenting on this specific procedure, President Lincoln admitted that "Agents to execute it, contrary to the great [Lord's] Prayer, were led into temptation. Some might, while others would not resist that temptation." Some lined their pockets, the President acknowledged.[53] Here is a clear reference by

President Lincoln to Christ's teachings. And yet, he did not actually inscribe the Savior's name in this written reply to the Missouri delegation on October 5. Again, Lincoln often alluded to the principles and philosophy expounded by Jesus Christ in the New Testament without acknowledging Him as the source of the quotation or citation. However, his audience made the connection easily since most of them had read the Bible, at least in their youth. But it seems clear that Lincoln did not put Christ on the same footing as he did Almighty God. The latter was the one he worshipped and prayed to.

When representatives of the Presbyterian Synod of Pennsylvania (New School) paid their respects to President Lincoln on October 22, 1863, he received them in the East Room of the White House. Lincoln told them that he could only do his duty if God assisted him and supplied the necessary means to carry out his mission. "If God be with us," he declared, "we will succeed; if not, we will fail." These Presbyterians assured the President of their loyalty and support.[54]

Just two days later, at 2:00 p. m., Dr. Phineas D. Gurley—pastor to the Lincolns—escorted the Moderator, Dr. Septimus Tustin, and delegates from the Presbyterian Synod of Baltimore (Old School), to the Executive Mansion and introduced these men to Lincoln. After thanking them for their support, the President expounded briefly upon his own faith. "Without the direct assistance of the Almighty," confessed Lincoln, "I was certain of failure." "I sincerely wish that I was a more devoted man than I am," he confessed. "Sometimes in my difficulties I have been driven to the last resort to say God is still my only hope. It is still all the world to me," he admitted. He thanked them for coming and said that "in the name of our common Father" he appreciated their encouragement and succor.[55] It should be noted that Lincoln referred to "our common Father," meaning the one and only Almighty God, by whatever name He might be called. There was no mention of Christ in these cogent remarks to those men of the cloth. By declaring his hope was in God, Lincoln voiced the motto of the Scottish Rite Masons who proclaim Spes Mea in Deo Est, "My hope is in God." However, Lincoln never joined the Masonic Fraternity, although many of his friends were members of the Craft, and he quite naturally picked up the phrases and words used by Freemasons.[56]

A close study of Lincoln reveals that he often suffered from fits of gloom and hopelessness. In April of 1862, Lincoln told a personal friend that he was "not of a very hopeful temperament." But in the next breath he disclosed his remedy: he was "relying on God for help" and believed that the

Union cause was right. Furthermore, he stated that "It has pleased Almighty God to place me in my present position, and looking up to Him for wisdom and divine guidance I must work my destiny as best I can."[57]

Lincoln sometimes suffered from severe depression and often his legendary humor helped save his very being. Even supreme successes oft-times brought him but scant happiness. "Being elected to Congress, though I am very grateful to our friends, for having done it," Lincoln revealed in 1846, "has not pleased me as much as I expected."[58] He told J. G. Nicolay in 1860 "that for personal considerations I would rather have a full term in the Senate—a place in which I would feel more consciously able to discharge the duties required, and where there was more chance to make a reputation and less chance of losing it—than four years in the presidency."[59] In addition to Lincoln's severe ups and downs, he remained a fatalist. What would be, would be. However, he had a saving grace which counteracted these problems. He informed a man once that he could "take hold of a thing and hold on a good while."[60] Indeed, for perseverance, he had few equals. Once Lincoln started a project, he generally finished it, no matter what the cost, social or political.

Most of Washington gossiped excitedly about the coming social event of the year. Katherine Jane Chase (Aug. 13, 1840-July 31, 1899), the oldest daughter of Secretary Salmon Portland Chase—thrice a widower—was scheduled to marry Senator William Sprague (Sept. 12, 1831-Sept. 11, 1915), on the evening of November 12, 1863. Senator Sprague, a rich young man, had already served as Governor of Rhode Island before entering the United States Senate that year. He was a handsome fellow, and the vivacious "Kate" Chase reigned as a social queen in her own salon at Washington. It seemed that all the country followed her every movement and dress style. She competed with Mary Lincoln for the most distinguished guest list, etc. A talented slender beauty of just twenty-three years, "Kate" had light auburn hair, white skin and large hazel eyes. Since the tender age of sixteen, she had acted as her illustrious father's hostess. In marked contrast, Mary (Todd) Lincoln was now almost forty-five, quite plump and motherly in appearance. Both ladies waded up to their ears in politics, with "Kate" laboring unceasingly to promote her father into the White House over the second-term claims of Abraham Lincoln. Quite naturally, Mary Lincoln disliked and distrusted the competitive "Kate" Chase. Like Mary Lincoln, "Kate" had studied French and had attended fashionable academies. "Kate" even went to New York City for schooling before enrolling in Heyl's Seminary at Columbus, Ohio, where she majored in music and languages. Over the years, however, Mary Lincoln had forgotten most of the French which she had once used. Not "Kate." It was still fresh in her mind, and she entertained the members of the foreign embassies regularly.

Although the nuptials were scheduled for 8:30 p. m. in her father's mansion at the corner of Sixth and E streets, distinguished guests began arriving an hour early to find a choice seat. After all, five hundred invitations had been issued, and Secretary Chase had spent $4,000 for this grand affair—money, by the way, that he could not afford to spend. Of course, President Lincoln had received one of the coveted bids. He donned his best dress suit and a white cravat. But nothing could persuade Mary Lincoln to accompany him. She declared that she was still in mourning for Willie "and had an opportune chill betimes." So, alone, the President arrived at the Chase residence promptly at 8:30. Inside, he joined Seward, Stanton, Usher, Welles, Blair and Bates of his Cabinet. When the dividing doors to an adjoining room were thrown open, there stood the lovely bride in a white velvet dress with a full train, white lace veil, and a tiara of diamonds and pearls on her pretty head. Indeed, she no doubt thought of herself as the social queen of Washington.

Thomas March Clark of Rhode Island then stepped forward and united the famous couple in holy wedlock using the full Episcopal service. This was at least the second time the President had seen this particular Anglican in a religious setting. And once more he witnessed the Episcopal ritual of marriage. A formal reception followed the stately ceremony. It lasted from 9 to 12 with dancing on the first floor and an impressive banquet on the second. For this auspicious occasion, none other than the U. S. Marine Band played. "To take the cuss off" and make up for Mary Lincoln's most conspicuous absence, the President remained for two and a half hours and seemed to enjoy himself with the principals and the noted guests. Yet, Father Abraham refrained from dancing with any of the attractive ladies.[61] If he had, Mary Lincoln's anger would have known no bounds when she heard of it. She was even particular about whom he conversed with at such elegant parties. On the other hand, Mary could sometimes be seen dancing with other men. One might easily say that there was very little "Christian Charity" in her makeup where her husband and other women were concerned.

More important matters faced Lincoln in November of 1863. In Gettysburg, there remained the problem of the many dead left strewn about the battlefield. Finally, the Northern States formed a commission to see to the burial of their valiant soldiers at a suitable spot near where they had fallen. Thus came about the Soldiers' National Cemetery.

Pennsylvania Governor Andrew Gregg Curtin, quite naturally, took the lead in this gigantic endeavor. He insisted upon a proper consecration of the burial site and named David Wills of Gettysburg, his agent—a position of great responsibility—to accomplish this purpose. As the plans matured, President Lincoln was invited, in person, to attend the ceremonies. David Wills then followed this up with a written invitation on November 2. Edward Everett, he explained, would deliver the main oration, but he petitioned Lincoln to "formally set apart these grounds to their Sacred use by a few appropriate remarks."

In conning over Wills' letter, President Lincoln quickly determined exactly what was expected of him. In fact, Lincoln perhaps used this invitation as a sort of outline for the type of speech he would make. It must be short and yet have a deeply religious tone for the dedication of these hallowed acres. No doubt he thought for several days about what he would say before even putting pencil to paper. All his constituents, he rightly knew, would be watching and listening to his "few appropriate remarks." His address must be a very polished and memorable communication. Everett would give the long flowery history of the battle, but Lincoln would be expected to preach a requiem over the newly-dug graves of the brave men in blue who had given their lives for the preservation of the Union.

Lincoln began to compose his vital message several days before he left for Gettysburg. His first draft is on Executive Mansion stationery, proving that he did not merely jot it down in a few minutes on the back of an envelope while bouncing along on the train. Rather, it was born from many hours of thought and careful revision. It turned out to be unlike any of Lincoln's many little extemporaneous talks given both before and after Gettysburg. However, he did express, extemporaneously, one of the thoughts in response to a serenade on July 7, 1863. Said Lincoln: "How long ago is it?—eighty odd years—since on the Fourth of July for the first time in the history of the world a nation by its representatives, assembled and declared as a self-evident truth that 'all men are created equal.'" How different this small thesis became when President Lincoln polished it and refined it on paper.

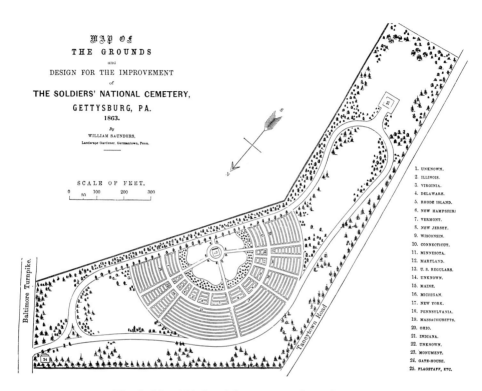

The Soldiers' National Cemetery at Gettysburg.
William Saunders' design of The Soldiers' National Cemetery at Gettysburg,
Pennsylvania, 1863.
Copied from Judge David Wills' own copy of the proceedings,
now owned by Michael J. McKee.

Note:
The following two pages include the second page of Abraham Lincoln's
actual reading copy of his Gettysburg Address and his signature as it appears on
the reading copy. Note the inserted words "under God."

The original is owned by Dr. Lloyd Ostendorf of Dayton, Ohio.

When Judge David Wills asked the President for his original manuscript on
November 23, 1863, Lincoln complied with his request. As asked, Lincoln also
appended his certificate to the document. Note that Lincoln identified the manuscript
exactly as he did House bills when he sat in the Illinois General Assembly.
The manuscript had been folded in fourths—just like his old House bills in the
Legislature! It also fit easily into his coat pocket.

for us to be here dedicated to the great task remaining before us— that from these honored dead we take increased devotion to that cause for which they here gave the last full measure of devotion—, that we here highly resolve that these dead shall not have died in vain; that this nation, under God shall have a new birth of freedom; and that this government of the people, by the people, for the people, shall not perish from the earth.

For Hon Judge
David Wills
from
A Lincoln
Nov 19, 1863

The keystone to Abraham Lincoln's political creed was Freedom. His touchstone for testing everything dealing with Freedom was the Declaration of Independence. "I have never had a feeling politically," declared Lincoln, "that did not spring from the sentiments embodied in the Declaration of Independence."[62] And in this setting, President Lincoln commenced writing his immortal Gettysburg Address. Being an inveterate reader of the Bible, his first sentence is styled after the method of calculating time as found in Psalm 90:10 which says, "The days of our years are threescore and ten; and if by reason of strength they be fourscore years . . . ." From these beautiful and lyrical words of the old King James version of the Holy Scriptures, Lincoln started his requiem for the dead. But it had to inspire the living, too, since funerals are really for the quick more than the dead. Another of Lincoln's basic beliefs was patriotism for one's country and its history. His inspirational message would have to play upon the "mystic chords of memory, stretching from every battle-field, and patriot grave, to every living heart and hearthstone, all over this broad land" so as to "swell the chorus of the Union."[63]

With this address partially completed, Lincoln scrutinized the timetable for his train trip to Gettysburg as planned by the War Department. The President rejected the schedule immediately. "I do not like this arrangement," complained Lincoln. "I do not wish to so go that by the slightest accident we fail entirely, and, at the best, the whole to be a mere breathless running of the gauntlet," he scolded Stanton.[64] Lincoln fully realized the importance of his part in the ceremony, and he wanted to let the whole world hear his remarks through the medium of the press. He did not wish to miss this important engagement whereby he hoped to inspire the public to an even greater war effort on behalf of the Federal Government as well as bury its heroes with fitting dignity. Lincoln probably also wished to view portions of the great battlefield.

After approving a revised and more feasible travel plan, Lincoln implored and "strongly urged" the members of his Cabinet to accompany him to Gettysburg. However, Bates decided he simply "could not go," and Welles felt "compelled to decline" because he "could not spare the time."[65] Evidently they did not think this dedication was as important as Lincoln did, nor did Chase or Stanton want to go. Taking Seward, Usher and Blair with him—as well as his private secretaries, Nicolay and Hay—the President departed from Washington at noon on November 18 aboard a special train consisting of four cars. Among those going along were the Marine Band, some foreign dignitaries, and a special escort from the First Regiment of the Invalid Corps. Amidst the members of the famous Marine Band was a trombonist by the name of Antonio Sousa. His son was none other than John Philip Sousa (1854-1932) who would later command this same band and become one of the greatest musicians the world has ever known. Certainly Antonio described his trip with President Lincoln to his nine-year-old son, John. The Marine Band frequently played for the President, and Antonia Sousa must have seen the President quite often.

For the first leg of the journey, the Baltimore & Ohio Railroad furnished the locomotive and crew, with Reuben Kepp operating Engine No. 236. When the Presidential Special reached Baltimore at 2:00 p. m., the cars were switched over to the Northern Central Railroad where another engine was coupled to them and more dignitaries clambered aboard the train. A baggage car, which had been fitted up as a diner, was also added at this point.

With Lincoln was his personal servant, William H. Johnson, a black man who held employment at the Treasury Department as a laborer and messenger. He has previously received scant attention in the telling of this tale, and even been misidentified. But he certainly made the trip more pleasant for the President who treated him more like a friend than a valet. Finally, at 6:30 p. m., the special train pulled into Gettysburg. Lincoln and Johnson were taken immediately to the home of David Wills where they would spend the night.[66] During his stay there, the President finished his address, polished it through two drafts and wrote out a clean copy to take with him to the dedication ceremonies. The second page of the final copy has finally surfaced and is owned by Dr. Lloyd Ostendorf of Dayton, Ohio.[67]

November 19 turned out to be a bright and beautiful sunny day at Gettysburg with the maximum temperature reaching 52 degrees. This little town of approximately 2,500 residents was crowded to overflowing with perhaps as many as 15,000 people who had come on special trains from long distances or in private conveyances from the surrounding areas. Dressed in a plain black suit and wearing a black band of mourning on his top hat, and with white, kid, riding gauntlets on his large hands, President Lincoln mounted "a beautiful bay charger." His horse had most probably been provided by Quartermaster Captain Henry Bloyden Blood who furnished mounts for other dignitaries that day.

Mounted in style, Lincoln joined the funeral-like parade out to the cemetery. At 12 o'clock he climbed onto the 12' x 20' temporary platform and took his seat in the middle of the front row amidst a thunderous applause from the vast crowd assembled about him. Out of sincere respect for Lincoln, the men immediately removed their hats, and the ladies gave him their undivided attention when he appeared. Many unprejudiced women thought of Lincoln as a handsome, virile male.[68]

Commander-in-Chief Lincoln had analyzed the event correctly. It would be patterned like a funeral service. And it would have a very religious air to it. Birgfield's Band from Philadelphia opened the consecration of the burial grounds with a dirge. The Rev. Dr. Thomas Hewlings Stockton (1808-1868) then arose and gave a long prayer. He had started his career as a physician after graduating from Jefferson Medical College. Yet he soon became a minister, being ordained in the Methodist Church. Dr. Stockton followed an extremely anti-slavery bent even while he edited a Methodist journal. When he was not allowed to express his sincere beliefs against slavery, he quit and organized his own independent, non-sectarian congregation. He was now the Chaplain of the United States Senate and a most talented orator. In greatly embellished language, Dr. Stockton read a long impressive eulogy saluting the fallen soldiers who had given their precious lives to save mankind. He also noted that the Chief Magistrate of the Nation would soon reply with an "honest tribute" to them. He reminded his listeners that the honored dead had shown their "devotion to liberty, religion, and God."

Prayer of Rev. Dr. Stockton

O God our Father, for the sake of Thy Son our Saviour, inspire us with Thy Spirit, and sanctify us to the right fulfillment of the duties of this occasion.

We come to dedicate this new historic centre as a National Cemetery. If all departments of the one government which Thou has ordained over our Union, and of the many governments which Thou has subordinated to our Union, be here represented,—if all classes, relations, and interests of our blended brotherhood of people stand severally and thoroughly apparent in Thy presence,—we trust that it is because Thou hast called us, that Thy blessing awaits us, and that Thy designs may be embodied in practical results of the incalculable and imperishable good.

And so, with Thy holy Apostle, and with the Church of all lands and ages, we unite in the ascription, "Blessed be God, even the Father of our Lord Jesus Christ, the Father of mercies, and the God of all comfort, who comforteth us in all our tribulation, that we may be able to comfort them which are in any trouble, by the comfort wherewith we ourselves are comforted by God."

In emulation of all angels, in fellowship with all saints, and in sympathy with all sufferers, in remembrance of Thy works, in reverence of Thy ways, and in accordance with Thy word, we laud and magnify Thine infinite perfections, Thy creative glory, Thy redeeming grace, Thy providential goodness, and the progressively richer and fairer developments of Thy supreme, universal, and everlasting administration.

In behalf of all humanity, whose ideal is divine, whose first memory is Thine image lost, and whose last hope is Thine image restored, and especially of our own nation, whose history has been so favored, whose position is so peerless, whose mission is so sublime, and whose future is so attractive, we thank Thee for the unspeakable patience of Thy compassion and the exceeding greatness of Thy loving-kindness. In contemplation of Eden, Calvary, and Heaven, of Christ in the Garden, on the Cross, and on the Throne, nay, more, of Christ as coming again in all-subduing power and glory, we gratefully prolong our homage. By this Altar of Sacrifice, on this Field of Deliverance, on this Mount of Salvation, within the fiery and bloody line of these "munitions of rocks," looking back to the dark days of fear and trembling, and to the rapture of relief that came after, we multiply our thanksgivings, and confess our obligations to renew and perfect our personal and social consecration to Thy service and glory.

Oh, had it not been for God! For lo! our enemies, they came unresisted, multitudinous, mighty, flushed with victory, and sure of success. They exulted on our mountains, they reveled in our valleys; they feasted, they rested; they slept, they awaked; they grew stronger, prouder, bolder, every day; they spread abroad, they concentrated here; they looked beyond this horizon to the stores of wealth, to the haunts of pleasure, and to the seats of power in our capital and chief cities. They prepared to cast the chain of Slavery around the form of

Freedom, binding life and death together forever. Their premature triumph was the mockery of God and man. One more victory, and all was theirs! But behind these hills was heard the feebler march of a smaller, but still pursuing host. Onward they hurried, day and night, for God and their country. Foot-sore, wayworn, hungry, thirsty, faint,—but not in heart,—they came to dare all, to bear all, and to do all that is possible to heroes. And Thou didst sustain them! At first they met the blast on the plain, and bent before it like the trees in a storm. But then, led by Thy hand to these hills, they took their stand upon the rocks and remained as firm and immovable as they. In vain were they assaulted. All art, all violence, all desperation, failed to dislodge them. Baffled, bruised, broken, their enemies recoiled, retired and disappeared. Glory to God for this rescue! But oh, the slain! In the freshness and fullness of their young and manly life, with such sweet memories of father and mother, brother and sister, wife and children, maiden and friends, they died for us. From the coasts beneath the Eastern star, from the shores of Northern lakes and rivers, from the flowers of Western prairies, and from the homes of the Midway and the Border, they came here to die for us and for mankind. Alas, how little we can do for them! We come with the humility of prayer, with the pathetic eloquence of venerable wisdom, with the tender beauty of poetry, with the plaintive harmony of music, with the honest tribute of our Chief Magistrate, and with all this honorable attendance: but our best hope is in thy blessing, O Lord, our God! O Father, bless us! Bless the bereaved, whether present or absent; bless our sick and wounded soldiers and sailors; bless all our rulers and people; bless our army and navy; bless the efforts for the suppression of the rebellion; and bless all the associations of this day and place and scene forever. As the trees are not dead, though their foliage is gone, so our heroes are not dead, though their forms have fallen. In their proper personality they are all with Thee. And the spirit of their example is here. It fills the air; it fills our hearts. And, long as time shall last, it will hover in these skies and rest on this landscape; and the pilgrims of our own land, and from all lands, will thrill with its inspiration, and increase and confirm their devotion to liberty, religion, and God.

Our Father, who art in heaven, hallowed be Thy name, Thy kingdom come. Thy will be done on earth as it is in heaven.

Give us this day our daily bread. And forgive us our debts, as we forgive our debtors. Lead us not into temptation, but deliver us from evil. For Thine is the kingdom, the power, and the glory, forever. Amen.

When he closed, he had spoken at least a thousand words. John Hay confided to his diary that this minister had "made a prayer which thought it was an oration."[69] But it was in keeping with the intended length of the program. Next, a band played the hymn "Old Hundred."

After a few announcements, the Hon. Edward Everett (1794-1865) was introduced by Benjamin Brown French—an Aide to the Chief Marshal. Then Everett stepped forward to give his oration, the main speech of the day. It was well past noon when he began. A renowned scholar, Everett had graduated from Harvard, studied theology and been ordained in the Unitarian Church. He had taught Greek at Harvard and even been its President before launching off in a career of politics which carried him to Congress, to the Governor's chair in Massachusetts, to be the successor to Daniel Webster as Secretary of State in Washington, D. C., and finally into the United States Senate. He had favored Bell in the election of 1860 but was to become an elector for President Lincoln in 1864. With his theological background, Dr. Everett—the first American to receive a Ph.D. from the University of Göttingen (in 1817)—launched into an eloquent dissertation which was sprinkled with religious meaning. He outlined the battle, its causes and the objectives of the Civil War. He ended nearly two hours later with a benediction over the sacrificed dead who lay just behind the speaking platform. It had been a masterful performance, closely listened to by the President. Yet, when Everett died on January 15, 1865, Lincoln asked an intimate friend, "What great work of Everett do you remember?" When this New Englander could not recall any, Lincoln retorted, "Now, do you know, I think Edward Everett was very much overrated. He hasn't left any enduring monument."[70]

Next, the National Union Musical Association of Baltimore sang a dirge which had been composed especially for this occasion by the many-talented Major Benjamin Brown French (1800-1870), the Commissioner of Public Buildings in Washington and the Past Grand Master of Freemasons in the District of Columbia as well as the then current Grand Master of all the Knights Templar in the United States, the latter a Christian fraternity.

HYMN.
Composed by B. B. French, Esq. at Gettysburg

Tis holy ground—
This spot, where, in their graves,
We place our country's braves,
Who fell in Freedom's holy cause,
Fighting for liberties and laws;
Let tears abound.

Here let them rest;
And summer's heat and winter's cold
Shall glow and freeze above this mould—
A thousand years shall pass away—
A nation still shall mourn this clay,
Which now is blest.

Here, where they fell,
Oft shall the widow's tear be shed,
Oft shall fond parents mourn their dead;
The orphan here shall kneel and weep,
And maidens, where their lovers sleep,
Their woes shall tell.

Great God in Heaven!
Shall all this sacred blood be shed?
Shall we thus mourn our glorious dead?
Oh, shall the end be wrath and woe,
The knell of Freedom's overthrow,
A country riven?

It will not be!
We trust, O God! thy gracious power
To aid us in our darkest hour.
This be our prayer—"O Father! save
A people's freedom from its grave.
All praise to Thee!"

When this glee club finished singing, Col. Ward Hill Lamon (1828-
1893), as the Chief Marshal for the dedication program and the U. S. Marshal
for the District of Columbia, arose and introduced Lincoln with one simple
sentence: "The President will now make a few remarks." This great honor fell

to Lamon not only because of his official capacity that day but also because he was Lincoln's "particular friend."[71] A large burly man, Col. Lamon was perceived by some as a vulgar person, and he may have been one of the least religious ones on the dais, yet he was completely devoted to Lincoln, even to the point of leaving Everett's name off the program and merely printing "Oration" at the point where Everett was to speak.

President Lincoln sidled to the front of the platform. His extreme height shocked one Union officer who stood within one hundred feet of the stand. Lincoln, he wrote the following day, "towered above everybody on the platform." "After he stood," reported this close observer, Lincoln "reached inside his coat pocket and removed t[w]o large papers and a pair of spectacles." Back on March 4, 1861, when Lincoln gave his First Inaugural Address, Senator Stephen A. Douglas had held the President-elect's top hat, but now if anybody took charge of his "tile" and riding gloves, it was probably either his attendant, William H. Johnson, or Brig. Gen. James Barnet Fry, the military aide assigned to him that day by Secretary Stanton.[72]

After adjusting his glasses, Lincoln began to speak. The Union officer mentioned above was surprised. "You would not expect a voice from one so big to be so high pitched, but so very clear," he divulged in a letter to his wife. "He looked so very sad and deep in thought like his mind was some where else," this officer observed. It was apparent that Lincoln had mostly memorized his words for the consecration of the cemetery. He only referred to his sheets once, vouched this officer. Another observer said Lincoln looked at his message only once and returned it to his pocket. Thus it is easy to explain why his words were slightly different from those on his reading copy. According to a reporter who captured only part of the declamation in shorthand, President Lincoln said:

> Four score and seven years ago our fathers brought forth
> upon his continent a new nation, conceived in liberty and
> dedicated to the proposition that all men are created equal.
> [Applause.] Now, we are engaged in a great civil war, testing
> whether that nation, or any other nation so conceived and so
> dedicated can long endure. We are met on a great battlefield
> of that war; we are met to dedicate a portion of it as the final
> resting-place of those who here gave their lives that the
> nation might live. It is altogether fitting and proper that we
> should do this. But, in a larger sense, we cannot dedicate, we
> cannot consecrate, we cannot hallow this ground. The brave

men, living and dead, who struggled here have consecrated it far above our poor power to add or detract. [Applause.] The world will little note nor long remember what we may say here, but it can never forget what they did here. [Applause.] It is for us, the living, rather to be dedicated here to the unfinished work that they have thus far so nobly carried on. [Applause.] It is rather for us here to be dedicated here to the great task remaining before us; that from these honored dead we take increased devotion to that cause for which they here gave the last full devotion; that we here highly resolve that those dead shall not have died in vain. [Applause.] That the nation shall under God, have a new birth of freedom; and that Government of the people, by the people and for the people, shall not perish from the earth. [Long continued applause.][73]

Joseph L. Gilbert, the Associated Press correspondent who sent out the above text on the wire service, had been on the ground just in front of the speakers, but he became so absorbed in Lincoln's cogent remarks that he neglected to take down all of the President's words in shorthand. So, at the end of the dedication he borrowed the President's own reading copy in order to correct or add to his incomplete notes. Once compiled, Gilbert dispatched his hybrid version over the telegraph line. Many newspapers subscribed to the AP service, but what they received was not exactly what Lincoln had actually uttered. Lincoln spoke from memory, but Gilbert neglected to record each spoken word.

If Gilbert failed to catch Lincoln's address in full, how could he have had time to insert—while Lincoln spoke—all of those references to "applause" on his copy before releasing it? Years later, he admitted that he hadn't had time, that he had fabricated the notations. This was an old journalistic trick; reporters merely scattered the word "applause" throughout any speech they were covering.

That Union officer who heard Lincoln and wrote to his wife the next day, testified that there was a "slight applause after he [Lincoln] took his seat." This missive is in private hands and has never been quoted previously. Such contemporary reports are more to be believed than reminiscences written years later.

Eyewitnesses corroborate the account written by that Union officer on the day following Lincoln's Gettysburg Address. Clark E. Carr, the Gettysburg Agent representing the State of Illinois, had a seat on the platform. He recalled that it was "the invariable custom in those days" to simply add the word "applause" to any speech. "I did not observe it," testified Carr, "and at the close the applause was not especially marked." William Yates Selleck, Gettysburg Agent for the State of Wisconsin, sat upon the speaking stand with Lincoln. He, too, insisted that "It has been repeatedly published that the address was received by the assembled multitude with loud demonstrations of approval. Such was not the case."

There may be a very plausible explanation for the light applause. Another eyewitness recalled that "Mr. Lincoln's sad face and the solemnity of the occasion, seemed to forbid any excessive demonstration."

President Lincoln's address would read so much better than it sounded at its original oral presentation. It was so short that the tired audience did not have time to savor it fully. Lincoln sensed the non-exuberance of his listeners. John Palmer Usher, Secretary of the Interior, also occupied a chair very near to Lincoln when he spoke at Gettysburg. Usher related that President Lincoln "was disappointed with the apparent indifference with which the assemblage received his remarks."

As soon as he returned to his seat, Lincoln whispered to the Chief Parade Marshal, "Lamon, that speech won't *scour*! It is a flat failure, and the people are disappointed." Using an old farmer's expression, Lincoln referred to the fact that if a plowshare and moldboard are rusty on a plow, the earth will not pass smoothly over them, and a proper furrow cannot be turned.

Actually, President Lincoln had prepared his short message with much care. He had delivered it very well and with great composure, except when he pronounced, "The world will little note nor long remember what we may say here, but it can never forget what they did here." At this point, his "lips quivered, and there was a tremor in his voice."

For various purposes, Lincoln later indited three more copies of his Gettysburg Address, each one slightly different. The speech, in its various versions, would quickly be accepted as perhaps the world's greatest example of English prose. Certainly, however, the most important early manuscript change which he made was the addition of the phrase "under God." He put that insertion in the third draft—his reading copy—before leaving the Wills house for the dedication ceremonies. Back on July 4, when he personally announced the Union success at Gettysburg, he had said, "And that for this," the President "especially desires that on this day, He whose will, not ours, should ever be done, be everywhere remembered and reverenced with

Photo Courtesy of Adams County Historical Society

John Lawrence Burns was privileged to accompany President Lincoln
and Secretary Seward to the Presbyterian Church at Gettysburg
late on the afternoon of November 19, 1863.

Photo by Alto and Hilda Sneller

Presbyterian Church at Gettysburg, Pennsylvania.

In this Presbyterian Church at Gettysburg, Abraham Lincoln sat after making his famous Gettysburg Address previously that afternoon, November 19, 1863.

profoundest gratitude."[74] This small yet vital insert onto his reading copy—just recently discovered—certainly was in keeping with the religious tone of the entire ceremony and Lincoln's true gratitude to God for His manifold blessings.

Knowing Abraham Lincoln's obvious obsession with death, he probably gleaned several historical facts when he took his announced tour of the battle site in the early hours that November morning. Troopers from Illinois' Eighth Cavalry had fired the first shots in the battle of Gettysburg. They had run into elements of General A. P. Hill's Confederate soldiers on the very first day of the battle. Lincoln would also have discovered that three Illinois soldiers lay interred in the burial area just behind where he would speak. Eventually, three more bodies of Illinois warriors would be identified and entombed there by 1864, bringing the total number to six. At the time of the dedication there were 1,188 graves in this necropolis, arranged in a semi-circle.[75] This fact must have been in his thoughts as he addressed the huge crowd which had grown restless during Everett's long oration.

That Union officer previously quoted who was present at this immortal occasion, explained that when Lincoln "finished speaking the people were silent for a time[;] many not knowing his speech was finished." John Hay stated, in his usual flippant style, that the President performed "in a fine, free way, with more grace than is his wont, said his half dozen words of consecration, and the music wailed . . . ."[76] Hay meant that as soon as Lincoln sat down, a dirge was rendered by a volunteer chorus composed of church choirs from Gettysburg. After this song of mourning there came a benediction given by the Rev. Dr. Henry Louis Baugher (1804-1868), the President of a local academy, Pennsylvania College—now known as Gettysburg College. A Lutheran minister, Dr. Baugher had been at this institution since 1832, first as a professor of Greek and Rhetoric, and from 1850 until his death, as the President. His words continued the deeply religious atmosphere of the dedication ceremony.

BENEDICTION
BY
REV. H. L. BAUGHER, D. D.,
President of Pennsylvania College, Gettysburg.

O Thou King of kings and Lord of lords, God of the nations of the earth, who by Thy kind providence hast permitted us to engage in these solemn services, grant us Thy blessing. Bless this consecrated ground, and these holy graves. Bless the President of these United States, and his Cabinet. Bless the Governors and the Representatives of the States here assembled with all needed grace to conduct the affairs committed into their hands, to the glory of Thy name, and the greatest good of the people.

May this great nation be delivered from treason and rebellion at home, and from the power of enemies abroad. And now may the grace of our Lord Jesus Christ, the love of God our Heavenly Father and the fellowship of the Holy Ghost, be with you all. <u>Amen</u>.

President Lincoln had actually taken part in a huge ecumenical church burial service at Gettysburg. His deathless words had been the sermon of the day, although unseemly short for sermons in those days. Everett's lengthy and more colorful discourse turned out to be mostly obituary in nature, plus a lengthy history of the battle and how it had unfolded. Because of its sheer length, Edward Everett's elocution lesson was shortly forgotten and left mostly unread in the aging pages of contemporary newspapers. It was Lincoln who had captured the very essence of the Gettysburg dedication in just two long paragraphs—as published in the newspapers—which took barely three minutes or so to deliver. This notable accomplishment was typical of Lincoln's mind which quickly grasped the significance of the historical battlefield and what the victory there meant to the Union and the future generations of Americans.

Edward Everett expressed his "great admiration of the thoughts" which Lincoln had spoken at this exercise. He declared that they had been full of "eloquent simplicity & appropriateness." The President, he said, had revealed the "central idea of the occasion" in approximately two minutes while he had taken two hours. With becoming modesty, President Lincoln replied that Everett "could not have been excused to make a short address, nor I a long one." It pleased Lincoln that Everett thought "the little I did say was not entirely a failure."[77] It would appear that even Lincoln had not as yet realized how great his address had been.

To conclude the program of dedication, a battery of artillery fired a salute over the revered dead, and the President's military escort units formed into a column and conducted him in a carriage back to the home of

David Wills, which he reached about 3:00 p. m. After a very late lunch there, he shook hands with well-wishers and talked to his many visitors for well over an hour.[78] At some point in his informal conversations with the citizens of Gettysburg, President Lincoln heard about an old resident of that little village who had become a local folk hero because of his brave actions as a civilian on July 1, the first day of the bloody engagement. Further inquiry revealed that this ancient one was John Lawrence Burns and that he had actually joined the enlisted ranks of the Union forces and fought against the Rebels. As a veteran of the Black Hawk War, the Commander-in-Chief exhibited an immense interest in this tale of derring-do. Immediately, he demanded to meet this gallant volunteer, and David Wills and Secretary Seward were dispatched to fetch him. Upon being introduced to Burns, Lincoln exclaimed, "God bless you, old man," a very religious greeting from the Chief Magistrate.

If President Lincoln questioned John L. Burns about his past, he would have discovered that the small old warrior was then seventy years of age, having been born in Burlington, New Jersey, on September 5, 1793. His father, Joseph, had emigrated to this country from Aberdeenshire, Scotland. About 1813, John settled down at Gettysburg after leading a rather wild life, as he later admitted. He married Barbara Hagerman on January 1, 1820. She had been born in 1799. By trade, Burns was a boot and shoe cobbler, but he had a wide military streak in his nature. Before the War of 1812 ended, he enlisted, on August 27, 1814, as a Private in Captain Christopher van Orsdel's Company of the 2nd Pennsylvania Volunteer Regiment. He was sworn in on September 3 and served until December 4, 1814. During this time, he experienced combat at Plattsburg and perhaps at other engagements.

When fifty-three years old, Burns signed up to fight in the Mexican War, but he never got out of camp. Although he went off in 1861 with Company K of the 1st Pennsylvania Reserves, commanded by Captain Edward McPherson, he could not actually enlist for duty in the Civil War because of his extreme age. Not daunted by this rebuff, he joined the wagon service as a teamster and drove his rig at Washington and Frederick, Maryland. Whenever he got near any skirmish, the old man would borrow a rifle and engage the enemy! Soon, however, his failing health would not permit him to remain in the field, and he was sent back to Gettysburg in the spring of 1862. To make him feel he was still contributing to the welfare of his community, the electorate again chose him as a town constable even though a few of the citizens thought he drank too much and was quite irascible by nature. He and his wife resided in a frame house, two stories tall, at the corner of West and Chambersburg streets. It was rented from his old captain, Edward McPherson. Since 1853, Burns had held intermittent terms as constable. He had little money, but did own forty-six acres of land at Mount Pleasant.

Upon the appearance of Major General Jubal A. Early, it has been said, Constable Burns, carried the news to the town council, and when the Union forces arrived, he guided the staff officers to show them the lay of the land. Before noon on July 1, Burns determined that a great battle was about to take place near his home. So, he seized his obsolescent flintlock rifle, stuffed his powder horn, as well as some lead bullets, into his pockets and marched into the Federal lines. Dressed in his old swallowtail coat with smooth brass buttons, Burns offered to fight with the 150th Pennsylvania Volunteers. They advised him to take a stand in the woods where there was more cover, but his unit soon withdrew to the rear under enemy pressure. Burns did not retreat. He coolly took up with Companies F and K of the 7th Wisconsin, a segment of the famous Iron Brigade, a real fighting outfit. They presented him with an Army issue rifle of more recent vintage, as well as ammunition.

A true inspiration to the embattled and battered Army of the Potomac, Burns confronted the enemy out in the open with elements of the Iron Brigade. He was shot three times and was left upon the battlefield when the Brigade withdrew to Cemetery Ridge. Captured by the Confederates, he was taken to his home which stood beside the battlefield. Little did his captors realize that this little, old, blue-eyed gentleman had killed at least three of their companions while firing off eighteen rounds at them. Word of his valiant stand against the Rebels spread up and down the Union lines and stiffened the resolve of the Federal soldiers during the next two days. As soon as General Lee withdrew his beaten army, a chaplain and a surgeon of the 24th Michigan Volunteer Regiment called upon John Burns, bandaged his wounds and congratulated him on his performance in the face of enemy fire. Bands from the Army of the Potomac marched to his house to serenade him. Officers paid homage to this aged patriot, and his fame spread throughout the region.

Major General Abner Doubleday even included Burns' name in his official report of the campaign at Gettysburg. "My thanks are specially due to a citizen of Gettysburg named John Burns," wrote Doubleday, "who, although [almost] seventy years of age, shouldered his musket, and offered his services to Colonel [Langhorne] Wister, One hundred and fiftieth Pennsylvania Volunteers. Colonel Wister advised him to fight in the woods, as there was more shelter there, but he preferred to join our line of skirmishers in the open fields. When the troops retired, he fought with the Iron Brigade. He was wounded in three places."[79]

After hearing this saga of the "Hero of Gettysburg," President Lincoln immediately determined to add one more honor to Burns' record. He invited Burns to accompany him to a special service scheduled for 5:00 p. m. in the edifice of the Upper Presbyterian Church of Marsh Creek—called The Presbyterian Church of Gettysburg after 1865—located on the southeast corner of South Baltimore and East High streets. The Rev. Henry Graham Finny was the pastor, having graduated from Princeton Theological Seminary in 1859. It was a very ancient congregation, stemming from the year 1740. However, the building which Lincoln saw had only been completed in 1843. Its members adhered to the New School faith. During the bloody fighting at Gettysburg, the sanctuary had been converted into a hospital for cavalry casualties by laying boards across the pew tops. Here, the wounded were placed, row upon row. This heroic shrine had been a part and parcel of the terrible conflict lasting from July 1 to 3 in 1863. Of course, the suffering patients had occupied this building for many days after the gory battle ended.[80]

David Wills, a member of this Presbyterian congregation,[81] had planned a special service to conclude the commemoration of the National Cemetery. Descended from a Scotch-Irish ancestor who came to America in 1730, Wills had been born on February 3, 1831, in Menallen Township of Adams County, Pennsylvania, the son of James Jack and Ruth (Wilson) Wills. He would die in Gettysburg on October 27, 1894. Until he reached the age of thirteen, David lived with his family on a farm. Then in 1846, he entered the preparatory department of Pennsylvania College (now Gettysburg College) and the following year matriculated at this institution where he graduated in 1851 with honors. For one year, he served as principal of an academy in Cahalia, Alabama, but in 1853, he became a student of the law in the office of none other than Thaddeus Stevens of Lancaster, Pennsylvania. After a year of study, he was admitted to the bar and began to practice law in Gettysburg. At that same time, he was elected as the first superintendent of schools in Adams County. He also won election as a director of the Bank of Gettysburg until succeeded by James Jack Wills, his own father. Later, he became a director of the Gettysburg National Bank and eventually its president.

An active Whig, and later a Republican, Wills actively participated in politics. He quickly was chosen as an acting justice of the peace and eventually became President Judge of the 42nd Judicial District which included Adams and Fulton counties. He also became widely involved in railroad building. On June 19, 1856, at Norristown, Pennsylvania, he married Catherine Jane "Jennie" Smyser. She had been born in Gettysburg on August 22, 1834, and bore her husband seven children. She died on December 27, 1891. It was "Jennie" Wills who served as President Lincoln's hostess during his memorable stay at Gettysburg. Around her dinner table, nearly twenty-five guests assembled on the evening of November 18, 1863.[82]

When it came time for the special service, with appropriate fanfare, President Lincoln placed himself on Burns' right, and Secretary Seward took up his position on Burns' left. Together, they proceeded on foot, under escort of the Marshals, over to the Presbyterian Church where they sat down in Pew No. 64, Lincoln taking the aisle position. What an impressive experience Burns would have to recall as long as he lived. He had occupied a church seat with President Lincoln on one hand and Secretary Seward on the other. Nor did the congregation forget this momentous event. This historic pew remains carefully persevered and appropriately marked in the same old church building which still stands in honored glory at Gettysburg. Three tablets marking this old pew were unveiled on the evening of November 19, 1914. One of them commemorates the spot occupied by John L. Burns. There is also a tablet fastened to the front of the church building. It announces that Abraham Lincoln occupied a seat in this Presbyterian church on the evening of November 19, 1863.

Although held in a church, the service was more patriotic than religious in nature. Chief orator for this overflowing audience was a former Colonel of the 93rd Ohio Infantry and the Lt. Governor-elect of Ohio, the Hon. Charles Anderson, who was the brother of the well-known Major General Robert Anderson, commanding officer of Fort Sumter when the Civil War started. He narrated the causes of the conflict and explained why it needed to be ended quickly.

Upon the conclusion of these proceedings, President Lincoln returned briefly to the residence of the Wills family before leaving on his

Presidential Special some time before 7:00 p. m.[83] Secretary Usher, however, did not return with the President. Instead, he left Gettysburg for a tour of the West.[84] By 1:00 a. m. of the 20th, the Chief Executive, quite ill by then with a case of varioloid, a mild form of smallpox, had steamed back into Washington.[85] His faithful valet, William H. Johnson, had kept cold towels upon his fevered brow until the trip was concluded. In doing so, he perhaps contacted the disease from the Chief Executive. Although Lincoln at first quipped, "Now I have something I can give everybody," the illness proved quite serious and hung on for approximately three weeks.[86] In the beginning, the President met with his Cabinet, but soon his physician forbade him from contacting other people for fear he would spread the malady.

Because of President Lincoln's recognition of John Burns, the press spread in ever widening circles the account of Burns' military service at Gettysburg. Congress then enacted a private law on his behalf, granting the old veteran a pension of eight dollars per month, beginning on the date of his wounds, July 1, 1863. This act was approved on March 14, 1864,[87] and David Wills assisted Burns in filling out the necessary governmental forms to enable him to start collecting it. Mrs. Burns died on July 1, 1868, the exact anniversary of her husband's bravery at Gettysburg! It has been stated that after her death, John's mind wandered—and he did, too. In December of 1871, he was spotted in New York City, ill and needing assistance. Upon his recovery, he was sent back home where he died of pneumonia on February 4, 1872, at the residence of his nephew, Nathaniel Hagerman, at Bonneauville, Pennsylvania. His frail corpse was buried beside his wife in Evergreen Cemetery at Gettysburg, near the site of his famous military exploits. A most suitable monument was erected over both husband and wife. There is also a heroic statue of him atop West McPherson Ridge on the battlefield.[88]

Abraham Lincoln's visitation to Gettysburg had been an emotional event for the President. Seeing the fresh graves of the fallen defenders of the Union, who had sacrificed their lives so their country might live, had moved the spirit of Lincoln deeply. He related to Mary Lincoln that he had felt a great religious experience at that time. God had caused this feeling, he revealed to his wife.[89] Lincoln had here encountered another religious experience that many thought necessary for church membership. One witness claimed the President actually told a friend that he had "then and there consecrated myself to Christ." Lincoln vowed, "I do love Jesus."[90]

Perhaps Lincoln did make this statement, but there was no visible change in Lincoln's later references to deity in his public utterances and writings. He still referred to God—not to Christ. And the honest President did not rush to join a church after speaking at Gettysburg. For a number of years he had been a God-fearing mortal, and he often referred to the United States as a Christian nation, yet Lincoln still did not publicly acknowledged himself to be a Christian. Indeed, Lincoln's attitude toward Christ is most difficult to evaluate. As President, Lincoln had many times experienced signs, dreams and prophecies which one could easily interpret as religious experiences. Sometimes he even acted and governed according to what he thought were God's wishes, revealed to him in various ways. Astrology, however, played no part whatsoever in his belief in the supernatural. Lincoln's religious experience at Gettysburg was not greatly different from those he had often felt in the past. He seems to have continued to give more credence to the Old Testament than the New.

Back on October 3, 1863, President Lincoln had beseeched his countrymen to observe Thanksgiving with religious services on November 26. But when this day arrived, Lincoln was still ailing and unable to leave his room.[91] Secretary Bates, however, followed the President's advice and attended the 4th Presbyterian Church (New School), where he listened to Dr. John C. Smith preach. Bates thought this minister's message was "particularly dull."[92] At least the President was spared this experience as he continued to labor over his annual message to Congress. When Major B. B. French called upon Lincoln on December 2, he found him still confined to his quarters.[93]

Lincoln's illness not withstanding, he managed to complete his annual message and send it over to Congress on December 8, 1863. It had a decidedly religious tone, beginning with these two sentences: "Another year of health, and of sufficiently abundant harvests has passed. For these, and especially for the improved condition of our national affairs, our renewed, and profoundest gratitude to God is due."[94] That same day he indited an epistle to General Grant, once more invoking the benison of Deity. "Understanding that your lodgment at Chattanooga and Knoxville is now secure," Lincoln complimented, "I wish to tender you, and all under your command, my more than thanks—my profoundest gratitude—for the skill, courage, and perseverance, with which you and they, over so great difficulties, have effected that important object. God bless you all."[95]

As the war progressed, the President continued to experience dreams which often expressed profound philosophy when he revealed them. During the night of December 21-22, 1863, Lincoln had a fantasy in which he found himself among a large group of ordinary folks. When one of these discovered who Lincoln was, he remarked, "He is a very common-looking man." To this, Lincoln retorted, "Common-looking people are the best in the world; that is the reason the Lord makes so many of them."[96] If Lincoln actually used the word "Lord," as John Hay recorded it, this would be a rather rare occasion when the President did not say "God" or some other name for the Supreme Being. It was to Him that Lincoln pledged his allegiance—again, not to Christ.

The War Department continued to get into difficult situations by mixing in the control of a Methodist Episcopal Church on Pine Street in St. Louis where the supposedly-disloyal Rev. Dr. Samuel B. McPheeters preached. When the President heard of this interference, he wrote again on December 22, "I have never interfered, nor thought of interfering as to whom shall or shall not preach in any church; nor have I knowingly, or believingly, tolerated any one else to so interfere by my authority . . . . I will not have control of any church on any side."[97] Such a statement seems very plain, and yet the military continued at times to meddle in the government of some churches. Lincoln must have felt exasperated when his orders were not followed in such matters. He continually had to chide over-zealous commanders in the field who attempted to replace Confederate sympathizers in the pulpits. Yet, he would not tolerate anybody who openly preached treason.

Although occupied by many weighty matters on January 14, 1864, President Lincoln took time from his busy schedule to accommodate the Episcopal Bishop of Ohio, Charles Pettit McIlvaine (1799-1873). Bishop McIlvaine requested Lincoln's autograph, and the President duly complied. Back in 1861, after the Trent Affair ruffled the feathers of Great Britain, Lincoln had sent Bishop McIlvaine to England to soothe the feelings of the government officials there.[98] Churchmen sometimes served the President in political affairs, and he appreciated their efforts.

In commenting to Secretary Stanton concerning an oath of allegiance required to muster former office holders in Confederate States into Federal regiments, President Lincoln expressed a religious solution to the problem. "On principle," explained Lincoln, "I dislike an oath which requires a man to swear he <u>has</u> not done wrong. It rejects the Christian principle of forgiveness on terms of repentance. I think it is enough if the man does no wrong <u>hereafter</u>."[99] In this case, Lincoln clearly was referring to the New Testament and its code of forgiveness. It is another of his mentions of Christian philosophy based upon Christ's teachings.

Such difficult issues greatly taxed the President's mental and physical well-being. On February 6, 1864, the day after he had told Stanton his solution to oaths of allegiance, Lincoln agonized, "This war is eating my life out. I have a strong impression that I shall not live to see the end." Again, Lincoln had a prophetic view of his own demise.[100]

Of all his manifold problems, the ones dealing with religious matters caused Lincoln some of his most difficult times. On November 30, 1863, the War Department had issued an order giving Bishop Edward Raymond Ames control and possession of all Methodist churches in certain Southern Military Districts where the pastors had been appointed by other than loyal Union Bishops. The military forces were furthermore ordered to assist him in taking charge of such churches. When the issue came to Lincoln's attention on February 11, 1864, he asked Stanton what he intended to do about this command. Once again, Lincoln told the Secretary of War that the government must not attempt to run the churches. It would seem officials in Stanton's department did not listen too closely to the Commander-in-Chief in such matters.[101]

On that same day, the Hon. John Armor Bingham (1815-1900), a Representative from Ohio until he failed of election in 1862, brought a delegation to the White House and introduced them to the President. These clerics, S. O. Wyle, R. W. Sloan and William Browne, came from Philadelphia and represented the Synod of the Reformed Presbyterian Church. They urged the President to amend the U. S. Constitution so that freedom for the slaves would be guaranteed permanently. Lincoln promised to give the matter his most earnest consideration. On the previous day, eighteen men from Pittsburgh, Pennsylvania, had asked for the same measure to be adopted.[102] Of course, the President had been thinking along these same lines prior to this visitation, and he soon requested Senator Lyman Trumbull to introduce the Thirteenth Amendment, which the Senator did in April of 1864.

Repeatedly, President Lincoln reiterated his thesis in regard to churches. On March 4, 1864, he sat down and indited another memorandum. "I have written before," Lincoln ordered, "and now repeat, the United States Government must not undertake to run the churches. When an individual in a church or out of it becomes dangerous to the public interest he must be checked, but the churches as such must take care of themselves. It will not do for the United States to appoint trustees, supervisors, or other agents for the churches. I add, if the military have military need of the church building, let them keep it; otherwise let them get out of it, and leave it and its owners alone except for causes that justify the arrest of any one."[103] This Presidential decree seems straightforward, to the point and impossible to misinterpret, but the military commanders in the field probably did as they pleased since they were so far removed from the desk of the Commander-in-Chief.

In his quest for a general who could win battles, President Lincoln finally picked U. S. Grant to take command of all Union forces. Although they had never met face to face, Lincoln had closely followed Grant's campaigns. When the President personally presented Grant with his commission as Lieutenant General on March 9, 1864, Lincoln said to him: "With this high honor devolves upon you also, a corresponding responsibility. As the country herein trusts you, so, under God, it will sustain you."[104] Again, note the President's reliance upon and trust in God in his struggle to save the Union.

In closing the Sanitary Fair at Washington on March 18, 1864, President Lincoln remarked, "And the chief agents in these fairs are the women of America." "I am not accustomed to the use of language of eulogy," he continued, "but I must say that if all that has been said by orators and poets since the creation of the world in praise of woman were applied to the women of America, it would not do them justice for their conduct during this war. I will close by saying God bless the women of America!"[105] Here, was another of the benedictions pronounced by Lincoln.

While addressing Albert G. Hodges of Frankfort, Kentucky, on April 4, 1864, President Lincoln revealed a vital portion of his religious philosophy. "I claim not to have controlled events," admitted Lincoln, "but confess plainly that events have controlled me. Now, at the end of three years struggle the nation's condition is not what either party, or any man devised, or expected. God alone can claim it. Whither it is tending seems plain. If God now wills the removal of a great wrong [slavery], and wills also that we of the North as well as the South, shall pay fairly for our complicity in that wrong, impartial history will find therein new cause to attest and revere the justice and goodness of God."[106]

On the following day, Lincoln replied to Mrs. Horace Mann concerning this same matter. She had forwarded a petition from young folks who asked the President to free all slave children. "While I have not the power to grant all they ask," Lincoln concluded, "I trust they will remember that God has, and that, as it seems, He wills to do it."[107]

Speaking before the Sanitary Fair at Baltimore on April 18 that year, President Lincoln confessed that he had been surprised that the war had lasted so long. Then he repeated a profound maxim. "So true is it," Lincoln said, "that man proposes, and God disposes." As to the use of colored troops in the United States armed forces and the massacre of some of them at Fort Pillow by Confederates, the Commander-in-Chief told his audience: "I am responsible for it to the American people, to the christian world, to history, and on my final account to God."[108] Such a revelation certainly proves that Lincoln believed in a final judgment at the hands of God. He also repeated his conviction that major portions of the world followed the teachings of Jesus Christ, and thus he termed these believers as being in "the christian world," with a small "c." Of course, Lincoln took liberties with punctuation. He did not, for instance, always capitalize the days of the week.

It seems appropriate that Lincoln—seemingly the most truly religious man ever to sit in the White House—was the Chief Executive who approved a bill on April 22, 1864, which, for the very first time, placed the slogan "In God We Trust" upon United States coinage. It first appeared on the two-cent piece.[109]

More and more, the President mentioned the name of Deity in his statements. In writing to General Grant on April 30, 1864, Lincoln told him, "And now with a brave Army, and a just cause, may God sustain you."[110] To Mrs. Abner Bartlett of Medford, Massachusetts, who had knitted a pair of socks for Lincoln, he acknowledged her most appreciated gift by saying, "May God give you yet many happy days."[111] He addressed all the friends of Union and Liberty on May 9, 1864, with these remarks: "Enough is known of Army operations within the last five days to claim our especial gratitude to God; while what remains undone demands our most sincere prayers to, and reliance upon, Him, without whom, all human effort is vain. I recommend that all patriots, at their homes, in their places of public worship, and wherever they may be, unite in common thanksgiving and prayer to Almighty God."[112] Here, Lincoln referred to the Battle of the Wilderness. Although Grant suffered a huge number of casualties, the Confederates lost a large number also and could not replace their losses as Grant could. In response to the serenade on May 9, tendered the President because of Grant's victory, Lincoln offered thanks to the brave men, their commanders, and "especially to our Maker." He reminded his listeners to "be very grateful to Almighty God, who gives us victory."[113]

The sharpest religious thorn which constantly pricked Lincoln was the quarrel over church property. Once more, on May 13, 1864, the President stated his policy clearly and distinctly. In regard to a church in Memphis, the Commander-in-Chief endorsed a complaint with these words: "I say again, if there be no military need for the building, leave it alone, neither putting any one in or out, of it, except on finding some one preaching or practicing treason, in which case lay hands upon him just as if he were doing the same thing in any other building, or in the streets or highways."[114]

And yet, by and large, religious denominations in the North supported Abraham Lincoln and his holy cause, as he saw it. On May 18, 1864, Lincoln paid tribute to them. "Nobly sustained as the government has been by all the churches," Lincoln confessed, "I would utter nothing which might, in the least, appear invidious against any. Yet, without this, it may fairly be said that the Methodist Episcopal Church, not less devoted than the best, is, by it's *[sic]* greater numbers, the most important of all. It is no fault in others that the Methodist Church sends more soldiers to the field, more nurses to the hospital, and more prayers to Heaven than any. God bless the Methodist Church— bless all the churches—and blessed be God, Who, in this our great trial, giveth us the churches."[115] When the Methodist clergy and their parishioners saw this praise, they must have been very proud. Since Bishop Matthew Simpson was a great favorite of Lincoln's, one wonders if the good Bishop may not have shown the above statistics to the President. Such figures would not have been compiled by the Federal Government.

When a delegation representing the American Baptist Home Missionary Society came to the Executive Mansion on May 28, 1864, the President received them kindly, telling them he "had great cause of gratitude for the support so unanimously given by all Christian denominations of the country." "I have had occasion so frequently to respond to something like this assemblage, that I have said all that I had to say," Lincoln explained to them. He informed them that "this particular body is in all respects as respectable as any that have been presented to me." After hearing the resolutions which they brought, Lincoln promised to reply in writing later.[116]

This he did on May 30, thanking them for the support which the Christian communities had so zealously given to the Union and to the cause of Liberty. "Indeed," reasoned Lincoln, "it is difficult to conceive how it could be otherwise with any one professing christianity, or even having ordinary perceptions of right and wrong. To read in the Bible, as the word of God himself, that 'In the sweat of <u>thy</u> face shalt thou eat bread,' [Genesis 3:19] and to preach therefrom that, 'In the sweat of <u>other</u> <u>mans</u> faces shalt thou eat bread,' to my mind can scarcely be reconciled with honest sincerity. When brought to my final reckoning, may I have to answer for robbing no man of his goods; yet more tolerable even this, than for robbing one of himself, and all that was his." "When, a year or two ago those professedly holy men of the South," Lincoln pointed out, "met in the semblance of prayer and devotion, and, in the name of Him who said 'As ye would all men should do unto you, do ye even so unto them' appealed to the christian world to aid them in doing to a whole race of men, as they would have no man do unto themselves, to my thinking, they condemned and insulted God and His church, far more than did Satan when he tempted the Saviour with the Kingdoms of earth. The devil[']s attempt was no more false, and far less hypocritical. But let me forbear, remembering it is also written 'Judge not, lest ye be judged.'"[117] (Matthew 7:1.)

Here is an excellent insight into Abraham Lincoln's personal conception of organized religion. Without doubt, he felt that all too often men used it merely to suit their own purposes and not what God willed. Yet, he must have thought that churches—as imperfect as they were—did much good in the nation. He frequently praised all of those in the North for their anti-slavery stand and their prayers for the President and the Union. Indeed, he was most grateful to them. Nevertheless, Lincoln did not choose to affiliate with one. A hypocrite he was not. He dealt with his Maker directly and not through any intermediary, and he referred to the Bible as "the word of God himself."

Typical of President Lincoln's fairness was his request that Attorney General Edward Bates assist black chaplains in the Federal service to receive pay the same as white chaplains. On May 26, 1864, both Lincoln and Senator Charles Sumner of Massachusetts thanked Bates for his assistance in this important decision. If colored chaplains "sweat," they should be allowed their "bread," too.[118]

Speaking at the Great Central Sanitary Fair at Philadelphia on June 16, 1864, Lincoln told those in attendance: "We accepted this war for an object, a worthy object, and the war will end when that object is attained. Under God, I hope it never will until that time." Great cheering followed this statement. Upon being presented a medal by the women who organized the Fair, the President replied, "I have only to say that I accept this present of the ladies as an additional token of your confidence, but I do not need any further evidence of the loyalty and devotion of the women of America to the cause of the Union and the cause of Christian humility."[119]

A great tragedy occurred at ten minutes before noon on June 17, 1864, in the Arsenal at Washington, D. C. One hundred and eight young women were working in the main laboratory making cartridges for small arms. Somehow a pile of fireworks stacked outside the building ignited, and a burning fuse flew through an open window into one of the rooms where twenty-nine of the women were making ammunition. It fell into some powder which exploded and spewed fire onto the dresses of numerous workers. In the panic that followed, the metal hoops under these women's skirts prevented co-workers from quickly putting out the flames.

When the catastrophe ended, nineteen bodies were recovered. Most of the young women who were burned to death had no families to claim the bodies. It was determined to hold religious services for fifteen of them at the Arsenal. At 3:00 p. m. on June 19—a very hot day—various public officials assembled to pay tribute to the patriotic dead who had given their young lives while aiding the Union's war effort. Among those present were President Lincoln, Secretary of War Stanton and Stanton's son. Because a number of the victims had been Roman Catholics, Father A. Bokel, of St. Dominick's Catholic Church on F Street between 6th and 7th, conducted a Catholic burial rite, including the sprinkling of the coffins with holy water. Such a ceremony was an unusual observance for Lincoln who had rarely—if ever before—attended a Catholic mass for the deceased.

Next, the Rev. S. V. Leech of Gorsuch Methodist Episcopal Chapel, located on the corner of L and 4 1/2 streets, presided over a Protestant funeral, including the final prayer. At the conclusion of the obsequies, President Lincoln sadly joined the procession which left about 4:00 p. m. by the north gate of the Arsenal Grounds and wound its way slowly to the Congressional Burial Grounds on the Eastern Branch of the Potomac River, about one and a half miles from the Capitol.[120] There, interment took place.

On June 30, President Lincoln participated in a more pleasant event. He gave his assent for the St. Matthews' Colored Sunday School to use the government grounds between the White House and the War Department on July 4 for a celebration. B. B. French had told Gabriel Coakley that this organization might assemble there, provided the President agreed.[121] St. Matthews was a Roman Catholic Church at H and 15th streets. As the

Washington directories do not list this as a colored church, this must have been a separate Sunday School for children of Color.

Sometime after July 2, 1864, when the Lincolns again took up their summer quarters at the Soldier's Home,[122] Joshua Fry Speed stayed overnight with the First Family. In this temporary residence, Speed found the President reading his Bible. Since Speed had known Lincoln to be a skeptic in his early life at Springfield when they had roomed together above Speed's store, this old Kentucky guest expressed some amazement at this strange turn of events. Speed volunteered that he himself had not recovered from his own skepticism. Whereupon Lincoln retorted, "You are wrong[,] Speed, take all of this book upon reason that you can, and the balance on faith, and you will live and die a happier and better man."[123] Lincoln had greatly modified his religious beliefs since Speed left Springfield in 1841. It appears, the longer Lincoln lived, the closer he felt to God and the more he relied upon God for sustenance.

Rarely did President Lincoln miss an opportunity to mention his reliance upon God. When, on July 2, 1864, Congress asked for a proclamation setting aside a day of prayer, Lincoln complied on July 7 with a beautiful tribute to his Maker. Referring to the "pious sentiments expressed" by Congress, the President heartily approved and appointed August 4 as the date for "national humiliation and prayer." He invited and requested the "Heads of the Executive Departments of this Government, together with all Legislators,—all Judges and Magistrates, and all other persons exercising authority in the land, whether civil, military or naval,—and all soldiers, seamen and marines in the national service,—and all the other loyal and law-abiding People of the United States, to assemble in their preferred places of public worship on that day, and there and then to render to the Almighty and Merciful Ruler of the Universe, such homages and such confessions, and to offer to Him such supplication, as the Congress of the United States have, in their aforesaid Resolution, so solemnly, so earnestly, and so reverently recommended."[124]

Ohio had sent a three-months infantry regiment into the fray, and when these soldiers were preparing to return to their families after serving out their enlistment, President Lincoln addressed them on August 31, 1864. He pointed out to them that his government was trying to maintain the Union and the institutions which their fathers enjoyed, which they themselves enjoyed, and which, he hoped, their children would enjoy, as well as their grandchildren. Nowhere in the world, Lincoln declared, was there another government with so much liberty and equality. "The present moment finds me at the White House," he commented, "yet there is as good a chance for your children as there was for my father's." He admonished them to stand fast to the Union and the old Flag. Then he gave the departing veterans his benediction: "I bid you God-speed to your homes."[125] It is doubtful that any of these officers and men ever forgot Lincoln's inspirational speech to them and his parting remarks which prayed for their safe return to their loved ones anxiously awaiting their coming. Like a prophet of old, Lincoln dispatched the 148th back to the State of Ohio with his blessing as well as his thanks to these loyal Buckeyes.

With the coming of more notable Union victories in the field, President Lincoln waxed even more religious on September 3, 1864, and issued another proclamation for thanksgiving and prayer. "The signal success that Divine Providence has recently vouchsafed to the operations of the United States fleet and army in the harbor of Mobile and the reduction of Fort-Powell, Fort-Gaines, and Fort-Morgan, and the glorious achievements of the Army under Major General Sherman in the State of Georgia, resulting in the capture of the City of Atlanta," Lincoln began, "call for devout acknowledgment to the Supreme Being in whose hands are the destinies of nations. It is therefore requested that on next Sunday [probably meaning September 11], in all places of public worship in the United States, thanksgiving be offered to Him for His mercy in preserving our national existence against the insurgent rebels who so long have been waging a cruel war against the Government of the United States, for its overthrow; and also that prayer be made for the Divine protection to our brave soldiers and their leaders in the field, who have so often and so gallantly periled their lives in battling with the enemy; and for blessing and comfort from the Father of Mercies to the sick, wounded, and prisoners, and to the orphans and widows of those who have fallen in the service of their country, and that he will continue to uphold the Government of the United-States against all the efforts of public enemies and secret foes."[126]

This eloquent supplication by the President was composed like a prayer to God. A minister could have easily altered this message into his own ode of thanksgiving and delivered it before his congregation.

When Eliza P. Gurney sent a message to the President from her home near Atlantic City, New Jersey, by way of a mutual friend—Isaac Newton—she rejoiced to Lincoln that the Almighty had led him to free the slaves and vouched that she assuredly believed God "did design to make thee instrumental in accomplishing, when he appointed thee thy present post of vast responsibility, as the Chief Magistrate." In replying to this famous Quaker writer, Lincoln told her on September 4, 1864: "In all, it has been your purpose to strengthen my reliance on God. I am much indebted to the good christian people of the country for their constant prayers and consolations; and to no one of them, more than to yourself. The purposes of the Almighty are perfect, and must prevail, though we erring mortals may fail to accurately perceive them in advance. We hoped for a happy termination of this terrible war long before this; but God knows best, and has ruled otherwise. We shall yet acknowledge His wisdom and our own error therein. Meanwhile we must work earnestly in the best light He gives us, trusting that so working still conduces to the great ends He ordains. Surely he intends some great good to follow this mighty convulsion, which no mortal could make, and no mortal could stay." He ended by stating: "That you believe this I doubt not; and believing it, I shall still receive, for our country and myself, your earnest prayers to our Father in Heaven."[127] Here is another example of President Lincoln's open statements regarding his faith in God.

The Loyal Colored People of Baltimore purchased an expensive Bible and inscribed it "To Abraham Lincoln, President of the United States, the Friend of universal Freedom . . . as a token of respect and Gratitude. Baltimore, 4th July, 1864." Because of his duties concerning the war, however, Lincoln was unable to receive the Bible personally from their hands at this time. Finally, the Revs. A. W. Wayman, S. W. Chase, and W. H. Brown, accompanied by William H. Francis, were able to obtain an audience with the President on September 7. After thanking them, Lincoln said, "In regard to this Great Book, I have but to say, it is the best gift God has given to man. All the good the Saviour gave to the world was communicated through this book. But for it we could not know right from wrong. All things most desirable for man's welfare, here and hereafter, are to be found portrayed in it." This is one of Lincoln's rare comments upon Jesus Christ and his teachings. But he began his statement by recognizing God as the giver of the Bible. This precious volume is now in the Fisk University Library at Nashville, Tennessee.[128]

Shortly after Lincoln received this Bible, Henry Champion Deming (May 23, 1815-Oct. 8, 1872) called at the White House. He was then a congressman from the 1st District of Connecticut after having been Colonel of the 12th Regiment from his home state and a mayor of New Orleans while it was

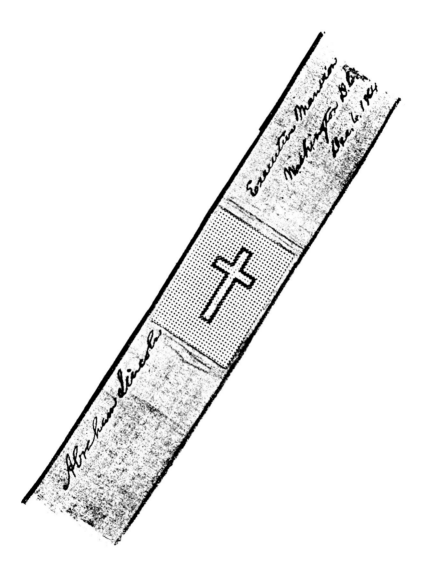

For some reason or other, President Abraham Lincoln signed this bookmark at the Executive Mansion on December 6, 1864. It is of crimson silk with an embroidered cross on a white background and was once owned by the noted collector, Oliver R. Barrett. Since Lincoln rarely used his full name unless he was signing a legal document, this sacred bookmark might have been endorsed by the President for a friend or visitor to the White House. It cannot be proved that Lincoln used it himself as a bookmark in his Bible, etc.

under martial law. A Republican, Deming had graduated from Yale and then taken a law degree from Harvard. Literary matters greatly interested him, and as a result, the President showed him the new Bible. Both men began to recite passages from the Scriptures, checking their memory by looking them up in this sacred volume.

Soon Congressman Deming asked Lincoln why he had never joined a church since he exhibited such a knowledge of the Bible and often expressed a deep interest in religious and moral issues. Lincoln replied that "he had never united himself to any church, because he found difficulty in giving his assent, without mental reservation, to the long complicated statements of Christian doctrine, which characterize their Articles of belief and Confessions of Faith. 'When any church,' he continued, 'will inscribe over its altar, as its sole qualification for membership the Saviour's condensed statement of the substance of both law and Gospel, "Thou shalt love the Lord thy God with all thy heart, and with all thy soul and with all thy mind, and thy neighbor as thyself," that church will I join with all my heart and all my soul.'"[129] (Deuteronomy 6:5 and Leviticus 19:18).

To set aside Thanksgiving Day once more, a devout President issued his proclamation on October 20, 1864. It read like a short sermon and was certainly better than many preached by trained ministers. "It has pleased Almighty God," Lincoln began, "to prolong our national life another year, defending us with his guardian care against unfriendly designs from abroad, and vouchsafing to us in His mercy many and signal victories over the enemy, who is of our own household. It has also pleased our Heavenly Father to favor as well our citizens in their homes as our soldiers in their camps and our sailors on the rivers and seas with unusual health. He has largely augmented our free population by emancipation and by immigration, while he has opened to us new sources of wealth, and has crowned the labor of our working men in every department of industry with abundant rewards. Moreover, he has been pleased to animate and inspire our minds and hearts with fortitude, courage and resolution sufficient for the great trial of civil war into which we have been brought by our adherence as a nation to the cause of Freedom and Humanity, and to afford to us reasonable hopes of an ultimate and happy deliverance from our dangers and afflictions. Now, therefore, I, Abraham Lincoln, President of the United States, do hereby, appoint and set apart the last Thursday in November next, [the 24th] as a day, which I desire to be observed by all my fellow-citizens wherever they may then be as a day of

Thanksgiving and Praise to Almighty God the beneficent Creator and Ruler of the Universe. And I do further recommend to my fellow-citizens aforesaid that on that occasion they do reverently humble themselves in the dust and from thence offer up penitent and fervent prayers and supplications to the Great Disposer of events for a return of the inestimable blessings of Peace, Union and Harmony throughout the land, which it has pleased him to assign as a dwelling place for ourselves and for our posterity through all generations."[130]

This proclamation was one which emphasized the benefits received from God in his mercy and the necessity to thank Him for bestowing them upon His faithful subjects in the North. It was a religious message from a reverential President.

Just prior to the Presidential election of 1864, Elizabeth S. Comstock, a Quaker minister, obtained an audience with Lincoln on the evening of November 7. She read to him from the Bible, choosing passages from the Book of the Prophet Isaiah. Upon the conclusion of their talk, the minister knelt in prayer, and President Lincoln got down on his knees.[131] Certainly this choice of Scripture was most fortuitous. By then, Lincoln was as sure that God was right as was the Prophet Isaiah.[132] In fact, the Civil War President was just as committed to his God as was this Prophet of Old Testament times.

But Lincoln was not always prophetic. After the votes had been tallied for the Presidential election held November 8, 1864, it was discovered that Major General George B. McClellan had carried only New Jersey, Delaware and Kentucky for a total of just 21 electoral votes. Lincoln was entitled to 212 electoral votes, a sweeping victory for the President who had written on August 23 that year: "This morning, as for some days past, it seems exceedingly probable that this Administration will not be re-elected."[133] In response to a group of serenaders from Pennsylvania who assembled at the White House on the evening of November 8, Lincoln told them, "I am thankful to God for this approval of the people." He then remarked, "I give thanks to the Almighty for this evidence of the people's resolution to stand by free government and the rights of humanity."[134]

By November 10, it was generally known that Lincoln had won another term in office. On that evening, another group of serenaders appeared at the Executive Mansion, and Lincoln was prepared for them. He had written a speech which he read from a window of the White House. "While I am deeply sensible to the high compliment of a re-election; and duly grateful, as I trust, to Almighty God for having directed my countrymen to a right conclusion, as

I think, for their own good," Lincoln confided to them, "it adds nothing to my satisfaction that any other man may be disappointed or pained by the result."[135] Here was a very Christian attitude expressed by the President to those who had not supported him. But above all, he thanked God for the victory at the hands of the people.

Earlier that same day, those who favored women's rights suffered yet another defeat. However, Lincoln himself supported those ladies who sought equality. As early as June 13, 1836, he had declared openly, "I go for all sharing the privileges of the government, who assist in bearing its burdens. Consequently I go for admitting all whites to the right of suffrage, who pay taxes or bear arms, (by no means excluding females.)"[136] Ella E. (Gibson) Hobart, an ordained minister, had been elected as Chaplain of the First Wisconsin Heavy Artillery. Even the Colonel had given his permission for her to be mustered into his unit. She presented her credentials to President Lincoln and asked for his help in obtaining her commission. The Chief Executive avowed that he had "no objection to her appointment" but admitted that Secretary-of-War Stanton would have to give his approval. Stanton later refused to accept her because she was a woman.[137] But the President had earnestly tried to reform the chaplaincy; after all, he had gotten Jews, Catholics and Negroes approved for this office. It would seem that the Army was simply not ready for women to soldier with the men.

President and Mrs. Lincoln invited their pastor, Dr. Phineas D. Gurley, and his wife to have dinner with them at the White House on the evening of November 18, 1864.[138] Various sources have declared that this minister frequently visited the Lincolns. What is not so well-known is that sometime prior to this date, Lincoln even had a preacher on his own staff at the Executive Mansion. As Major John Milton Hay (1838-1905) became more actively engaged in running military errands for his boss and John George Nicolay (1832-1901) suffered from ill health and was asked to do various assignments away from his post, these two private secretaries to the President needed additional assistance with the voluminous correspondence and administrative duties. As a result, Lincoln hired the Rev. Edward Duffield Neill (Aug. 9, 1823-Sept. 26, 1893) as another White House secretary. Neill had been born in Philadelphia; he graduated from Amherst College as well as Andover Theological Seminary. The Presbyterian Church had ordained him to preach in 1848. Having a literary flair, in 1858 he wrote a history of Minnesota where he lived. When the Civil War began, he became a Chaplain of the First Minnesota Volunteer Infantry Regiment and later served as a hospital chaplain in the United States Military Hospital at Philadelphia.[139]

While there were no other ministers, there were other secretaries who served in the White House. Since July 15, 1861, William Osborn Stoddard (Sept. 24, 1835-Aug. 29, 1925) had been working in the Executive Mansion as Lincoln's land patent secretary and doing other secretarial duties, such as handling Mary Lincoln's mail. He had graduated from the University of Rochester with an A. B. in 1858 and an A. M. in 1861. He, too, was not always in the best of health, but sometimes traveled on official assignments for the President. Eventually, he quit to become a United States Marshal for the Eastern District of Arkansas.[140]

To fill in for Stoddard, Lincoln, on September 14, 1864, engaged Charles H. Philbrick (Apr. 9, 1837-Oct. 17, 1885) as a private secretary. Philbrick had graduated from Illinois College in 1858 with an A. B. degree. Few people today even recognize the name Philbrick, but he was an important cog in the operation of President Lincoln's personal staff. Unfortunately, he never wrote his memoirs.[141]

Although Abraham Lincoln had little formal schooling, he never shied away from securing college men for his secretarial work. Of his known secretaries, only Nicolay had never been to college. If the harried Chief Executive discussed religious philosophy or history with his White House secretaries, it was probably Neill who answered questions or expounded upon the theory of religion with Lincoln after he came aboard in 1864.

After very faulty and inadequate research in the military records of his state, the Adjutant General of Massachusetts determined that Lydia (Parker) Bixby (1801-1878), a Boston widow since 1854, had lost five sons in the Civil War. General William Schouler passed on his information, orally, to Governor John A. Andrew who, in turn, wrote to the War Department in Washington requesting that President Lincoln communicate with Mrs. Bixby because "a noble mother of five dead sons so well" deserved a letter from the Chief Magistrate. Secretary Stanton called the matter to the attention of Lincoln who seems to have asked John Hay to help him compose a missive of deep condolence for Widow Bixby. It reads like a pastor giving solace to a parishioner who has been bereft of a loved one and needs the sustaining hand of God in order to carry on with life. Lincoln examined and signed the letter to her, thus making it his own.

This composition was a masterpiece, and the mention of human sacrifices upon an altar must have come from a reading of the Old Testament.

But the original and priceless document has never been found after it was released to the local Boston press. It is quoted here from a contemporary newspaper which received it on November 25 from the wire service out of Boston.

Executive Mansion,
Washington, Nov. 21, 1864.

DEAR MADAM: I have been shown in the files of the War Department a statement of the Adjutant General of Massachusetts that you are the mother of five sons who have died glorious on the field of battle. I feel how weak and fruit-less must be any words of mine which should attempt to beguile you from the grief of a loss so overwhelming. But I cannot refrain from tendering to you the consolation that may be found in the thanks of the republic—they died to save. I pray that our Heavenly Father may assuage the anguish of your bereavement, and leave you only the cherished memo-ry of the loved and lost, and the solemn pride that must be yours to have laid so costly a sacrifice upon the altar of free-dom. Yours, very sincerely and respectfully,

To MRS. BIXBY, Boston, Mass.   A. LINCOLN[142]

Alas, it was not true. Mrs. Bixby did not lose five sons. Sgt. Charles N. Bixby was killed May 3, 1863. Pvt. Oliver Cromwell Bixby was killed July 30, 1864. Corp. Henry Cromwell Bixby was discharged on December 19, 1864. Pvt. George Way Bixby was captured July 30, 1864, and then desert-ed to the enemy. After the war, he moved to Cuba. Edward Bixby also deserted from his unit. An alleged sixth son was probably Henry Cromwell Bixby who *was* wounded before his honorable discharge in 1864.[143] Nevertheless, President Lincoln's message deserves to be read and reread because of its beautiful language and religious comfort. It is certainly one of his best known letters, and numerous forgeries of it have been made and distributed widely. Upon occasion, the text has even been reproduced with-out identification.

For example, when the American Battle Monuments Commission decided in 1955 to construct a huge stone memorial at the National Memorial Cemetery of the Pacific in the Punchbowl Crater at Honolulu, Hawaii, President Abraham Lincoln's famous letter to Widow Bixby again entered the scene. After carving a huge stone figure of a sorrowing female, standing thirty feet tall, on the prow of a United States Navy aircraft carrier, the planners cut these words, without quotation marks or attribution, under this native lady who holds a branch of laurel in her left hand:

THE SOLEMN PRIDE
THAT MUST BE YOURS
TO HAVE LAID
SO COSTLY A SACRIFICE
UPON THE ALTAR
OF FREEDOM.

She stands guard over the heroic dead who are actually buried in this hallowed soil or whose names are incised in the Trani marble walls which form the Courts of the Missing. These Italian marble courtyards contain the names of those American servicemen who are missing, lost or buried at sea. It is one of the most impressive National Cemeteries in the world, and the tribute to both the living and their dead came from the deathless pens of John Hay and Abraham Lincoln who composed these majestic words thousands of miles from the Hawaiian Island.

It matters not that Mrs. Bixby did not suffer the loss of five sons in battle. President Lincoln thought she had, and his epistle of consolation will live forever in the annuals of literature.[144]

Thanksgiving Day November 24, 1864, which had been set aside by President Lincoln as a national day of prayer, dawned clear and bright. The weather was cool, and crowds of pedestrians thronged the principal streets of Washington as all governmental offices were closed. A feeling of hope ran through the city. Even the temporary framework that had been in the Rotunda of the Capitol during the construction of the new dome was removed, and artists had commenced to fresco the beautiful ceiling as it was to be finished before Congress reassembled.[145]

Heeding his own proclamation, President Lincoln attended a special Thanksgiving service at the New York Avenue Presbyterian Church where Dr. P. D. Gurley talked for an hour. His sermon came from the Sixty-Ninth Psalm, Verse 30: "I will praise the name of God with a song, and will magnify him with thanksgiving." For special music, the choir sang "The President's Hymn," being actually "Give Thanks, All Ye People." In conclusion, they rendered a fine performance of the "Hallelujah Chorus." Lincoln promised to contribute a

Photo by Herbert C. Ruckmick

President Abraham Lincoln sat in this settee when attending prayer meetings at
The New York Avenue Presbyterian Church in Washington, D. C.,
on Thursday evenings.

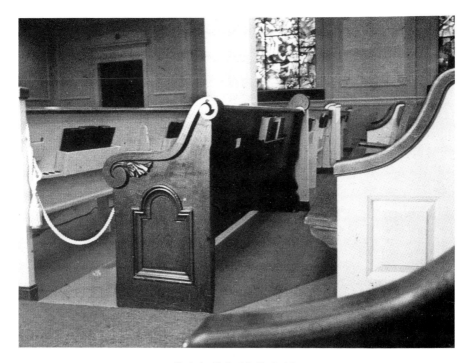

Photo by Herbert C. Ruckmick.

The Lincoln Family Pew, No. B-14,
in The New York Avenue Presbyterian Church, Washington, D. C.

very suitable sum for the work of the Christian Commission if somebody would call at the White House for it. A special collection had been taken at this service for its benefit.[146]

President Lincoln started off his Annual Message to Congress on December 6, 1864, in a religious tone. "Again, the blessings of health and abundant harvests claim our profoundest gratitude to Almighty God," declared Lincoln.[147] That same day he wrote out a little story for Noah Brooks to publish. It, too, contained a portion of Lincoln's religious philosophy and helps to explain why he could not accept membership in a church. When two ladies from Tennessee asked the President to release their husbands who were being held as prisoners, one of them affirmed that her husband "was a religious man." After several interviews with these wives, Lincoln finally acquiesced to their supplications and ordered the discharge of their husbands. However, he chided one of them with these words: "You say your husband is a religious man; tell him when you meet him, that I say I am not much of a judge of religion, but that, in my opinion, the religion that sets men to rebel and fight against their government, because, as they think, that government does not sufficiently help <u>some</u> men to eat their bread on the sweat of <u>other</u> men's faces, is not the sort of religion upon which people can get to heaven!"[148] Lincoln took this text from Genesis 3:19: "In the sweat of thy face shalt thou eat bread . . . ."

Once more, the President condemned the formal practice of a religion which too often—he thought—was twisted to conform to the selfish interests of the practitioners. It also reveals his belief in a hereafter. Yet despite Lincoln's knowledge that churches were organized and operated by frail human beings who often did not act in a Godly manner, he conceded on September 6, 1864, that he "relied very much upon the religious element for the support of his administration."[149]

While President Lincoln's Annual Message was being read to Congress, more black citizens in New Orleans, Louisiana, were holding a meeting to make arrangements for the presentation of a gold and silver mounted Bible to Abraham Lincoln in recognition of his Emancipation Proclamation. The Bible was bound in red morocco with silver bands and bosses. A gold plate on the front announced that it was presented to "His Excellency A. Lincoln, President, U. S. By the Colored People, New Orleans, La." In due course, Thomas Jefferson Durant, a lawyer and political leader in New Orleans, delivered the sacred volume to the White House. It eventually came into the famous collection of Oliver Rogers Barrett and was later sold when his assemblage was auctioned off. Its history is documented in the Barrett Catalogue issued for this sale.

President Lincoln ordered the protection of religious facilities which had in no way hindered his war effort. On January 17, 1865, he acted upon a request from Senator Lazarus Whitehead Powell who wished to safeguard a Mother House at Nazareth, Kentucky, from further harm by the military. These nuns had asked their Kentucky Senator, who had been educated at Bardstown, Kentucky, to intercede for them. Accordingly, Lincoln picked up his pen and wrote on a small card: "Let no depredation be committed upon the property or possessions of the 'Sisters of Charity' at Nazareth Academy, near Bardstown, Ky."[150]

A Philadelphia delegation headed by the Rev. William Suddards presented Lincoln a superb vase filled with skeleton leaves from the Gettysburg battlefield. To them, Lincoln replied on January 24, 1865, thanking the ladies and gentlemen for their gift. After paying tribute to American women, the President dismissed the assemblage by giving them his benediction: "May God bless you all." He had declined to give any remarks on Gettysburg because he declared that so "much has been said about Gettysburg" already and "that for me to attempt to say more may, perhaps, only serve to weaken the force of that which has already been said."[151] The President's "few appropriate remarks" delivered there on November 19, 1863, had covered the subject very well.

Always supporting the work of the U. S. Christian Commission, the President appeared at its third anniversary meeting held during the evening of January 29, 1865, in the Hall of the House of Representatives. Although not a singer, Lincoln appreciated music and asked in writing that Philip Philips of Cincinnati render an encore of the hymn "Your Mission" which this musician did between the hours of 11 and 12 midnight. Evidently, this number greatly impressed the weary Chief Magistrate of the Union.[152]

The eloquent Rev. Henry Ward Beecher, whom Lincoln had heard preach at least twice in Brooklyn at the former's home church, obtained an interview with Lincoln February 1, 1865. While speaking with the President, Rev. Beecher declared, "I am grateful to God, for raising you up. I believe that you are in His hand. That he may guide you is my daily & almost hourly prayer."[153] Here again was a man of the cloth who believed President Lincoln to be God's man and His servant on this earth. Indeed, Lincoln sought to do

God's will as far as it was made known to him. And others noticed this, too. Always Lincoln looked for a divine sign, a prophetic dream or an intuition which stemmed from the Heavenly Father.

In writing to Governor Thomas C. Fletcher of Missouri, President Lincoln asked him to encourage the local communities to hold meetings which might combat the destruction of life and property by the guerrilla elements running rampant throughout his state although no organized enemy military force was present. Prophesied Lincoln on February 20, 1865, "At such meetings old friendships will cross the memory; and honor and Christian Charity will come in to help."[154] It would seem that Father Abraham put great stock in the philosophy of Christ even if he did not specifically recognize his divinity.

When Thomas W. Conway, General Superintendent of the Freedmen in the Department of the Gulf, related the success he'd had in elevating the physical and moral condition of the former slaves, Lincoln declared "The blessing of God and the efforts of good and faithful men will bring us an earlier and happier consummation than the most sanguine friends of the freedmen could reasonably expect."[155]

To the Joint Notification Committee from Congress who called on March 1, 1865, to officially inform him of his re-election, President Lincoln expressed his belief that the voting public had thought that he could finish a difficult task because of his previous four years of experience. "In this view," Lincoln continued, "and with assured reliance on that Almighty Ruler who has so graciously sustained us thus far; and with increased gratitude to the generous people for their continued confidence, I accept the renewed trust, and it's [sic] yet onerous and perplexing duties and responsibilities."[156] Without doubt, the President renewed his contract with the Northern people and announced that again he would depend upon God for assistance.

March 4, 1865, began very inauspiciously with violent rain and howling winds. Avenues and streets ran with mud. It appeared to be a very inclement day for Lincoln's Second Inaugural. But when the tall President stepped forward to take the oath of office, the rain miraculously ceased, and a bright sun burst forth upon the august scene at the Capitol. Some of those present declared that this was an omen. B. B. French had constructed a special little table for this historic event. It had been fashioned with iron scraps and iron pieces left over from the reconstruction of the Capitol dome. For the shaft, French selected an extra baluster not needed for the completion of the dome work. A piece of paneling formed the top of the table. An ornament from the inner portion of the dome served as a base, and a long bolt fastened the parts together. After a coat of paint, one could not readily tell the provenance of this small metal stand which now had a glass of water resting upon it for the convenience of the President if he needed a drink while speaking. Commissioner French later gave this artifact to the Massachusetts Historical Society in Boston.[157]

Daniel W. Middleton, the Clerk of the Supreme Court, opened the Bible without premeditation and discovered that the separation of the pages fell at the fifth chapter of Isaiah.[158] While repeating the oath with his hand resting on this Bible, President Lincoln, of course, noted the sudden appearance of the bright sunlight, and the following day he commented to a close friend that he was "just superstitious enough to consider it a happy omen."[159]

With great care, Lincoln had prepared his address. It was quite short and actually read like a sermon with numerous references to God and the Bible. It would appear that Abraham Lincoln's Presbyterian experiences with that particular denomination's theories of religion helped to shape this magnificent oration. It could have been read from one of their pulpits. This President was so familiar with the Scriptures that he often incorporated whole sentences and phrases into his own writings without quotation marks.

Lincoln explained there was no need for a long speech. Both the North and South deprecated war, Lincoln thought, "but one of them would make war rather than let the nation survive; and the other would accept war rather than let it perish. And the war came." Each side looked "for an easier triumph, and a result less fundamental and astounding," admitted the President. Then Lincoln launched into his religious message to the Nation— and perhaps the world—each sentence a perfect gem of preparation, experience and thought.

> Both read the same Bible, and pray to the same God; and each invokes His aid against the other. It may seem strange that any men should dare to ask a just God's assistance in wringing their bread from the sweat of other men's faces [Genesis 3:19]; but let us judge not that we be not judged [Matthew 7:1]. The prayers of both could not be answered; that of neither has been answered fully. The Almighty has His own purposes [2 Timothy 1:9]. "Woe unto the world because of offenses! for it must needs be that offenses come; but woe to that man by whom the offense cometh!" [Luke 17:1] If we shall suppose that American Slavery is one of those offenses

which, in the providence of God, must needs come, but which, having continued through His appointed time, He now wills to remove, and that He gives to both North and South, this terrible war, as the woe due to those by whom the offense came, shall we discern therein any departure from those divine attributes which the believers in a Living God always ascribe to Him? Fondly do we hope—feverently do we pray—that this mighty scourge of war may speedily pass away. Yet, if God wills that it continue, until all the wealth piled by the bondman's two hundred and fifty years of unrequited toil shall be sunk, and until every drop of blood drawn with the lash, shall be paid by another drawn with the sword, as was said three thousand years ago, so still it must be said "the judgments of the Lord, are true and righteous altogether." [Psalm 19:9]

With malice toward none; with charity for all; with firmness in the right, as God gives us to see the right, let us strive on to finish the work we are in; to bind up the nation's wounds; to care for him who will have borne the battle, and for his widow, and his orphan—to do all which may achieve and cherish a just, and a lasting peace, among ourselves, and with all nations.[160]

If there had been a slight doubt in Lincoln's mind about the effectiveness of his Gettysburg Address, there was absolutely none in regard to his Second Inaugural. Eleven days after delivering his masterpiece at the Capitol, President Lincoln asserted that it would "wear as well as—perhaps better than—any thing I have produced; but I believe it is not immediately popular. Men are not flattered by being shown that there has been a difference of purpose between the Almighty and them. To deny it, however, in this case, is to deny that there is a God governing the world. It is a truth which I thought needed to be told; and as whatever of humiliation there is in it, falls most directly on myself, I thought others might afford for me to tell it."[161]

Here, again, is Abraham Lincoln's religious creed in writing: God governed the world. And he was God's instrument. Who could still say that Lincoln was not a religious man?

Knowing that Mary Lincoln would cherish the Bible which her husband had handled while taking his oath of office, Salmon Portland Chase—now Chief Justice of the Supreme Court and the officer who had administered the oath—carefully marked the exact spot where President Lincoln's lips had touched the Bible and presented this sacred volume to Mrs. Lincoln. He indicated that Lincoln had saluted with a kiss the 27th and 28th verses of the 5th Chapter of Isaiah: "None shall be weary nor stumble among them; none shall slumber nor sleep; neither shall the girdle of their loins be loosed, nor the latchet of their shoes be broken: Whose arrows <u>are</u> sharp, and all their bows bent, their horses' hoofs shall be counted like flint, and their wheels like a whirlwind."[162]

But President Lincoln *was* weary and tired. Still, he certainly could see that the end of the terrible conflict was in sight. And his army of the faithful was becoming invincible. These portions of the Bible verses were prophetic. So, too, were Lincoln's comments to Harriet Beecher Stowe when she remarked to him that he must look forward to the end of hostilities. "No, Mrs. Stowe, I shall never live to see peace; this war is killing me."[163]

A tradition was broken by the Lincolns at their evening reception in the White House on March 4, 1865. Many colored people had been invited, including the noted Mr. and Mrs. Frederick Douglass.[164] Such actions bespeak a very charitable and Christian spirit on the part of the First Family considering the previous attitudes held by occupants of the Executive Mansion.

As part of the inaugural festivities, Bishop Matthew Simpson of the Methodist Episcopal Church preached in the Capitol building on Sunday, March 5. A large and attentive audience assembled to hear him deliver a masterly sermon which proved to be very moving. Among those present were President and Mrs. Abraham Lincoln as well as Secretary Stanton, Chief Justice Chase, Admiral David Glasgow Farragut and numerous other dignitaries.[165] Lincoln liked the Bishop, who—it has been said—helped the President modify the harsher policies of Stanton—both came from Cadiz, Ohio. And Bishop Simpson openly campaigned for Lincoln's re-election.[166]

On the evening of March 6, the Inaugural Ball took place in the Patent Office. Mary Lincoln appeared "most elegantly dressed" in a rich, white, silk gown, heavily flounced and trimmed with beautiful pointlace. Around her shoulders she wore a white lace shawl. Upon her head were "delicate lilac and white flowers." She wore a necklace and carried a fan, among other appointments. Many dances were scheduled on the program, and no doubt certain Washington ladies criticized this Presbyterian First Lady for sponsoring such an event with its "sinful" dancing.[167]

References

1   Basler, ed., *The Collected Works*, V, 146; Lincoln thought that $400 per slave would be about the right amount to offer. *Ibid.*, V, 160.

2   *Ibid.*, V, 185-186.

3   *Ibid.*, V, 212.

4   *Ibid.*, V, 212-213.

5   *Ibid.*, V, 213.

6   *Ibid.*, V, 215-216.

7   *Ibid.*, V, 279.

8   *Ibid.*, V, 327.

9   *Ibid.*, V, 343.

10   *Ibid.*, V, 356.

11   *Ibid.*, V, 403-404.

12   *Ibid.*, V, 419-421.

13   Beale, ed., *Diary of Gideon Welles*, I, 143; J. P. Usher's statement in Allen Thorndike Rice, ed., *Reminiscences of Abraham Lincoln* (N. Y.: North American Review, 1888), 91; Basler, ed., *The Collected Works*, VI, 30; Donald, ed., *Diaries of Salmon P. Chase*, 150.

14   Lincoln memo dated Sept. 22, 1862, in collection of Dr. George M. Oldenbourg, Jr., Berkeley, Cal.

15   Chittenden, *Recollections of Lincoln,* 448.

16   Basler, ed., *The Collected Works*, V, 438.

17   Charles M. Segal, ed., *Conversations with Lincoln* (N. Y.: G. P. Putnam's Sons, 1961), 245.

18   Basler, ed., *The Collected Works*, V, 445-446.

19   Washington *Evening Star*, Oct. 6, 1862, p. 1, c. 6; N. Y. *Herald*, Oct. 6, 1862, p. 5, c. 4.

20   Basler, ed., *The Collected Works*, V, 452.

21 Donald, ed., *Diaries of Salmon* P. Chase, 166.

22 Beale, ed., *Diary of Gideon Welles*, I, 161.

23 Dorothy Lamon Teillard, ed., *Recollections of Abraham Lincoln* (Washington: Pub. by author, 1911), 151.

24 Philip Whitwell Wilson, *An Unofficial Statesman—Robert C. Ogden* (Garden City: Doubleday, Page & Co., 1924), 60-61.

25 Basler, ed., *The Collected Works*, V, 478; VII, 535. I have used the contemporary newspaper account for the dating of this interview as being much more reliable than recollections.

26 *Ibid.*, V, 497-498.

27 *Ibid.*, V, 518, 537.

28 *Ibid.*, VI, 34.

29 *Ibid.*, VI, 39-40.

30 *Ibid.*, VI, 42.

31 *Ibid.*, IV, 550, V, 12; Shelby M. Cullom, *Fifty Years of Public Service* (Chicago: A. C. McClurg & Co., 1911), 135; Turner and Turner, eds., *Mary Todd Lincoln*, 571.

32 *Daily National Intelligencer*, Jan. 17, 1863, p. 1, c. 6.

33 *Ibid.*, Jan. 19, 1863, p. 3, cc. 1, 3; "F. T. B." in *Decatur (Ill.) Republican*, May 19, 1870, p. 1, c. 4, an observer of this important event; Homer L. Calkin, *Castings from the Foundry Mold: A History of Foundry Church, Washington, D. C., 1814-1964* (Washington: Foundry Methodist Church, 1965), 127. The late William H. Townsend once had possession of this important document and allowed it to be published in Edgar DeWitt Jones, *Lincoln and the Preachers* (N. Y.: Harper & Bros., 1948), 138-139.

34 Edwin Erle Sparks, ed., *The Lincoln-Douglas Debates of 1858* (Springfield: Ill. State Hist. Lib., 1908), 479-480.

35 Basler, ed., *The Collected Works*, VI, 114-115.

36 RTL Coll., Ser. 1, No. 22215-6, The Library of Congress.

37 Basler, ed., *The Collected Works*, VI, 152-153.

38   Wayne C. Temple, *Lincoln and Grant: Illinois Militiamen* (Springfield: Illinois Military and Naval Dept., 1981).

39   Basler, ed., *The Collected Works*, VI, 155-157.

40   *Ibid.*, VI, 199.

41   Nicolay and Hay, *Abraham Lincoln: A History*, IV, 469n.

42   Basler, ed., *The Collected Works*, VI, 226-227.

43   *Ibid.*, VI, 244-245.

44   James F. Rusling, *Men and Things I Saw in Civil War Days* (N. Y.: Eaton & Mains, 1899), 12-18, 358. A facsimile of the certified document is in Johnson, *Abraham Lincoln the Christian*, 113.

45   Basler, ed., *The Collected Works, VI, 319-320.*

46   *Ibid.*, V, 537.

47   *Ibid.*, VI, 332-333.

48   Dennett, ed., *Diaries and Letters of John Hay*, 74. The poem is in Basler, ed., *The Collected Works Supplement*, 194-195.

49   Basler, ed., *The Collected Works*, III, 145. For the sermon, see David Hein, "A Sermon Lincoln Heard . . . ," *Lincoln Herald*, LXXXIX, 161-166 (Winter, 1987).

50   Basler, ed., *The Collected Works*, VI, 401.

51   *Ibid.*, VI, 410. When Lincoln saw his address published in the Eastern newspapers several days before it was to be released in Springfield, he was furious. He telegraphed Conkling and asked for an immediate explanation, saying he was mortified. Also, the papers had botched it up. *Ibid*, VI, 430.

52   *Ibid.*, VI, 496-497.

53   *Ibid.*, VI, 501.

54   *Ibid.*, VI, 531; N. Y. *Herald*, Oct. 23, 1863, p. 7, c. 2.

55   Basler, ed., *The Collected Works*, VI, 535-536.

56   Turner and Turner, eds., *Mary Todd Lincoln,* 67.

57   N. W. Miner, "Personal Recollections of Abraham Lincoln," 42, 44.

58   Basler, ed., *The Collected Works*, I, 391.

59   Helen Nicolay, *Lincoln's Secretary* (N. Y.: Longmans, Green & Co., 1949), 42.

60   N. W. Miner, "Personal Recollections of Abraham Lincoln," 42.

61   Washington *Evening Star*, Nov. 12, 1863, p. 2, c. 1, Nov. 13, 1863, p. 2, c. 5; "Castine," Washington, D. C., Nov. 14, 1863, in *Sacramento Union*, Dec. 12, 1863; Dennett, ed., *Diaries of John Hay*, 119.

After her regal wedding, "Kate" Chase Sprague had a tragic life. By 1866, her marriage was in great difficulty. Her husband drank excessively, was extremely jealous—perhaps with some cause—and lost his fortune in the Panic of 1873. The Spragues were divorced in 1882. Of their four children, one daughter was mentally ill, and the only son committed suicide in 1890. "Kate" ended her life toiling like a poor farmer's wife, selling what produce she could raise on a small tract of land.

62   Basler, ed., *The Collected Works*, IV, 240.

63   *Ibid.*, IV, 271.

64   *Ibid.*, VII, 16.

65   Beale, ed., *Diary of Edward Bates*, 316; Beale, ed., *Diary of Gideon Welles*, I, 480.

66   N. Y. *Herald*, Nov. 20, 1863, p. 4, c.1; Washington *Evening Star,* Nov. 18, 1863, p. 2, c. 4, Nov. 19, 1863, p. 1, c. 5, Nov. 20, 1863, p. 2, cc. 2-3; Basler, ed., *The Collected Works Supplement,* 210.

President Lincoln was noted for his kindness to blacks. For instance, he thought the widows and children of "colored soldiers" should have the same benefits whether or not the soldier's marriage could be supported by legal documents. He reasoned that "wives" and their children were certainly de facto. Many slave owners had never allowed legal marriages of their slaves. Many others had split up slave families, etc.*Ibid.*, 243.

67   Louis A. Warren, *Lincoln's Gettysburg Declaration* (Fort Wayne: Lincoln National Life Foundation, 1964), 70-73.

68   Washington *Evening Star*, Nov. 19, 1863, p. 2, c. 6, Nov. 20, 1863, p. 2, cc. 2-3; N. Y. *Daily Tribune*, Nov. 20, 1863, p.1, cc. 5-6; Harvey Sweney to Andrew Sweney, Gettysburg, Pa., Nov. 29, 1863, *Jour. Ill. State Hist. Soc.* LI, 106 (Spring, 1958); Basler, ed., *The Collected Works*, VII, 23.

69   Dennett, ed., *Diaries of John Hay*, 121.

70   Brooks, *Washington in Lincoln's Time*, 304-305.

71   Gov. Richard Yates of Illinois had commissioned Lamon on Feb. 9, 1861, as his Aide de Camp with the rank of Colonel in the Artillery, to take rank from Feb. 4 that year. Executive Record, VIII, 196, MS., Ill. State Archives.

Lincoln called him "my particular friend" in a recommendation dated May 28, 1862. Basler, ed., *The Collected Works*, V, 247.

72   Abraham Lincoln had known William H. Johnson about a year before he took him with the Presidential party to Washington in 1861. But Johnson departed on Mary Lincoln's train and joined the President at Indianapolis. He served Lincoln not only as a valet but also as a barber, messenger, etc. At the White House, on March 4, Johnson became a fireman tending the furnace at $600 per year. However, trouble developed between him and the rest of the black staff. When the President sought another job for him, Lincoln stated that the "difference of color between him & the other servants is the cause of our separation." Historians have assumed from this letter that Johnson was very dark and the staff was very light. Yet he was not extremely black. A correspondent for the *New York Herald* observed this valet in the Presidential suite of travelers and identified him as "William, a likely Mulatto." Johnson was slightly darker than most of the other servants at the White House, some of whom appear in photographs owned by Dr. Lloyd Ostendorf to be so light that they could have almost passed for white. However, the real cause probably lay mostly with the attitudes of the old help who had held positions at the Executive Mansion over several administrations. These blacks were extremely clannish; most even attended the same black church, the 15th Street Presbyterian. They were notorious for boycotting any new employee who was hired in the White House. They were very jealous and most fearful of losing their employment whenever a new President took up residence in their domain.

Johnson was finally hired on November 30, 1861, in the Treasury Department as a laborer and messenger for the librarian in this division. In the mornings he still served the President; in the afternoons he worked at his post in the Treasury. Whenever Johnson was needed for a full day or more, the President simply sent a notice to Johnson's supervisor, as he did for the Gettysburg trip. Johnson may have caught the smallpox from Lincoln on this excursion. At any rate, Johnson died of this disease sometime before January 28, 1864. Lincoln informed his son Robert that there was "a good deal of small-pox here" when he wrote him on January 19, 1864. Wm. Johnson was buried in Arlington National Cemetery in Section 27, Grave No. 3346 at Lincoln's own expense. There was no obituary in the newspapers of his life. Yet he rests with the heroes of the Nation and was much trusted and befriended by President Lincoln. Basler, ed., *The Collected Works*, IV, 277, 288, V, 33, 446-447, 474, VI, 8-9, 69, 125n, VII, 137, 156-157; *Supplement*, 210-211; N. Y. *Herald*, Feb. 20, 1861, p. 1, c. 5; John E. Washington, *They Knew Lincoln* (N. Y.: E. P. Dutton & Co., 1942), 107. This last study identifies the wrong "William" as Lincoln's personal servant, manager of his wardrobe, barber, etc. It was not William Slade. Basler, "Did President Lincoln Give the Smallpox to William H. Johnson?" *Huntington Library Quarterly*, XXXV, 279-284 (May, 1972).

Secretary of War Stanton ordered Brig. Gen. James B. Fry to go with Pres. Lincoln to Gettysburg "as a sort of special escort." James B. Fry in Rice, ed., *Reminiscences of Abraham Lincoln*, 402-403.

73   Washington *Evening Star*, Nov. 20, 1863, p. 2, cc. 2-3.

74   Warren, *Lincoln's Gettysburg Declaration*, 140; Philip B. Kunhardt, Jr., *A New Birth of Freedom: Lincoln at Gettysburg* (Boston: Little, Brown & Co., 1983), 215; Robert to his wife, Gettysburg, Penn., Nov. 20, 1863, MS., Dr. Lloyd Ostendorf Coll.; Clark E. Carr, *Lincoln at Gettysburg* (Chicago: A. C. McClurg & Co., 1907), 60, 72; Selleck's Reminiscences in *Milwaukee Evening Wisconsin*, Feb. 6, 1909, p. 12, cc. 4-6; Elmo R. Richardson and Alan W. Farley, *John Palmer Usher* (Lawrence: Univ. of Kansas Press, 1960), 66; Dorothy Lamon Teillard, ed., *Recollections of Abraham Lincoln 1847-1865 by Ward Hill Lamon* (Washington: Privately Published, 1911), 173.

B. B. French was silent about the audience's reactions to Lincoln's address, merely stating there was a "hurricane of applause that met his every movement at Gettysburg . . . ." But he never mentioned the crowd's reaction when he spoke at the dedication ceremonies. Cole and McDonough, ed., *B. B. French Journal*, 435-436; Basler, ed., *The Collected Works*, VI, 314.

75   Washington *Evening Star,* Nov. 20, 1863, p. 2, c. 3. The State of Illinois had but three military units that fought at Gettysburg: the 8th Cavalry; four companies of the 12th Cavalry; and the 82nd Infantry. By 1864, there were a total of 3,355 Union soldiers buried at Gettysburg in the National Cemetery. Illinois' dead were: J. Wallikeck, John Ellis, Charles Wm. Miner, David Dieffenbaugh, Corp. John Ackerman and an unknown man from the 8th.

76   Dennett, ed., *Diaries of John Hay*, 121.

77   Basler, ed., *The Collected Works*, VII, 24-25.

78   Washington *Evening Star*, Nov. 20, 1863, p. 2, c. 3.

79   *The National Cyclopaedia of American Biography* (Ann Arbor: Univ. Microfilms, 1967, reprint ed.), II, 30-31; *Battles and Leaders of the Civil War*, III, 276n, 284n; *Official Records* (Washington: Govt. Print. Office, 1889), Ser. I, XXVII, Pt. I, p. 255; Donald L. Smith, *The Twenty-Fourth Michigan of the Iron Brigade* (Harrisburg: The Stackpole Co., 1962), 149-150.

80   *History of the Church 1740-1931* (Gettysburg: The Church, 1931), 9-16.

81 On October 5, 1873, Wills would be ordained as an Elder of this congregation. "The Church Register of the Presbyterian Church Gettysburg, Pennsylvania begun April 1867," p. 2, MS., The Presbyterian Church of Gettysburg.

82 *History of Cumberland and Adams Counties, Pennsylvania* (Chicago: Warner, Beers & Co., 1886), 375-376. Often called Judge, he was not elected to this position until 1874. He died on Oct. 27, 1894.

83 Washington *Evening Star*, Nov. 20, 1863, p. 2, cc. 2-3.

84 N. Y. *Herald*, Nov. 19, 1863, p. 7, c. 4.

85 Washington *Evening Star*, Nov. 20, 1863, p. 2, cc. 2-3.

86 Beale, ed., *Diary of Gideon Welles*, I, 480.

87 *U. S. Statutes at Large* (Boston: Little, Brown & Co., 1866), XIII, 577.

88 *National Cyclopaedia*, II, 30-31; Robert L. Bloom, "'I Know How to Fight . . . .' John Burns of Gettysburg," *Adams County Historical Society Newsletter*, XVII, 2-4 (June, 1990); Burns' pension file, No. 31776, MSS., The National Archives.

89 Wm. H. Herndon interview with Mrs. A. Lincoln at the St. Nicholas Hotel, Springfield, Ill., Sept. 5, 1866 [misdated 1871], Herndon-Weik Coll., Group IV, No. 1561, MS., The Library of Congress.

90 *Freeport (Ill.) Weekly Journal*, Dec. 7, 1864, p. 1, c. 3. At least this account was related while Lincoln still lived.

91 Dennett, ed., *Diaries of John Hay*, 128. Hay went to hear Rev. Hale.

92 Beale, ed., *Diary of Edward Bates*, 318, 257.

93 Cole and McDonough, eds., *Benjamin Brown French Journal*, 439.

94 Basler, ed., *The Collected Works*, VII, 36.

95 *Ibid.*, VII, 53.

96 Dennett, ed., *Diaries of John Hay*, 143.

97 Basler, ed., *The Collected Works*, VII, 86.

98 *Ibid.*, VII, 128.

99 *Ibid.*, VII, 169.

100   Miers, ed., *Lincoln Day by Day*, III, 238.

101   Basler, ed., *The Collected Works*, VII, 179.

102   Washington *Evening Star*, Feb. 12, 1864, p. 3, c. 1.

In 1864, Pres. Lincoln named Bingham a Major and assigned him to be a Judge Advocate in the Union Army. He would later become Special Judge Advocate in the trial of the conspirators who were charged with assassinating Lincoln in 1865.

103   Basler, ed., *The Collected Works*, VII, 223.

104   *Ibid.*, VII, 234.

105   *Ibid.*, VII, 254.

106   *Ibid.*, VII, 282.

107   *Ibid.*, VII, 287.

108   *Ibid.*, VII, 301-302.

109   *U. S. Statutes at Large*, XII, 54.

110   Basler, ed., *The Collected Works*, VII, 324.

111   *Ibid.*, VII, 331.

112   *Ibid.*, VII, 333.

113   *Ibid.*, VII, 334.

114   *Ibid.*, VII, 339.

115   *Ibid.*, VII, 350-351.

116   *Ibid.*, VII, 365.

117   *Ibid.*, VII, 368.

118   Beale, ed., *Diary of Edward Bates*, 371.

119   Basler, ed., *The Collected Works*, VII, 395, 396.

120   Washington *Evening Star*, June 17, 1864, p. 2, c. 4, June 20, 1864, p. 1, cc. 5-6.

121   Basler, ed., *The Collected Works*, VII, 419n.

122   N. Y. *Herald*, July 3, 1864, p. 5, c. 1.

123   Speed, *Reminiscences of Abraham Lincoln*, 32-33.

Before Speed died, he finally joined Trinity Methodist Church in his home town. Robert L. Kincaid, *Joshua Fry Speed* (Harrogate: Lincoln Memorial Univ. Press, 1943), 32.

124   Basler, ed., *The Collected Works*, VII, 431-432.

125   *Ibid.*, VII, 528-529.

126   *Ibid.*, VII, 533-534.

127   *Ibid.*, VII, 535-536.

128   *Ibid.*, VII, 542-543.

129   Deming, *Eulogy of Abraham Lincoln*, 41-42. Deming revealed these facts on June 8, 1865, at Allyn Hall in Hartford, Conn., before the General Assembly of Connecticut. Less than a year had passed since he'd heard Pres. Lincoln utter these very personal sentiments.

130   Basler, ed., *The Collected Works*, VIII, 55-56.

131   *Armory Square Hospital Gazette*, Nov. 26, 1864.

132   G. George Fox, *Abraham Lincoln's Religion* (N. Y.: Exposition Press, 1959), 117.

133   Basler, ed., *The Collected Works*, VII, 514.

134   *Ibid.*, VIII, 96.

135   *Ibid.*, VIII, 101.

136   *Ibid.*, I, 48.

137   *Ibid.*, VIII, 102-103.

138   *Ibid.*, VIII, 567.

139   Theodore C. Blegen, ed., *Abraham Lincoln's Mailbag: Two Documents by Edward D. Neill, One of Lincoln's Secretaries* (St. Paul: Minn. Hist. Soc., 1964).

140   William O. Stoddard, Jr., ed., *Lincoln's Third Secretary* (N. Y.: Exposition Press, 1955). One of his commissions is facing p. 74.

141   The author has studied Philbrick's life from primary sources and will publish his finds at a later time. There is no doubt of Philbrick's service to Lincoln. Both Nicolay and Hay mention his duty, and Philbrick's father supplied the exact date of his appointment when Phi Alpha Fraternity requested information on their alumni. MSS., Illinois College, Jacksonville, Ill.

142   N. Y. *Herald*, Nov. 26, 1864, p. 5, c. 5. This Boston source explained that Mrs. Bixby was a poor widow living in the 11th Ward and even had a sixth son lying wounded in Readville Hospital at that very time. But Widow Bixby did not have a sixth son in the service.

    Michael Burlingame, "New Light on the Bixby Letter," *Jour. of the Abraham Lincoln Assoc.*, XVI, 59-71 (Winter, 1995).

143   William E. Barton, *A Beautiful Blunder* (Indianapolis: The Bobbs-Merrill Co., 1926).

144   Millions of tourists read this inscription at the Punchbowl Crater and never realize the source. Even this author visited the site many times before it dawned upon him that it was a long phrase from the immortal Bixby letter. For the story of this cemetery, see Milly Singletary, *Punchbowl: National Memorial Cemetery of the Pacific* (Honolulu: Sunset Publications, 1981).

145   N. Y. *Herald*, Nov. 25, 1864, p. 8, c. 4, p. 1, cc. 3-4.

146   *Washington Daily Morning Chronicle*, Nov. 25, 1864, p. 2, c. 5.

147   Basler, ed., T*he Collected Works*, VIII, 136.

148   *Ibid.*, VIII, 154-155.

149   *The Congregationalist* (Boston), XVIII, No. 13, p. 50, c. 7, p. 51, c. 1 (Mar. 30, 1866).

150   Basler, ed., *The Collected Works*, VIII, 219.

151   *Ibid.*, VIII, 236.

152   *Ibid.*, VIII, 245-246.

153   *Ibid.*, VIII, 318-319n.

154   *Ibid.*, VIII, 308.

155   *Ibid.*, VIII, 325.

156   *Ibid.*, VIII, 326.

157   N. Y. *Herald,* Mar. 6, 1865, p. 4, c. 6; Cole and McDonough, eds., *Benjamin Brown French Journal*, 460-461, 514-515.

158   N. Y. *Herald*, Mar. 8, 1865, p. 4, c. 5.

159   Brooks, *Washington in Lincoln's Time*, 74.

160   Basler, ed., *The Collected Works*, VIII, 332-333.

161   *Ibid.*, VIII, 356.

162   Salmon P. Chase to Mary T. Lincoln, Washington, D. C., Mar. 4, 1865, MS., Ser. I, No. 41049, RTL Coll., The Library of Congress.

163   Rice, ed., *Reminiscences of Abraham Lincoln*, 251.

164   N. Y. *Tribune*, Mar. 6, 1865, p. 4, cc. 4-5.

165   Washington *Evening Star*, Mar. 6, 1865, p. 3, c. 1.

166   Jones, *Lincoln and the Preachers*, 57-58.

167   *Daily National Intelligencer*, Mar. 7, 1865, p. 2, c. 4.

Photo Courtesy of the Illinois State Historical Library.

President Abraham Lincoln in his casket at the New York City Hall on April 24, 1865, by Jeremiah Gurney whose photographic studio was at 707 Broadway. Gurney was in a gallery twenty feet higher than the casket and forty feet away from it. Rear Adm. Charles Henry Davis was standing at the head, and Brig. Gen. Edward Davis Townsend was at the foot of the casket. A description of this event is found in O. R., Ser. I, Vol. XLVI, Pt. 3, pp. 965-967.

When Lt. Gen. U. S. Grant saw that the end of the long conflict was near, he invited President Lincoln to visit him at City Point, Virginia, and witness the last days of the war. Accordingly, Lincoln accepted this gracious invitation and steamed out of Washington on March 23. Jefferson Davis fled from Richmond on the night of April 2, and Major General Godfrey Weitzel, a West Point graduate in the Class of 1855, occupied the capital city of the Confederacy on the following day. General Weitzel commanded the 25th Army Corps in the Army of the James.

Lincoln went to the front on the *River Queen* but transferred to the *U. S. S. Malvern* with Admiral David Dixon Porter for his excursion into Richmond. When shallow water forced the *Malvern* to heave to, Admiral Porter put the Commander-in-Chief aboard his barge which landed at Rocketts on April 4. With twelve sailors as his military escort, the President disembarked to walk into Richmond with no great show of ceremony. At the landing stood a small house where about twelve Negroes were digging with their spades. One of them proved to be an old man. When he caught sight of Lincoln, he stood up straight and dropped his spade. He rushed up and threw himself at Lincoln's feet. His fellow workers followed.

With great embarrassment, the President spoke quickly to these poor black men. "Don't kneel to me," he instructed them. "That is not right," he told them. "You must kneel to God only, and thank him for the liberty you will hereafter enjoy. I am but God's humble instrument; but you may rest assured that as long as I live no one shall put a shackle on your limbs, and you shall have all the rights which God has given to every other free citizen of this Republic." After saying this, Lincoln's face lit up "with a divine look." The President appeared to be at that time "of another world."

After visiting the Army's headquarters, Lincoln returned to his ship for the night but came back to Richmond for an extended visit on April 5. He walked through the streets without any disturbance being created by the citizens of that city. Also present was the U. S. Assistant Secretary of War, Charles A. Dana. On Friday night, the 7th, Dana questioned General Weitzel whether or not divine services in the local churches would be allowed on Sunday. Weitzel replied that he would permit them to open if no disloyalty would be uttered by the ministers. He also declared that he would require the preachers to pray for President Lincoln just as they had previously prayed for President Jefferson Davis. However, after giving this answer to Dana, General Weitzel talked to a local judge who objected to such a prayer. Giving in to Judge John Campbell, the Union General said the clergy would only be required not to pray for Jefferson Davis. When Secretary Stanton learned this fact, he was furious with Weitzel. He insisted the clergy pray for President Lincoln.

The Chief Magistrate departed from the front on the evening of April 8 and did not witness any church services in Richmond on the following day. When the Secretary of War pressed the issue and threatened to discipline Weitzel, the General carried his plea to Lincoln on April 12. The Commander-in-Chief replied that same day, saying, "I do not remember hearing prayers spoken of while I was in Richmond; but I have no doubt you have acted in what appeared to you to be the spirit and temper manifested by me while there." The President had told Weitzel not to press petty points with the defeated Confederates.[1] He was not vindictive and wished for a lenient reconstruction among his former enemies.

During the entire day of April 9, President Lincoln and his party sailed up the Potomac toward Washington. To his guests, the President read aloud from the writings of Shakespeare. He concentrated upon the tragedy *Macbeth* and expounded several times on the murder of Duncan and what must have gone on in the murderer's mind.[2] In retrospect, this appears to have been most prophetic. In the coming days President Lincoln would think even more about his own death.

Upon docking in Washington that evening, the President learned that Robert E. Lee had surrendered to Grant about 1:00 p. m. that day. By means of the military telegraph, the Washingtonians had learned of Lee's capitulation before the President had, since his vessel had not communicated with any ports on the return voyage. People thronged through the streets, lit bonfires and rejoiced that the cruel war had finally terminated with a Union victory.

In responding to a crowd who visited him on April 10, the President pleaded with them to wait until the evening of the following day when he would make a more formal speech. Meanwhile, he noted that the revelers had several bands with them and remarked that he had "always thought 'Dixie' one of the best tunes" he had ever heard. Therefore, he asked one of the bands to play it since it had been "fairly captured" by the Union forces. His Attorney General, he vouched, had given his legal opinion that "Dixie" was now their "lawful prize." In the blush of victory, these statements caused much laughter and applause. Accordingly, the musicians performed this request and followed it up with "Yankee Doodle" while the President listened from a window of the White House. When the music ended, Lincoln proposed three cheers for General Grant and his Army and three more for the gallant Navy. Lincoln seemed in a cheerful mood.[3]

At the President's last public address, given on the night of April 11, Lincoln told his listeners that "We meet this evening, not in sorrow, but in gladness of heart. The evacuation of Petersburg and Richmond, and the surrender of the principal insurgent army, give hope of a righteous and speedy peace whose joyous expression.can not be restrained." "In the midst of this, however," Lincoln informed the gleeful crowd, "He, from Whom all blessings flow, must not be forgotten. A call for national thanksgiving is being prepared, and will be duly promulgated."[4] As usual, his hopeful message started off with words of praise for God; this time from the Doxology.

Next day, the Chief Executive informed Gen. Weitzel at Richmond that as Lee's Army had surrendered, there was no need for the old Virginia Legislature to assemble and recall its Virginia troops. These men were already prisoners of General Grant, and Lincoln forbid the legislators to convene as a legitimate body for the enactment of any business whatsoever in this occupied state of the Confederacy.[5]

Although it appeared the President was happily carrying on his executive duties, fits of melancholy still crept into his tired mind. At about this time, the President seemed pensive and silent in the presence of two or three other people, including Mary Lincoln and Marshal Ward Hill Lamon. Finally, the President aroused himself under the prodding of his wife and exclaimed, "It seems strange how much there is in the Bible about dreams." "If we believe the Bible," continued Lincoln, "we must accept the fact that in the old days God and His angels came to men in their sleep and made themselves known in dreams. Nowadays dreams are regarded as very foolish, and are seldom told, except by old women and by young men and maidens in love." Mary Lincoln then queried her husband if he believed in dreams.

"I can't say that I do," replied Lincoln, "but I had one the other night which has haunted me ever since. After it occurred, the first time I opened the Bible, strange as it may appear, it was at the twenty-eighth chapter of

Genesis [verses 12-16], which relates the wonderful dream Jacob had. I turned to other passages, and seemed to encounter a dream or vision wherever I looked. I kept on turning the leaves of the old book, and everywhere my eye fell upon passages recording matters strangely in keeping with my own thoughts,—supernatural visitations, dreams, visions, etc."

Seeing that he had frightened Mary, the President remarked that he should not have mentioned the subject at all. But, he admitted, "the thing has got possession of me, and, like Banquo's ghost, it will not down." Such a statement merely made Mary more curious, and she urged him to repeat the dream to her. After hesitating for a bit, the President finally commenced this tale:

"About ten days ago," he said, "I retired very late. I had been waiting for important dispatches from the front. I could not have been long in bed when I fell into a slumber, for I was weary. I soon began to dream. There seemed to be a death-like stillness about me. Then I heard subdued sobs, as if a number of people were weeping. I thought I left my bed and wandered downstairs. There the silence was broken by the same pitiful sobbing, but the mourners were invisible. I went from room to room; no living person was in sight, but the same mournful sounds of distress met me as I passed along. It was light in all the rooms; every object was familiar to me; but where were all the people who were grieving as if their hearts would break? I was puzzled and alarmed. What could be the meaning of all this? Determined to find the cause of a state of things so mysterious and so shocking, I kept on until I arrived at the East Room, which I entered. There I met with a sickening surprise. Before me was a catafalque, on which rested a corpse wrapped in funeral vestments. Around it were stationed soldiers who were acting as guards; and there was a throng of people, some gazing mournfully upon the corpse, whose face was covered, others weeping pitifully. 'Who is dead in the White House?' I demanded of one of the soldiers. 'The President,' was his answer; 'he was killed by an assassin!' Then came a loud burst of grief from the crowd, which awoke me from my dream. I slept no more that night; and although it was only a dream, I have been strangely annoyed by it ever since."[6]

In referring to this vivid and horrible dream once more to Lamon, the President ended by quoting from *Hamlet*: "To sleep; perchance to dream! ay, there's the rub!" This matter still hung heavily upon Lincoln's mind.[7] Even though he might publicly deny that he believed in dreams, Lincoln actually put great store in such revelations as being messages from God. He tended to treat them as did the prophets of old. He even revealed his dreams to his Cabinet.

Early in the morning of April 14, the Commander-in-Chief summoned General Grant to meet with the Cabinet members at 11:00 a. m. that day.[8] Talk soon turned to Major General William T. Sherman. Since Secretary Stanton was late—as usual—somebody asked if Lt. General Grant had heard from Sherman. "No," replied Grant, but he expected a message any hour. Whereupon the President exclaimed that there soon would be word from Sherman, and it would be favorable to their cause. Just last night, the President explained, he'd had the same dream which he always had just before every big battle. Turning to Secretary Welles, the President informed him that it involved his element: the water. Lincoln revealed that he always seemed to be on an indescribable vessel which was sailing rapidly towards some indefinite shoreline. Thus, Lincoln predicted that very quickly they would receive "great news" from General Sherman. His thoughts were "in that direction," said Lincoln, and he was sure some great event would soon take place.[9] Actually, Sherman had already occupied Raleigh, North Carolina, on April 13th, but this information had not yet reached Washington. However, another great event occurred that very evening—the assassination of Lincoln himself!

April 14 being the exact fourth anniversary of the day when Major Robert Anderson had lowered the Flag in surrender at Fort Sumter in Charleston Harbor, South Carolina, Secretary Stanton had selected noon of this very day for Anderson—now a Major General—to raise once again the same old Colors over the battered fort where the Civil War had started back in 1861. On March 25, Stanton, with Lincoln's approval, had selected the Rev. Henry Ward Beecher to make the patriotic address upon this gala occasion.[10] Rev. Beecher spoke most eloquently. But President Lincoln would not live to read this address by a minister whom he admired greatly for his oratory and delivery.

At three o'clock in the afternoon of that day, President Lincoln took his wife for a leisurely ride in an open carriage. He seemed quite happy and told Mary that they must be more cheerful in the future. Willie's tragic death had caused them both great pain and sorrow. The terrible war had haunted the President's very soul and turned his facial features into those of a much older man. Now, husband and wife could lay plans for the future. They eagerly looked forward to the end of his second term. Lincoln expressed a desire, Mary said, to travel after leaving office. Europe, he promised, they would visit, but he especially wished to see the Holy Land and walk in Jerusalem where so much of the Bible history had taken place.[11] For many years he had read and studied the Scriptures, and his natural curiosity led him to desire a first-hand experience in those famous places mentioned in the Bible. However, it was Mary Lincoln who generally exhibited an insatiable bent for traveling. After her husband's death, she would rove around endlessly.

At 5:00 p. m. the Lincolns' carriage returned to the White House where Governor Richard J. Oglesby and Brigadier General Isham Nicholas Haynie of Illinois awaited them. These old friends sat with Lincoln in his reception room where he read to them four chapters from Petroleum V. Nasby's book, *The Nasby Papers*. After an hour, somebody called Lincoln to dinner, and he left. He seemed in great humor.[12] Nevertheless, he confided to his personal bodyguard, William H. Crook, that he was going to be assassinated. Lincoln had no special desire to attend Ford's Theatre that night, but he felt it was necessary since his attendance had already been advertised in the newspapers.[13] Lincoln's pronouncement parallels that of Jesus Christ when he informed his disciples that he must go to Jerusalem and be killed (Matthew 16:21).

Somewhere near 8:00 p. m. the Lincolns departed in their carriage from the Executive Mansion and picked up their two guests for the evening— Major Henry Reed Rathbone and Clara Harris, Rathbone's fiancée. In due course they arrived at Ford's Theatre to witness the play "Our American Cousin," an English farcical comedy written by Tom Taylor. Guarding the President that night was John Parker, a Washington City police officer of doubtful reputation.

Being in a theatre on Good Friday was not the thing to do, according to many churchgoers in the Nation's capital city. Strangely enough, this site was originally where the First Baptist Church had been constructed in 1833. When it, and another church of this same denomination, combined in 1859, this building on Tenth Street was abandoned for a new location. John T. Ford leased the edifice on December 10, 1861, for five years with an option to purchase. Then early in 1862, the operator closed his theatre, which he had established there, and remodeled the premises. Unfortunately for Ford, fire later swept through it on December 30 of that year. After reconstruction, it opened on August 27, 1863, as Ford's New Theatre.[14]

When the audience recognized the Presidential party on their way to the state box, a chorus of cheers went up. William Withers, conductor of the house orchestra, immediately led his musicians in rendering "Hail to the Chief." Lincoln acknowledged this warm greeting with a bow while holding his right hand over his heart. Then he led his party to the state box, actually numbers 7 and 8 which had been combined for more room, and which had been especially rearranged for them. Still the audience clapped and cheered until the President stood and bowed, again, to them.

The drama proceeded in a timely manner. Not being overly interested in this play, President Lincoln sat holding Mary's hand in his and repeating his desire to journey over to Palestine and actually walk in the places which the Bible mentioned. He thought that if would be most interesting to tread in the paths trod by Christ so many years before. He believed that Jerusalem would be the most interesting city in the world to see. Since it was Good Friday, it was quite natural that Lincoln's thoughts were on the last hours of Jesus Christ, at least as a historical figure and a philosopher. What more, we cannot state at this late date. Lincoln also expressed his relief that the cruel war had finally come to the point that General Joseph E. Johnston had no other recourse but to surrender to Sherman very soon. That would, for all practical purposes, bring to a close the bloody four-year conflict of brother against brother.[15]

While the President was thinking and talking of these matters at about 10:13 p. m., John Wilkes Booth, the actor, stole quietly into the Presidential box; raised his .44-caliber Deringer pistol made in Philadelphia; fired its single round, consisting of Britannia metal, into Lincoln's head, just behind his left ear; and shouted, "Sic semper tyrannis," the state motto of Virginia. With such a display and oath, "thus ever to tyrants," the Federal Government immediately concluded that the Confederacy had somehow sponsored Booth's violent act of seeming madness, and they probably had aided his original plan to capture Lincoln. However, as time passed and the North experienced a mellowing toward the South, revisionist historians and writers attempted to change the previously accepted view of this tragic event. These authors declared that the assassin was insane, or was losing his voice and thus needed an exploit to insure his place in history, or was certainly acting alone with his gang of thugs, etc. A recent work of scholarship severely damages the theses of the revisionists who held the Confederate authorities blameless in President Lincoln's death.[16] These apologists ignored the facts turned up at the conspiracy trial of Booth's cohorts. If not a Southern agent, why did Booth have a Confederate cipher book in his hotel room? Why did he constantly associate with known

Confederate agents and spies? Why did he even travel to Canada to see them? Why did he refer to the Confederacy as his country? When he escaped from Washington after killing Lincoln, why did he follow the route used by Confederate spies and utilize Confederate agents and sympathizers? Why did his fellow conspirator, Louis Thornton Powell, alias Lewis Paine (or Payne), confide to his jailer, Colonel Levi A. Dodd, and his minister, Rev. A. D. Gillette, just before he was hanged, that he "believed that he was acting under an order from the rebel authorities . . ." if it were not true?[17]

John Wilkes Booth was certainly in the pay of the Confederate Government, at least at the beginning of his association with them. For six months prior to the assassination, Booth had attempted to seize President Lincoln and take him south. His own journal revealed this fact. What unattached private citizen would attempt such a feat in wartime without monetary assistance and access to an underground network sponsored by the Confederate Army? In his journal, Booth explained that "our cause being almost lost, something decisive and great must be done." His kidnapping plan had failed, Booth declared, "owing to others who did not strike for their country with a heart." He had no desire, he admitted, "to out live my country."

Of course, it may have been that the Confederate officials in charge of clandestine operations did not dream Booth would continue his activities even after Lee had surrendered. The war was lost for them, but evidently Booth decided to act out his revenge upon the leader of the North, regardless of the altered circumstances between the two countries.

If Abraham Lincoln could have read Booth's journal, he would probably have shaken his head in disbelief. Booth had inscribed on one page: "Our country [the Confederacy] owed all her troubles to him, and God simply made me the instrument of his punishment." President Lincoln had long declared that *he* was God's instrument, and here was an actor—not in a governmental position of leadership—proclaiming that *he* was an instrument of God, too. Long before, Lincoln had puzzled out loud over this dilemma. In his Second Inaugural Address, referring to the warring parties, he had pointed out that "Both read the same Bible, and pray to the same God; and each invokes His aid against the other." Here was another example of this conundrum. But Lincoln would not have believed Booth's claim, because he had questioned how "any men should dare to ask a just God's assistance in wringing their bread from the sweat of other men's faces." Slavery was certainly wrong, and God condemned it, too. "The prayers of both could not be answered," Lincoln had decided.

Booth also confided to his journal, "God try and forgive me, and bless my mother." Being a baptized Episcopalian, it seems he was asking for forgiveness after making his confession on paper. "God <u>cannot</u> pardon me if I have done wrong," Booth wrote. He also noted a statement that even his victim would have understood perfectly: "God's will be done."[18] The martyred Lincoln had known all along that everything would be done according to God's design. "With malice toward none," Lincoln had pointed out, the United States must bind up its wounds so as to "achieve and cherish a just, and a lasting peace." Lincoln would probably have forgiven his own assassin so long as the United States lived on in freedom and prospered and bound up its terrible deep wounds and healed itself.

Although the heavy handmade ball from Booth's pistol had plowed a half-inch-wide path across Lincoln's brain and rendered him completely unconscious, the physically-powerful "Railsplitter" did not die immediately.[19] With several physicians in attendance, the President was hurried across the way to 453 Tenth Street, NW, a building owned by William Petersen who, in turn, rented out rooms to at least five other people. There, Lincoln was laid across the bed of a boarder and examined by a number of physicians, including the Lincoln family doctor, Robert K. Stone who informed Robert T. Lincoln upon his arrival at the scene that there was no hope for his father's recovery. Mary Lincoln became so distraught that those in charge tried to keep her confined in another room of the house. By the request of Robert Lincoln, a number of women were brought to comfort her. Among them were Elizabeth Lord (Cogswell) Dixon, wife of Senator James Dixon of Connecticut; her sister, Mary Kinney; and the latter's daughter, Constance Kinney.

Gradually, a number of high governmental officials were called or simply appeared at the scene. Quite naturally, the family minister, Dr. Phineas D. Gurley, was also summoned to Lincoln's bedside. Very early the next morning, B. B. French arrived at Petersen's building and was immediately asked to take the President's carriage, which stood at the curb, and fetch Mary Jane (Hale) Welles, wife of Secretary of the Navy; and Emma (Brooks) Gurley, wife of Dr. Gurley. It was hoped that these two understanding ladies could cope with Mary Lincoln much better than the women already sitting with her. Mary Lincoln had not gotten along well with many of the women in Washington. However, she did like Mary Jane Welles and Emma Gurley. In due course, these two intimate friends of Mary's arrived.[20]

At 7:22:10 on the morning of April 15, 1865, Dr. Charles S. Taft observed that President Lincoln's pulse had ceased to beat. This woeful news caused a sudden deathly hush to fall over the entire bedroom for several minutes. At last Stanton broke the silence, turned to Dr. Gurley, and asked him to pray. This kindly minister responded with "one of the most impressive prayers ever uttered." When he concluded, all those assembled around the deceased President answered "amen," and Secretary Stanton remarked to his tearful audience, "Now he belongs to the ages."[21] Quite appropriately, the first notice which the general public received of Lincoln's death was the solemn tolling of church bells throughout Washington.

The President's thoroughly broken widow was then taken back to the White House and put to bed with only Mary Jane Welles at her side.[22] Finally, a messenger located Elizabeth Keckley and escorted her to the Executive Mansion where she relieved Mrs. Welles who had been ill prior to the assassination of Lincoln. Alone with her sorrowing mistress, Elizabeth Keckley attempted to soothe her, but Mary would not be consoled. She let out "unearthly shrieks," had "terrible convulsions," and "tempestuous outbursts of grief." Like the roar of a tornado, her clamorous voice of terrible affliction swept through the White House. She flatly refused to see any of her friends who called upon her. Only Tad seemed able, at times, to calm her. He pointed out to his mother that his father had been a good man and certainly had gone to Heaven.[23]

Abraham Lincoln's body had been borne in a flag-draped pine box to the guest room of the White House on the north side of the second floor, opposite Mary Lincoln's room. There, medical examiners and surgeons performed their bloody autopsy by sawing open the skull, removing the brain and retrieving the spent pistol ball. Undertakers later went about the ghoulish preparation of the corpse for the funeral services. Several friends of the First Family observed all of these procedures. Elizabeth Keckley, a woman of color, upon reflection during the tragedy, exclaimed that President Lincoln had been the Moses of her race.[24] She, too, had seen the Biblical connection in Lincoln's life.

With Mary Lincoln lying in her bedroom *non compos mentis*, Robert Todd Lincoln—at twenty-one years of age—became the responsible head of the Lincoln household. On April 15 he telegraphed Justice David Davis of the U. S. Supreme Court, who happened to be in Chicago, and implored him, "Please come at once to Washington & take charge of my father's affairs."[25]

Regarding the photo on the preceding page:

On April 16, 1865, Secretary of War Edwin M. Stanton ordered that "The headquarters of every department, post, station, fort, and arsenal will be draped in mourning for thirty days . . . ."
O. R. Ser. I, XLVI, Pt. 3, p. 788.

The Illinois State Arsenal at 430 N. 5th Street in
Springfield was so draped.
Illinois State Journal, Apr. 17, 1865, p. 3, c. 3.

C. M. Smith later announced that he had 30,000 yards of mourning goods
for sale at cost.
Ibid., Apr. 27, 1865, p. 3, c. 3.

In charge of the guard at this Arsenal was Sgt. Edward M. Brooks, Co. D, 113th
Infantry Regiment, Illinois Volunteers.
E. M. Brooks to Rev. Dr. [Thomas Dale] Logan, of Springfield, Ill.

Copy in Author's Collection

Some preparations were already underway. Dr. Charles B. Brown and his partner, Dr. John Alexander, who was actually an upholsterer at times, had quickly taken charge of Lincoln's body after the autopsy and accomplished their difficult task of preservation with great skill. Since these two were the same ones who had embalmed Willie Lincoln's remains in February of 1862, their selection had not been a difficult decision to make. Perhaps Mary Lincoln had even mentioned them to Stanton or French immediately after her husband died. These undertakers dressed the martyred Chief Magistrate in the same suit of clothing that he had worn at his second inauguration.

On Sunday, April 16, B. B. French, acting in his capacity as Commissioner of Public Buildings, called at the White House to oversee the funeral arrangements. He had already closed the Capitol and ordered it draped in mourning. George Harrington (1815-1892) assisted French in formulating the program for the funeral. The former, from Massachusetts, was the Assistant Secretary of the Treasury. His church affiliation is not recorded, but French—like Lincoln—shunned a formal church membership. He emphatically believe in God and often read his Bible, but he disliked the dogma of organized religions. Instead, he found his necessary solace and comfort in Masonry, although he sometimes accompanied his second wife to her church services. She was a Roman Catholic. However, French and Harrington tried not to permit their personal feelings to dictate the arrangements. Instead, they followed the wishes of the Lincoln family, so far as they could determine them. French had been able to consult with Mary Lincoln briefly after she returned to the White House on the morning of April 15 concerning funeral arrangements. After that, Secretary Stanton was the only Cabinet official who could gain entrance to Mary Lincoln's room. And yet, there was one touch to the funeral trimmings which had its origin in French's Masonic background. He place evergreen around the casket,[26] a symbol of eternal life to members of Craft Masonry.

Noah Brooks decided to worship at the New York Avenue Presbyterian Church on that Sunday, April 16th, and discovered that the Lincoln pew, as well as the entire building, had been draped in black cloth. All the musical numbers were dirges. Sadness hung heavily over the grieving congregation and the stunned minister. Dr. Gurley directed his parishioners to look from the hand of the assassin to the hand of God. He agreed that it was a difficult burden of pain to bear but opined that God had his purpose in this tragic event.[27]

Much later—about 1883—the sacred pew of the Lincolns was removed from the sanctuary and placed in the Bible Class Rooms of the Sunday School portion of the building. But at the annual meeting of the congregation on the evening of March 9, 1893, "the question arose as to the advisability of replacing President Lincoln's pew in its original form in the main auditorium." Although a few hinted that this ancient piece of furniture would look out of place amidst the new seats, Dr. William Alvin Bartlett, the pastor at that time, arose and declared that "There is no greater religious relic in the world, and no greater relic anywhere, than this pew where Abraham Lincoln sat to worship his God." Rev. Bartlett vowed that he "would rather sit [in] it than another of pure gold." Following this moving oration, the Trustees immediately ordered the custodian to take out one of the new pews and install Lincoln's seat at its previous location in the sanctuary where it belonged. A silver identification plate was then attached to it.[28]

When the old 1859 house of worship could no longer serve the needs of its congregation, a new structure was erected upon the same plot of ground. President Harry S. Truman, a Past Grand Master of Masons in Missouri, laid the cornerstone on April 3, 1951, and the new edifice—looking much like the old building—was formally dedicated on December 20, 1951. Needless to say, the Lincoln Family pew was retained in this "Church of the Presidents" and can still be found today in the beautiful sanctuary. It carries the number B-14. Not only does the New York Avenue Presbyterian Church have a Lincoln Committee, but it also sponsors a special Lincoln program in the church every year with a noted speaker and a patriotic program with a religious theme.

To mark President Lincoln's passing, church bells immediately tolled a mourning tribute to his greatness. That response was a common audible sound throughout the Nation. However, the reaction expressed by ministers varied widely. The Rev. John Chester, at his Capitol Hill Presbyterian Church (O. S.) on 4th between B and Pennsylvania Avenue in Washington, pronounced on April 16 that Lincoln might have been removed from the governmental scene because he was too lenient. Here was a man of the cloth who sought vengeance against the secessionists.[29] Other preachers repeated this same theme. There needed to be a harsher reconstruction visited upon the errant South, they said. Some agonized over the President's being in the theatre on Good Friday instead of at church. Yet all of them thought he should be forgiven, because he only went to satisfy the curiosity of the electorate who wished to cast their eyes upon him. He was only serving the people that he loved and cared for in his capacity as Chief Magistrate. Pastors explained to their flocks that God would allow President Lincoln to enter Heaven because of his good works and his religious faith.[30] One friend vouched for Lincoln's religious observances and asserted that Lincoln attended the New York Avenue Presbyterian Church "frequently."[31] Some ministers took their text from the Old Testament and declared that slavery had caused Lincoln's demise, and the Confederacy had been deeply involved in the plot. Of course, there was a natural comparison of Lincoln to Christ. The day Christ died became Good Friday. Both died on Good Friday and both gave their lives for mankind.[32]

One old colleague felt it was necessary to publish his feeling and his alibi that Lincoln had actually given his life to Christ and accepted the Christian religion. "For myself," divulged Noah Brooks, "I am glad to say that I have a firm belief in Mr. Lincoln's saving knowledge of Christ; he talked always of Christ, his cross, his atonement; he prayed regularly, cast all his cares on God and felt inexpressible relief thereby; was almost as familiar with the Bible as our old friend Field . . . ."[33] Lincoln did read the Bible and prayed constantly, but it is extremely doubtful that he talked openly to anybody about Christ's atonement for man's sins, etc. Lincoln spoke mainly of God and to God.

Rabbi Samuel Meyer Isaacs saw no problem with Abraham Lincoln's faith and his life eternal. He prayed on Wednesday, April 19, "We beseech Thee receive the soul of our lamented President, as Thou hast accepted all those who have served Thee in truth."[34] Rabbi Max Lilienthal prayed on Saturday, April 22, "Farewell, till God grants us a meeting in eternity."[35] Those of the Jewish faith had no doubt at all but what Lincoln had been saved by God's grace and rested in Heaven at that very moment. None of them faulted Lincoln for not having a church membership.

Sands & Harvey on 7th Street, constructed the special walnut coffin for President Lincoln's body, and immediately billed the Federal government for $1,500. The coffin was covered with fine broadcloth and lined with satin and silk. It contained a thick lead lining so that after the last viewing it might be soldered shut airtight. Heavy silver fringe hung from the black cloth covering, complete with tassels. There were four massive handles on each side for carrying the casket.[36] Into this magnificent box of death the corpse of Lincoln was placed and carried into the great East Room on the evening of the 17th. At 9:30 a. m. on Tuesday, April 18, the anxious public was admitted to view their martyred leader. They were allowed to enter at one of the gates, proceed through the Green Room and on into the East Room. Visitation ceased at 5:30 p. m. that afternoon. No lingering was permitted in the White House after viewing the body.

It had been most difficult to arrange the formal funeral ceremonies, because Mary Lincoln remained secluded in her private chamber and refused all interviews except to two or three people. With these, she had discussed the necessary rites only on the afternoon of April 16. Dr. R. K. Stone continued to treat her physical and mental condition.[37] Congress, of course, selected the pallbearers to attend the casket in an honorary capacity. The Senate chose Lafayette S. Foster of Connecticut, Edwin D. Morgan of New York, Reverdy Johnson of Maryland, Richard Yates of Illinois, Benjamin F. Wade of Ohio and John Conness of California. The House picked Henry L. Dawes of Massachusetts, Alexander H. Coffroth of Pennsylvania, Green C. Smith of Kentucky, Schuyler Colfax of Indiana, Henry Gaither Worthington of Nevada and Elihu Benjamin Washburne of Illinois.[38] At first it was announced that the rites at the Executive Mansion would be held at 11:00 a. m. on April 19, Wednesday, and only those with tickets would be admitted. Later, the hour was changed to noon, and the service actually began at 12:10. Those with passes did not quite fill the great East Room.[39]

By eleven, some of the mourners began arriving. About sixty clergymen from all parts of the country appeared in a body and were the first to enter. Then came heads of government bureaus, etc. Prominent officers of the Army and Navy appeared, including U. S. Grant. Members of the Diplomatic Corps wore their impressive costumes. Congressmen and Senators found their places in the seating chart and took their seats. Joining them were officers of local governmental bodies, the Christian Commission, and the Union League from Philadelphia and New York. Precisely at noon, President Andrew Johnson led his Cabinet into the somber chamber. Of course, Secretary Seward was not present since an assassin had attempted to kill him with a knife on the same night Lincoln was shot, and he was still confined to his bed. Hannibal Hamlin returned for the funeral, and Chief Justice Chase was there, also.

Many of President Lincoln's friends from Springfield, Illinois, did not arrive in time for the funeral. However, some of Mary Lincoln's relatives were present: Ninian Wirt Edwards; Clark Moulton Smith; Dr. Lyman Beecher Todd of Lexington, Kentucky; and General John Blair Smith Todd of the Dakota

Territory. Nicolay and Hay, naturally, were present, but Mary (Todd) Lincoln did not appear. She remained sequestered in her room upstairs. Both Robert and Tad Lincoln took their places in the audience and were the only members of Lincoln's immediate family present. Only seven women attended this service: Mrs. Kate (Chase) Sprague, Mrs. John Palmer Usher, Mrs. Edwin (McMasters) Stanton, Mrs. Gideon Welles, Miss Hattie Chase, and Mrs. William Dennison and her daughter.

At ten minutes past noon, the Rev. Dr. P. D. Gurley arose and walked to the head of the catafalque and announced the order of service.[40] It would seem that each celebrant had been carefully chosen to represent a denomination which had touched Abraham Lincoln's life in a particular way. Gurley, being the Lincoln Family minister, had been placed in the position of moderator. First, he introduced the Rev. Dr. Charles H. Hall, the Episcopal minister from the Church of the Epiphany on G Street between 13th and 14th, presumably because an Episcopal Priest had married the Lincolns on November 4, 1842, in Springfield. Dr. Hall read from the Episcopal burial service:

> I am the resurrection and the life saith the Lord; he that believeth in me, though he were dead, yet shall he live, and whosoever liveth and believeth in me shall never die—John xi: 25, 26.

> I know that my Redeemer liveth, and that He shall stand at the latter day upon the earth and though after my skin worms destroy this body, yet in my flesh shall I see God, who I shall see for myself, and mine eyes shall behold and not another.—Job xix: 25, 26, 27.

> We brought nothing into this world, and it is certain we can carry nothing out. The Lord gave and the Lord hath taken away. Blessed be the name of the Lord.—1 Timothy vi: 7, and Job i: 21

> Lord, let me know my end and the number of my days, that I may be certified how long I have to live. Behold, Thou hast made my days as it were but a span long, and mine age is even as nothing in respect of Thee. And verily every man living is altogether vanity; for man walketh in a vain shadow, and disquieteth himself in vain. He heapeth up riches, and cannot tell who shall gather them. And now, Lord, what is my hope? Truly my hope is ever in Thee; deliver me from all my

offenses, and make me not a rebuke unto the foolish. When Thou, with rebukes dost chasten man for sin, Thou makest his beauty to consume away, like as it were a moth fretting a garment. Every man is, therefore, but vanity. Hear my prayer, O Lord, and with Thine ears consider my calling. Hold not Thy peace at my tears, for I am a stranger with thee and a sojourner, as all my fathers were. O, spare me a little, that I may recover my strength before I go hence and be no more seen. Lord, Thou hast been our refuge from one generation to another. Before the mountains were brought forth, or even the earth and the world were made, Thou art God from everlasting, and world without end. Thou turnest man to destruction; again thou sayest, come again, ye children of men, for a thousand years As soon as Thou scatterest them, they are even as sheep, and fade away suddenly like the grass. In the morning it is green and groweth up, but in the evening it is cut down, dried up, and withered. For we consume away in Thy displeasure, and are afraid at thy wrathful indignation. Thou hast set our misdeeds before Thee, and our secret sins in the light of Thy countenance; for when thou art angry all our days are gone. We bring our years to an end, as it were a tale that is told. The days of our age are threescore years and ten, and though men be so strong that they come to fourscore years, yet is their strength then but labor and sorrow, so soon passeth it away, and we are gone. So teach us to number our days that we may apply our hearts unto wisdom. Glory be to the Father, and to the Son, and to the Holy Ghost; as it was in the beginning, is now, and ever shall be, world without end. Amen.

Then was read the lesson from the 15th chapter of St. Paul to the Corinthians, beginning with the 20th verse:

But now is Christ risen from the dead, and become the first-fruits of them that slept.

For since by man came death, by man came also the resurrection of the dead.

For as in Adam all die, even so in Christ shall all be made alive.

But every man in his own order; Christ the first-fruits; afterward they that are Christ's at his coming. Then cometh the end, when he shall have delivered up the kingdom to God,even the Father; when he shall have put down all rule, and all authority, and power.

For he must reign, till he hath put all enemies under his feet.

The last enemy that shall be destroyed is death.

For he hath put all things under his feet. But when he saith, all things are put under him, it is manifest that he is excepted which did put all things under him.

And when all things shall be subdued unto him, then shall the Son also himself be subject unto him that put all things under him, that God may be all in all.

Else what shall they do, which are baptized for the dead, if the dead rise not at all? why are they then baptized for the dead?

And why stand we in jeopardy every hour?

I protest by your rejoicing which I have in Christ Jesus our Lord, I die daily.

If after the manner of men I have fought with beasts at Ephesus, what advantageth it me, if the dead rise not? let us eat and drink; for tomorrow we die.

Be not deceived; evil communications corrupt good manners.

Awake to righteousness, and sin not; for some have not the knowledge of God. I speak this to your shame.

But some man will say, How are the dead raised up? and with what body do they come?

Thou fool, that which thou sowest not that body that shall be, but bare grain; it may change of wheat, or of some other grain: But God giveth it a body as it hath pleased him, and to every seed his own body.

All flesh is not the same flesh; but there is one kind of flesh of men, another flesh of beasts, another of fishes, and another of birds.

There are also celestial bodies, and bodies terrestrial: but the glory of the celestial is one, and the glory of the terrestrial is another.

There is one glory of the sun, and another glory of the moon, and another glory of the stars; for one star differeth from another star in glory.

So also is the resurrection of the dead. It is sown in corruption, it is raised in incorruption:

It is sown in dishonor, it is raised in glory: it is sown in weakness, it is raised in power:

It is sown a natural body, it is raised a spiritual body. There is a natural body, and there is a spiritual body.

And so it is written, The first man Adam was made a living soul, the last Adam was made a quickening spirit.

Howbeit, that was not first which is spiritual, but that which is natural; and afterward that which is spiritual.

The first man is of the earth, earthy: the second man is the Lord from Heaven.

As is the earthy, such are they also that are earthy: and as is the Heavenly, such are they also that are heavenly.

And as we have borne the image of the earthly, we shall also bear the image of the heavenly.

Now this I say, brethren, that flesh and blood cannot inherit the Kingdom of God; neither doth corruption inherit incorruption.

Behold, I shew you a mystery: We shall not all sleep, but we shall all be changed.

In a moment, in the twinkling of an eye, at the last trump: for the trumpet shall sound, and the dead shall be raised incorruptible, and we shall be changed.

For this corruptible must put on incorruption, and this mortal must put on immortality.

So when this corruptible shall have put on incorruption, and this mortal shall have put on immortality, then shall be brought to pass the saying that is written, Death is swallowed up in victory.

O death, where is thy sting? O grave, where is thy victory?

The sting of death is sin; and the strength of sin is the law.

But thanks be to God, which giveth us the victory, through our Lord Jesus Christ.

Therefore, my beloved brethren, be ye steadfast, unmovable, always abounding in the work of the Lord, forasmuch as ye know that your labor is not in vain in the Lord.

Next came Bishop Matthew Simpson from Philadelphia representing the Methodist Episcopal Church. Well did Abraham Lincoln's colleagues remember that the deceased President had held this man in great esteem. He had enjoyed this Bishop's eloquence and friendship. On May 18, 1864, Lincoln had said, "God bless the Methodist Church." His immediate friends also recalled that Lincoln had accepted a Life Directorship in the Missionary Society of the Methodist Episcopal Church in 1863. Rarely had he ever allowed himself to be officially associated with any denomination's religious activities. Bishop Simpson now came forward to render the opening prayer:

Almighty God, our Heavenly Father, as with smitten and suffering hearts we come into Thy presence, we pray, in the name of our blessed Redeemer, that Thou wouldst pour upon us Thy Holy Spirit, that all our thoughts and acts may be acceptable in Thy sight. We adore Thee for all Thy glorious perfections. We praise Thee for the revelation which Thou hast given us in Thy works and in Thy Word. By Thee all worlds exist. All beings live through Thee. Thou raisest up Kingdoms and empires, and castest them down. By Thee kings reign and princes decree righteousness. In Thy hand are the issues of life and death. We confess before Thee the magnitude of our sins and transgressions, both as individuals and as a nation. We implore Thy mercy for the sake of our Redeemer. Forgive us all our iniquities. If it please Thee, remove Thy chastening hand from us; and, though we be unworthy, turn away from us Thine anger, and let the light of Thy countenance again shine upon us.

At this solemn hour, as we mourn for the death of our President, who was stricken down by the hand of an assassin, grant us also the grace to bow in submission to Thy holy will. May we recognize Thy hand high above all human agencies, and Thy power as controlling all events, so that the wrath of man shall praise Thee, and that the remainder of wrath Thou wilt restrain.

Humbled under the suffering we have endured, and the great afflictions through which we have passed, may we not be called upon to offer other sacrifices. May the lives of all our officers, both civil and military, be guarded by Thee; and let no violent hand fall upon any of them. Mourning as we do, for the mighty dead by whose remains we stand, we would yet lift our hearts unto Thee in grateful acknowledgment for Thy kindness in giving us so great and noble a commander.

Thou art glorified in good men, and we praise Thee that Thou didst give him unto us so pure, so honest, so sincere, and so transparent in character. We praise Thee for that kind, affectionate heart, which always swelled with feelings of enlarged benevolence. We bless Thee for what Thou didst enable him to do; that Thou didst give him wisdom to select for his advisers, and for his officers, military and naval, those men through whom our country has been carried through an unprecedented conflict.

We bless Thee for the success which has attended all their efforts, and victories which have crowned our armies; and that Thou didst spare Thy servant until he could behold the dawning of that glorious morning of peace and prosperity which is about to shine upon our land; that he was enabled to go up as Thy servant of old upon Mount Pisgah, and catch a glimpse of the promised land. Though his lips are silent and his arm is powerless, we thank Thee that Thou didst strengthen him to speak words that cheer the hearts of the suffering and the oppressed, and to write that declaration of emancipation which has given him an immortal reward; that though the hand of the assassin has struck him to the ground, it could not destroy the work which he has done, nor forge again the chains which he has broken. And while we mourn that he has passed away, we are grateful that his work was so fully accomplished, and that the acts which he has performed will forever remain.

We implore Thy blessing upon his bereaved family, Thou husband of the widow. Bless her who, broken-hearted and sorrowing, feels oppressed with unutterable anguish. Cheer the loneliness of the pathway which lies before her, and grant to her such consolations of Thy spirit, and such hopes, through the resurrection, that she shall feel that "Earth hath no sorrows which Heaven cannot heal."

Let Thy blessing rest upon his sons; pour upon them the spirit of wisdom; be Thou the guide of their youth; prepare them for usefulness in society, for happiness in all their relations. May the remembrance of their father's counsels, and their father's noble acts, ever stimulate them to glorious deeds, and at last may they be heirs of everlasting life.

Command Thy rich blessings to descend upon the successor of our lamented President. Grant unto him wisdom, energy, and firmness for the responsible duties to which he has been called; and may he, his cabinet, officers and generals who shall lead his armies, and the brave soldiers in the field, be so guided by Thy counsels that they shall speedily complete the great work which he had so successfully carried forward. Let Thy blessing rest upon our country. Grant unto us all a fixed and strong determination never to cease our efforts until our glorious Union shall be fully re-established.

Around the remains of our loved President may we covenant together by every possible means to give ourselves to our country's service until every vestige of this rebellion shall have been wiped out, and until slavery, its cause, shall be forever eradicated.

Preserve us, we pray Thee, from all complications with foreign nations. Give us hearts to act justly toward all nations, and grant unto them hearts to act justly toward us, that universal peace and happiness may fill our earth. We rejoice, then, in this inflicting dispensation Thou hast given, as additional evidence of the strength of our nation. We bless Thee that no tumult has arisen, and in peace and harmony our government moves onward; and that Thou hast shown that our republican government is the strongest upon the face of the earth.

In this solemn presence, may we feel that we too are immortal! May the sense of our responsibility to God rest upon us; may we repent of every sin; and may we consecrate anew unto Thee all the time and all the talents which Thou hast given us; and may we so fulfill our allotted duties that finally we may have a resting-place with the good, and wise, and the great, who now surround that glorious throne! Hear us while we unite in praying with Thy Church in all lands and in all ages, even as Thou hast taught us, saying:

Our Father which art in heaven; hallowed by Thy name. Thy kingdom come. Thy will be done in earth as it is in heaven. Give us this day our daily bread. And forgive us our trespasses, as we forgive those who trespass against us. And lead us not into temptation, but deliver us from evil. For Thine is the kingdom, and the power, and the glory, forever. Amen!

To deliver the funeral sermon, Dr. Gurley mounted the first step of the catafalque and stood near Lincoln's head.[41] He had received this high honor because the Lincolns had chosen his Presbyterian Church as their regular place of worship. It will be remembered, also, that Mary Lincoln was actually a member of this denomination back in Springfield, Illinois.

Dr. Gurley gave this message which he captioned "Faith in God," its title taken from Mark 11:22:

AS WE STAND HERE TODAY, MOURNERS AROUND THIS COFFIN, AND AROUND THE LIFELESS REMAINS OF OUR BELOVED CHIEF MAGISTRATE, WE RECOGNIZE AND WE ADORE THE SOVEREIGNTY OF GOD. His throne is in the heavens, and His kingdom ruleth over all. He hath done, and He hath permitted to be done, whatsoever He pleased. "Clouds and darkness are round about Him; righteousness and judgment are the habitation of His throne." His way is in the sea, and His path in the great waters, and His footsteps are not known. "Canst thou by searching find out God? Canst thou find out the Almighty unto perfection? It is as high as heaven; what canst thou do? Deeper than hell; what canst thou know? The measure thereof is longer than the earth, and broader than the sea. If He cut off and shut up, or gather together, then who can hinder Him? for He knoweth vain men; He seeth wickedness also; will He not then not consider it?"—We bow before His Infinite Majesty, we bow, we weep, we worship.

> "Where reason fails, with all her powers,
> There faith prevails, and love adores."

It was a cruel, cruel hand, that dark hand of the assassin, which smote our honored, wise, and noble President, and filled the land with sorrow. But above and beyond that hand there is another which we must see and acknowledge. It is the chastening hand of a wise and a faithful Father. He gives us this bitter cup. And the cup that our Father has given us, shall we not drink it?

> "God of the just, thou gavest us the cup:
> We yield to thy behest, and drink it up."

"Whom the Lord loveth He chasteneth." O how these blessed words have cheered and strengthened and sustained us through all these long and weary years of civil strife, while our friends and brothers on so many ensanguined fields were falling and dying for the cause of Liberty and Union! Let them cheer, and strengthen, and sustain us to-day. True, this new sorrow and chastening has come in such an hour and in such a way as we thought not, and it bears the impress of a rod that is very heavy, and of a mystery that is very deep. That such a life should be sacrificed, at such a time, by such a foul and diabolical agency; that the man at the head of the nation, whom the people had learned to trust with a confiding and loving confidence, and upon whom more than upon any other were centered, under God, our best hopes for the true and speedy pacification of the country, the restoration of the Union, and the return of harmony and love; that he should be taken from us, and taken just as the prospect of peace was brightly opening upon our torn and bleeding country, and just as he was beginning to be animated and gladdened with the hope of ere long enjoying with the people the blessed fruit and reward of his and their toils, care, and patience, and self-sacrificing devotion to the interests of Liberty and the Union—O it is a mysterious and a most afflicting visitation! But it is our Father in heaven, the God of our fathers, and our God, who permits us to be so suddenly and sorely smitten; and we know that His judgments are right, and that in faithfulness He has afflicted us. In the midst of our rejoicings we needed this stroke, this dealing, this discipline; and therefore He has sent it. Let us remember, our affliction has not come forth out of the dust, and our trouble has not sprung out of the ground. Through and beyond all second causes let us look, and see the sovereign, permissive agency of the great First Cause. It is His prerogative to bring light out of darkness and good out of evil. Surely the wrath of man shall praise Him, and the remainder of wrath He will restrain. In the light of a clearer day we may yet see that the wrath which planned and perpetrated the death of the President, was overruled by Him, whose judgments are unsearchable, and His ways past finding out, for the highest welfare of all those interests which are so dear to the Christian patriot and philanthropist, and for which a loyal people have made such an unexampled sacrifice of treasure and of blood. Let us not be faithless, but believing.

> "Blind unbelief is prone to err,
> And scan His work in vain;
> God is his own interpreter,
> And He will make it plain."

We will wait for his interpretation, and we will wait in faith, nothing doubting. He who has led us so well, and defended and prospered us so wonderfully, during the last four years of toil, and struggle, and sorrow, will not forsake us now. He may chasten, but He will not destroy. He may purify us more and more in the furnace of trial, but He will not consume us. No, No! He has chosen us, as He did his people of old in the furnace of affliction, and He has said of us as He said of them, "This people have I formed for myself; they shall show forth My praise." Let our principal anxiety now be that this new sorrow may be a sanctified sorrow; that it may lead us to deeper repentance, to a more humbling sense of our dependence upon God, and to the more unreserved consecration of ourselves and all that we have to the cause of truth and justice, of law and order, of Liberty and good government, of pure and undefiled religion. Then, though weeping may endure for a night, joy will come in the morning. Blessed be God! despite this great and sudden and temporary darkness, the morning has begun to dawn—the morning of a bright and glorious day, such as our country has never seen. That day will come and not tarry, and the death of an hundred Presidents and their Cabinets can never, never prevent it. While we are thus hopeful, however, let us also be humble. The occasion calls us to prayerful and tearful humiliation. It demands of us that we lie low, very low, before Him who has smitten us for our sins. O that all our rulers and all our people may bow in the dust to-day beneath the chastening hand of God! and may their voices go up to Him as one voice, and their hearts go up to Him as one heart, pleading with Him for mercy, for grace to sanctify our great and sore bereavement, and for wisdom to guide us in this our time of need. Such a united cry and pleading will not be in vain. It will enter into the ear and heart of Him who sits upon the throne, and He will say to us, as to His ancient Israel, "In a little wrath I hid my face from thee for a moment: but with everlasting kindness will I have mercy upon thee, saith the Lord, thy Redeemer."

I have said that the people confided in the late lamented President with a full and loving confidence. Probably no man since the days of Washington was ever so deeply and firmly imbedded and enshrined in the very hearts of the people as Abraham Lincoln. Nor was it a mistaken confidence and love. He deserved it—deserved it well—deserved it all. He merited it by his character, by his acts, and by the whole tenor, and tone, and spirit of his life. He was simple and sincere, plain and honest, truthful and just, benevolent and kind. His perceptions were quick and clear, his judgments were calm and accurate, and his purposes were good and pure beyond a question. Always and everywhere he aimed and endeavored to *be* right and to *do* right. His integrity was thorough, all-pervading, all-controlling, and incorruptible. It was the same in every place and relation, in the consideration and the control of matters great or small, the same firm and steady principle of power and beauty that shed a clear and crowning luster upon all his other excellences of mind and heart, and recomended him to his fellow citizens as *the* man, who, in a time of unexampled peril, when the very life of the nation was at stake, should be chosen to occupy, in the country and for the country, its highest post of power and responsibility. How wisely and well, how purely and faithfully, how firmly and steadily, how justly and successfully he did occupy that post and meet its grave demands in circumstances of surpassing trial and difficulty, is known to you all, known to the country and the world. He comprehended from the first the perils to which treason had exposed the freest and best Government on the earth, the vast interests of Liberty and humanity that were to be saved or lost forever in the urgent impending conflict; he rose to the dignity and momentousness of the occasion, saw his duty as the Chief Magistrate of a great and imperiled people, and he determined to do his duty, and his whole duty, seeking the guidance and leaning upon the arm of Him of whom it is written, "He giveth power to the faint, and to them that have no might He increaseth strength." Yes, he leaned upon His arm. He recognized and received the truth that the "kingdom is the Lord's, and He is the governor among the nations." He remembered that "God is in history," and he felt that nowhere had His hand and His mercy been so marvelously conspicuous as in the history of this nation. He hoped and he prayed that that same hand would continue to guide us, and that same mercy continue to abound to us in the time of our greatest need. I speak what I know, and testify what I have often heard him say, when I affirm that that guidance and mercy were the props on which he humbly and habitually leaned; they were the best hope he had for himself and for his country. Hence, when he was leaving his home in Illinois, and coming to this city to take his seat in the executive chair of a disturbed and troubled nation, he said to the old and tried friends who gathered tearfully around him and bade him farewell, "I leave you with this request: *pray for me.*" They did pray for him; and millions of other people prayed for him; nor did they pray in vain. Their prayer was heard, and the answer appears in all his subsequent history; it shines forth with a heavenly radiance in the whole course and tenor of his administration, from its commencement to its close. God raised him up for a great and glorious mission, furnished him for his work, and aided him in its accomplishment.

Nor was it merely by strength of mind, and honesty of heart, and purity and pertinacity of purpose, that He furnished him; in addition to these things, He gave him a calm and abiding confidence in the overruling providence of God and in the ultimate triumph of truth and righteousness through the power and the blessing of God. This confidence strengthened him in all his hours of anxiety and toil, and inspired him with calm and cheering hope when others were including to despondency and gloom. Never shall I forget the emphasis and the deep emotion with which he said in this very room, to a company of clergymen and others, who called to pay him their respects in the darkest day of our civil conflict: "Gentlemen, my hope of success in this great and terrible struggle, rests on that immutable foundation, the justice and goodness of God. And when events are very threatening, and prospects very dark, I still hope that in some way which man cannot see all will be well in the end, because our cause is just, and God is on our side." Such was his sublime and holy faith, and it was an anchor to his soul, both sure and steadfast. It made him firm and strong. It emboldened him in the pathway of duty, however rugged and perilous it might be. It made him valiant for the right; for the cause of God and humanity, and it held him in a steady, patient, and unswerving adherence to a policy of administration which he thought, and which we all now think, both God and humanity required him to adopt. We admired and loved him on many accounts—for strong and various reasons: we admired his childlike simplicity, his freedom from guile and deceit, his stanch and sterling integrity, his kind and forgiving temper, his industry and patience, his persistent, self-sacrificing devotion to all the duties of his eminent position, from the least to the greatest; his readiness to hear and consider the cause of the poor and humble, the suffering and the oppressed; his charity toward those who questioned the correctness of his opinions and the wisdom of his policy; his wonderful skill in reconciling differences among the friends of the Union, leading them away from abstractions, and inducing them to work together and harmoniously for the common weal; his true and enlarged philanthropy, that knew no distinction of color or race, but regarded all men as brethren, and endowed alike by their Creator "with certain inalienable rights, among which are life,Liberty, and the pursuit of happiness;" his inflexible purpose, that what freedom had gained in our terrible civil strife should never be lost, and that the end of the war should be the end of slavery, and, as a consequence of rebellion; his readiness to spend and be spent for the attainment of such a triumph—a triumph, the blessed fruits of which shall be as wide-spreading as the earth, and as enduring as the sun:—all these things commanded and fixed our admiration, and the admiration of the world, and stamped upon his character and life the unmistakable impress of *greatness*. But more sublime than any or all of these, more holy and influential, more beautiful, and strong, and sustaining, *was his abiding confidence in God and in the final triumph of truth and righteousness, through him, and for his sake.* This was his noblest virtue, his grandest principle, the secret alike of his strength, his patience, and his success. And this, it seems to me, after being near him steadily, and with him often, for more than four years, is the principle by which, more than by any other, "he, being dead, yet speaketh." Yes; by his steady enduring confidence in God, and in the complete ultimate success of the cause of God, which is the cause of humanity, more than by any other way, does he now speak to us and to the nation he loved and served so well. By this he speaks to his successor in office, and charges him to "have faith in God." By this he speaks to the members of his cabinet, the men with whom he counseled so often and associated with so long, and he charges them to "have faith in God." By this he speaks to the officers and men of our noble army and navy, and, as they stand at their posts of duty and peril, he charges them to "have faith in God." By this he speaks to all who occupy positions of influence and authority in these sad and troublous times, and he charges them all to "have faith in God." By this he speaks to this great people as they sit in sackcloth to-day, and weep for him with a bitter wailing, and refuse to be comforted, and he charges them to "have faith in God." And by this he *will* speak through the ages, and to all rulers and peoples in every land, and his message to them will be, "Cling to Liberty and right; battle for them; bleed for them; die for them, if need be; and have confidence in God." O that the voice of this testimony may sink down into our hearts to-day and every day, and into the heart of the nation, and exert its appropriate influence upon our feelings, our faith, our patience, and our devotion to the cause of freedom and humanity—a cause dearer to us now than ever before, because consecrated by the blood of its most conspicuous defender, its wisest and most fondly-trusted friend.

He is dead; but the God in whom he trusted lives, and He can guide and strengthen his successor, as He guided and strengthened him. He is dead; but the memory of his virtues, of his wise and patriotic counsels and labors, of his calm and steady faith in God lives, is precious, and will be a power for good in the country quite down to the end of time. He is dead; but the cause he so ardently loved, so ably, patiently, faithfully represented and defended—not for himself only, not for us only, but for all people in all their coming generations, till time shall be no more—that cause survives his fall, and will survive it. The light of its brightening prospects flashes cheeringly to-day athwart the gloom occasioned by his death, and the language of God's united providences is telling us that, though the friends of Liberty die, Liberty itself is immortal. There is no assassin strong enough and no weapon deadly enough to quench its inextinguishable life, or arrest its onward march to the conquest and empire of the world. This is our confidence, and this is our consolation, as we weep and mourn to-day. Though our beloved President is slain, our beloved country is saved. And so we sing of mercy as well as of judgment. Tears of gratitude mingle with those of sorrow. While there is darkness, there is also the dawning of a brighter, happier day upon our stricken and weary land. God be praised that our fallen Chief lived long enough to see the day dawn and the daystar of joy and peace arise upon the nation. He saw it, and he was glad. Alas! alas! He only saw the *dawn*. When the *sun* has risen, full-orbed and glorious, and a happy re-united people are rejoicing in its light,—alas! alas! it will shine upon his grave. But that grave will be a precious and a consecrated spot. The friends of Liberty and of the Union will repair to it in years and ages to come, to pronounce the memory of its occupant blessed, and, gathering from his very ashes, and from the rehearsal of his deeds and virtues, fresh incentives to patriotism, they will there renew their vows of fidelity to their country and their God.

And now I know not that I can more appropriately conclude this discourse, which is but a sincere and simple utterance of the heart, than by addressing to our departed President, with some slight modification, the language which Tacitus, in his life of Agricola, addresses to his venerable and departed father-in-law: "With you we may now congratulate; you are blessed, not only because your life was a career of glory, but because you were released when, your country safe, it was happiness to die. We have lost a parent, and, in our distress, it is now an addition to our heartfelt sorrow that we had it not in our power to commune with you on the bed of languishing, and receive your last embrace. Your dying words would have been ever dear to us; your commands we should have treasured up, and graved them on our hearts. This sad comfort we have lost, and the wound for that reason, pierces deeper. From the world of spirits behold your disconsolate family and people; exalt our minds from fond regret and unavailing grief to contemplation of your virtues. Those we must not lament; it were impiety to sully them with a tear. To cherish their memory, to embalm them with our praises, and, so far as we can, to emulate your bright example, will be the truest mark of our respect, the best tribute we can offer. Your wife will thus preserve the memory of the best of husbands, and thus your children will prove their filial piety.

By dwelling constantly on your words and actions, they will have an illustrious character before their eyes, and, not content with the bare image of your mortal frame, they will have what is more valuable—the form and features of your mind. Busts and statues, like their originals, are frail and perishable. The soul is formed of finer elements, and its inward form is not to be expressed by the hand of an artist with unconscious matter—our manners and our morals may in some degree trace the resemblance. All of you that gained our love and raised our admiration still subsists, and will ever subsist, preserved in the minds of men, the register of ages, and the records of fame. Others, who have figured on the stage of life and were the worthies of a former day, will sink, for want of a faithful historian, into the common lot of oblivion, inglorious and unremembered; but you, our lamented friend and head, delineated with truth, and fairly consigned prosperity, will survive yourself, and triumph over the injuries of time."

To close the service, the Rev. Dr. E. H. Gray from the E Street Baptist Church gave the final prayer. It seems logical to suppose that a pastor of this denomination was included in the funeral services because Abraham Lincoln had grown up in a Baptist atmosphere. Both of his parents were members of this faith. Dr. Gray prayed:

> God of the bereaved, comfort and sustain this mourning family. Bless the new Chief Magistrate. Let the mantle of his predecessor fall upon him. Bless the Secretary of State and his family. O God, if possible, according to Thy will, spare their lives that they may render still important service to the country. Bless all the members of the Cabinet. Endow them with wisdom from above. Bless the commanders in our Army and Navy and all the brave defenders of the country. Give them continued success. Bless the Embassadors from foreign courts, and give us peace with the nations of earth. O God, let treason, that has deluged our land with blood and desolated our country, and bereaved our homes and filled them with widows and orphans, which has at length culminated in the assassination of the nation's chosen ruler,—God of justice, and Avenger of the nation's wrong, let the work of treason cease, and let the guilty perpetrators of this horrible crime be arrested, and brought to justice! O hear the cry and the prayer and the wail rising from the nation's smitten and crushed heart, and deliver us from the power of our enemy, and send speedy peace into all our borders. Through Jesus Christ our Lord. Amen.[42]

At the conclusion of this prayer, the casket was closed, and a special detachment of Veteran Reserve Corps soldiers carried their former Commander-in-Chief to the waiting hearse at the main entrance of the White House. Two previous Presidents, William Henry Harrison and Zachary Taylor, had died in office, and their state funerals had also been held in the East Room. But Lincoln's service was the most elaborate one ever conducted up to that time. Great pains had been taken to decorate the room in fine taste, and the ceremonies had been carefully planned. President Lincoln's cruel assassination at the pinnacle of his successful prosecution of the Civil War relegated him to the status of martyr and folk hero. His sorrowing country would pay him the very highest respect in its power to give. This particular service in the White House had lasted two hours.[43]

On Pennsylvania Avenue the funeral cortège formed behind the 10th Regiment of the Veterans Reserve Corps accompanied by its band whose drums had been muffled. Next came a detachment of Marines and the famed Marine Band under the command of Prof. Francis Scala. After them were elements of several artillery batteries and a marching column of various regiments of infantry. The clergy rode in carriages. Behind the honorary pallbearers and distinguished individuals, such as U. S. Grant, O. H. Browning and many others, came the funeral car pulled by six gray horses, each one led by a man wearing a white sash. Behind the hearse was President Lincoln's gray horse, completely saddled and displaying his owner's boots reversed in the stirrups. Then came the Senate, House and Supreme Court members, and other groups too numerous to list. Among the many fraternal bodies marching were the Knights Templar, a Christian fraternity of Freemasons of which B. B. French was the Grand Commander of all the Knights in the United States. No doubt they marched at the special invitation of French who actually led the entire funeral column toward the Capitol. He was in charge of this procession from beginning to end. Thirty thousand marched behind the military escort.

At the east portico the hearse stopped, and the same eight soldiers from the Veterans Reserve Corps carefully removed the coffin and carried it into the Rotunda where at exactly 3:30 p. m. they placed it upon the catafalque designed especially for this use by B. B. French, Jr., son of the Commissioner of Public Buildings. Then the clergy assembled at the head of the casket "which was turned to the west." The honorary pallbearers arranged themselves in a circle about the coffin while various officials, such as President Andrew Johnson, U. S. Grant and Admiral Farragut, took a station at the foot of the body. When all those entitled to be present had assembled, Dr. Gurley stepped forward and gave a Presbyterian burial service:

> It is appointed unto men once to die. The dust returns to the earth as it was, and the spirit to God who gave it. All flesh is as grass, and all the glory of man as the flower of grass. The grass withereth, and the flower thereof falleth away. We know that we must die and go to the house appointed for all living. What is our life? It is even a vapor that appeareth for a little time, and then vanisheth away. Therefore be ye also ready: for in such an hour as ye think not, the Son of Man cometh. Let us pray.

> Lord, so teach us to number our days that we may apply our hearts unto wisdom. Turn us from this transitory world. Turn

away our eyes from beholding vanity. Help us to seek true things which are above, where Christ sitteth on the right hand of God. Wash us in the blood of Christ, clothe us in the righteousness of Christ, renew and sanctify us by His word and spirit, lead us in the ways of peace and piety for His name's sake, gently, Lord, Oh! gently lead us through all the duties, changes, and trials of our earthly pilgrimage; dispose us to pass the time of our sojourning here in fear, denying ungodliness and worldly lusts, and living soberly, righteously, and godly in this present world; and when at the last our turn shall come to die, may we be gathered to our fathers, having the testimony of a good conscience; a communion of the Christian Church; in the confidence of a certain faith; in the comfort of a reasonable religious and holy hope; in favor with Thee our God, and in perfect charity with the world; all which we ask through Jesus Christ, our blessed Lord and Redeemer, Amen.

Forasmuch as it hath pleased Almighty God, in His wise providence, to take out of this clay tabernacle the soul that inhabited it, we commit its decaying remains to their kindred element; earth to earth, ashes to ashes, dust to dust, looking for the general resurrection through our Lord Jesus Christ, at whose coming to judge the world, earth and sea shall give up their dead, and the corruptible bodies of them that sleep in Him shall be fashioned like unto His glorious body, according to the working whereby He is able even to subdue all things unto Himself. Wherefore, let us comfort one another with these words.

And now may the God of Peace, that brought again from the dead our Lord Jesus, that great shepherd of the sheep, through the blood of the everlasting covenant make you perfect in every good work to do His will, working in you that which is well pleasing in His sight through Jesus Christ, the Resurrection and the life, our Redeemer and our Hope, to whose care we now commit these precious remains and to whose name be glory forever and ever, Amen.

Dr. Gurley had presented this prayer "in a very impressive manner, and many of the auditors" were moved to tears. It was not from the standard burial services printed in Shields' *Book of Common Prayer* . . . .[44] Therefore, Rev. Gurley had drafted his own particular version for this occasion.

When Gurley concluded his remarks, the mourners quietly drifted away. The Capitol Police and a special detail from the 24th Veterans Reserve Corps remained to watch over Lincoln's body. Job W. Angus had constructed the catafalque. "The base," said a reporter, "is one foot high, eight and a half feet long, and four feet wide, and is covered with fine black cloth." Above that was the dais which was "two feet high, seven feet long, and two and a half feet wide. At each corner of the dais is a sloping union column, representing bundles of fasces tied with silver lace. This dais is also covered with black cloth and heavy festoons of the same material, which is edged with silver fringe hung on either side, being gathered in the center with a black rosette of satin ribbon, with a silver star, and from this falls a fold of cloth, the end of which containing three stars. On either side of the dais are two muskets with bayonets, two carbines and two sword bayonets crossed."

All the large panel pictures in the Rotunda of the Capitol were completely covered in mourning cloth. All statuary was likewise enveloped except that of George Washington which had a black sash tied across the body. A heavy drapery of black mourning cloth hung from the corridor at the base of the dome.[45] In silence the coffin rested in the Rotunda under guard until the doors of the Capitol were opened on the morning of April 20 when thousands and thousands of citizens and military personnel thronged into the building to view for the last time the body of their late lamented leader. As if the heavens were weeping in sympathy with the mourners, drizzling rain fell all day. Because of the huge turnout, the doors remained open that evening until 9:00 p. m., although the schedule had called for them to be closed at six.

Then, at about 6:00 a. m, April 21, Friday, various important officials, who had been invited to be present, assembled about the casket. Dr. Gurley once more offered a brief prayer:

> Lord, Thou hast been our dwelling place in all generations. Before the mountains were brought forth, or ever Thou hadst formed the earth and the world, even from everlasting to everlasting Thou art God. Thou turnest man to destruction, and sayest, return, ye children of men. We acknowledge Thy hand in the great and sudden affliction that hast befallen us as a nation, and we pray that in all these hours and scenes of sorrow through which we are passing we may have the guidance of Thy counsel and the consultation of Thy spirit. We commit to Thy care and keeping this sleeping dust of our fallen Chief Magistrate, and pray Thee to watch over it as it

passes from our view and is borne to its final resting place in the soil of that State which was his abiding and chosen home. And grant, we beseech Thee, that as the people in different cities and sections of the land shall gather around this coffin and look upon the fading remains of the man they loved so well, their love for the cause in which he fell may kindle into a brighter, intenser flame, and, while their tears are falling, may they renew their vows of eternal fidelity to the cause of justice, liberty, and truth. So may this great bereavement redound to Thy glory and to the highest welfare of our stricken and bleeding country; and all we ask is in the name and for the sake of Jesus Christ, our blessed Lord and Redeemer. Amen.

Quietly, the same twelve sergeants from the Veterans Reserve Corps appeared. Four with drawn swords always acted as the Guard of Honor while the other eight carried the heavy casket upon their shoulders. These veterans bore it once more to the hearse at twenty minutes before seven o'clock. This somber vehicle carried its precious burden of death toward the Baltimore & Ohio train station on New Jersey Avenue. Abraham Lincoln's casket appeared in front of the depot at the same time that Willie Lincoln's smaller coffin arrived from the Carroll vault at Georgetown's Oak Hill Cemetery. Willie's original metallic burial case was now hidden inside a black walnut box, and together—Father and Son—were placed gently aboard the funeral car attached to the special train which would return them to Springfield, Illinois. Mary Lincoln had made it plain that the body of Willie was not to be displayed on the mournful trip home.[46] She remained closeted in the White House. She did not plan to journey back to Illinois for the funeral and burial there.

Before the train departed, the Rev. Dr. Gurley once more offered a prayer from the station platform:

O Lord our God, strengthen us under the pressure of this great national sorrow as Thou only canst strengthen the weak, and comfort us as Thou only canst comfort the sorrowing and sanctify us as Thou only canst sanctify people when they are passing through the fiery furnace of trial. May Thy grace abound to us according to our need, and in the end may the affliction that now fills our hearts with sadness and our eyes with tears work for us a far more exceeding and eternal weight of glory.

And now may the God of peace that brought again from the dead our Lord Jesus that Great Shepherd of the sheep, through the blood of the everlasting covenant, make you perfect; in every good work to do His will working in you that which is well pleasing in His sight; through Jesus Christ, the Resurrection and the Life our Redeemer and our Hope, our fathers' God and our God in whose care we now leave these precious remains, to whose blessing we renewedly commit our bereaved and beloved country, and to whose name be glory forever and ever. Amen.[47]

Even as Gurley addressed God, the pilot engine started up and moved down the track. It would run ahead of the funeral train to insure that the right-of-way was not only clear but also safe. Rev. Gurley then swung aboard the train; he would make the entire trip, occupying his time in writing verses which were to be sung at Springfield.

Precisely at eight a. m. on that morning of April 21, Brig. General Daniel Craig McCallum, Superintendent of Military Railroads, gave the signal for the engineer to pull the train out of the station. With a hissing of live steam from the new engine—No. 238—and a grinding of metal wheels upon iron rails, the nine cars jerked forward on a journey which would cover 1,654 miles. Among those making this long circuitous journey were Dr. Charles B. Brown, the embalmer who would keep a careful watch over the two corpses aboard the funeral car, and Frank T. Sands, the undertaker.[48] Robert T. Lincoln would also start out on the train as the only member of the Lincoln family present.[49] But Robert would ride with friends Nicolay and Hay only to Baltimore where they would all turn around and head back to Washington. There was still much planning to be done in the Capital City, and Robert could help with it. Justice David Davis would also accompany these three on their short trip.

Since this funeral train was traveling under orders from the War Department, Secretary Stanton and his administrators had been the ones who determined that the route would follow roughly the itinerary that the Presidential Special had taken back in February of 1861 with three major exceptions. This time the cars would not pass through Pittsburgh or Cincinnati and would return to Springfield, Illinois, from the north by way of Chicago. Those close to the deceased President knew also that he had thought of Senator Henry Clay as his "beau ideal of a statesman." Clay had died in Washington on June 29, 1852. After lying in state at the Senate Chamber and in the Rotunda of the Capitol, Clay's corpse on July 1 commenced a funeral trek of approximately 1,200 miles. It passed through Wilmington, Baltimore, Philadelphia, Trenton, New York City, Albany, Schenectady, Utica, Rome, Syracuse, Rochester, Buffalo, Cleveland, Columbus, Cincinnati, Louisville, Frankfort and finally arrived at Lexington, Kentucky, where the "Sage of Ashland" was buried on July 10.[50] Never before in the history of the United States had such a funeral pageant taken place. Now, Abraham Lincoln's embalmed body would also be taken on an even longer circuit. And Lincoln had surpassed Clay in political honors, too. Although a Presidential candidate, Clay never made it to the White House.

Obsequies for Lincoln along the way were to be under the direction of the Governor of each State but subject to approval from the military officer in charge of that particular division, department or district, so ordered the Secretary of War. Operating under these instructions, the funeral train began its sad journey, first pausing only briefly at Annapolis Junction where Governor Augustus Williamson Bradford, his aide and suite boarded the cars before this special train made its initial stop in Baltimore at 10 a. m. Under escort, the casket was borne to the Mercantile Exchange building where the public was allowed to view the martyred President for an hour and a half. However, no religious services took place here.

Similar observances were held at Harrisburg, Philadelphia, New York City, Albany and Buffalo. At New York City, Rabbi Samuel Myer Isaacs of the Broadway Synagogue was invited to read passages from the Bible and to offer a brief prayer. This may have been the only time that one of the Jewish faith participated in the various services along the route. Lincoln would have rejoiced that a Rabbi had taken part in this manner.

But when the funeral train reached its designated spot inside Cleveland at 7:20 a. m. on Friday, April 28, Lincoln's body was transported to the Public Square where the Right Reverend Charles Pettit McIlvaine, Episcopal Bishop of Ohio, performed the full and regular burial service of his denomination. Somehow, he had received special permission to hold a complete religious burial service—not just a prayer—over the body. This certainly was a unique happening in the long journey of the corpse back to Springfield, Illinois. Although married by an Episcopal minister, President Lincoln had never been an Episcopalian, nor was Cleveland the final destination of the deceased. Nevertheless, Bishop McIlvaine repeated these words as pact of the ceremony:

I am the resurrection and the life, saith the Lord; he that believeth in me, though he were dead, yet shall he live; and whosoever liveth and believeth in me shall never die.

We brought nothing into the world and it is certain we can carry nothing out. The Lord gave, and the Lord hath taken away; blessed be the name of the Lord.

Man that is born of a woman, hath but a short time to live, and is full of misery. He cometh up, and is cut down, like a flower; he fleeth as it were a shadow and never continueth in one stay.

In the midst of life we are in death; of whom may we seek for succor, but of thee, O Lord, who for our sins art justly displeased?

Then the Bishop uttered an eloquent prayer, asking succor for the Lincoln family; the wounded Secretary of State, whom an assassin had also attempted to kill; and for President Andrew Johnson; as well as for all the American people. When he had concluded his religious remarks, the public was allowed to file past the coffin in this Pavilion erected on the Square.[51]

On ran the funeral train with stops in Columbus, Indianapolis, and Chicago until at last it rolled somberly into Springfield on May 3 at 8:40 a. m.[52] It was a bright day, and thousands awaited the arrival of the casket. Illinois' Capital City had prepared very carefully for its reception.

In the State Library Room of the Capitol on the afternoon of April 17, State officers, City Council members and prominent citizens of the town had assembled to formulate plans. Since Governor Richard James Oglesby was in Washington, D. C., Lt. Gov. William Bross took the chair and presided. Upon a motion being made, seconded and duly passed, Bross appointed a Committee of Arrangements which would have the power to name subcommittees for all the tasks which needed to be accomplished. The chair chose John T. Stuart, who became the chairman, Sharon Tyndale, Col. John Williams, Judge S. H. Treat, Brig. Gen. John Cook, O. M. Hatch, Thomas J. Dennis, O. H. Miner and J. C. Conkling.[53]

Because Mary Lincoln remained in seclusion at the White House and gave but few instructions for the funeral, this Committee of Arrangements must also have chosen the honorary pallbearers who would be seen most prominently by the assembled throngs. As Lincoln's body was taken from the train, these appointed citizens of distinction marched on either side of the coffin. All had been known by Lincoln. They were: John Wood, W. B. Archer, Jesse K. Dubois, S. T. Logan, William F. Elkin, Gustavus P. Koerner, James L. Lamb, S. H. Treat, Dr. Gershom Jayne, Col. John Williams, Erastus Wright, Capt. Jas. N. Brown, Jacob Bunn and Charles W. Matheny. The remains, though, were actually carried by the Honor Guard of Veteran Sergeants.[54]

With great dignity the coffin was taken carefully upstairs to the Hall of the House of Representatives in the State House and placed upon an ornate catafalque. For an hour the Philharmonic Association, which had been formed in June of 1860, sang in the Hall, evidently from the balcony.

Meanwhile, great masses of people crowded into the Capitol to view the body of the martyred President.[55] That evening Capt. Robert T. Lincoln arrived in Springfield, accompanied by John George Nicolay, Lincoln's secretary. They were close friends. Robert immediately went to the residence of John Todd Stuart where he had been invited to stay. Coming in at the same time was Bishop Matthew Simpson whom the Committee of Arrangements had invited to give the main oration on the following day. This prominent cleric dismounted from the train feeling quite unwell.[56]

After countless mourners had continuously passed by Lincoln's bier since the morning of May 3, the line was finally shut off at 10 a. m. on the following day. Samuel S. Elder, a local tinsmith, then soldered shut the lead lining of the casket.[57] As had been done all along the funeral train route, fresh flowers were heaped upon the casket, and the Springfield Ladies Aid Society also placed a cross of flowers atop the lid long before the body left the State House.[58] The fact that Abraham Lincoln had never claimed to be a Christian did not stop the admiring public from decorating his coffin with symbols of this particular religion. It would seem that since the President had declared himself a man of God, the citizens of the United States simply concluded that he was also a Christian. Lincoln, himself, had often described his country as a land of Christians, although he knew perfectly well that there were small numbers of other religions being practiced in America.

At 11:30 a. m. on May 4, the casket of Abraham Lincoln was placed into a borrowed hearse from St. Louis. This elaborate hearse had previously borne the bodies of Brig. Gen. Nathaniel Lyon, who had helped keep Missouri out of Confederate hands, and Senator Thomas Hart Benton. The huge funeral cortège of ten thousand people then began its slow solemn trek to Oak

Ridge Cemetery under the leadership of Maj. Gen. Joseph Hooker who served as the Marshal-in-Chief. The honorary pallbearers this time were John Wood, W. B. Archer, Jesse K. Dubois, S. T. Logan, G. P. Koerner, James L. Lamb, S. H. Treat, John Williams, Erastus Wright, J. N. Brown, Jacob Bunn, C. W. Matheny, Elijah Iles and J. T. Stuart. The latter two replaced Dr. Gershom Jayne and William F. Elkin who had marched in the procession to the State House from the station on the morning of May 3rd.[59] A band began to play "Lincoln's Funeral March," a special piece of music composed for the occasion. As the procession moved on to the cemetery, other bands rendered the "Dead March of Saul." In addition to numerous military units, there were eight divisions with people from the legal profession, the clergy, the medical profession, and many civic and fraternal groups, including the Masons. Firemen and educators also paraded in the column. Rounding out the long assemblage at the tail end were citizens-at-large and persons of color. It was, indeed, a most impressive scene that day. Each division had its own marshal who, in turn, had several aides to assist him. Needless to recount, all the marshals and aides were persons of notable social standing and prominence. May 4th proved to be an usually hot day for that time of the year. A clear sky allowed the sun's torrid rays to beat down upon the marchers. Several members of the military and even the Mayor of Springfield suffered mild sunstrokes but later recovered. When the procession reached Oak Ridge Cemetery at 1:00 p. m., the President's coffin was placed upon a huge slab of elevated stone inside the Public Receiving Vault at the north end of the graveyard. There, it rested beside that of William Wallace Lincoln's which had also been returned to Springfield from Washington on the same funeral car. To the left of the Vault's gates had been erected a platform for the speakers and the press. To the right was one for the choir singers. Robert T. Lincoln—the only member of the President's immediate family who attended the services—took a seat near the open door of the Vault. Other dignitaries were seated nearby.[60]

To open the religious service, the choir sang from the Dead March of Saul, "Unveil Thy Bosom." Then the Rev. Albert Hale, pastor of the Second Presbyterian Church, gave a lengthy opening prayer. He had known Lincoln well. He prayed earnestly:

> Father of Heaven, we acknowledge Thee as the author of our being and the giver of every good and perfect gift. Thou givest life, and Thou takest it away. The lives of men and the lives of nations are in Thy hands as the drop of a bucket.

Father in Heaven, we bow down before Thee to-day, believing in Thy promises, and asking that with submissive hearts we may acknowledge Thee in the serious thoughts that press upon the millions to-day. Father in Heaven, we thank Thee that Thou didst give to this nation Thy servant, so mysteriously and maliciously taken from us. We acknowledge Thy hand in all these providences which Thou has suffered from time to time to unfold themselves, by which we have been blessed with his private and public influence. We thank Thee, Father of Heaven, that Thou didst give him to this people, and that he was raised to a position of power and authority, and that through him Thou hast led them through storm and strife to the present hopeful condition of our public affairs.

And now Father in Heaven, we bow to that stroke by which, suddenly, and contrary to our desires and expectations, he is taken from the high place where he stood, and we are now called upon to deposit his remains in the grave.

Father in Heaven, we mourn before Thee; our hearts bow in grief and in sorrow unto Thy stroke, but he helped us to say "It is the Lord, let Him do what seemeth good for us." And we do entreat Thee, Father in Heaven, to remember especially the bereaved widow and family. We pray that in this hour of their trial, God will give to them those blessings that they need, and so open the fountains of Divine consolation, that they in their grief shall make this event not only a sorrow, but under God, the opening day of numberless blessings.

To Thee we commit them and all personal relatives who mourn in consequence of this distressing event, and, Father in Heaven, to Thee we commit the people of the city and of the state in which he has grown up, whose affection he holds to-day in his death, stronger than in the most powerful moment of his life.

Merciful God, bless us, and we pray Thee help us to cherish the memory of his life, and the worth of the high example he has shown us. Sanctify the event to all in public office; may they learn wisdom from that example, and study to follow in the steps of him whom Thou hast taken away. We do pray and beseech Thee to grant that the high purpose for which he lived and in which, by the blessing of God, he had far succeeded, may be carried to a completion, and the time soon come when the good in heaven and on earth shall unite in shouts of joy and praise to the everlasting God. And, O God, we thank Thee for that other example which he acted in a steady adherence to truth, a love of freedom and opposition to wrong and injustice, and slavery; and we pray that God will grant that the policy of our government touching these great issues may be successfully carried through, when not a slave shall clank his shackles in the land, and not a soul be found that will not rejoice in universal freedom, in righteousness established, in pure religion revived, in Christ manifested in his glory and reigning with power in the hearts of this nation.

We mourn in sorrow to-day, yet we would rejoice in that "nor life, nor death, not things present, nor things to come" can check this continuation. Give us grace, we pray Thee, to plead for Thy blessing on all men throughout the land, and for the dawning of that day in which righteousness and truth, and freedom, and pure religion, and humanity, shall reign triumphant.

Oh God, our Father, give grace and wisdom to him who so mysteriously is called to occupy the chair of state, from which, by the hand of malice, he whom the country and the nation mourn, has been taken away. Give unto him humility; give him wisdom to direct his steps; give him a love of righteousness, and help him to cherish the freedom of the people, while he sits at the head of the nation; and may God give him, and all associated with him, grace to perceive the right, and to bear the sword of justice so as to serve the nation's welfare and to redound to the honor of truth and the honor of God; and may they conduct themselves patiently and courageously to the end.

Our Father in Heaven, smile we pray Thee, upon the millions that have come out of bondage. Remember them, we pray Thee, our brethren, dear to him who is taken from us. May God grant that they may be able to act worthily of the privileges which Providence opens before them, and may all the people unite their prayers, their patience, their self-denial, so that these may come up and take their place in the nation as citizens, rejoicing in new born privileges, and the rights which God gave, and which man cannot rightfully take away.

Father in Heaven we ask Thy blessing upon all those who are endeavoring, to-day, to secure the public interest against the hands of an assassin, and to prevent the murder of those in high places. Oh, God, let Thy justice, Thy righteousness and power, speedily rid the nation of those lusts out of which all these evils arise, and the Union rise up from this great trial, and become a light among the nations of the earth in all future time.

Father in Heaven, Thou are just and righteous in all Thy ways, holy in all Thy doings; we are sinful and unworthy of our privileges, but Thou hast not dealt with us after our sins, nor rewarded us according to our iniquities. Hear us, and aid us in the services still to be performed here; and accept us, through Christ our Redeemer, to whom, with the Father and the Holy Spirit, be glory everlasting. Amen.

Next, the assembled choir sang "Farewell Father, Friend and Guardian," the music having been composed by George F. Root, and the words by L. M. Dawes. Following this rendition, the Rev. N. W. Miner, minister at the First Baptist Church on the southwest corner of 7th and Adams, who had once lived just across the street from the Lincolns, read passages from the first chapter of the Book of John and also some of the writings of St. Paul. One reporter thought he also read from the Book of Job. Perhaps Miner and the next minister to follow him were chosen to participate partly because of their friendship for the fallen President and partly because Lincoln's parents had also been Baptists.

Once more the singers sang a piece, "To Thee, O Lord" from the *Oratorio of St. Paul.* Rev. A. C. Hubbard, pastor of the Second Baptist Church—generally called the North Baptist Church, being at the southwest corner of 6th and Madison—delivered President Lincoln's Second Inaugural Address. Following this, came a dirge by the choir, the music by Otto and the special words by a local artist, George F. Wright, entitled "As When Thy Cross Was Bleeding."[61]

At last it was time for the Methodist Episcopal Bishop Matthew Simpson to render his flowery oration. Evidently, he had recovered from his illness first noted when he alighted in Springfield the night before. As Dr. Mark E. Neely, Jr., has so aptly remarked, it was rather ironic that Bishop Simpson had been asked to deliver the final funeral sermon at Springfield. Although

President Lincoln knew Simpson very well and appeared to be his friend, the good Bishop had frequently found fault with Lincoln's patronage appointments. He constantly cajoled Lincoln to name more Methodists to top posts. A Radical in politics, Simpson had the backing of not only Edwin M. Stanton but also of Salmon P. Chase.[62] It is entirely possible that Stanton suggested Simpson for the honor of preaching in Oak Ridge Cemetery at the entombment of Abraham Lincoln.

Bishop Simpson gave a brief history of the Civil War and declared that "Mr. Lincoln was no ordinary man." He was, vowed Simpson, picked by the hand of God to "guide our government in these troublesome times, and it seems to me that the hand of God may be traced in many of the events connected with his history." Furthermore, Simpson stated that "Abraham Lincoln was a good man. He was known as an honest, temperate, forgiving man; a just man; a man of noble heart in every way. As to his religious experience, I cannot speak definitely, because I was not privileged to know much of his private sentiments." But Simpson did know that Lincoln "read the Bible frequently." Then Simpson went beyond his personal knowledge to aver that Lincoln "believed in Christ the Saviour of sinners." Simpson certainly could not prove this last statement, and perhaps for this and other reasons Nicolay and Hay termed Bishop Simpson's address "a pathetic oration."[63] Nicolay had been present when this message had been given at the mouth of the Public Receiving Vault. The full oration is as follows:

FUNERAL ADDRESS

FELLOW-CITIZENS OF IllINOIS, AND OF MANY PARTS Of OUR ENTIRE UNION: Near the capitol of this large and growing State of Illinois, in the midst of this beautiful grove, and at the open mouth of the vault which has just received the remains of our fallen chieftain, we gather to pay a tribute of respect and to drop the tears of sorrow around the ashes of the mighty dead. A little more than four years ago he left his plain and quiet home in yonder city, receiving the parting words of the concourse of friends who in the midst of the dropping of the gentle shower gathered around him. He spoke of the pain of parting from the place where he lived for a quarter of a century, where his children had been born, and his home had been rendered pleasant by friendly associations; and, as he left, he made an earnest request, in the hearing of some who are present at this hour, that, as he was about to enter upon responsibilities which he believed to be greater than any which had fallen upon any man since the days of Washington, the people would offer up prayers that God would aid and sustain him in the work which they had given him to do.His company left your quiet city, but as it went snares were in waiting for the chief magistrate. Scarcely did he escape the dangers of the way or the hands of the assassin as he neared Washington; and I believe he escaped only through the vigilance of officers and the prayers of the people, so that the blow was suspended for more than four years, which was at last permitted, through the providence of God, to fall.

How different the occasion which witnessed his departure from that which witnessed his return! Doubtless you expected to take him by the hand, and to feel the warm grasp which you had felt in other days, and to see the tall form walking among you which you had delighted to honor in years past. But he was never permitted to come until he came with lips mute and silent, the frame encoffined, and a weeping nation following as his mourners. Such a scene as his return to you was never witnessed. Among the events of history there have been great processions of mourners. There was one for the patriarch Jacob, which went up from Egypt, and the Egyptians wondered at the evidences of reverence and filial affection which came from the hearts of the Israelites. There was mourning when Moses fell upon the heights of Pisgah, and was hid from human view. There have been mournings in the kingdoms of the earth when kings and warriors have fallen. But never was there in the history of man such mourning as that which has accompanied this funeral procession, and has gathered around the mortal remains of him who was our loved one, and who now sleeps among us. If we glance at the procession which followed him, we see how the nation stood aghast. Tears filled the eyes of manly, sun-burnt faces. Strong men, as they clasped the hands of their friends, were not able in words to find vent for their grief. Women and little children caught up the tidings as they ran through the land, and were melted into tears. The nation stood still.

Men left their plows in the fields and asked what the end should be. The hum of manufactories ceased, and the sound of the hammer was not heard. Busy merchants closed their doors, and in the exchange gold passed no more from hand to hand. Though three weeks have elapsed, the nation has scarcely breathed easily yet. A mournful silence is abroad upon the land; nor is this mourning confined to any class or to any district of country. Men of all political parties, and of all religious creeds, have united in paying this mournful tribute. The archbishop of the Roman Catholic Church in New York and a Protestant minister walked side by side in the sad procession, and a Jewish rabbi performed a part of the solemn services.

Here are gathered around his tomb the representatives of the army and navy, senators, judges, governors, and officers of all the branches of the government. Here, too, are members of civic processions, with men and women from the humblest as well as the highest occupations. Here and there, too, are tears as sincere and warm as any that drop, which come from the eyes of those whose kindred and whose race have been freed from their chains by him whom they mourn as their deliverer. More persons have gazed on the face of the departed than ever looked upon the face of any other departed man. More have looked on the procession for sixteen hundred miles, by night and by day, by sunlight, dawn, twilight, and by torchlight, than ever before watched the progress of a procession.

We ask why this wonderful mourning, this great procession? I answer, first, a part of the interest has arisen from the times in which we live, and in which he that has fallen was a principal actor. It is a principle of our nature that feelings once excited turn readily from the object by which they are excited to some other object which may for the time being take possession of the mind. Another principle is, the deepest affections of our hearts gather around some human form in which are incarnated the living thoughts and ideas of the passing age. If we look then at the times, we see an age of excitement. For four years the popular heart has been stirred to its inmost depth. War had come upon us, dividing families, separating nearest and dearest friends, a war the extent and magnitude of which no one could estimate; a war in which the blood of brethren was shed by a brother's hand. A call for soldiers was made by this voice now hushed, and all over the land, from hill to mountain, from plain to valley, there sprung up thousands of bold hearts, ready to go forth and save our national Union. This feeling of excitement was transformed next into a feeling of deep grief because of the dangers in which our country was placed. Many said, "Is it possible to save our nation?" Some in our country, and nearly all the leading men in other countries, declared it to be impossible to maintain the Union; and many an honest and patriotic heart was deeply pained with apprehensions of common ruin; and many, in grief and almost in despair, anxiously inquired, What shall the end of these things be? In addition to this, wives had given their husbands, mothers their sons, the pride and joy of their hearts. They saw them put on the uniform, they saw them take the martial step, and they tried to hide their deep feeling of sadness. Many dear ones slept upon the battle-field never to return again, and there was mourning in every mansion and in every cabin in our broad land. Then came a feeling of deeper sadness as the story came of prisoners tortured to death or starved through the mandates of those who are called the representatives of the chivalry, and who claimed to be the honorable ones of the earth; and as we read the stories of frames attenuated and reduced to mere skeletons, our grief turned partly into horror and partly into a cry for vengeance.

Then this feeling was changed to one of joy. There came signs of the end of this rebellion. We followed the career of our glorious generals. We saw our army, under the command of the brave officer who is guiding this procession [Hooker], climb up the heights of Lookout Mountain, and drive the rebels from their strongholds. Another brave general swept through Georgia, South and North Carolina, and drove the combined armies of the rebels before him, while the honored Lieutenant-General held Lee and his hosts in a deathgrasp.

Then the tidings came that Richmond was evacuated, and that Lee had surrendered. The bells rang merrily all over the land. The booming of cannon was heard; illuminations and torchlight processions manifested the general joy, and families were looking for the speedy return of their loved ones from the field of battle. Just in the midst of this wildest joy, in one hour, nay, in one moment, the tidings thrilled throughout the land that Abraham Lincoln, the best of presidents, had perished by the hands of an assassin. Then all the feelings which had been gathering for four years in forms of excitement, grief, horror, and joy, turned into one wail of woe, a sadness inexpressible, an anguish unutterable.

But it is not the times merely which caused this mourning. The mode of his death must be taken into the account. Had he died on a bed of illness, with kind friends around him; had the sweat of death been wiped from his brow by gentle hands, while he was yet conscious; could he have had power to speak words of affection to his stricken widow, or words of counsel to us like those which we heard in his parting inaugural at Washington, which shall now be immortal, how it would have softened or assuaged something of the grief! There might at least have been preparation for the event. But no moment of warning was given to him or to us. He was stricken down, too, when his hopes for the end of the rebellion were bright, and prospects of a joyous life were before him. There was a cabinet meeting that day, said to have been the most cheerful and happy of any held since the beginning of the rebellion. After this meeting he talked with his friends, and spoke of the four years of tempest, of the storm being over, and of the four years of pleasure and joy now awaiting him, as the weight of care and anxiety would be taken from his mind, and he could have happy days with his family again. In the midst of these anticipations he left his house never to return alive. The evening was Good Friday, the saddest day in the whole calendar for the Christian Church, henceforth in this country to be made sadder, if possible, by the memory of our nation's loss; and so filled with grief was every Christian heart that even all the joyous thought of Easter Sunday failed to remove the crushing sorrow under which the true worshiper bowed in the house of God.

But the great cause of this mourning is to be found in the man himself. Mr. Lincoln was no ordinary man. I believe the conviction has been growing on the nation's mind, as it certainly has been on my own, especially in the last years of his administration, that by the hand of God he was especially singled out to guide our government in these troublesome times, and it seems to me that the hand of God may be traced in many of the events connected with his history. First, then, I recognize this in the physical education which he received, and which prepared him for enduring herculean labors. In the toils of his boyhood and the labors of his manhood, God was giving him an iron frame. Next to this was his identification with the heart of the great people, understanding their feelings because he was one of them, and connected with them in their movements and life. His education was simple. A few months spent in the schoolhouse gave him the elements of education. He read few books, but mastered all he read. Pilgrim's Progress, Aesop's Fables, and the Life of Washington were his favorites. In these we recognize the works which gave the bias to his character, and which partly molded his style. His early life, with its varied struggles, joined him indissolubly to the working masses, and no elevation in society diminished his respect for the sons of toil. He knew what it was to fell the tall trees of the forest and to stem the current of the broad Mississippi. His home was in the growing West, the heart of the republic, and, invigorated by the wind which swept over its prairies, he learned lessons of self-reliance which sustained him in seasons of adversity.

His genius was soon recognized, as true genius always will be, and he was placed in the legislature of his state. Already acquainted with the principles of law, he devoted his thoughts to matters of public interest, and began to be looked on as the coming statesman. As early as 183[7] he presented resolutions in the legislature asking for emancipation in the District of Columbia, when, with but rare exceptions, the whole popular mind of his state was opposed to the measure. From that hour he was a steady and uniform friend of humanity, and was preparing for the conflict of later years.

If you ask me on what mental characteristic his greatness rested, I answer, On a quick and ready perception of facts; on a memory unusually tenacious and retentive; and on a logical turn of mind, which followed sternly and unwaveringly every link in the chain of thought on every subject which he was called to investigate. I think there have been minds more broad in their character, more comprehensive in their scope, but I doubt if ever there has been a man who could follow step by step, with more logical power, the points which he desired to illustrate. He gained this power by the close study of geometry, and by a determination to perceive the truth in all its relations and simplicity, and when found, to utter it.

It is said of him that in childhood when he had any difficulty in listening to a conversation, to ascertain what people meant, if he retired to rest he could not sleep till he tried to understand the precise point intended, and when understood, to frame language to convey in it a clearer manner to others. Who that has read his messages fails to perceive the directness and the simplicity of his style? And this very trait, which was scoffed at and decried by opponents, is now recognized as one of the strong points of that mighty mind which has so powerfully influenced the destiny of this nation, and which shall, for ages to come, influence the destiny of humanity.

It was not, however, chiefly by his mental faculties that he gained such control over mankind. His moral power gave him pre-eminence. The convictions of men that Abraham Lincoln was an honest man led them to yield to his guidance. As has been said of Cobden, whom he greatly resembled, he made all men feel a *sense of himself,* a recognition of individuality; a self-relying power. They saw in him a man whom they believed would do what is right, regardless of all consequences. It was this moral feeling which gave him the greatest hold on the people, and made his utterances almost oracular. When the nation was angered by the perfidy of foreign nations in allowing privateers to be fitted out, he uttered the significant expression, "One war at a time," and it stilled the national heart. When his own friends were divided as to what steps should be taken as to slavery, that simple utterance, "I will save the Union, if I can, with slavery; if not, slavery must perish, for the Union must be preserved," became the rallying word. Men felt the struggle was for the Union, and all other questions must be subsidiary.

But after all, by the acts of a man shall his fame be perpetuated. What are his acts? Much praise is due to the men who aided him. He called able counselors around him, some of whom have displayed the highest order of talent united with the purest and most devoted patriotism. He summoned able generals into the field, men who have borne the sword as bravely as ever any human arm has borne it. He had the aid of prayerful and thoughtful men everywhere. But, under his own guiding hands, wise counsels were combined and great movements conducted.

Turn toward the different departments. We had an unorganized militia, a mere skeleton army, yet, under his care, that army has been enlarged into a force which, for skill, intelligence, efficiency, and bravery, surpasses any which the world had ever seen. Before its veterans the fame of even the renowned veterans of Napoleon shall pale, and the mothers and sisters on these hillsides, and all over the land, shall take to their arms again braver sons and brothers than ever fought in European wars. The reason is obvious. Money, or a desire for fame, collected those armies, or they were rallied to sustain favorite thrones or dynasties; but the armies he called into being fought for liberty, for the Union, and for the right of self-government; and many of them felt that the battles they won were for humanity everywhere, and for all time; for I believe that God has not suffered this terrible rebellion to come upon our land merely for a chastisement to us, or as a lesson to our age.

There are moments which involve in themselves eternities. There are instants which seem to contain germs which shall develop and bloom forever. Such a moment came in the tide of time to our land, when a question must be settled which affected all the earth. The contest was for human freedom, not for this republic merely, not for the Union simply, but to decide whether the people, as a people, in their entire majesty, were destined to be the government, or whether they were to be subjects to tyrants or aristocrats, or to class-rule of any kind. This is the great question for which we have been fighting, and its decision is at hand, and the result of the contest will affect the ages to come. If successful, republics will spread, in spite of monarchs, all over this earth.

I turn from the army to the navy. What was it when the war commenced? Now we have our ships-of-war at home and abroad, to guard privateers in foreign sympathizing ports, as well as to care for every part of our own coast. They have taken forts that military men said could not be taken; and a brave admiral, for the first time in the world's history, lashed himself to the mast, there to remain as long as he had a particle of skill or strength to watch over his ship, while it engaged in the perilous contest of taking the strong forts of the rebels. Then again I turn to the treasury department. Where should the money come from? Wise men predicted ruin, but our national credit has been maintained, and our currency is safer to-day than it ever was before. Not only so, but through our national bonds, if properly used, we shall have a permanent basis for our currency, and an investment so desirable for capitalists of other nations that, under the laws of trade, I believe the center of exchange will speedily be transferred from England to the United States.

But the great act of the mighty chieftain, on which his fame shall rest long after his frame shall molder away, is that of giving freedom to a race. We have all been taught to revere the sacred characters. Among them Moses stands pre-eminently high. He received the law from God, and his name is honored among the hosts of heaven. Was not his greatest act the delivering of three millions of his kindred out of bondage? Yet we may assert that Abraham Lincoln, by his proclamation, liberated more enslaved people than ever Moses set free, and those not of his kindred or his race. Such a power, or such an opportunity, God has seldom given to man. When other events shall have been forgotten; when this world shall have become a network of republics; when every throne shall be swept from the face of the earth; when literature shall enlighten all minds; when the claims of humanity shall be recognized everywhere, this act shall still be conspicuous on the pages of history. We are thankful that God gave to Abraham Lincoln the decision and wisdom and grace to issue that proclamation, which stands high above all other papers which have been penned by uninspired men.

Abraham Lincoln was a good man. He was known as an honest, temperate, forgiving man; a just man; a man of noble heart in every way. As to his religious experience, I cannot speak definitely, because I was not privileged to know much of his private sentiments. My acquaintance with him did not give me the opportunity to hear him speak on those topics. This I know, however, he read the Bible frequently; loved it for its great truths and its profound teachings; and he tried to be guided by its precepts. He believed in Christ the Saviour of sinners; and I think he was sincere in trying to bring his life into harmony with the principles of revealed religion. Certainly if there ever was a man who illustrated some of the principles of pure religion, that man was our departed president. Look over all his speeches; listen to his utterances. He never spoke unkindly of any man. Even the rebels received no word of anger from him; and his last day illustrated in a remarkable manner his forgiving disposition. A dispatch was received that afternoon that Thompson and Tucker were trying to make their escape through Maine, and it was proposed to arrest them. Mr. Lincoln, however, preferred rather to let them quietly escape. He was seeking to save the very men who had been plotting his destruction. This morning we read a proclamation offering $25,000 for the arrest of these men as aiders and abettors of his assassination; so that, in his expiring acts, he was saying, "Father, forgive them, they know not what they do."

As a ruler I doubt if any president has ever shown such trust in God, or in public documents so frequently referred to Divine aid. Often did he remark to friends and to delegations that his hope for our success rested in his conviction that God would bless our efforts, because we were trying to do right. To the address of a large religious body he replied, "Thanks be unto God, who, in our national trials, giveth us the Churches." To a minister who said he hoped the Lord was on our side, he replied that it gave him no concern whether the Lord was on our side or not, "For," he added, "I know the Lord is always on the side of right;" and with deep feeling added, "But God is my witness that it is my constant anxiety and prayer that both myself and this nation should be on the Lord's side."

In his domestic life he was exceedingly kind and affectionate. He was a devoted husband and father. During his presidential term he lost his second son, Willie. To an officer of the army he said, not long since, "Do you ever find yourself talking with the dead?" and added, "Since Willie's death I catch myself every day involuntarily talking with him, as if he were with me." On his widow, who is unable to be here, I need only invoke the blessing of Almighty God that she may be comforted and sustained. For his son, who has witnessed the exercises of this hour, all that I can desire is that the mantle of his father may fall upon him.

Let us pause a moment in the lesson of the hour before we part. This man, though he fell by an assassin, still fell under the permissive hand of God. He had some wise purpose in allowing him so to fall. What more could he have desired of life for himself? Were not his honors full? There was no office to which he could aspire. The popular heart clung around him as around no other man. The nations of the world had learned to honor our chief magistrate. If rumors of a desired alliance with England be true, Napoleon trembled when he heard of the fall of Richmond, and asked what nation would join him to protect him against our government under the guidance of such a man. His fame was full, his work was done, and he sealed his glory by becoming the nation's great martyr for liberty.

He appears to have had a strange presentiment, early in political life, that some day he would be president. You see it indicated in 1839. Of the slave power he said, "Broken by it I too may be; bow to it I never will. The probability that we may fail in the struggle ought not to deter us from the support of a cause which I deem to be just. It shall not deter me. If ever I feel the soul within me elevate and expand to those dimensions not wholly unworthy of its Almighty architect, it is when I contemplate the cause of my country, deserted by all the world besides, and I standing up boldly and alone and hurling defiance at her victorious oppressors. Here, without contemplating consequences, before high Heaven, and in the face of the world, I swear eternal fidelity to the just cause as I deem it, of the land of my life, my liberty, and my love." And yet, recently, he said to more than one, "I never shall live out the four years of my term. When the rebellion is crushed my work is done." So it was. He lived to see the last battle fought, and dictate a dispatch from the home of Jefferson Davis; lived till the power of the rebellion was broken; and then, having done the work for which God had sent him, angels, I trust, were sent to shield him from one moment of pain or suffering, and to bear him from this world to the high and glorious realm where the patriot and the good shall live forever.

His career teaches young men that every position of eminence is open before the diligent and the worthy. To the active men of the country his example is an incentive to trust in God and do right. To the ambitious there is this fearful lesson: Of the four candidates for presidential honors in 1860, two of them—Douglas and Lincoln—once competitors, but now sleeping patriots, rest from their labors; Bell abandoned to perish in poverty and misery, as a traitor might perish; and Breckinridge is a frightened fugitive, with the brand of traitor on his brow.

Standing, as we do to-day, by his coffin and his sepulcher, let us resolve to carry forward the policy which he so nobly begun. Let us do right to all men. Let us vow, in the sight of Heaven, to eradicate every vestige of human slavery; to give every human being his true position before God and man; to crush every form of rebellion, and to stand by the flag which God has given us. How joyful that it floated over parts of every state before Mr. Lincoln's career was ended! How singular that, to the fact of the assassin's heels being caught in the folds of the flag, we are probably indebted for his capture. The flag and the traitor must ever be enemies.

Traitors will probably suffer by the change of rulers, for one of sterner mould, and who himself has deeply suffered from the rebellion, now wields the sword of justice. Our country, too, is stronger for the trial. A republic was declared by monarchists too weak to endure a civil war; yet we have crushed the most gigantic rebellion in history, and have grown in strength and population every year of the struggle. We have passed through the ordeal of a popular election while swords and bayonets were in the field, and have come out unharmed. And now, in an hour of excitement, with a large minority having preferred another man for President, when the bullet of the assassin has laid our President prostrate, has there been a mutiny? Has any rival proffered his claims? Out of an army of near a million, no officer or soldier uttered one note of dissent; and, in an hour or two after Mr. Lincoln's death, another leader, under constitutional forms, occupied his chair, and the government moved forward without one single jar. The world will learn that republics are the strongest governments on earth.

And now, my friends, in the words of the departed, "with malice toward none," free from all feelings of personal vengeance, yet believing that the sword must not be borne in vain, let us go forward even in painful duty. Let every man who was a senator or representative in Congress, and who aided in beginning this rebellion, and thus led to the slaughter of our sons and daughters, be brought to speedy and to certain punishment. Let every officer educated at the public expense, and who, having been advanced to high position, perjured himself and turned his sword against the vitals of his country, be doomed to a traitor's death. This, I believe, is the will of the American people. Men may attempt to compromise, and to restore these traitors and murderers to society again. Vainly may they talk of the fancied honor or chivalry of these murderers of our sons—these starvers of our prisoners—these officers who mined their prisons and placed kegs of powder to destroy our captive officers. But the American people will rise in their majesty and sweep all such compromises and compromisers away, and will declare that there shall be no safety for rebel leaders. But to the deluded masses we will extend arms of forgiveness. We will take them to our hearts, and walk with them side by side, as we go forward to work out a glorious destiny.

The time will come when, in the beautiful words of him whose lips are now forever sealed, "The mystic cords of memory, stretching from every battlefield and patriot grave to every living heart and hearthstone all over this broad land, will yet swell the chorus of the Union, when again touched, as surely they will be, by the better angels of our nature."

Chieftain, farewell! The nation mourns thee. Mothers shall teach thy name to their lisping children. The youth of our land shall emulate thy virtues. Statesmen shall study thy record and learn lessons of wisdom. Mute though thy lips be, yet they still speak. Hushed is thy voice, but its echoes of liberty are ringing through the world, and the sons of bondage listen with joy. Prisoned thou art in death, and yet thou art marching abroad, and chains and manacles are bursting at thy touch. Thou didst fall not for thyself. The assassin had no hate for thee. Our hearts were aimed at, our national life was sought. We crown thee as our martyr, and humanity enthrones thee as her triumphant son. Hero, Martyr, Friend, FAREWELL![64]

When Bishop Simpson concluded his hour-long oration, the choir chanted a dirge composed especially by G. F. Wright and sung to a tune written by Storch. It was entitled, "Over the Valley the Angels Smile." A concluding prayer was assigned to Prof. Simeon W. Harkey, D. D., Professor of

Theology and German at the Illinois State University in Springfield. He was asked to officiate, no doubt, because on June 28, 1860, Abraham Lincoln had been elected a Trustee of this institution where not only Robert T. Lincoln had attended but also John M. Hay, the President's Assistant Secretary.[65] Many reporters ignored this participant entirely in their coverage of the funeral. The Rev. Dr. Harkey was a Lutheran clergyman.

Then a requiem was sung, "Peace, Troubled Souls." Following this came the Rev. P. D. Gurley, the Lincolns' pastor in Washington, D. C. He gave a few brief remarks and then uttered a Benediction to the obsequies. To close the long program, the choir sang a funeral hymn which the Rev. Dr. Gurley had composed himself while riding the funeral train on its long journey from the Nation's Capital to Springfield. It began, "Rest, noble martyr! rest in peace." Upon its conclusion, the audience and the choir sang a Doxology:

> To Father, Son, and Holy Ghost,
> The Gods whom we adore,
> By glory as it was, is now,
> And shall be evermore.[66]

Thus came to a close the greatly extended funeral service for the beloved Abraham Lincoln. In life, he had had many detractors; in death, he had very few who were willing to express any dislike for this immortal martyr.

Sadly, the General officers of the Honor Guard saw to it that the ponderous doors of the Public Receiving Vault were swung closed and locked. The massive key was then presented to Capt. Robert T. Lincoln, the representative head of the Lincoln family now. Since he would soon be returning to Washington, he handed it over to John Todd Stuart for safekeeping.

At 10:00 p. m. that evening, the tired Honor Guard, under the direction of Brig. Gen. E. D. Townsend, departed by train from Springfield and headed back to Washington.[67] It had been thirteen days since they had left the Capital City on the Potomac, and they were not home yet. Certainly, the United States has never witnessed such a funeral pageant of that magnitude in its entire history. By order of the War Department, General John Cook, Commander of the Military District, detailed a company of soldiers to stand guard at the Vault where Lincoln's body had temporarily been placed until a monument could be erected over the sacred remains.[68] Nearby Camp Butler had a number of units still in quarters there and furnished the guards.

From that moment forward, philosophers, scholars, infidels, agnostics and clerics have debated whether or not Abraham Lincoln was a church member or even a religious man. Mary Lincoln divulged to John Todd Stuart on December 15, 1873, that her husband's heart "was naturally religious." However, she carefully pointed out to William H. Herndon in the St. Nicholas Hotel at Springfield, Illinois, on September 5, 1866, that her husband had never joined any church. Gleefully, Billy Herndon announced in his lecture on Lincoln's Religion, published in the *Illinois State Register* as a supplement on December 13, 1873, that the sorrowing widow had admitted that Abraham Lincoln had not technically been a Christian. True enough; Lincoln had never joined any denomination, and that should have put the matter to rest, but it did not.

Perhaps an old Springfield friend and neighbor, Dr. William Jayne, gave one of the best answers when he declared that "Mr. Lincoln was by nature a deeply religious man. But I have no evidence that he ever accepted the formulated creed of any sect or denomination. I know that all churches had his profound respect and support." Lincoln, said Dr. Jayne, had an "enduring and abundant religious faith in the relations between God and his immortal soul." "It is now beyond the realm of controversy," explained Dr. Jayne, "that Lincoln loved, honored and revered Almighty God."[69]

As time passed, the memory of Abraham Lincoln became more and more honored by the world. His was a name to conjure with and repeat over and over again. This humble servant of God became a folk hero, much larger than life itself. He had indeed been a very uncommon common man with a unique gift of honesty and ability and humbleness, all combined into one tall human being. Yet it was not until June 17, 1891, that his home state of Illinois added Lincoln's birthday to its official list of legal holidays.[70] In those days, the General Assembly was quite loath to create more holidays which closed the counting houses and businesses. And the United States Congress still has not given Abraham Lincoln his own day of honor, although it has set aside days for much lesser figures. Politics in the 20th Century has created a set of "politically correct" politicians.

Courtesy of the Illinois State Historical Library.

Mourners file past the casket of Abraham Lincoln in the Hall of the House of
Representatives in the State House at Springfield, Illinois.
W. Waud sketched this scene which was
published in *Harper's Weekly*, May 27, 1865, IX, No. 439, p. 328.

Drawing by Thomas Hogan

The last funeral service for President Abraham Lincoln at the Receiving Vault in Oak Ridge Cemetery, Springfield, Illinois, on May 4, 1865,

From *Frank Leslie's Illustrated Newspaper*, May 27, 1865, p. 156.

Lamentations

References

1   David Dixon Porter, *Incidents and Anecdotes of the Civil War* (N. Y.: D. Appleton & Co., 1885), 294-297; Basler, ed., *The Collected Works*, VIII, 405-406.

2   de Chambrun, *Impressions of Lincoln*, 83.

3   Basler, ed., *The Collected Works*, VIII, 393-394.

4   *Ibid.*, VIII, 399-400.

5   *Ibid.*, VIII, 406-407.

6   Dorothy Lamon Teillard, ed., *Recollections of Abraham Lincoln by Ward Hill Lamon* (Washington: pub. by the editor, 1911), 114-117.

7   *Ibid.*, 117.

8   Basler, ed., *The Collected Works*, VIII, 411.

9   Beale, ed., *Diary of Gideon Welles*, II, 282-283.

10   Basler, ed., *The Collected Works*, VIII, 375.

11   Turner and Turner, eds., *Mary Todd Lincoln*, 285, 400.

12   W. Emerson Reck, *A. Lincoln: His Last 24 Hours* (Jefferson: McFarland & Co., 1987), 49-50.

13   Margarita Spalding Gerry, ed., *Reminiscences of Colonel William H. Crook* (N. Y.: Harper & Bros., 1910), 76.

14   George J. Olszewski, *Restoration of Ford's Theatre* (Washington: National Park Service, 1963), 5-13.

15   Miner, "Personal Recollections of Abraham Lincoln." Ford's Theatre has been restored by the Federal government and is under the direction of the National Park Service. Recently, the museum section of the building has been remodeled and tells the story of the assassination and its aftermath.

16   William A. Tidwell, James O. Hall and David Winfred Gaddy, *Come Retribution* (Jackson: Univ. Press of Mississippi, 1988).

17   N. Y. *Times*, July 8, 1865, p. 1, c. 5; For the minister's report see Thomas Reed Turner, *Beware the People Weeping* (Baton Rouge: Louisiana State Univ. Press, 1982), 200.

18   William Hanchett, "Booth's Diary," *Jour. Ill. State Hist. Soc.*, LXXII, 40-42 (Feb., 1979).

19   Some confusion has resulted due to the various contemporary accounts of where the bullet stopped. Dr. Charles S. Taft reported discoloration in the right eye area, indicating that the slug had lodged behind Lincoln's right eye. Some physicians who had been at the autopsy even gave conflicting accounts. John K. Lattimer, *Kennedy and Lincoln* (N. Y.: Harcourt, Brace, Jovanovich, 1980), 33. But two contemporary diary entries corroborate Taft's testimony. B. B. French observed "the bloodshot appearance of the cheek directly under the right eye." Cole and McDonough, eds., *Benjamin Brown French Journal*, 471. Senator Browning attended the autopsy and recorded that the surgeons found the ball behind the right eye. James G. Randall, ed., *The Diary of Orville Hickman Browning* (Springfield: Ill. State Hist. Lib., 1933), II, 20. An inquiring reporter obtained a copy of the official autopsy report and published the fact that the bullet was found behind the right eye of Lincoln. Washington *Evening Star*, Apr. 17, 1865, p. 4, c. 1. Dr. Joseph K. Barnes, the Surgeon General of the United States and a witness to the Lincoln autopsy, testified at the trial of John H. Surratt on June 17, 1867, that he found the pistol ball behind Lincoln's right eye. By that date, he certainly had time enough to clear up any confusion in the various medical reports filed with him. *Trial of John H. Surratt in the Criminal Court for the District of Columbia* (Washington: Govt. Printing Office, 1867), I, 121, 122.

20   Cole and McDonough, eds., *Benjamin Brown French Journal*, 470.

21   Beale, ed., *Diary of Gideon Welles*, II, 288; Lattimer, *Kennedy and Lincoln*, 32; Reck, *A. Lincoln*, 157.

22   Cole and McDonough, eds., *Benjamin Brown French Journal*, 470.

23   Keckley, *Behind the Scenes*, 196.

24   *Ibid.*, 187-192; Randall, ed., *Browning Diary*, II, 20.

25   R. T. Lincoln to David Davis, Washington, D. C., Apr. 15, 1865, MS., David Davis Papers, Ill. State Hist. Lib.

26   Cole and McDonough, eds., *Benjamin Brown French Journal*, 470, 471, 85, 371-372, 407, 414, 595; Washington *Evening Star*, Apr. 18, 1865, p. 2, c. 5.

27   "Castine" [Noah Brooks], Washington, D. C., Apr. 16, 1865, in *Sacramento (Cal.) Daily Union*, May 17, 1865; Washington *Evening Star*, Apr. 17, 1865, p. 4, cc. 1-2.

28   *The Washington (D. C.) Post*, Mar. 12, 1893, p. 2, c. 7.

29 Randall, ed., *Browning Diary*, II, 21; *Boyd's Directory of Washington 1867* (Washington: Wm. H. Boyd, 1867), n. p.

30 Rollin W. Quimby, "Lincoln's Character as Described in Sermons at the Time of His Death," *Lincoln Herald*, LXIX, 178-186 (Winter, 1967).

31 Bates, *Lincoln in the Telegraph Office*, 215.

32 Turner, *Beware the People Weeping*, 77-83.

33 Noah Brooks to the Rev. Isaac P. Langworthy, Washington, D. C., May 10, 1865,privately printed as a separate item.

34 Hertz, ed., *Abraham Lincoln*, 77.

35 *Ibid.*, 121.

36 "Commissioner of Public Buildings, Funeral Accounts, Abraham Lincoln," pp. 84-85, MS., Record Group 48, The National Archives, Washington, D. C. See also Wayne C. Temple, "Tinsmith to the Late Mr. Lincoln: Samuel S. Elder," *Jour. Ill. State Hist. Soc.*, LXXI, 176-184 (Aug., 1978). R. F. & G. W. Harvey had actually fashioned the coffin.

37 N. Y. *Herald*, Apr. 17, 1865, p. 1, c. 3; Washington *Evening Star*, Apr. 18, 1865, p. 2, c. 5.

38 Washington *Evening Star*, Apr. 18, 1865, p. 1, c. 6.

39 Randall, ed., *Browning Diary*, II, 23.

40 Washington *Evening Star*, Apr. 20, 1865, p. 1, c. 2.

41 *Ibid.*, p. 1, c. 3.

42 Prayers and sermon have been taken from *Sermons Preached in Boston on the Death of Abraham Lincoln Together with the Funeral Services in the East Room of the Executive Mansion at Washington* (Boston: J. E. Tilton & Co., 1865), 7-29, and Dr. Gurley's address corrected from *Faith in God: From the Original Manuscript* (Phila.: Presbyterian Church, 1940).

43 de Chambrun, *Impressions of Lincoln*, 113.

44 Charles W. Shields, D. D., LL. D., *The Book of Common Prayer . . . of the Presbyterian Church in the United States.* (N. Y.: Anson D. F. Randolph & Co., 1864), 325—.

45 *Washington Daily National Intelligencer*, Apr. 22, 1865, p. 2, c. 6; Washington *Evening Star*, Apr. 20, 1865, p.1, c.6.

46   Washington *Evening Star*, Apr. 21, 1865, p. 2, c. 1; N. Y. *Herald*, Apr. 22, 1865, p. 1, c. 2; *Washington Daily National Intelligencer*, Apr. 22, 1865, p. 2, c. 7.

47   *Washington Daily National Intelligencer*, Apr. 22, 1865, p. 3, c. 1.

48   N. Y. *Herald*, Apr. 20, 1865, p. 5, c. 4.

49   *Washington Daily National Intelligencer*, Apr. 22, 1865, p. 3, c. 1.

50   J. Winston Coleman, Jr., *Last Days, Death and Funeral of Henry Clay* (Lexington: Winburn Press, 1951).

51   William T. Coggeshall, *The Journeys of Abraham Lincoln* (Columbus: Ohio State Journal, 1865), 218-225.

52   *Official Records*, Ser. I, Vol. XLVI, Pt.3, p. 1081.

53   *Illinois Daily State Journal*, Apr. 18, 1865, p. 2, c. 2.

54   *Ibid.*, May 4, 1865, p. 2, c. 2. It is often asked just who the official Honor Guard were. Nine General officers were assigned to escort the remains of Abraham Lincoln to their final resting place: Bvt. Brig. Gen. Edward Davis Townsend, Assistant Adjutant General, representing Edwin McMasters Stanton, Secretary of War; Bvt. Brig. Gen. Charles Thomas, Assistant Quartermaster General; Brig. Gen. Amos Beebe Eaton, Commissary General of Subsistence; Bvt. Major Gen. John Gross Barnard, Corps of Engineers; Brig. Gen. George Douglas Ramsey, Ordinance Dept.; Brig. Gen. Albion Parris Howe, Chief of Artillery; Bvt. Brig. Gen. Daniel Craig McCallum, Superintendent of Military Railroads; Maj. Gen. David Hunter; and Brig. Gen. John Curtis Caldwell.

Gideon Welles, Secretary of the Navy, ordered Rear Admiral Charles Henry Davis, Chief of the Bureau of Navigation; Capt. William Rogers Taylor, U. S. Navy; and Maj. Thomas Y. Field, U. S. Marine Corps, to join the military escort on the funeral train.

Under General Orders No. 72, Secretary Stanton declared that an Army Captain and twenty-five enlisted men would also accompany the body of President Lincoln. However, Stanton gave General Townsend the authority to "change or modify details not conflicting with the general arrangement." *Official Records*, Ser. I, Vol. XLVI, Pt. 3, pp. 845-846.

There were twelve Union officers in addition to the four company-grade officers who commanded the funeral detail of veteran sergeants. Three of the field-grade officers from this elite group of twelve were always on duty in the funeral car, guarding the bodies. (Engraving of this scene in Kean Archives, Philadelphia.)

Army officials turned to the Veterans Reserve Corps for the company-grade officers and enlisted men—all sergeants. They also added three Lieutenants to the roster. The Honor Guard was thus composed of the following veterans:

Name	Unit	Former Unit
Capt. James M. McCamly	Co. A, 9th VRC	70th N. Y. Vol. Inf.
1st Lt. Joseph H. Durkee	Co. E, 7th VRC	146th N. Y. Vol. Inf.
2nd Lt. Edward Murphy	Co. B, 10th VRC	148th Penn. Vol. Inf
2nd Lt. Edward Hoppy	Co. C, 12th VRC	44th & 9th U. S. Inf. and 2nd U. S. Art.
1st Sgt. Chester Swinehart	Co. D, 7th VRC	14th Ohio Vol. Inf.
Sgt. John R. Edwards	Co. E, 7th VRC	21st Wis. Vol. Inf.
Sgt. Samuel T. Carpenter	Co. K, 7th VRC	35th Mo. Vol. Inf.
Sgt. Addison Cornwell	Co. I, 7th VRC	134th N. Y. Vol. Inf.
Sgt. Jacob F. Nelson	Co. A, 9th VRC	150th Penn. Vol. Inf.
Sgt. Luther E. Bulock	Co. E, 9th VRC	97th N. Y. Vol. Inf.
Sgt. Patrick Callaghan	Co. H, 9th VRC	69th N. Y. Vol. Inf.
Sgt. A. Judson Marshall	Co. K, 9th VRC	94th N. Y. Vol. Inf.
Sgt. William T. Daly	Co. A, 10th VRC	
Sgt. James Collins	Co. D, 10th VRC	12th Mass. Vol. Inf.
Sgt. William W. Durgin	Co. F, 10th VRC	1st & 9th Maine Vol. Inf.
Sgt. Frank T. Smith	Co. C, 10th VRC	5th Wis. Vol. Inf.
Sgt. George E. Goodrich	Co. A, 12th VRC	124th Ohio Vol. Inf.
Sgt. Augustus E. Carr	Co. D, 12th VRC	140th N. Y. Vol. Inf.
Sgt. Frank Carey	Co. E, 12th VRC	51st Ohio Vol. Inf.
Sgt. William Henry Noble	Co. G, 12th VRC	21st Wis. Vol. Inf.
Sgt. John Karr	Co. D, 14th VRC	1st Mich. Vol. Inf.
Sgt. John P. Smith	Co. I, 14th VRC	119th Ill. Vol. Inf.
Sgt. John Hanna	Co. B, 14th VRC	40th N. Y. Vol. Inf. & 2nd U. S. Cav.
Sgt. Lloyd D. Forehand	Co. I, 18th VRC	5th N. H. Vol. Inf.
Sgt. Irvin M. Sedgwick	Co. H, 18th VRC	8th Mass. Vol. Inf.& 93rd N. Y. Vol. Inf.
Sgt. Rufus W. Lewis	Co. E, 18th VRC	15th Conn. Vol. Inf.
Sgt. John P. Barry	Co. A, 24th VRC	118th Penn. Vol. Inf.
Sgt. William H. Wiseman	Co. E, 24th VRC	139th Penn. Vol. Inf.
Sgt. James M. Pardun	Co. K, 24th VRC	93rd Ind. Vol. Inf.

An incomplete and inaccurate list is in Coggeshall, *The Journeys of Abraham Lincoln*, 141. Because of numerous spelling errors in Coggeshall's list, this roster has been checked in the National Archives against the original manuscripts by Paul Kallina who has corrected and added to the information gleaned by Coggeshall.

Because the Honor Guard had performed their difficult task with great fidelity to duty, all twenty-nine members—from the Captain on down through all the Sergeants—were awarded the Congressional Medal of Honor. However, a Board of Review struck their names from the rolls on February 15, 1917, since their deeds were not performed in combat. Editors of the Boston Publishing Company, *Above and Beyond: A History of the Medal of Honor from the Civil War to Vietnam* (Boston: Boston Pub. Co., 1985), 122-123.

55   "Diary of Anna Ridgely" printed in *Jour. Ill. State Hist. Soc.*, XXII, 444-445 (Oct., 1929).

56   *Illinois Daily State Journal*, May 4, 1865, p. 2, c. 1.

57   Temple, "Tinsmith to the Late Mr. Lincoln: Samuel S. Elder," *Jour. Ill. State Hist. Soc.*, LXXI, 176-184 (Aug., 1978).

58   *Illinois Daily State Journal*, May 5, 1865, p. 2, c. 1.

59   *Ibid.*; *Daily Illinois State Register*, May 5, 1865, p. 4, c. 2.

Two of the pallbearers were omitted from the first published lists: Wood and Archer. See the *Illinois Daily State Journal*, May 8, 1865, p. 3, c. 3.

Wood was a Republican Ex-Governor who had allowed Lincoln to use his office in the State House while a candidate for the Presidency and as President-elect. He became Illinois' Quartermaster General in the Civil War and later was Colonel of Illinois' 137th Infantry Regiment (a 100-day unit). Col. William B. Archer had been one of the first Commissioners for the Illinois & Michigan Canal; Lincoln later served as a Commissioner, too. Jesse Kilgore Dubois, a Republican, had been Illinois State Auditor from 1857 to 1864 and was a close friend of Lincoln's. Stephen Trigg Logan had been Lincoln's second law partner. Dr. Gersham Jayne had been the first physician in Springfield; he, too, had been a Commissioner on the I & M. Canal; and his daughter, Julia, was the wife of Senator Lyman Trumbull. Col. John Williams, a merchant and President of the First National Bank, was a Republican and Commissary General for State of Illinois during the Civil War. Erastus Wright was an early settler in Sangamon County and was an early Abolitionist. Capt. James Nicholas Brown had sat in the House of Representatives with Lincoln from 1840-1841; he lived in Island Grove Township and was an early political ally of Lincoln's; he was a farmer. Jacob Bunn, of course, was one of the most prominent citizens of Springfield; he had been Lincoln's banker and had supported him as a Republican partisan. Charles W. Matheny was a local merchant, soon to become a bank president. William F. Elkin had sat with Lincoln in the Illinois General Assembly as a member of the famous "Long Nine;" he was later Sheriff of Sangamon County; Pres. Lincoln had named him Register of the U. S. Land Office at Springfield in 1861. Gustavus Phillip Koerner had been Lt. Gov. of Illinois, from 1853 to 1857. James L. Lamb was a merchant and pork packer; he was an Elder in the First Presbyterian Church where the Lincolns attended. Samuel Hubbel Treat had been a Circuit Judge, a Justice on the Illinois Supreme Court and Judge of the U. S. District Court; he was also a prominent Mason. Elijah Iles had been the first merchant in Springfield when he settled there in 1821; he had been one of the four men who owned the land where Springfield was founded. Maj. Iles had soldiered with Lincoln in the Black Hawk War, too. John Todd Stuart had been Lincoln's first law partner; he had been a Major in the Black Hawk War where he first met Lincoln; they had later served together in the Illinois General Assembly; Stuart had encouraged Lincoln to study law; and he was a cousin of Mary (Todd) Lincoln.

Rather strangely, William Henry Herndon, Lincoln's third and last law partner, and former mayor of Springfield, was not asked to be a pallbearer. Instead, he was merely the Marshal of the Sixth Division in the funeral cortege.

60   *Chicago Tribune*, May 6, 1865, p.2, c. 4; N. Y. *Herald*, May 5, 1865, p. 1, c. 3.

61   *Illinois Daily State Journal*, May 5, 1865, p. 2, cc. 1-4. Rev. Hale's prayer was first printed in the *Daily Illinois State Register*, May 5, 1865, p. 4, c. 3.

62   *The Abraham Lincoln Encyclopedia* (N. Y.: McGraw-Hill, 1982), 277-278.

63   Nicolay and Hay, *Abraham Lincoln: A History*, X, 323.

64   *Funeral Address Delivered at the Burial of President Lincoln, at Springfield, Illinois, May 4, 1865 By Rev. Matthew Simpson, D. D.* (N. Y.: Carlton & Porter, 1865).

65   *Illinois Daily State Journal*, July 3, 1860, p. 3, cc. 2-3.

66   *Ibid.*, May 5, 1865, p. 2, cc. 1-4; *Daily Illinois State Register*, May 3, 1865, p. 4, c. 3.

67   *Official Records*, Ser. I, Vol. XLVI, Pt. 3, p. 1090.

68   *Illinois Daily State Journal*, May 6, 1865, p. 3, c. 3.

69   Mary Lincoln also told Herndon that her husband was "a religious man by nature." His religion, she said, "was a kind of poetry in his nature." W. H. Herndon & Jesse Wm. Weik, *Herndon's Lincoln* (Springfield: The Herndon's Lincoln Pub. Co., n. d.), III, 445. Herndon had taken notes during his interview with Mary Lincoln on Sept. 5, 1866.

William Jayne, *Personal Reminiscences of the Martyred President Abraham Lincoln* (Chicago: Grand Army Hall and Memorial Assoc., 1908), 51.

70   *Laws of the State of Illinois* (Springfield: H. W. Rokker, 1891), 173.

Interior of Lincoln's Church

Corner Third and Washington Streets, Springfield, Illinois,
taken after the assassination of President Lincoln.
Note the Lincoln pew is draped in mourning.

Chapter Twelve—Judges

How did Christian ministers view the life of Abraham Lincoln after his death? Perhaps one typical example will suffice to answer this vital question. The Session of the First Presbyterian Church in Springfield, where the Lincolns had worshipped, invited the Rev. Dr. Henry Addison Nelson, who held the pulpit of the First Presbyterian Church in St. Louis, Missouri, to preach in their pulpit on May 7, 1865, the first Sunday after President Lincoln's burial. First Church was at that time in between ministers and needed one to fill in. Rev. Nelson accepted the invitation and announced that he would speak on the topics "Life, Character and Death of President Lincoln" and the "Condition of the Country." Evidently, he would lecture both at the morning and evening services.[1]

In the same old church building known to the Lincolns at Third and Washington, the Rev. Dr. Nelson took his morning text from Psalm 79:70-72 where God chose David, His humble servant who had tended sheep to lead His people. Then he compared Abraham Lincoln to King David. Both had been brought from "humble circumstances and occupations of a peasant, to the high position and responsibilities of a monarch." God guided them both, he said. Could any Christian doubt that Lincoln "was signally guided and helped by God?" Some of Lincoln's "most conspicuous and important acts of his administration were not contemplated when he took the reins of government." The "Providence of God" led Lincoln to do them.

"I understand," Dr. Nelson said, "that his name had never been enrolled on your list of communicants, and that he had never here been known as a professor of religion." "But," continued Nelson, "that he was an honest believer in not only theoretical, but experimental Christianity, is generally understood." Rev. Nelson recalled that President Lincoln's public addresses and papers impressed him as having been composed by a Christian. God had indeed made him His instrument in accomplishing His goals. This Presbyterian pastor had the "precious hope that" Lincoln "was a child of God, and an heir, through grace in Christ Jesus, of the bliss of Heaven."[2] Therefore, Lincoln was probably in Heaven because of his good works and his belief, although holy water had never touched his noble head.

Dr. Nelson's addresses were well received, and ten of his listeners petitioned him to allow them to be published. He agreed with their request but changed both the titles prior to publication.[3]

Most Protestant ministers gave similar sermons which declared that Abraham Lincoln was actually in Heaven, even though he had never been an official or technical member of any denomination. Evidently, the American public also accepted this general thesis. Countless admiring and loyal Union citizens in the North purchased commercial carte-de-visite views depicting Abraham Lincoln being welcomed into Heaven by George Washington. There were at least four variations upon this theme. In three of them, angels also join Washington in honoring the martyred Lincoln in his Heavenly home. These carte-de-visite creations were acquired and placed in family photographic albums, usually kept and displayed in the front parlors of private residences.[4] A common custom was for a family to start their album with a photo of the President of the United States and follow it with various pictures of prominent public figures and heroes. Next, they added photographs of their own family members.

As many of Lincoln's contemporaries soon discovered, their tall friend rarely divulged much personal information about himself. Some thought him extremely "shut-mouthed." Even such a close associate as Governor Richard James Oglesby admitted, "I could never discover why Mr. Lincoln[']s views on religion or on christianity were so sedulously kept to himself."[5] By observation, however, some could at least repeat what they had seen. Ward Hill Lamon insisted, quite correctly, that Lincoln had never belonged to any church. Nevertheless, he had to concur that Lincoln "was as conscientiously religious as any man."[6] In a practical sense, David Homer Bates, who labored in the telegraph office at the War Department, declared that "if love be the fulfilling of the law of Christ, Abraham Lincoln, in his day and generation, was the nearly perfect human example of the operation of that law." Furthermore, Bates revealed that about the strongest swearing he ever heard Lincoln do was to utter "damn" when extremely provoked by some action.[7]

Perhaps Nicolay and Hay summed up their understanding of President Lincoln's religion the best of any of his intimate companions when they revealed that he "was a man of profound and intense religious feeling." "We have no purpose of attempting to formulate his creed," they confessed; "we question if he himself ever did so."[8] One could easily argue that they were exactly correct in their analysis of this difficult matter.

Although not a creed, Abraham Lincoln once wrote on a calendar for Judge David Davis, "God is the only being who has time enough, but a prudent man, who knows how to seize occasions, can commonly make a shift to find as much as he needs."[9] Certainly this statement points out Lincoln's acknowledgment of God as the supreme ruler and regulator of the universe. And it was to him that Lincoln pledged his allegiance. As we have seen, rarely did he mention Jesus Christ except as a historical figure. It would seem that the Trinity meant little to Lincoln. God was the one to whom he prayed; He was the one true God that revealed things to him. And Lincoln believed the dreams which he experienced to be divine revelations.[10] One might compare Lincoln to Benjamin Franklin and Thomas Jefferson, except that Lincoln openly stated that God guided the outcome of worldly events. Perhaps a better definition for Lincoln would be Monotheist.

Given what we know of his religious philosophy, Abraham Lincoln would have found much enjoyable communion with Freemasons. This oldest of fraternities only requires that a man believe in one Supreme Being. It accepts good men and tries to make them better through its teachings about the Fatherhood of God and the Brotherhood of Men. Although not a religion, Masonry might have given great solace, comfort and pleasure to Lincoln. Many of his dearest friends were Masons. Through them, he picked up some of the language used in Masonic ritual. He, upon occasion, referred to God as the "Almighty Architect."[11] Calling God the Architect of the Universe is a common practice of Masons. It is probably unique with them, too.

Yet Abraham Lincoln never was a Mason.[12] He simply was not much of a "joiner;" however, he had promised his Masonic colleagues in Springfield that he would petition the Craft for membership when his Presidency was finished. Immediately upon Lincoln's death, Orlin H. Miner, Master of one of Springfield's Masonic Lodges, gave to the local press a copy of the resolutions which his Brothers had passed. It read: "Resolved, That the decision of President Lincoln to postpone his application for the honors of Masonry, lest his motives should be misconstrued, is in the highest degree honorable to his memory."[13]

This fact was common knowledge among his Masonic friends in town. They longed for the time when they could call him Brother Lincoln and sit with this distinguished man in a tiled Lodge where neither religion nor politics are ever discussed.

Somebody went so far as to draw a Masonic apron and sash upon a photograph of Lincoln. But, it was only a misguided artist's imagination, perhaps originating in France where Lincoln was often considered a Mason.[14] It is even thought that some foreign Lodges elected Lincoln to membership posthumously. He was a man they wished to have on their rolls. But although Abraham Lincoln never joined the Masonic Fraternity, his great-grandson, Robert Todd Lincoln Beckwith, became a Mason and a Shriner. Beckwith openly wore his membership pin.

During the program at the Illinois State House prior to the removal of Lincoln's body to Oak Ridge Cemetery, an assembled choir sang "Pleyel's Hymn." Somebody on the Committee of Arrangements had to have been a Mason who knew of the late President's interest in Masonry, because this musical number is utilized in the Symbolic Lodge during the enactment of one of its degrees. It is not a common musical piece and is generally associated only with Masonry.[15]

Abraham Lincoln's life came full circle. He was born on a Sunday and was shot on a Good Friday. His religious experience had developed very slowly. He began life in a Christian home and then drifted away from formal-ized worship services. It would appear that he put little faith in religious doc-trines promulgated by earthly clerics over the ages. A reading of history would have shown him how inhumane religious leaders had been to their opponents who followed other faiths, and how cruel had been the actions of one sect against another—all in the name of religion.

There were, nevertheless, a few personal preachers for whom Abraham Lincoln expressed some liking, even if he would not bind himself to their congregation in a formal manner. One of them was Dr. James Smith; another was the Rev. Dr. P. D. Gurley. After Lincoln's death, his distraught widow penned a note to Dr. Gurley on May 22 and informed him that her late husband had entertained a "very kind regard" for him. With this note, she sent him Lincoln's top hat, the one which he had worn to his Second Inauguration. When Gurley failed even to acknowledge the receipt of the precious memen-to, Mary Lincoln, months later, implored Alexander Williamson to check on this man-of-the-cloth and find out why he had not replied to her.[16] He got the message and therefore had to have received the hat. Mary Lincoln would soon discover that with her husband's death, many sycophants, who had pre-tended great allegiance to Father Abraham prior to his demise, now found no profit in paying court to Mary Lincoln, a common citizen with no political influ-ence whatsoever. Whether or not Dr. Gurley fell in this category will never be known. He had already experienced the glory of traveling with Lincoln's body to Springfield and appearing upon the platform during the final burial service. Was he merely forgetful or was he just ignoring the pitiful widow? We shall probably never know the answer. We do know that during the Civil War, Dr. Gurley sometimes pestered the President for favors, just as did many others.

One true friend of the Lincolns would have greatly appreciated the gift which Mary Lincoln intended to give him. When Dr. Anson G. Henry was in Chicago during June of 1865, Mary could not get to some boxes in a warehouse which contained "a large family Bible." She had intended to present the precious book to Dr. Henry, but before she could retrieve it, this faithful physician had been killed. Yet, she promised to send it to Dr. Henry's widow, Eliza.[17] Mary Lincoln gave away many items closely associated with President Lincoln. Most of the recipients cherished these artifacts and greatly appreciated the kindness of Mrs. Lincoln in remembering them.

Not all political figures in the Republican Party admired President Lincoln's philosophy. Senator Benjamin Franklin Wade (1800-1878) became very critical of Lincoln. He once blurted out that he wished the Devil had Abraham Lincoln. Senator Zachariah Chandler (1813-1879) also found great fault with Lincoln. Upon the President's death, Senator Chandler opined that the "Almighty continued Mr. Lincoln in office as long as he was useful." When invited to accompany Lincoln's body back to Springfield on the funeral train, Chandler flatly refused the honor.[18] Such men were in the minority, and history has largely forgotten these critics.

Broken in health as well as in spirit and with but a weak grasp on reality, Mary Lincoln finally took her belated departure from the White House aboard the 6:00 p. m. train on May 22—thirty-seven days after her beloved husband had been assassinated. She was bound for Chicago, not Springfield. In truth, she had but few admiring friends left in her old home town. B. B. French confided to his diary that "the sudden and awful death of the President somewhat unhinged her mind, for at times she has exhibited all the symptoms of madness." "She is a most singular woman," he concluded, "and it is well for the nation that she is no longer in the White House." "She has given me a world of trouble," French complained.[19] Indeed, Mary (Todd) Lincoln often made it extremely difficult for people to feel comfortable around her. One relative in Springfield recalled from experience that Mary could be "sarcastic and severe."[20] That was most probably a mild assessment of her personality.

Perhaps, because Mary Lincoln had largely remained in her bedroom and was not able to administer the White House after the assassination of her husband, the Executive Mansion was stripped of its costly furnishings and furniture. Even beds disappeared! It was gossiped around the Capital City that Mary had either stolen or sold government property. The fact that she took from seventy-five to one hundred boxes of possessions with her to Chicago added fuel to the accusations. Congress, quite naturally, held several investigations to uncover the truth. Its committee of inquiry concluded that it was impossible to state that Mrs. Lincoln had actually purloined Federal property, but she certainly had not guarded it.[21] Servants and interlopers, no doubt, simply walked off with, or carted off, valuable items. However, Judge David Davis told O. H. Browning that Mary Lincoln was a thief whose stealing was a part of her insanity complex. Davis further reported that Mrs. Lincoln had solicited bribes from office-seekers, such as Simeon Draper of New York. Even these bribes were not enough to pay for the extremely expensive jewelry which she had purchased on credit. Indeed, Mary Lincoln was not beloved by those who knew her best.[22]

When Mary (Todd) Lincoln definitely needed a religious anchor to hold her in the channel of reason during her time of greatest need, did she rely upon her church or its ministers? That is a most difficult question to answer. We do know that she appeared to believe in certain ceremonies of churches. During the summer of 1861, the First Lady sent a bottle of water from the River Jordan in Palestine to Springfield, Illinois, with instructions that her infant great nephew, Edward Lewis Baker, Jr., could now be baptized properly and in great style.[23] She also once declared that "God is just." She was positive, too, that her husband now dwelt in Heaven. His eyes, she felt, were constantly observing her and protecting her. Her belief in Heaven was so sure that she thought that death would be only a "blessed transition." It comforted her to know that the dead, "though unseen by us," are "very near."[24] Spiritualism had once more invaded her Presbyterian upbringing and experience. It bolstered her orthodox worship and perhaps even gave added comfort to her tortured mind and soul. But it also opened her purse to charlatans who took advantage of a distraught widow with a very troubled mind.

Dressed in mourning and heavily veiled, Mary Lincoln sometimes frequented the Third Presbyterian Church at Washington and Carpenter in Chicago. The Rev. Dr. David Swing, of the Westminster Presbyterian Church at the corner of West Jackson and Peoria, later paid her visits.

In June of 1867, Mary Lincoln, in the absence of Robert and Tad, paid a visit to Racine, Wisconsin, to examine personally Racine College—

later called DeKoven Foundation. She was contemplating sending Tad to school there. From the head of this institution, she quickly discovered that it was an Episcopalian academy. From the sound of the music in the chapel, she concluded that it was a very high church place. In the end, she decided against the school because she would be separated from Tad. Her Presbyterian background may also have figured in the decision.[25]

Tad eventually was enrolled in the Chicago Academy at Number 11 Eighteenth Street where H. H. Babcock was the principal. Young Tad attended Sunday School in several churches, but finally decided upon that held in the First Baptist Church on Wabash Avenue between Hubbard and Peck. Like his namesake, Grandfather Thomas Lincoln, Tad cast his lot with these Baptists and formally joined their Sunday School with a friend. Dr. William W. Everts, the pastor, reported that Tad attended faithfully after joining.[26] At this time, Mary and Tad Lincoln were living at 375 West Washington Street in Chicago.

When Robert T. Lincoln married Mary Harlan at Washington, D. C., on the evening of September 24, 1868, Mary (Todd) Lincoln and Tad determined to witness this momentous event and then leave for Europe. After the wedding, they journeyed over to Baltimore and sailed on October 1 aboard the steamer *Baltimore*.[27] Their eventual destination was Frankfurt-am-Main where Mary had decided to enter Tad into an excellent school referred to as Dr. D. Hohagen's Institute on Kettenhofstrasse. She took up simple quarters in the Hotel d' Angleterre, not far away. While Tad studied, she visited the various health resorts of Europe. By May of 1870, Tad was attending a school in Oberursel, near Frankfurt, Germany.

For the first time in his life, Tad Lincoln was exposed to a rigorous education. Some of his instruction was in German. With strict practice, he overcame his speech impediment which had plagued him since birth. Becoming very serious, he determined not to drink beer or wine, unlike his brother, Robert, who liked his glass of spirits. It was even reported that Tad was studying medicine.[28] But when the Franco-Prussian War threatened to engulf them, the Lincolns fled to England in the late summer of 1870. By the ninth of September that year, Mary Lincoln had secured a tutor for Tad. She had taken up living quarters in Leamington, a noted spa about ninety-eight miles northwest of London in Warwickshire. Her stay in Leamington had been prompted by the opportunity to take the healing baths, and they had put her in better spirits. On the Continent, she had frequented towns famous for their mineral-water baths. While Tad studied, Mary traveled about the country, often taking trips to London and other locations.[29] After a number of months, she simply moved down to London.

As time passed, Tad yearned to see his brother, Robert, and Mary longed to see her new granddaughter. Therefore, on April 29, 1871, mother and son sailed from Liverpool aboard the steamship *Russia*.[30] It steamed into New York harbor on May 10. Included on the passenger list was Maj. Gen. P. H. Sheridan. Since the revenue cutter *Bronx* sailed out to take this famous Civil War officer off before the *Russia* docked, this official vessel also picked up the Lincolns. Thus, they avoided customs and also shared in the gala reception tendered General Sheridan. A reporter noted that Mrs. Lincoln was still wearing her mourning clothes. After the party, she took Tad to the Everett House for a brief stay before continuing on their way. Mary Lincoln had decided to let Tad finish his education in the United States.[31]

On the morning of May 15, 1871, Mary and Tad Lincoln took their leave of New York City and boarded a train for Chicago. Observers noted that Tad had grown tall and had acquired a good knowledge of both French and German. He reminded them of Robert T. Lincoln at the time the Civil War began.[32] Mother and son may have stopped at least once on their way to Chicago, because they did not arrive until about May 19.[33]

Little is known of their religious experience while in Europe, although Mary Lincoln sometimes was visited by well-known divines who happened to be sojourning near her. While in London, she had contact with Bishop Matthew Simpson and his wife. And she once went with Paul Shipman to hear the Rev. Charles Haddon Spurgeon (1834-1892) preach. He had been born in Essex and began his ministry as a Baptist, but he became a non-conformist, had his own Tabernacle constructed in 1861 at Newington Causeway, and tended to preach in the Puritan style. In 1865, he withdrew from the Evangelical Alliance.

Although Mary pretended to seek anonymity, she seemed flattered when famous people—such as Spurgeon—recognized her despite her veils. She enjoyed receiving attention for what she considered her exalted station in life. Her religious beliefs seem to have been quite standard for a Presbyterian woman in her era—except for her practice of Spiritualism. And she did believe in luck. In November of 1869, she declared that "Certainly ill luck presided at my birth—certainly within the last few years it has been a faithful attendant."[34]

Even though Mary Lincoln had told reporters that she intended to live with Robert and his little family in Chicago at 653 Wabash Avenue, Mary could not get along with her daughter-in-law and departed from under their roof to find living accommodations in Room 21 at the Clifton House where W. A. Jenkins and J. A. Holmes were the proprietors. This hostelry stood at Wabash Avenue and Madison.[35] Never a completely healthy child, Tad, by May 23, was reported to be confined to his bed "with a severe cold."[36] Dr. Charles Gilman Smith, a physician residing at 792 Wabash Avenue, treated Tad who suffered—so the doctor proclaimed—from "dropsy of the chest." Dr. H. A. Johnson and Dr. N. S. Davis also consulted with Dr. Smith. This malady first developed in his left lung area and then spread to the right. Dropsy was a term then used for liquid filling the lungs and causing compression to the heart. Tad might have been suffering from tuberculosis which certainly killed his brother, Edward Baker Lincoln, in 1850. Robert reported that water was accumulating on Tad's chest, and he hired two nurses to care for him around the clock. Pleurisy was also reported as a cause of his demise. This malady produces fever and very difficult breathing.

By July 7, 1871, the world was informed that Tad had been "at the point of death for the last week and cannot possibly recover."[37] At 7:30 a. m. on July 15, he succumbed in the Clifton House. At eighteen years of age, Tad Lincoln was no more. After the body was embalmed, it was taken to the home of his brother, Robert, at 653 Wabash Avenue. As was usual with Mary Lincoln in a crisis, her grief appeared to be beyond expression. Her personal physician thought "the blow may cause insanity in her." She would not participate in the brief religious service held over the body at 4:30 p. m. on July 16.[38]

Despite the fact that the Lincoln family invited only a few personal friends for the abbreviated obsequies at the Robert Todd Lincoln mansion, the house was completely filled—parlours, hall, steps, balcony and every place where a person could stand. The Rev. Dr. William W. Everts from the First Baptist Church took charge of this brief observance. He had been an organizer of the Baptist Theological Union in 1863 which sponsored the Chicago Baptist Theological Seminary at Morgan Park.[39] Tad had greatly admired him since he first attended Everts' Sunday School. Dr. Everts was the logical choice for an intimate religious tribute. This minister read from the Scriptures and commented about the shortness of life. Then he related to his audience the fact that Tad had taken the temperance pledge. After a prayer and a hymn, the short service ended.[40]

Following these private religious rites, Tad's impressive rosewood casket was conveyed to the train station where a special railway car had been added to the "Lightning Express" of the Chicago, Alton & St. Louis Railroad to accommodate the mourners on their two-hundred-mile trip to Springfield where the main funeral services would be held. Mary Lincoln was still a member of the First Presbyterian Church there, and burial would take place in Oak Ridge Cemetery where Tad's father and two of his brothers lay in temporary quarters.[41] Mary Lincoln, however, did not accompany the remains down to Springfield; she stayed closeted in her room just as she had done in the White House after her husband's tragic death. Robert left her with a nurse and departed.

Capt. Robert Lincoln alone shouldered the heavy responsibilities and assembled a contingent of friends to help him escort Tad's body on its sad journey by night. They filled the special railway car. Among those whom the press recognized were: The Rev. Dr. John H. Brown; Senator Lyman Trumbull of Illinois; Senator James Harlan of Iowa; United States Supreme Court Judge David Davis; Major General James Allen Hardie and Lt. Colonel Michael Vincent Sheridan, both of the U. S. Army; J. Y. Scammon; William Butler Ogden; Isaac N. Arnold; Dr. C. G. Smith; Edward Swift Isham; Norman Williams; a Mr. Bishop; a Major Eaton; and several others.[42] At 3:50 a. m. on the morning of July 17, the "Lightening Express" pulled into the C. A. & St. L. station with a hissing of steam and a grinding of steel wheels. Quickly, the somber casket was taken from the baggage car and conveyed to the opulent residence of Mr. and Mrs. N. W. Edwards who then lived where the Centennial Building now stands in Springfield.[43] The tired travelers probably hurried to hotels for a few hours rest before the funeral later that morning. Robert Lincoln, no doubt, found accommodations with one of his numerous relatives.

The final funeral service for Tad Lincoln was scheduled for July 17 at 9:00 a. m. in the First Presbyterian Church at Third and Washington. This very building had been where the Lincolns attended church and Sunday School; the venerable sanctuary would not be sold to another denomination until December 2, 1871.[44] It would be a sentimental worship experience for all of the older members who had—before the Civil War—often observed the Lincolns there in their particular pew. Some may have even witnessed Tad's baptism there on April 4, 1855.

Since the obsequies had been well announced by the local press, this ancient structure was crowded to overflowing prior to 9: 00 a. m. However, ample space had been reserved for the several relatives and intimate friends of Mary Lincoln's still residing in Springfield. Especially mentioned by the newspapers as being present were her sisters, Mrs. N. W. Edwards, Mrs. C. M. Smith and Mrs. Dr. William S. Wallace. From an analysis of the newspaper accounts, it would appear that Captain William H. Hayden commenced playing organ music at 9:00 a. m. A most talented man, Hayden was an Elder of First Church, since October 13, 1867, was also its Sunday School Superintendent and found pleasure in working with the youth of the community. Hayden had been born July 11, 1825, in Boston. With his parents, he moved to Alton, Illinois, in 1831 and graduated from Shurtleff College in 1846. After pursuing a mercantile career in St. Louis, he drifted up to Springfield, Illinois, where he became the chief bookkeeper of the First National Bank. During the Civil War, he soldiered with a Missouri outfit and then became an instructor in tactics at Camp Butler and Camp Dement.[45]

At approximately 9:30, the casket—decorated with a cross and wreaths of immortelles —was borne into the sanctuary and deposited in front of the pulpit by six young pallbearers: William Lewis, William Jayne, William Campbell, Treat Campbell, Addison Booth and George W. Chatterton, Jr. After another dirge on the organ, Dr. John H. Brown—formerly one of the two pastors of this church while the Lincolns worshipped there, but now preaching in Chicago— invoked the divine blessing upon friends and relatives assembled together that morning. Then the choir sang Hymn No. 610, commencing, "How shall the young secure their hearts and guard their lives from sin." Next, the Rev. Brown read the 12th Chapter of Ecclesiastes: "Remember now thy Creator in the days of thy youth. . . ." Following him to the pulpit was the Rev. Dr. John G. Bergen— the initial pastor of First Church, starting from 1828 to 1848—who gave a prayer. Dr. Brown then opened his sermon with a text from Isaiah 40: 30-31, "Even the youth shall faint and be weary, and the young men shall utterly fall. But they that wait upon the Lord shall renew their strength; they shall mount up with wings as eagles; they shall run, and not be weary; and they shall walk, and not faint." His message was that only with divine assistance could one sustain "the dispensations of divine providence." He directed the first part of his discourse to the congregation and the second, to the mourning family and close friends. Brown exhorted them to seek comfort from God in their hour of need. He implored the young people present to dedicate themselves to God and help others to find their way to God. Following this, Hymn No. 781 was sung, commencing, "When death appears before my eyes." Dr. Bergen then spoke the benediction.

A solemn funeral procession was then formed at the church for the long trek to Oak Ridge Cemetery on the north end of the city. This cortège was noted to be "one of the largest that has been seen in this city in many years." Upon reaching Oak Ridge, the coffin was slipped into the western-most one of the five crypts in the wall of the catacomb room within the new Lincoln Monument. Just before the funeral, this portion of the grand memorial tomb had been completed, although there remained much architectural work to be done.[46] Tad Lincoln rested alone in this truncated edifice.

During the summer of 1865, a private tomb had been begun on the hill southeast of the Public Receiving Vault where the bodies of President Lincoln and William Wallace Lincoln had been placed on May 4, 1865. Upon the completion of this temporary mausoleum, Edward Baker Lincoln was transferred to it from Hutchinson Cemetery on December 13, 1865. The bodies of President Lincoln and William Wallace Lincoln were next taken from the Public Receiving Vault and placed in the temporary vault on December 21 of that year. Finally, between 3:00 and 4:00 p. m. on September 19, 1871, the caskets of Abraham Lincoln, Willie Lincoln and Eddie Lincoln were removed from their temporary sepulcher and transported to the rising Lincoln Monument. There, President Lincoln's body was slid into the center one of the five crypts. The bodies of Willie and Eddie were then put, together, into the one remaining crypt to the west.[47] The entire western half of the burial niches were filled. Only two burial crypts remained empty: those to the east of Abraham Lincoln. And only two of the original Presidential family still survived: Mary Todd and Robert.

Tad's death greatly affected both Mary and Robert. Robert's physician advised him to get out of Chicago for awhile and rest. Mary (Todd) Lincoln's personal physician prognosticated that Tad's death could easily bring insanity upon her. He was correct. Mary began to write, begging a few select friends to come stay with her. She continually cried that she had been prostrated by illness and grief which only the grave could soften. Within a year, she began to wander about the country, going first to Boston, then to Wisconsin, and then on up to Canada. She sought out Spiritualists, health resorts, baths, and physicians who would listen to her complaints and treat her many aches. Although she always returned to Chicago after these strange excursions, her actions grew to be more and more bizarre. Fearing for her safety, Robert engaged a nurse-companion to travel with her. After more trips to Wisconsin and elsewhere, she determined to spend the winter of 1874-75 in Jacksonville, Florida. While there, she had hallucinations and exhibited the most eccentric conduct. If Mary was taking her usual paregoric or laudanum, these drugs could have increased her hallucinations and illusions, because they both contained opium. William B. Ober, M. D., has studied the effects of opium in his fine treatise entitled *Boswell's Clap and Other Essays: Medical Analyses of Literary Men's Afflictions* (Carbondale: Southern Illinois University Press, 1979). Finally, Mary Lincoln came back to Chicago on March 15, 1875.[48] Friends of hers who were entirely realistic, acknowledged that her "mind was somewhat unbalanced."[49] Mary's embarrassing actions had driven another wedge between herself and Robert and his wife.

Dr. Ralph N. Isham, her personal physician, and five other doctors, advised Robert that his mother was indeed insane. Leonard Swett counseled Robert to have a hearing and commit her to an asylum for her own good. An insanity hearing was scheduled on May 19, 1875, before Cook County Judge M. R. M. Wallace. A jury of twelve men pronounced her insane. That evening Mary tried to commit suicide but failed because the druggist knew her and omitted the laudanum from her prescription. The following day, she was taken to Dr. Richard J. Patterson's Bellevue Place, a private insane asylum at Batavia, Illinois. Soon, however, Judge and Myra Bradwell began to stir up public sympathy for Mary Lincoln. Robert Lincoln described Myra as "a high priestess in a gang of Spiritualists." She denied Robert's charge. Greatly embarrassed, Robert Lincoln finally agreed to let his mother live in Springfield with her sister and brother-in-law, the Ninian W. Edwardses, who were paid one hundred dollars a month to care for her, and later, at Mary's insistence, $150.

On September 10, 1875, Robert escorted Mary to Springfield, Illinois. There, Mary again made contact with Spiritualists. In the meantime, Robert determined to wash his hands of the whole worrisome mess. On June 15, 1876, he arranged for a jury in Chicago to restore his mother to reason. She remained living with the Edwardses until about September 10 that year when she slipped out of Springfield for a pleasant jaunt back to her childhood home, and other scenic spots. She coaxed her great-nephew, Edward Lewis Baker, Jr., to accompany her. Young Lewis, as he was called, resided with his grandparents while his own parents were away in Argentina. Mary had come to rely on this seventeen-year-old, who had just graduated from Springfield High School earlier that year, as a substitute for her estranged son, Robert, although she detested his parents, E. L. Baker, Sr., and Julia Cook (Edwards) Baker.

Mary and Lewis journeyed down to the beautiful Blue Grass country where they toured Lexington and looked at the places still standing which were sentimental to Mary from her childhood days. Mary showed him the burial places of their Todd ancestors. They also went to see impressive Mammoth Cave. Next, they traveled up to Philadelphia to experience the sights of the Centennial Exposition. Then, after a week in New York City, Mary was ready to sail for Europe. After Lewis saw her safely aboard, she handed him $27 for his return railroad fare back to Springfield.

Her steamship, the *S. S. Labrador*, departed from New York on October 1, 1876, and headed for Le Harve, France. A vessel of the French Line, she had been originally constructed in 1865 and boasted of two smokestacks and two masts for sails, when and if needed. She carried just forty-eight paying voyagers, most of them French, in addition to Mary Lincoln who managed to keep her name off the passenger list published in the newspapers. Before leaving Springfield, Mary had sworn her sister, Elizabeth Edwards, to secrecy about her planned escape to Europe. Out of respect for her wishes, the local Springfield papers had omitted any reference to her departure.

After a rough crossing of the Atlantic, Mary stepped ashore in Le Harve, twelve days out of New York City. After recuperating for awhile, she resumed her journey down to Bordeaux on the new ship *Columbia*. By rail, she proceeded to her final destination, Pau, France. Pau was a famous health resort, with curative baths, at the foot of the picturesque Pyrenees. From this hub, Mary made numerous excursions to other interesting places. Mary still complained constantly about her health, but she managed to continue to travel extensively. And she had put an ocean between herself and her enemy, Robert Todd Lincoln.[50]

Numerous writers have stated or implied that there was little wrong with Mary (Todd) Lincoln other than her obsession with money and her ill-advised shopping sprees for objects which she—in many instances—could not use at all. Some authors have even suggested that her commitment as a lunatic was no doubt the result of male chauvinism. But a careful study of original sources indicates that Mary was mentally unstable. President Lincoln had pointed out to his wife in 1862, that if she did not get a grip upon herself, he might have to have her admitted to the insane asylum.[51] Dr. R. J. Patterson testified that she was insane.[52] Dr. Willis Danforth—just one of several physicians who came to this same conclusion—confirmed that Mary "was suffering from debility of the nervous system."[53] Her own cousin, John Todd Stuart, stated in writing that she was insane.[54] Her nephew, Albert Stevenson Edwards, revealed that "Mrs. Abraham Lincoln was insane from the time of her husband['s] death until her own death." R. T. Lincoln, Albert confided, had asked Albert's wife, Josephine (Remann) Edwards, to help care for Mary Lincoln while she resided with the Ninian Edwardses, Albert's parents. Albert knew first-hand the facts concerning Mary's condition.[55] After 1875, Robert Todd Lincoln explained to a correspondent that his mother suffered from an "unhappy mental condition in which she lived during the years following my father's death."[56] At the time of her 1875 trial, he had actually testified that his mother was insane. A Springfield historian observed that "Death to her was a merciful release after more than seventeen years of mental and physical torture."[57]

A partial examination of Mary's genealogy sheds new light on this question. Her grandmother, Elizabeth Ann Porter Parker, married a cousin, Robert Parker. Their daughter, Eliza Ann Parker, married her cousin, Robert Smith Todd (born February 25, 1791) on November 26, 1812. Consequently, Mary Todd had parents who had the same great-grandfather. Such marriages of cousins is often discouraged, either by law or custom. Robert S. Todd was nearly six feet tall, with brown hair and ruddy complexion. He was said to have been impetuous, high-strung and very sensitive.[58] He died at 1:00 a. m. on July 17, 1849, on his farm in Franklin County, Kentucky, before Abraham and Mary Lincoln became nationally known.[59] Therefore, his life was never widely scrutinized by the press.

Among Robert S. Todd's children was Confederate Capt. David Todd, half-brother to Mary Lincoln. David seems to have been an unpredictable person. As a warden at Libby Prison, he one day took his sword and slashed a prisoner without any provocation. George Todd, a physician and the youngest son of Robert S. Todd, was reported to be eccentric, high-tempered, egotistical and brutal. His first wife divorced him for cruelty. In the Civil War, he served as a Confederate surgeon. Prisoners testified that he had "fits of madness" and was "the most degraded of all the rebels" they had contact with during their confinement.[60] Mary's full brother, Levi, had a cruel nature, and his wife divorced him.

Were any of these mental characteristics evident in some of the succeeding generations? Elizabeth Porter (Todd) Edwards, Mary's oldest sister, confided to Robert T. Lincoln that "Insanity, although a new feature, in our family history, first appeared within my knowledge, in the case of my own daughter," Julia Cook Edwards, born in Springfield on April 29, 1837. Elizabeth first noted her daughter's peculiar traits "at the early age of thirteen." Julia married Edward Lewis Baker, Sr., on June 6, 1855. Her malady was "severely felt, particularly by her husband" and her mother. "At no time," Elizabeth divulged, "has she ever been natural in her demeanor." "God pity those who are the victims—and who are the anxious sufferers in such terrible afflictions!" exclaimed Elizabeth Edwards to her nephew Robert.[61] It is a matter of legal record that Julia Baker had a trustee, Christopher Columbus Brown, to manage her affairs.[62] Mary Lincoln once alluded to "poor, silly, Julia Baker!" when Julie visited her in the White House during 1864. "How unfortunate a Mother, must consider herself, to so rear, a child—Naturally weak, how much better, to have brought her up a good, domestic, woman," Mary observed. Mary Lincoln explained that Julia had so badly behaved as to disgrace the City of Washington.[63]

Elizabeth (Todd) and Ninian W. Edwards also had a son, Albert Stevenson Edwards, born December 16, 1839. He married Josephine E. Remann on June 3, 1863. Albert seems to have led a normal life and became Custodian of the Lincoln Home on July 1, 1897. He and his wife had a daughter named Georgie Hortense Edwards who was born on July 22, 1864. She never married and helped around the Lincoln Home after her father and mother became the official State caretakers of this historic site. She died on April 10, 1922, in The Norbury Sanitarium in Jacksonville, Illinois.[64] Ninian Edward's side of the family had some peculiarities, too. Ninian Wirt Edwards' parents, Governor and Mrs. Ninian Edwards, were first cousins.

Dr. Frank Parsons Norbury, A. M., M. D., served as the Medical Director of Norbury Sanitarium which was a "Private Residential Home For the Treatment of Nervous and Mental Disorders." Lest there be any doubt about the nature of his establishment, he identified himself as the President and Medical Director of a "Psychopathic hospital" at 1631 West Mound Avenue in Jacksonville.[65] Dr. Norbury had been born on August 5, 1863, in Beardstown, Illinois. He studied medicine and received his diploma on March 9, 1888, from the Long Island College Hospital. He was registered as a physician in Illinois on August 23, that same year. He died in Jacksonville on March 14, 1939.[66]

No further genealogical study has been made regarding the relatives of Mary Lincoln, but it certainly would appear that there was a serious abnormality in the Todd bloodline which manifested itself in some of the generations which followed Robert S. Todd. It is perfectly safe to say that Mary (Todd) Lincoln was adjudged legally insane in a court of law after the testimony of several physicians and other observers. It would further appear safe to conclude that she could have come by her insanity by inheriting a tendency towards it. Even Robert Todd Lincoln, himself, admitted to George N. Black, when writing from Augusta, Georgia, on March 20, 1906, that he had suffered "a nervous break-down." This letter is preserved in the Illinois State Historical Library. Robert perhaps hinted at this problem again on January 30, 1911, while explaining why he could not attend the festivities in Springfield, Illinois, on February 11, 1911. Said Robert to Judge J. Otis Humphrey: "my medical adviser tells me that I must, for a considerable time to come, refrain not only from attending to business, but from doing anything that would take me out of a very quiet life." This reply was printed in the program for that event. To an aunt in Lexington, Kentucky, Robert Lincoln frequently revealed that he suffered greatly from nervous problems. His blood pressure also soared to a reading of over two hundred. These valuable letters were later acquired by William H. Townsend of Lexington, Kentucky.

In Europe, Mary Lincoln continued to write her few remaining friends. To her sister, Elizabeth, she reported, "My 'Gethsemane' is ever with me & God, can alone, lighten the burden, until I am reunited to my dearly beloved husband, and children."[67] Most of her correspondence remained in this same vein. Her grief was ever present and never ending until she died. Nevertheless, she traveled to Paris, Naples, Rome, Sorrento, Marseilles, Biarritz, St. Jean de Luz, St. Sauver, Avignon, and other places. She fell twice, hurting her back and left side. In the midst of her suffering, she determined, at last, to return to the United States.

From Bordeaux, she journeyed up to Paris and sailed from Le Harve on October 16, 1880, aboard *l'Amerique*.[68] She arrived in New York City on October 27 and immediately proceeded to the Clarendon Hotel.[69] It was reported that she was so ill that "no one is allowed to call upon her."[70] That may have been one of her exaggerations, because a few days later she left by train for Springfield, Illinois, arriving by November 3 and taking up her abode with Elizabeth and Ninian Edwards.[71]

At this point in their lives, Ninian and Elizabeth Edwards were not young nor in the best of health. Neither were they wealthy anymore. So, Mary

Lincoln's boarding with them proved somewhat beneficial, since they charged her $150 a month. In addition, Mary paid $3 a month for the two rooms where her sixty-four trunks were stored. Since Mary had quarters on the second floor, the Edwardses' maid quit and moved out, her room having been directly below the spot where Mary's heavy trunks were stored. The maid feared she would be killed if the floor collapsed from all the weight. After a study of the meager evidence, it would appear that Mary also had access to a sitting room or parlor on the second floor. Her domain, then, must have encompassed about four rooms.[72]

While the Edwardses appreciated the board and room money, there were serious drawbacks to having sister Mary with them again. They experienced difficulties with their boarder. Mary proved to be "a lot of trouble." She argued and squabbled with Elizabeth. At times she even accused Elizabeth of stealing her cash. Of course, the "missing" bills and gold coins not kept in her money belt—which she constantly wore, even in bed—had been secreted by Mary herself under her own mattress or in her dresser. Whenever Mary made these false accusations, her sister and her helpers would have to search for the money and show it to Mary to prove their innocence.

The Edwards' renter had terrible headaches, too; her tired body became puffed and swollen; she took large quantities of paregoric to ease her pain; and it contained opium which may have given her even more illusions. When her fingers swelled, she removed her wide-banded wedding ring and hid it.[73] One could easily conclude that the Edwardses earned their rent money from Mary Lincoln. If feeling at her very best—providing the weather proved pleasant—Mary sometimes walked briefly in the neighborhood where the new State Capitol now stood, practically next door to the Edwards' house. Or she would ride down the streets in a closed carriage.[74]

When James A. Garfield became President in 1881, he appointed Robert T. Lincoln as Secretary of War, a post Robert held until 1885. While in route back from an official inspection trip to Fort Leavenworth in Kansas, Robert stopped at Springfield, Illinois, on the evening of May 28, 1881. He and his official party took up quarters at the Leland Hotel. On the following day, Robert called upon his mother at the home of the Edwardses. He had had little or no contact with her for years. How this meeting actually went, we do not know. We do know that on the 29th, Robert spent a pleasant evening at the Executive Mansion with Governor Shelby Moore Cullom, a fellow Republican, and left for Chicago at midnight on the Chicago, Alton & St. Louis Railroad.[75]

In the early fall of 1881, Mary Lincoln's physical ailments grew much worse. Her injured back caused her great suffering, and she decided to seek medical treatment as well as soothing baths at some spa. With her typical delight in confusing the press about her movements, she announced that she had determined to spend the coming *winter* in Canada.⁷⁶ Of course, in Europe she had found out that cold weather greatly aggravated her aches and pains, and she always migrated farther south when frigid temperatures arrived. Nevertheless, she informed the newshounds in Springfield that she had picked out St. Catherine's in the Province of Ontario, Canada, for her winter watering hole. This noted resort city lies just about eight miles northwest of Niagara Falls on the Canadian side. By October 5, Mary even mentioned casually to friends that she would leave town "within a few days" for St. Catherine's.⁷⁷

Soon after delivering this misleading bit of gossip, Mary slipped out of Springfield, about October 8th. As late as October 13th, a local newspaper still thought that Mary Lincoln had gone to St. Catherine's.⁷⁸ But if she actually visited this city of the baths, she did not stay long, because on October 11, she suddenly checked into the Clarendon Hotel in New York City.⁷⁹ It was a three-day train ride to New York. Upon arrival, Mary was unable to walk properly, and the hackman carried her into the hotel—not a difficult task since Mary now weighed only 100 pounds. But with her parsimonious nature, she quickly sought cheaper lodgings with baths. She chose Miller's Hotel at Numbers 37, 39, and 41 West Twenty-sixth Street where Dr. E. P. Miller reigned as proprietor. He advertised "Turkish, Electric and Roman Baths," whatever those might have been. Mary Lincoln selected the Electric Baths, and an employee carried her to and from these soothing encounters with hydrotherapy. For her personal medical specialist, she engaged Dr. Lewis Albert Sayre (1820-1900).⁸⁰ She evidently had first consulted him when she landed from Europe in October of 1880.

Dr. Sayre was a nephew of Lexington's David Austin Sayre who had once been Mary's Sunday School teacher.⁸¹ Lewis had been born February 29, 1820, in Morris County, New Jersey, but went to Transylvania University in Lexington, Kentucky, and graduated from there in 1839. Since his uncle was a very wealthy man, young Lewis Sayre may have been helped through school with financial aid from David Sayre. At any rate, Mary Todd first met Lewis while he was a college student in her home town, and she—quite naturally—had followed his brilliant career.⁸² After receiving his bachelor's degree, Lewis Sayre attended the College of Physicians and Surgeons in New York City and earned his M. D. degree in 1842. Staying in New York, he specialized in orthopedics and became one of the most famous surgeons of his day, having taught in both the United States and Great Britain. He also authored medical books and lectured widely. Mary Lincoln had made a fine choice when she selected Dr. Lewis A. Sayre, who treated spinal problems as one of his specialties.[83]

Calling upon Mary Lincoln quite frequently was Eliza Ann (Hall) Sayre, wife of Dr. Sayre. She evidently provided some cheer for Mary during her suffering.[84] Robert Lincoln also visited his mother during that time. A New York City newspaper reported that the Hon. Robert T. Lincoln, Secretary of War, had checked into the Gilsey House on November 21, 1881.[85] However, Robert probably made his visit because of rumors which threatened his very political life as a Cabinet member.[86]

Mary had been giving interviews to newsmen and had even persuaded her physician, Dr. Sayre, to make statements to the press concerning her "precarious" financial condition. One reporter started his column by announcing that Mrs. Lincoln was taking electrical treatments for her "spinal difficulty." She required constant attention, he declared, and had great difficulty in walking. After a two-hour interview with her, this reporter revealed that "Mentally Mrs. Lincoln is active and clear, talks with rapidity, and is pleased to meet her friends who may call to visit her." But what Mary Lincoln wanted to talk about was the possibility of an increase in her pension. She proclaimed that the Federal Government owed her a better pension income. She claimed she did not have enough money to maintain herself. She remarked that although Robert might take care of her, she did not desire that he should spend his own money to do so. He had, she confided, been paying her $1,500 a year for the house which she owned in Chicago. That property, she vouched, had cost her $18,000 when she originally purchase it, and now Robert was renting it out but not receiving the $1,500 which he was required to remit to her. Furthermore, Mary Lincoln told the newspapermen that she had "given" the old Lincoln homestead in Springfield to Robert. This statement was false. Robert had paid his mother $500 for her share in the house on April 16, 1874.[87] Of late, Mary cried that she had been forced to borrow money on her pension claim in order to live. Jacob Bunn, Mary said, did hold "a small amount" of her assets, but that fact was nobody's business but hers. It was, she proclaimed, the "duty of Congress" to increase her pension.[88]

Not only was Robert Lincoln greatly chagrined by these public statements of his mentally-unstable mother, but he was also threatened by both political parties. Many were calling for his resignation if he could not provide for the care of his ailing mother. Robert greatly disliked public notoriety, and he shrank from any open discussion of his private life. He must have been even more mortified than he had been back in 1867 when his demented mother tried to sell her old clothes at a shop in New York City. Then, at least, he had been a private citizen, but now he was a highly-visible Federal official. In that age, a family was expected to take care of its own without public money being expended unless the immediate family was penniless.

At long last, the *Illinois State Journal* sprang to Robert's defense. Those false statements printed in the New York papers justified the Springfield editor "in breaking the silence which, from motives of sympathy and respect for the feelings of the relatives and friends of the Martyred President, it has so long maintained on this subject, but makes it a duty to do so." While news stories gave the impression that Mary Lincoln was "in a state of virtual poverty, being without means to secure the medical attendance and the aid of nurses of which she greatly stands in need, notwithstanding the pension of $3000 per annum granted her by Congress." Such reports had become "the ground for an attack upon Secretary Lincoln, whose removal from the position of Secretary of War is to be demanded . . . ."

"The fact is," the editor revealed, "that while Mrs. Lincoln is, undoubtedly, physically and mentally ill, she is a hypochondriac as to her health and a monomaniac on the subject of money." She had previously gone berserk when the public raised a fund for General U. S. Grant, and she now exhibited the same symptoms and reactions when a like fund was started for the widow of Pres. James A. Garfield who had died from an assassin's bullet on September 19, 1881.[89] She demanded equal treatment because of what her husband had done for the Union. The nation owed her much more than what it was giving her. Being completely unbalanced, she never seemed to realize how ridiculous her poverty claims appeared to the reading public who had for years heard her complaints of being broke. Many of these laments had been released to the public while she traveled in style, with a maid, through Europe. To so travel, in their minds, equated her with wealthy tourists. They, for the most part, could not afford to see the world. If Mrs. Lincoln were truly destitute, why did she not remain living in Springfield where she once owned a home? Or why did she not reside in Chicago where she also owned an expensive residence? Mary Lincoln's pleas did not greatly move the voting public nor members of Congress.

In order to discredit the misrepresentations emanating from the East Coast concerning Mrs. Abraham Lincoln's finances, the editor of the *Illinois State Journal* used his influence to secure an accurate account of her personal estate. "Owing to the fact that Mrs. Lincoln's peculiarities are well known here," he stated, "her affairs have not been discussed by the local press" in Springfield "out of regard to that lady and her friends." Nevertheless, he felt it his duty to "lay aside personal consideration in order that the real facts may become known." "Instead of the paltry sum of $3,000 as an income," he continued, "Mrs. Lincoln to-day has an annual revenue of more than $5000. Mr. Jacob Bunn, of this city, holds in trust for her $60,000 of Government securities, that sum remaining from her share of the late President's estate and the money appropriated by Congress for Mrs. Lincoln soon after the assassination." "Besides the $3,000 interest on these bonds," he explained, "Mrs. Lincoln received while in Europe an annual rental on a Chicago residence of $1,500, making with her pension an income of over $8,000 per year." The previous winter, however, that Chicago property was sold. And when she replaced the old bonds, which had come due, the new bonds bore a lower rate of interest, giving her but $2,120 per year. At last count, her annual income was $5,120, a very nice sum indeed. But since returning to Springfield, she had saved $5,000, which she immediately invested in additional bonds. Thus, her total income amounted to $5,300.

Such a sum would have made numerous working families envious, because they earned far less than this amount. For instance, the Governor of Illinois received only $6,000 a year in salary. Certainly, Mary Lincoln was not destitute. The editor further proposed that although Mary Lincoln's announced purpose of traveling to the East was to receive medical care, it now appeared that she went there to "bring her case before the country and Congress." She was, the editor disclosed, "very jealous of the interest taken in Mrs. Garfield's behalf." To sum up the situation, the *Journal* exposed the fact that "Mrs. Lincoln's relatives and friends in this city believe her income is sufficient to procure everything necessary, and if it is not they are able and willing to supply the deficiency." They discountenanced and disapproved of her efforts to create excitement for financial gain.[90]

After these revelations, some of the New York papers copied the stories published in Springfield by the *Journal*.[91] Nothing more was said about

Robert Lincoln's *neglect* of his mother. However, Mary Lincoln must have been furious with these revelations. She was feverishly contacting politicians to plead her cause before Congress, and she convinced an old friend, Noyes W. Miner, to act as an "agent" in her lobbying efforts. She cautioned Rev. Miner not to mention his maneuverings to Congressman William M. Springer, nor Robert T. Lincoln, nor "the Springfield Clique" which she did not trust at all.[92] And yet, it was Congressman Springer, a Democrat from the Twelfth District of Illinois and a resident of Springfield, who was sponsoring Mary Lincoln's mighty efforts for an increase in her pension. In fact, it was Springer who was willing to submit a medical examination of Lincoln's widow in order to sway Congress when the vote came.

On January 1, 1882, four noted physicians came to examine Mary Lincoln at her quarters in the Miller Hotel. They were working even though it was New Year's Day. Their patient reported that she could walk but a few steps, and her vision was very poor and obscured.[93] Dr. Lewis A. Sayre, an orthopedist and her personal doctor, led the medical team; his offices were at 285 Fifth Avenue, a most prestigious address. Assisting him was Dr. Meredith Clymer of 65 West 38th Street; he graduated from the University of Pennsylvania with an M. D. degree in 1837. During the Civil War he was a Union surgeon and the Medical Director of the Department of the South; and since 1871, had been Professor of Mental and Nervous Diseases in Albany Medical College. Also on the evaluation team was Dr. Herman Knapp of 25 West 24th Street; he was a graduate in medicine from the University of Giessen in 1854. His specialty was the eyes, and he was the founder of the New York Ophthalmic and Aural Institute, and was one of the most celebrated eye surgeons in the country. Rounding out the examining committee was Dr. William H. Pancoast, an ophthalmologist whose office was at 1100 Walnut Street in Philadelphia.

They discovered that Mary Lincoln was "suffering from chronic inflammation of the spinal cord, chronic disease of the kidneys, and commencing cataract of both eyes." She was also afflicted with diabetes.[94] "The disorder of the spinal cord," they revealed, "is the consequence of an injury received some time since and has resulted in considerable loss of power of both lower extremities, so as to lessen their use and to render walking without assistance very unsafe, and going unaided down stairs impossible. The nature of the spinal trouble is progressive, and will end in paralysis of the lower extremities. Connected with the spinal disease and one of its evidences is the reflex paralysis of the iris of the eye, and the reduction of the sight to one tenth natural standard, together with much narrowing of the field of vision. The sight will gradually grow worse."

"There is no probability that there will be any permanent improvement in Mrs. Lincoln's condition," they all prognosticated, "considering her age and the nature of her diseases. She is now quite helpless, unable to walk with safety without the aid of an attendant, or indeed to help herself to any extent. She requires the continued service of a competent nurse, and also constant medical attendance." They neglected to state her mental condition since they were attempting to sway a hesitant Congress.

This frightening statement they directed to the attention of the Hon. Wm. M. Springer, House of Representatives, Washington, D. C.[95] However, Rhoda (White) Mack, a confidante of Mary Lincoln's, went to pick up the statement on the afternoon of January 3.[96] Such action indicates that Mary forwarded the statement to Springer's office in Washington. At last, Mary (Todd) Lincoln could prove to the world that she truly was suffering from numerous maladies.

On February 14, 1882, Mary Lincoln moved out of Miller's and took up a room at the Grand Central Hotel. She had been unable to continue with the Electric baths. True to form, she explained her reason for leaving: the miserable food and the fact that Mr. Miller had charged her $60 a week. Now, she suffered from severe chills and found herself in feeble health. Yet she continued to write letters and lobby with gusto for her pension increase.[97] Debilitating chills remained with her, and she contemplated cataract surgery upon her eyes.[98] But to our knowledge, she never underwent an operation. Congress did, however, pass her pension bill, and she immediately pestered Rev. Miner to get her the money and the new pension papers.[99]

Finding that she could not improve her health further and having managed to convince Congress of her financial need, Mary Lincoln informed Edward Lewis Baker, Jr., that she was taking a train out of New York City on March 22 at 5:30 p. m. She begged him to meet her in Springfield and take charge of her wheelchair, another box and a package of medicine. Her rail route lay up the Hudson to Buffalo and then west to Illinois. Her limbs, she wrote, were in a paralyzed state, and she greatly dreaded the long journey home.[100] Early on the morning of March 24, her railroad car on the Wabash Line pulled into Springfield after having passed through Indianapolis and Decatur. From the station she went to the Edwardses, "in as comfortable health as her friends had reason to expect."[101] A reporter observed that the baths had "considerably improved" her health, but she was "still feeble and will probably never recover her former activity." "Her eyes," he was told, "give her trouble yet[,] though they are not so bad as they were at one time."[102]

Although Mary Lincoln was still greatly ailing when she returned to Springfield, she adamantly refused to let a local physician treat her. But as she became much worse, the Edwardses persuaded her to let their own physician administer to her medical needs. This was Dr. Thomas Withers Dresser.[103] Although eminently qualified, he was rather a strange choice to attend Mary Lincoln.

Dr. Dresser was a Democrat and had actually fought in the Confederate Army. His sympathies lay with the South, and he had voted for Douglas, even though he was the son of the same Rev. Mr. Charles Dresser who had married the Lincolns and who had sold his house to them in 1844, and who had been born in Connecticut, and who had moved to Springfield from Virginia because he hated slavery. But Dr. Dresser's mother had been born in Dinwiddie County, Virginia, and perhaps influenced her son's attitude more than did his father.

Thomas W. Dresser had been born on January 11, 1837, at Halifax Court House, Virginia. After his schooling in Springfield, Illinois, Thomas graduated from Jubilee College in Peoria County, Illinois in 1855. From there he traveled down to New Orleans where he became principal of Fiske School. Then he attended two courses of medical lectures at the University of Louisiana, but the Civil War closed down this college, and Dresser enlisted in the Confederate Army. He was captured and eventually returned to Springfield during 1862. In September of 1863, he entered the medical department of the University of New York and graduated in March of 1864. Following the granting of his M. D. degree, Dresser again took up residence in Springfield where he practiced for many years. He died at the home of his daughter, Mrs. John Chandler White, in East St. Louis on April 27, 1907. His body was returned to Springfield on the following day, and the funeral took place at the home of his sister, Virginia Dresser, at 518 West Edwards, and in St. Paul's Episcopal Church on April 29 with burial in Oak Ridge Cemetery. Through financial speculation, he had become a very wealthy man.[104]

In 1851, Ninian Wirt Edwards had deserted the Whig Party and joined the Democrats. Judge David Davis, at that time, wrote to his wife on March 23 that Mr. Edwards had switched—so people said—because his ambitious wife wanted him to run for Congress and win since the district held so many Democrats. Ninian's desertion from the Whigs had "deeply mortified" Abraham Lincoln, the Judge confided to his spouse.[105] Ninian did not win but remained with the Democrats, receiving a choice appointment from Governor Joel Aldrich Matteson as Superintendent of Public Instruction on March 24, 1854. And when President Lincoln appointed him Commissary of Subsistence to serve Camp Butler, with the rank of Captain, on August 8, 1861, Ninian caused the President no end of trouble by letting most of his contracts with prominent Democrats. Lincoln remarked that Edwards had harassed him and also provoked his personal Republican friends.[106] As a result, the President changed Ninian's station to Chicago and kept him there. However, after Lincoln died, his distraught widow took sweet revenge upon Edwards for having embarrassed her husband with his partisan and questionable dealings which netted him a huge amount of profit which he used to pay his debts. She persuaded the War Department to have Capt. Edwards transferred to a faraway post.[107] Edwards, of course, resigned on June 22, 1865, rather than move to an undesirable location in the boondocks. On August 22, he retired and became a Major by brevet.

Mary Lincoln had once more returned to her lonely room at the Edwards' residence, but she would never again walk the Capitol grounds nor ride out in a carriage. Broken in health and mind, she remained closeted in her chamber where she demanded that the shades be kept drawn, claiming the light hurt her eyes. Only a candle was permitted in her quarters. She suffered from terrible headaches. From the time that Abraham Lincoln had first met her, she had been cursed with headaches, and as late as May 26, 1864, President Lincoln was still asking Dr. Robert K. Stone to furnish a medical prescription to ease his wife's "bilious headaches."[108] Now, Dr. Dresser discovered that his diffident patient could carry on a conversation and could even recall interesting events of the past. Nevertheless, she suffered from "a cerebral disease." She had "certain mental peculiarities," he testified.[109] She simply was not herself.[110] Sometimes she slept on just one side of her bed, reserving the other half for the President, she explained.[111] Quite naturally, it became common gossip that a crazy woman lived in the Edwards' house, and children avoided this place and ran by it in great haste if they had to pass that way.[112]

By the time summer came in 1882, Mary Lincoln was afflicted with not only boils but also carbuncles. These painful abscesses covered most of her frail body.[113] Only a very select few of the family were ever admitted into her presence. Steadily, she grew worse. On Friday, July 14, she arose from bed and walked across her room. On Saturday, the following day, she again walked with some assistance. But that evening at 9:00 p. m., she suffered a stroke of paralysis. Mary Lincoln could not speak, eat, nor move any part of her body. That day, the fifteenth, proved to be the anniversary of Tad's death at Chicago in 1871, and this fact, no doubt, increased her mental anguish. A member of the press learned on Sunday morning that Mary Lincoln was "semi-comatose." She was completely comatose for several hours, and then passed away at 8:15 p. m. July 16, 1882.[114]

Dr. Dresser termed the cause of her death "apoplexy." Mary Lincoln had lived approximately twenty-four hours after suffering a "paralytic stroke," the rupture or blockage of a blood vessel in the brain.[115] After studying several contemporary reports of her symptoms, Dr. W. A. Evans, in 1932, speculated that Mary Lincoln might have gone into a diabetic coma in addition to her other ailments.[116] She was just over sixty-three and one-half years of age, having been born in Lexington, Kentucky, on December 13, 1818. Said a local scribe, "Mrs. Lincoln's life has been an extremely sad one; and her death is a merciful release from an existence which she was poorly able to bear."[117]

Immediately, a wire was dispatched to Robert Lincoln in Washington, advising him of his mother's sudden demise. He determined to leave that evening for Chicago and then continue his journey on down to Springfield. Robert arrived on the afternoon of July 18 and proceeded to the Edwards' residence on Second Street. Observers noticed right away that his wife had not accompanied him for the funeral. Mary Eunice (Harlan) Lincoln had previously been recovering from an illness in Colorado but was in Chicago when the news came of her mother-in-law's death. Although she had been up and about since March of 1882, Mary (Harlan) Lincoln decided to take to her room because of "ill-health." This could have been the final snub to the lady who had caused her so much trouble and heartache—the woman who had broken up her marriage on at least one occasion, and the woman who on numerous occasions had accused her of taking household goods previously given outright to her.[118] In the Robert and Mary (Harlan) Lincoln collection of family pictures, there is only *one* of Mary (Todd) Lincoln.

Knowing that Robert could not make the necessary funeral arrangements from such a great distance, the Edwards family acted in his stead. They summoned Thomas C. Smith to take charge of the body and prepare it

Courtesy of the Illinois State Historical Library.

An unknown artist sketched this scene at the First Presbyterian Church in Springfield, Illinois, on July 19, 1882. Dr. James Armstrong Reed is sitting on the extreme right upon the dais, behind the "From the Citizens of Springfield" flower arrangement. To his immediate right is Rev. R. O. Post, and next to him is Dr. T. A. Parker. Sitting immediately in front of the casket is Robert T. Lincoln who is with his widowed aunt, Frances (Todd) Wallace, heavily veiled.

for burial. This noted undertaker kept his establishment and his home at 325 South 5th. After embalming, Mary's body was placed in a rosewood casket having a heavy lead inside lining. Outside, the coffin was covered with black velvet. When the undertaker had completed his labors, Mary Lincoln's "face bore the faint trace of a smile as though the troubled soul had been thrilled with a new joy." On Monday, July 17, friends assisting Elizabeth Edwards discovered Mary's wedding ring where she had hidden it. They took it to the funeral director who placed it once more upon Mary's finger so that it might be buried with her. The inscription read, "Love is Eternal."[119]

Early on Tuesday morning, July 18, the undertaker returned Mary Lincoln's body to the Edwards' house. There, the casket was opened and placed in the front parlour where Mary Todd had wed Abraham Lincoln on November 4, 1842. Her body reposed almost exactly where Mary and Abraham had taken their sacred vows nearly forty years before in front of that same beautiful hearth. Once more, the same old astral lamps were placed on that identical ancient mantle and lit; they had glowed with a bright light back on that fateful evening when Mary had taken as her husband that ambitious and rising lawyer as yet unpolished in the world of genteel society. This old mansion had witnessed numerous important incidents in Mary (Todd) Lincoln's life. Here, she had come to live in 1839; here, she was married; here—according to knowledgeable family members—she and Abraham as bride and groom had spent several nights before taking up living quarters in the Globe Tavern, evidently sleeping together in her old bed in the guest room; and here, she had died and was about to be buried from the protection of its historic walls that had known so many activities of Springfield's society circle.[120]

Although the press was kept in the dark at the time, the immediate family of Mary Lincoln quietly allowed their friends and neighbors to come to the Edwardses and view the body all day Tuesday and right up until the time the casket would be borne to the church for the final ceremonies on Wednesday. There, Mary lay in state and in solemn death while the elite of Springfield passed by and observed her for the last time. It turned out that "a large number of people who had known the deceased in her life-time" called to pay their respects.[121] While invited or accepted visitors queued sadly through the Edwards' mansion, John Flynn, who had once worked for the Edwardses but who normally labored at the Courthouse, took complete charge of this private residence.[122]

In the meantime, both the State and City officials held meetings to plan appropriate ceremonies, realizing that Mary Lincoln's only living son would not be on hand to guide them but agreeing to change anything which displeased him when he did arrive on the scene. On the 18th, the State officers convened and agreed to attend the funeral in a body; they would assemble in the new State House at 9:30 a. m. on the following day and proceed to the church from there. Mayor A. N. J. Crook issued a proclamation asking all business to cease during the funeral of Mary Lincoln. Of course, many prominent citizens were chosen for the Springfield Committee, and yet it was quickly pointed out that Judge James H. Matheny, who had stood up with Lincoln at his marriage, and the Hon. Samuel H. Jones had been omitted from the list. Those oversights were quickly remedied.[123] Jones was then President of the State National Bank and resided at 327 South Eighth Street, within a block of the old Lincoln Home. A Republican and a Mason, President Grant had appointed Jones as a Pension Agent; later, Jones was named a Commissioner of the State Penitentiary at Joliet.

Mary Lincoln's funeral was scheduled to be held in the First Presbyterian Church at 10:30 a. m. on July 19. Actually, the time was later changed to 10:00. Since November 28, 1871, this congregation had owned a new church building located at the northwest corner of Seventh and Capitol. It is very doubtful that Mary Lincoln had ever worshipped here, but, of course, she had remained a member of this church body since the day she had joined. By 9:00 a. m., hundreds of citizens sought to gain admission to the sanctuary. Knowing that seating would be inadequate for the expected crowd, the first six rows in the front of the sanctuary had been roped off for the family, pallbearers and distinguished guests. Although the local newspapers had not printed the notice of her death with black borders—as had been done for Abraham Lincoln—Mary Lincoln's passing had received wide notice for several days.[124] Upon seeing the grand crush of people attempting to enter the church, the doors were immediately closed after only a few had gotten inside. At fifteen minutes to ten, the doors were once more thrown open, and the available seats were quickly taken.

At some minutes before ten, Mary Lincoln's casket was closed, and the funeral procession started from the Edwards' house and moved directly to the First Presbyterian Church. Precisely at ten, Alice H. Knapp, a music teacher and the widow of Thomas L. Knapp, began to play a dirge upon the church organ. The pulpit had been draped in black, and down in front of it, on the floor level, stood a bier covered in white velvet, ready to receive the casket when it arrived.

Shortly thereafter, the funeral party entered the sanctuary to the strains of Beethoven's "Funeral March." First to appear were Judge S. H. Treat and Col. John Williams, honorary pallbearers. They led the way west, up the northernmost main aisle. In those days, there were two center aisles, making three sections of pews. Of course, there were also two very narrow aisles at the north and south walls of the church, but completely unsuited for a procession. Following these two men came the active pallbearers with Mary Lincoln's remains. Carrying the casket were Governor Shelby Moore Cullom; Hon. Milton Hay; Hon. James C. Conkling; Gen. John A. McClernand, substituting for O. M. Hatch who had originally been named; Jacob Bunn, Esq.; and Captain John S. Bradford. They carefully deposited the coffin upon the bier and were seated in the reserved section. Following them came the Hon. Robert T. Lincoln with Mrs. Dr. W. S. Wallace, his widowed aunt; the Hon. and Mrs. N. W. Edwards; Mr. and Mrs. C. M. Smith and numerous other relatives and old-time friends of the deceased. The state officers marched in and found pews on the north side of the church, very near the front. The citizen's committee delegates were shown to their places as were the members of the Lincoln Guard of Honor who had followed the immediate family behind the casket.

When the distinguished mourners were all seated, four members of the assembled Presbyterian Choir, in the organ loft, began to sing "God Is a Spirit." This special quartet consisted of Ellen (Huntington) Henkle, the wife of Thomas Condell Henkle who was a bookkeeper with J. W. Bunn & Co.; Carry Cullom or Ella Cullom. The newspapers could not agree as to which one of the Governor's daughters actually sang, and both lived in the Executive Mansion with their parents. Also in the choir were William L. Grimsley, a salesman with Herndon's and a second cousin of Mary Lincoln's, born March 17, 1852, to Elizabeth J. (Todd) Grimsley; and Fred F. Fisher, also a salesman at Herndon's.

The Rev. Roswell O. Post, pastor of the Congregational Church at Fifth and Edwards, read the 90th Psalm, beginning: "Lord, thou hast been our dwelling place in all generations." Then he gave a moving prayer after which William Grimsley, as soloist, sang, "Nearer My God to Thee," accompanied by the rest of the Choir. Following this musical number, the Rev. Dr. James Armstrong Reed, minister of the First Presbyterian Church, arose and read the text for his burial sermon from II Samuel 14:14, beginning, "For we must die, and are as water spilt on the ground, which cannot be gathered up again; neither doth God respect <u>any</u> person: yet doth he devise means, that his banished be not expelled from him."

Dr. Reed, a Republican and a fundamentalist, had been called to First Church on January 11, 1870, and had not known Abraham Lincoln as a worshipper in his congregation. Yet he had started his Springfield ministry in the same old building where the Lincoln pew still occupied its customary place, just as the Lincolns had left it back in 1861. It is extremely doubtful that Mary Lincoln ever heard him preach, but Reed did correspond with her. Emulating one of his predecessors, Dr. James Smith, Reed had composed a lengthy lecture on Lincoln's belief in God, denouncing what Ward Hill Lamon's biography of Lincoln in 1872 had stated about his religion. Utilizing this research, Reed then published a wordy article in *Scribner's Monthly*, outlining what he thought were Abraham Lincoln's religious beliefs.[125] This controversial piece caused Billy Herndon, whose research Lamon had purchased and used, to give another public lecture in the Courthouse at Springfield on the evening of December 12, 1873. Before a full house, Herndon belittled and criticized the writings of Josiah Gilbert Holland and James A. Reed, claiming that Lincoln had lived and died "a disbeliever."[126] After a few more fiery speeches, Rev. Reed finally ceased to spar with Herndon and abandoned the debate over Lincoln's religion. Now, this learned divine[127] was about to preach a final sermon for Mary (Todd) Lincoln who had been so very greatly pained by Herndon's rantings about her husband's lack of religion and supposed illegitimacy. The latter charge—of course—being entirely false, was eventually proved so by legal documents. The *Illinois State Journal* on October 14, 1876, p. 2, c. 4, announced that the marriage license of Thomas Lincoln and Nancy Hanks had finally been found.

After reading this chosen text, Rev. Dr. Reed began his lengthy remarks:

> These admonitory words fell from the lips of a princely woman pleading the common mortality to gain a merciful end with a princely man. They have their fitting repetition now, in the solemnities of this hour, when all that remains of the wife of a princely [man] lies before us. A poor, desolate, heart broken woman, whose sorrows have been too great for utterance even, has at last yielded to the withering hand of death, and entered upon that 'silent bourne whence no traveler returns.' This is only the climax of the shock of years ago.Death's doings have now only ripened unto maturity.

When among the Allegheny mountains last summer, I saw two tall and stately pines standing on a rocky ledge where they had grown so closely together as to be virtually united at the base, their interlocking roots entering the same rock cavities, and penetrating the same soil. There they had stood for years with intertwining branches, and interlocking roots braving in noble fellowship the mountain storms. But the taller of the two had, years before, been struck by a flash of lightning, that had gone to its very roots, shattering it from top to bottom, and leaving it scarred and dead.

The other apparently uninjured had survived for some years, but it was evident from the appearance of its leaves that it too was now quite dead. It had lingered in fellowship with its dead companion, but the shock was too much for it. In their sympathetic fellowship and union, both trees had suffered from the same calamity. They had virtually both been killed at the same time. With the one that lingered, it was only slow death from the same cause. So it seems to me today, that we are only looking at death placing his seal upon the lingering victim of a past calamity.

Years ago, Abraham Lincoln placed a ring on the finger of Mary Todd inscribed with these words: 'Love is Eternal.' Like two stately trees they grew up among us in the nobler, sweeter fellowship of wedded life. They twain became one flesh. Here they planted their home and, in domestic bliss their olive plants grew up around them. Here they were known and honored, and loved by an appreciative and admiring community, and when perilous times came, and the nation looked forth among the people for a steady hand to guide the ship of state, its heart went out after this tall and stately man that walked like a prince among us. He was their choice, and ascending to the chief place in the Nation's gift, he stood like some tall cedar amid the storm of National strife, and with a heroism, and a wisdom and a lofty prudence in his administration that won the wonder and respect of the world, he guided the Nation through its peril, back again to peace. But when at the height of his fame, when a grateful people were lauding him with just acknowledgment of his great services to the country, and when he was wearily trying to escape from their very adulation into the restful presence and company of his life partner, to be alone awhile in the hour of his triumphant joy, like lightning, the flash of a cruel and cowardly enemy's wrath struck him down by her side. The voice that cheered a nation in its darkest hour is hushed. The beauty of Israel is slain upon the high places. The Nation in its grief and consternation, is driven almost to madness. Strong men know not hardly how to assuage their sorrow or control themselves under it. And when the Nation so felt the shock what must it have been to the poor woman that stood by his side, who was the sharer of his joys, the partner of his sorrows, whose heart strings were wound about his great heart in that seal of eternal love. What wonder if the shock of that sad hour, that made a Nation reel, should leave a tender loving woman, shattered in body and in mind, to walk softly all her days. It is no reflection upon either the strength of her mind or the tenderness of her heart, to say that when Abraham Lincoln died, she died. The lightning that struck down the strong man, unnerved the woman. The sharp iron of this pungent grief went to her soul. The terrible shock, with its quick following griefs in the death of [another of] her children, left her mentally and physically a wreck, as it might have left any of us in the same circumstances. I can only think of Mrs. Lincoln as a dying woman through all these sad years of painful sorrow through which she has lingered since the death of her husband. It is not only charitable but just to her native mental qualities and her noble womanly nature, that we think of her and speak of her as the woman she was before the victim of these great sorrows. Drawing the veil over all these years of failing health of body and mind, which have been spent in seeking rest from sorrow in quiet seclusion from the world, I shall speak of her only as the woman she was before her noble husband fell a martyr by her side.

As the public may be interested in knowing something of the family history of the woman that shared the confidence and love of the lamented Lincoln, I have gleaned the following particulars concerning her ancestry. She was the third daughter of Robert S. Todd, and was born in Lexington, Kentucky, on the 13th of December 1818. The Todd family, which is distinguished in all its branches, is of Scotch-Irish descent. Robert Todd emigrated from Ireland about the beginning of the year 1700, and settled in Pennsylvania, on the Schuykill, a short distance above Philadelphia. Henry

Todd, one of his descendants, occupies the homestead on which he settled, and a long line of his descendants and family connections lie buried in the burial ground of the Presbyterian church in that vicinity, of which the family were members. The three daughters of Robert Todd married respectively into the Porter, the Findley and the Magow families of Pennsylvania. His son David married Hannah Owen, and they were the direct ancestors of Mrs. Lincoln. Through these marriages she was connected with the Porters, the Parkers, the Owens, the McFarlands, the Findleys and the Magow families of Pennsylvania.

John Todd, one of the sons of Robert Todd, graduated at Princeton, went to Virginia, and became distinguished as a Presbyterian clergyman, scholar and educator, and it has been said that no history of the Presbyterian Church of Virginia could be written without honorable mention of Dr. John Todd. Three of the sons of David Todd and Hannah Owen, after acquiring a fine education under the instruction of their uncle, Dr. John Todd, of Virginia, went to Kentucky in the year 1781, and made it their home. They were John, Robert and Levi. John Todd was a lawyer of fine abilities. He accompanied Gen. [George] Rogers Clark on his Western expedition; was at the capture of Kaskaskia, and afterwards appointed by Patrick Henry, then Governor of Virginia, the Lieutenant Commandant of the county of Illinois, and was then practically the First Governor of Illinois. Returning from Kaskaskia, and on his way to Virginia to remove his family to Illinois, he stopped at Lexington, and learning that the Indians had crossed the Ohio, he took command of the regiment of that district, of which he was Colonel, and was killed at the battle of Blue Licks.

Gen. Robert Todd was also with Gen. Clark at the capture of Kaskaskia, and in all the early wars with the Indians, and became the ancestor of a numerous family. The other brother, Gen. Levi Todd, the grandfather of Mr[s]. Lincoln, was married in the fort at Harrodsburg, to a niece of Gen. Benjamin Logan—said to be the first marriage in Kentucky. He was also with Gen. Clark at the capture of Kaskaskia. He was then a Lieutenant, and after the capture was ordered to take charge of a squad of the captured [British] Governor and conduct him to Jamestown, Va., which he did. He also participated in all the early Indian wars of the Bloody Ground. He was appointed Clerk of the Circuit Court of Fayette county, Ky., an office which he held to the time of his death, which happened at a highly advanced age. He died the father of twelve children, wealthy and highly respected.

Robert S. Todd, the son of Gen. Levi Todd, and the father of Mrs. Lincoln, was during his lifetime, a resident of Lexington, Ky. He was a merchant and manufacturer of considerable wealth. During the greatest part of his early manhood he was clerk of the House of Representatives of Kentucky. He was said to be, in person, a very handsome and dignified man: well educated and intelligent. His home was one of refinement and hospitality. At the time of his death he was one of the most popular men in his State, and had he lived to the next election after his death, would doubtless have been made Governor of the State.

His daughter, Mary Lincoln, who now lies before us, was his third daughter, was reared in Lexington, where she was finely educated, as young women were at that day. Soon after the death of her mother she came to Illinois and resided with her sister, Mrs. Ninian W. Edwards, till the time of her marriage with Mr. Lincoln. She has thus descended in the line of a gifted ancestry, which in its various branches has given, I am told, many talented ministers to the Presbyterian Church, and many noble men to the public service of the country.

Mrs. Lincoln possessed in a remarkable degree the mental characteristics that distinguished her ancestry. As a young woman, she was vivacious, brilliant and winning in her manners, social in her disposition, intellectual, and cultural. She was fond of literature, gifted in conversation and well posted on almost all subjects. Those who have been most associated with her in public life, speak of the ease and dignity with which she entertained her guests, and bore herself on all occasions, as well as her kindness and hospitality. While she, no doubt, had her faults like other women, and made mistakes, yet she had her excellencies and her virtues which shone with a luster all their own. When her husband went forth, an untried man, from among the people with the gravest responsibilities upon him, she went with him and stood by him in heroic fortitude through all the varying vicissitudes of his eventful career, till that glorious career of service and devotion was crowned with a martyr's death. For this wifely devotion to the man the Nation loves, for every gentle ministry of love she tendered him, for every word she spoke that cheered him, for every tear she wiped, and every solace she gave him, the people thank her as their hearts throb heavily again at the portals of his tomb. Of her gifts and qualities of heart and mind, I might here say much, but I know she would reproach me if I now bordered on eulogy, and that more than I have said would not be in [ke]eping with the more spiritual requirements of this service.

In regard to the history of her religious life, I find that she professed her faith in Christ, and united with the First Presbyterian Church of this city, on the 13th of April, 1852. This was under the ministry of the Rev. Dr. James Smith, who was the intimate and esteemed friend of Mr. Lincoln. Mrs. Lincoln and her husband and family regularly attended this church, from that time till they went to Washington City. While there they sat regularly under the ministry of the lamented Dr. Gurley, who was their pastor and intimate friend of the family, and their consoler in the time of their great sorrow. In keeping with her ancestral training, Mrs. Lincoln regarded the Presbyterian Church as her spiritual home, and it was her last request that she should be buried from the church where she professed her faith in Christ. Though in her weak and afflicted condition she was seldom able to appear in society or attend the sanctuary in later life, yet her faith and hope was in the grace of the Gospel. She believed in the Christian religion as that which had given her consolation in the hour of her sorrow, and now from the midst of a congregation where she once subscribed with her hand unto the Lord, we commit her to the hands of a faithful Creator; to the care and keeping of Him who said to the Mary of Bethany that sat at his feet, 'I am the Resurrection and the Life. He that believeth on me, though he were dead, yet shall he live.'

And now, dear friends, in the presence of these remains, let us hear the word of the Lord in the admonitory utterance of my text 'For we must needs die.' Death awaits us all, even as he has laid his cold hand upon this noble woman. It is the one event that is common to us. There are many things that are not common to us. Wealth is not common; health is not common;

eminence is not common; happiness is not common to us. But there is one thing that is common to us. We can all count upon it and look for it. That is death. It is the one lesson the solemnity of this occasion presses upon us, that 'we must needs die.' And this is the nature of it. It is an upsetting of our life vessels, a spilling out as upon the ground of all that we are; an [e]mptying of the fleshly tabernacle of mind and soul and all its powers. There is nothing so hard to gather up as water spilt upon the ground, and there is no repairing the ravages of death in this life. The upsetting of our life vessel by the Kin[g] of Terrors, is the frustrating of all our earthly plans and business, and projects, and hopes. There is no more recovery from the disa[s]ter here, when it once overtakes us, than 'there is hope of gathering up water spilt upon parched ground that eagerly drinks it up.' We must needs die. And why the needs be? Because God is no respecter of persons. Ah! here we see it in the presence of these remains. The person of Mrs. Lincoln is not respected. The person of Abraham Lincoln was not respected. These two persons [t]hat have stood so high in the esteem of the people, that have enjoyed such honors, and wielded such power, are not respected in the article of death. They lie as low as you and I must lie. The precious life vessel that held all this treasure of wisdom, and wealth of statesmanship that was exercised by the immortal Lincoln is overturned and spilled as water upon the ground, and who shall gather it up again[?] This grand woman who stood on the dizzy heights of fame beside him lies now on the same level with her gifted and honored husband. God is no respecter of persons, that any should escape death. The persons of the great, the wise, the noble, the honored, the powerful, the influential are not respected here. The statesman must die as well as the plebeian, the General as well as the soldier, the rich as well as the poor, the learned as well as the unlearned. 'There is no discharge in that war; we all do fade as a leaf, and our iniquities, like the wind, carry us away.' 'We must all needs die, and are as water spilled upon the ground, which cannot be gathered up again.'

But is there no brighter side to this spectacle of our approaching mortality? Yes, and this is it: Though God is no respecter of persons; though death is our common fate, and we must all go down to the grave, 'Yet doth he devise means that his banished be not expelled from him.' God deviseth means! Ah, there is the silver lining of the cloud. There is the rainbow of hope and promise. There is the gleaming of the blessed Gospel amid the shadows of death. We have banished ourselves from God by our sins. Like Absalom, we have turned our back upon our Father, and upon our Father's house. Like the prodigal, we have sinned and are no more worthy of Him. But, though banished, He would not expel us from Him, and abandon us to the wages of sin. He hath devised means whereby the ravages of death may be repaired; means whereby the spilled water of our life may be gathered up again; means whereby we may be saved, even to the redemption of soul and body into everlasting life. And what are the means a loving Father has so devised? Ah! we have it in the ring of this glorious Gospel of the blessed God to which we so often listen when we put death far from us: 'God so love the world that He gave His only begotten Son that whosoever believeth on Him might not perish, but have everlasting life.' That is the means devised. That is God's plan of salvation, by which he would restore us to Himself. He hath no pleasure in the death of the sinner, that any should perish, but would rather that all should repent and be saved. So [H]e hath devised the means. He hath let down the ladder with beckoning angels inviting us to mount the new and living Way. The means devised are ample, sufficient and available. But the means are for us to use. This is the will of God that you believe on Him whom He hath sent. Repent and believe the Gospel. 'Come unto me all ye that labor and are heavy laden and I will give you rest. In my Father's house are many mansions. If it were not so I would have told you. Follow me and I will show you the way. You believe in God; believe also in me.' This is the voice of the tender loving son of God to us all, to-day, in our affliction. He has gone to prepare a place for us just that he may bring us home, home to a land over which hangs no shadow of death, home to a land that is never invaded by sorrow, 'where the wicked cease from troubling and the weary are at rest.' Let us hear the heavenly voice, and as we give back to God our beloved dead, let us come back ourselves to the God who hath loved us, and the Saviour who hath washed us with His blood.

The last words Mr. Lincoln ever said to his wife were these, 'There is no city I desire so much to see as Jerusalem.' With these words half spoken on his tongue, the bullet of the assassin entered his brain. He was not spared to see the earthly Jerusalem, but I doubt not his spirit was carried by angels to:

> Jerusalem the Golden,
> Where all our birds that flew—
> Our flowers but half unfolded.
> Our pearls that turn to dew—
> And all that glad life music,
> Now heard no longer here,
> Shall come again to greet us
> As we are drawing near.

Death has given him back, I trust, the partner of his life, and their spirits bearing the image of the heavenly, walk the golden scenes in the sweet fellowship of the love that is eternal, and the life everlasting.

May we so use the means Heaven has devised to bring us home, that when 'we must needs die,' and be 'as water spilt upon the ground,' we may be gathered up again, body and soul, and restored to resurrection beauty and glory, mingle with all the loving and the loved, and sing the conqueror's song above the skies."[128]

Dr. Reed had delivered a very lengthy "discourse," as he termed it. Certainly, Elizabeth (Todd) Edwards had provided him with the detailed genealogy which he repeated. And despite his disclaimer, the Rev. Reed had certainly included a most adequate eulogy. He even gently alluded to her "clouded mentality," as her niece once called Mary's affliction.[129] Perhaps the crowded audience had squirmed and suffered from the heat of July during Reed's wordy message, but it was an historic occasion, and most listeners perhaps counted themselves extremely fortunate to be participating in the funeral service for a former First Lady.

If the mourners' minds wandered during the sermon, they might have carefully observed again the immense number of floral tributes in the sanctuary. Many of them had been designed and shipped down from Chicago. Among the flower arrangements were a cross and anchor, a pillow inscribed "From the Citizens of Springfield," a book of life with "Mary Lincoln" spelled out in flowers, several gates ajar, another pillow with "Lincoln" on it, a star of lilies suspended above the pulpit, a column with a dove upon it and many others. Upon the casket reposed a cross and crown composed of rosebuds, carnations and tuberoses. Whole areas of the church were draped with velvet and broadcloth. Mr. T. C. Smith had taken complete charge of all the arrangements.

Officials and citizens knew of Mary Lincoln's love of flowers, and in death they showered them with her. In life, she had not endeared herself with most of the general public, especially after her husband's assassination. To many, she appeared to be vain, aristocratic, untruthful and often emotional and erratic. If any of her detractors sat in the church that day, they may have been reminded of one of President Lincoln's own jokes. He had once told David R. Locke about an Illinois politician who had recently died. He, too, suffered because his "undeniable merit was blemished by an overweening vanity." Lincoln then postulated that had this deceased man "known how big a funeral he would have had, he would have died years ago."[130] In the case of Mary Lincoln, she had publicly announced that she could hardly wait until God called her to a grave beside her beloved husband.

While the service proceeded, an unnamed person in the east gallery attempted to take a photograph of the proceedings. It proved rather unsuccessful, and a sketch replaced the picture. It would be published later as a rare broadside. A reporter noted that a photographer had taken pictures of the floral arrangements, too.[131]

Following Dr. Reed's discourse, Mrs. Henkle sang "with characteristic sweetness and power, 'I Know That My Redeemer Liveth.'" Then the Rev. Dr. Thomas Asbury Parker (Feb. 22, 1838-June 18, 1921), pastor of the First Methodist Episcopal Church at the corner of Fifth and Monroe, prayed most impressively. Indeed, he was a most impressive gentlemen. Dr. Parker had come to Springfield just two years previously. After graduating from McKendree College in 1856, he studied medicine in St. Louis and received his license to practice. Then he went to Topeka, Kansas, but he labored as a professor of English at Baker University. In 1861, he became a minister with the Methodist Episcopal Church and soon thereafter joined the 12th Regiment of Kansas Volunteers where he became Chaplain with the rank of Captain. After the Civil War, he returned to the field of education and became President of St. Charles College. A year later, he advanced to be the Superintendent of Public Instruction for the State of Missouri. By 1871, however, he had returned to the ministry at Hannibal. Then he moved to

Illinois in the early 1870's and served several churches. For nineteen years he acted as Grand Prelate for the Grand Commandery of the Knights Templar in the State of Illinois. He also joined the Grand Army of the Republic and was recognized as a prominent member of that organization. He ended his career as Chaplain of the Soldiers' Home in Danville, Illinois.

When Dr. Parker finished speaking, the pallbearers came forward silently and bore the casket back through the sanctuary to the front doors. As the relatives and friends followed the remains of Mrs. Lincoln to the outside, the choir sang Rooke's "Rest, Spirit, Rest." Outside, the long procession reformed for the very warm march to Oak Ridge Cemetery. Superintendent of Streets, John F. Bretz, had been up before dawn leveling off the unpaved thoroughfares that were to be used by the funeral party. It was a dry, dusty, day, and a large crowd had very early taken the street railways or their own private conveyances out to Oak Ridge to await the long cortège's arrival at the Lincoln Monument.

Upon reaching the Tomb, the black hearse stopped at the south side, while the relatives and intimate friends of the deceased proceeded to the entrance of the Catacomb on the north side. The faithful pallbearers lifted their heavy burden from the somber vehicle and—escorted by the Lincoln Guard of Honor—carried it around to the opposite side where they could enter the burial chamber. Carefully, they deposited the casket down on the floor beside the stone sarcophagus constructed for President Abraham Lincoln. It had been strewn with flowers for the occasion of his wife's return to his side.[132] Since her husband's assassination, Mary Lincoln had constantly talked about patiently awaiting "the hour, when 'God's love,' shall place me, by his side again—where there are no more partings & no more tears shed."[133] At last her earthly remains rested near the Presidential sarcophagus, but his impressive marble sepulcher did not contain the mortal remains of Abraham Lincoln.

Although nearly everybody assumed confidently that Lincoln's precious reliquiae were housed in the marble case, such was not the fact. On September 19, 1871, the President's body had been taken from the temporary vault on the hill and placed in Crypt No. 1 of the Lincoln Monument. But on October 9, 1874, the casket was pulled out and encased within the showy sarcophagus erected in the middle of the burial chamber where viewers might see it and venerate it. However, on the night of November 7, 1876, thieves attempted to steal Lincoln's corpse, prompting the Guard of Honor to remove the casket on November 15 and hide it secretly within the area around the base of the obelisk. This unfinished space was, of course, closed to the public who were never informed of the removal in order to insure complete security.

After the mourners departed from the Lincoln Tomb on July 19, 1882, burly workmen openly slid Mary Lincoln's coffin into Crypt No. 4 of the inner wall. But on the night of July 21, the Guard of Honor secretly withdrew it and carried her body around the Monument on the outside, through the south door and into the hidden interior where President Lincoln's casket rested completely out of sight. Now, husband and wife were truly together once more. Robert Lincoln had asked that this wish of his mother's be carried out, and so the ruse continued for years until finally the two were actually buried in one final act, but that is another story in itself.[134]

Although the world would never forget Mary Lincoln, the lasting impression in the minds of the common citizens would come to be that she was a historical figure hard to admire. Her caustic tongue, fiery temper, imperious manner, jealous nature, insensitivity to the feelings of others, greed and insanity would mar her reputation down to the latest generation—despite those apologists who have written biographies of her. However, one tribute paid to her in this century would probably have pleased her no end. Mary loved parties, elaborate entertainment, travel, merriment, gourmet food and drink as well as personal aggrandizement from an adoring audience.

Just such an occasion occurred at New Orleans during Mardi Gras in 1987. At that time, the Krewe of Venus on March 1 threw "doubloons" to the festive throng assembled along Canal Street. On the obverse of one "coin" was the portrait of Mary (Todd) Lincoln. The theme of this krewe was "Honoring our Nation's First Ladies." Revelers prize two items thrown to the merrymakers along the parade route: doubloons and strings of cheap beads. The tribute may have pleased Mary Lincoln, but she might have objected to the small figure of a log cabin pictured to her left. It was her honored husband who had been born in a log cabin. Mary was raised in brick mansions in Lexington, Kentucky.

At Mary Lincoln's funeral, Robert Lincoln—once more—acted as the solitary representative of the Lincolns at a family funeral. After a day's rest in Springfield, he caught the midnight train for Chicago on July 20. There, he intended to remain for another day or two before continuing on to his office in Washington.[135] As the train wheels clicked over the splices in the steel rails, Robert perhaps thought of the numerous embarrassments which he had experienced because of insanity in some of those who had touched his life.

Less than two decades earlier, Robert Lincoln had attended law classes at the old University of Chicago and took a desk in the law firm of Scammon, McCagg & Fuller on Lake Street. His mentors would instruct him by the preceptor method—teaching him while he worked with them. These men were Jonathan Young Scammon, an old friend of President Lincoln, E. B. McCagg and Samuel W. Fuller. While studying with them, Robert would testify that Fuller had also been "an old personal friend of my father."

Robert obtained his law license on February 25, 1867, and shortly thereafter entered into a partnership with Charles Telfant Scammon, the son of Jonathan Young Scammon. Both of them were Civil War veterans. Robert had served briefly as a Captain on U. S. Grant's staff, and Charles had begun his military service on November 11, 1861, as a First Lieutenant in Company L of the 9th Cavalry Regiment, Illinois Volunteers. Charles won promotion to Captain of Company H on January 15, 1863, and then became a Major and Aide de Camp on June 7, 1864. He was mustered out on February 8, 1865.

These young lawyers should have had a lot in common, but shortly after their law firm commenced operation, Robert reported that Scammon had been on "a succession of 'sprees' since early in May." He told Judge David Davis that Major Scammon was "utterly worthless." Finally, Robert dissolved the partnership.[136] There must have been more to Scammon's unusual behavior than excessive drinking, because on August 23, 1876, he died in the Elgin Insane Asylum.[137] After his problems with Scammon, Robert had been forced to have his own mother committed to a private asylum. Robert experienced more than his share of personal tragedies and difficulties.

Did religion offer a solace to Robert T. Lincoln in times of trouble? Like his famous father, Robert never revealed a great quantity of personal information about his private life. However, old "Aunt" Ruth Stanton recalled that as a very small lad, Robert had attended Sunday School at the Episcopal Church in Springfield.[138] Of course, after his mother joined the First Presbyterian Church, he went there. But he was not baptized in that denomination's font; Tad received this sacrament, however.

While living away from home for the first time in Exeter, New Hampshire, Robert seems to have preferred the Second Congregational Church where the Rev. Orpheus T. Lanphear preached.[139] His church habits in Cambridge while attending Harvard are not so well known. However, among the courses which he studied during his first year at Harvard was "religious instruction."[140] Whenever he visited his parents at Washington during vacations, he attended the New York Avenue Presbyterian Church with his parents, especially with his mother.[141] Nevertheless, Bishop Matthew Simpson of the Methodist Episcopal Church performed the marriage ceremony for Robert and Mary Eunice Harlan on September 24, 1868, in Washington D. C.[142] This was most certainly the bride's choice, but she was not a member of this denomination, either.

As a resident of Chicago, Robert T. Lincoln frequented the Second Presbyterian Church at the northwest corner of Michigan Avenue and 20th Street (numbered 1936 S. Michigan), but he never applied for membership in this beautiful, stone, Neo-Gothic edifice designed by the noted architect, James Renwich (1818-1895), constructed after the great Chicago Fire in 1871. Building began on this sanctuary in 1872 and was completed two years later. Back in 1842, the Presbyterians had split over the issue of slavery. Those who favored abolition remained with the First Presbyterian Church, formed in 1835, and those who wished for a delay formed the Second Presbyterian Church. This offshoot branch built a structure at the northeast corner of Wabash and Washington, but it was destroyed by the Chicago Fire.

From 1874 until 1918, wealthy members contributed enough money to decorate Second Church with expensive art works which rivaled those in religious places of worship constructed in Europe during the Middle Ages. Its membership included the Armours, the Blackstones, the Cobbs, the Glessners, the Grays and the Pullmans. Into this clique stepped the Robert Lincolns. While Robert never joined, his wife, Mary (Harlan) Lincoln, did put her name on the membership rolls. She joined under the pastorship of the Rev. Dr. J. Munro Gibson by a profession of faith on January 12, 1877. Mary had not previously belonged officially to any other denomination. Her name remained on the membership lists until February 2, 1898, when it was "erased" because she had "joined another communion."[143] She, we know from other church records, had just joined the Christian Science Church. Robert was following the history of his own parents: his mother held church membership, but his father did not; Robert's wife held church membership, but he did not.

Strange as it might seem today, numerous churches in the Nineteenth Century chose trustees who were not communicants of their fellowship. These trustees were picked mostly because of their business experience. So, it came about that on December 30, 1878, the Board of Trustees for the Second Presbyterian Church elected R. T. Lincoln as a member of their board. He replaced G. W. Thompson who declined reelection. Robert served on the Music Committee, too. A few times the Trustees even met at Lincoln's home, and sometimes he served as Secretary. For the meeting of April 11, 1887, Robert took the minutes and submitted a signed and typed copy, probably the first typewritten minutes filed at this church. Among his fellow Board of Trustee members were: John Crerar, a Mason, a merchant and philanthropist associated with a railway supply house; John S. Gould, a real estate broker; George Clinton Clarke, an insurance agent; and Franklin D. Gray, a grocery dealer. At times, Robert's good friend Norman Williams, an attorney, sat in for him at these meetings. In the year 1888, Robert contributed $200 toward the renovation of the church building. He attended his last meeting of the Trustees on January 3, 1889.[144] In that year, R. T. Lincoln was appointed United States Minister to Great Britain and left for London.

As Minister to the Court of St. James, Robert Lincoln established his family at 2 Cromwell House, S. W. The Lincolns had two daughters, Mary and Jessie, and an idolized son named Abraham Lincoln, II, whom they called "Jack." He had been born on August 14, 1873, in Chicago. In the fall of 1889, they sent him to a school in Versailles, France, so that he might learn French and prepare himself for Harvard. Unfortunately, he became afflicted with a malignant carbuncle under one of his arms. A French surgeon removed the growth on November 6. However, "Jack" contracted blood poisoning (septicemia) and was returned to London for treatment. There, he died at just a few minutes after 11:00 a. m. on March 5, 1890, as his father sat at his side in their home. Like Tad's illness, "Jack's" lungs filled with fluid, and he struggled to breathe until death finally came. Although blood poisoning has been given repeatedly as the cause of his demise, the official death record states simply that pleurisy killed him.[145]

The Queen of England sent a message of condolence as did Governor Joseph W. Fifer of Illinois. On the day following "Jack's" death, the Lord Salisbury and his wife; the Duke of Marlborough; the Earl of Derby; the Lord Chief Justice Coleridge; and the Lord Randolph Churchill left their cards at Robert's residence. Quickly, Minister Lincoln announced that a private funeral service would be held on Friday, March 7, with invitations going only to personal friends of the family, plus Robert's employees and their wives.[146] On that oppressively sad morning this small group assembled at the Lincoln residence where the deceased Abraham Lincoln, II, lay in a costly casket of polished, antique, English oak with silver handles and trimmings. But the impressive coffin remained completely hidden under a huge bank of beautiful flowers. A reporter learned, nevertheless, that there was a heavy lead lining inside the burial case. There does not seem to have been any viewing of the body by the mourners present that day.[147]

Residing at this very time in England was the Rev. Dr. J. Munro Gibson who had been the minister of the Second Presbyterian's congregation back in Chicago part of the time that the Lincolns had attended this particular church. When the Rev. Dr. R. W. Patterson resigned from this Chicago church, after having ministered there since June of 1842, the Session and the membership called the Rev. Dr. J. Munro Gibson to fill their pulpit. Dr. Gibson had been preaching in Montreal, Canada, prior to his invitation to take charge of the Second Presbyterian Church. He was formally installed on May 6, 1874, and his wife, Lucy, joined later. But on April 28, 1880, Dr. Gibson informed his congregation that he was resigning to go to St. John's Woods Presbyterian Church in London, England.[148]

Knowing that he was in London, Robert and Mary (Harlan) Lincoln immediately asked Dr. Gibson to conduct the brief religious service for "Jack," indicating they still considered themselves Presbyterians. Upon the conclusion of these memorial services in the Lincoln home, Mr. Lincoln, together with Henry White, his chief of staff, and the Rev. Dr. Gibson, escorted the remains to the catacombs at Kensal Greens in London where the body would be kept until Robert could take it back to Springfield, Illinois.[149] The Lincolns did not wish to leave their only son interred in a foreign land.

On a journey of great sorrow, Robert Lincoln recrossed the Atlantic with the body of "Jack." He landed in New York City aboard the *City of New York* on November 5, 1890. There, he became the house guest of his old and dear friend, Edgar T. Welles, son of Gideon Welles, Secretary of the Navy under President Lincoln. As a Vice President of the Wabash line, Edgar arranged for a private car to take Robert and the remains on to Springfield, Illinois, and he personally accompanied Robert on this long trek of sadness which began two days later on the 7th. Once again, Robert assumed the entire family burden for burying a loved one. His wife had immediately taken their two daughters and departed for Mt. Pleasant, Iowa, where her father resided. She did not go with her husband to Springfield.

At 6 a. m. on November 8, the special railroad car pulled into Springfield and was run onto the siding at the depot. Here, Robert and Edgar rested until 9 a. m. when a special delegation from the Lincoln Monument

Association came to meet them. It consisted of S. M. Cullom, John M. Palmer, R. J. Oglesby, Milton Hay, C. C. Brown, O. M. Hatch, George N. Black, Lincoln DuBois and James C. Conkling (father of Clinton L. Conkling). Thomas C. Smith, the undertaker, took immediate charge of the casket which had been traveling in an iron-bound packing box. Members of the Lincoln Guard of Honor also appeared along with George Clayton Latham, E. D. Keys, A. S. Edwards and William Jones. Upon first learning of "Jack's" death, the Lincoln Monument Association had invited Robert to entomb his son in its magnificent edifice, and he had accepted the kind offer.

From the Wabash Depot, Smith's somber hearse and four carriages of mourners proceeded out to Oak Ridge Cemetery. George Latham accompanied Robert Lincoln. They had been close companions in childhood. Born May 16, 1842, to Phillip Clayton and Catherine Rue (Tabor) Latham, George was a year older than Robert. He had attended Estabrook's Academy with Robert Lincoln, and then both entered Illinois State University which opened its classes in the Mechanics' Union Building at Springfield. Following this rather dubious educational experience, they both matriculated as roommates at Phillips Exeter Academy in New Hampshire to prepare for entry into Harvard. Robert eventually passed the entrance exam at Cambridge, but George failed. Since George's father had been killed by lightning on May 25, 1844, Abraham Lincoln seems to have served as a trusted advisor to young Latham. Upon learning of George's failure, Abraham Lincoln, the extremely busy Presidential candidate, sat down on July 22, 1860, and indited a letter to the discouraged youth. Lincoln wrote that he had "scarcely felt greater pain in my life than on learning yesterday from Bob's letter, that you had failed to enter Harvard." Lincoln counseled him that "there is very little in it, if you will allow no feeling of <u>discouragement</u> to seize, and prey upon you." Lincoln declared that George "<u>must</u> succeed in it." "<u>Must</u>," he emphasized, "is the word."[150]

Robert went on to Harvard, but George Latham did not. Instead, he did gain admittance to Yale where he studied for two years before returning to Springfield and going into the shoe business. Yet, George and Robert— although separated physically—remained very much in each other's thoughts. Abraham and Mary had even invited George to accompany them to Washington on the inaugural train which left Springfield on February 11, 1861. He and Robert certainly kept each other company on this long excursion, and George remained in the White House with the First Family for over a week before returning to Yale. Nevertheless, the two men drifted apart as the years passed. Only when Robert Lincoln returned to Springfield on sporadic occasions did they get to renew their friendship. Robert came back mostly for funerals—except for once in 1909—but these old companions must have savored those rare moments. Latham was a Mason and also a Knight Templar, indicating that he believed in the Christian religion when he became a Templar. But they probably talked very little about religion in those brief meetings in afteryears. Latham would die before Robert, on February 1, 1921, but he probably never forgot the kindness shown to him by Robert's father who encouraged him and even allowed him to participate in the festivities of March 4, 1861. Few boys of his age could make the boast of having been so intimate with President Lincoln and his family. Latham became a noted businessman in Springfield.[151] On March 16, 1921, Robert Lincoln wrote Mary (Edwards) Brown that "Since the death of Mr. [Clinton L.] Conkling and later of Mr. George Latham, there is not now in Springfield, I feel quite sure, a single one of my old men friends or even acquaintances who might write to me."[152] Unknown to him, DeWitt Smith yet lived and would survive him by several years.

Since Robert Lincoln had decreed that no religious service or ceremony be held over "Jack's" body at this entombment, there was no minister present at the Lincoln Tomb when the burial party arrived. After stripping the protective case from the casket, strong arms carried it into the burial chamber and lifted it up and over the stone sarcophagus which had once contained the remains of President Lincoln but which now stood empty. One reporter was informed that both President and Mrs. Lincoln now rested under the Monument "in solid concrete." That was the story generally told the public for reasons of security; both probably still rested inside the Tomb in that area closed to visitors. "Jack" Lincoln's casket, with a simple wreath of flowers on its top, was then slipped into the center crypt, No. 1, where the President's casket had rested until removed to the sarcophagus. How appropriate to have another Abraham Lincoln fill his niche in the wall. Now, there were only two crypts vacant; one for Robert and the other for his wife. Of course, the Tomb would later be totally rebuilt, and the crypt arrangement completely changed once more.

Like his father, Robert did not stand too much on religious ceremony alone. When young "Jack" had been safely buried, Robert merely thanked all the gentlemen present who had assisted in the burial, and the same carriages returned the group to town. Robert checked into a room at the Leland Hotel where he remained all that afternoon with friends. That evening he boarded a train for Washington, D. C. The loss of his only son had caused intense mental pain to Robert. "Jack" had been such a promising lad with a fine intellect and a desire to study. Robert had intended to send him off to his own alma mater and then practice law with him in partnership. Lincoln & Lincoln would indeed have been an imposing law shingle outside any legal office.[153]

Robert spent Christmas of 1890 in Mount Pleasant, Iowa, with his wife and father-in-law before eventually returning to London and his duties there. When Grover Cleveland was elected President, Robert resigned on March 25, 1893, and returned to Chicago. He does not seem to have accepted any positions of leadership in the Presbyterian Church there.

In 1911, Robert sold his mansion in Chicago at 60 Lake Shore Drive and purchased a home in Washington, D. C., at 3014 N Street, N. W. Since 1905, he had also utilized an estate near Manchester, Vermont. This became his summer home, and he enjoyed it greatly. He could play golf and rest there. While in Washington as Secretary of War from 1881 to 1885, and after he once more took up residence there in 1911, Robert attended worship services at the New York Avenue Presbyterian Church upon occasion, just as he had done during the Civil War.[154] Little is known of his wife's worship activities at this time.

Like his father, Robert Lincoln supported some religious bodies even when he no longer had any close connection to them. In 1907 he contributed $1,000 to Westminster Presbyterian Church in Springfield, Illinois, at the urging of his childhood chum, Clinton L. Conkling.[155] Then, on June 21, 1919, he gave $100 to the First Presbyterian Church, in the same city, for its rebuilding fund.[156] The latter, of course, had a sentimental tie with his family and himself, but in his adult years he had done no more than attend funerals there. One more major restoration project would take place at First Church whereby the old historic structure was strengthened by steel buttresses and interior tie rods, and a new recreational facility constructed to the north. The First Presbyterian Church was then rededicated on April 12, 1970.

In his last years, observers described Robert T. Lincoln as of a "taciturn and retiring nature," and yet he frequently told anecdotes and joked with intimate colleagues and friends, just as his father had done. He delighted in telling a story about the time President Lincoln had chanced upon a column of marching soldiers and inquired, "What is it?" meaning in his parlance,

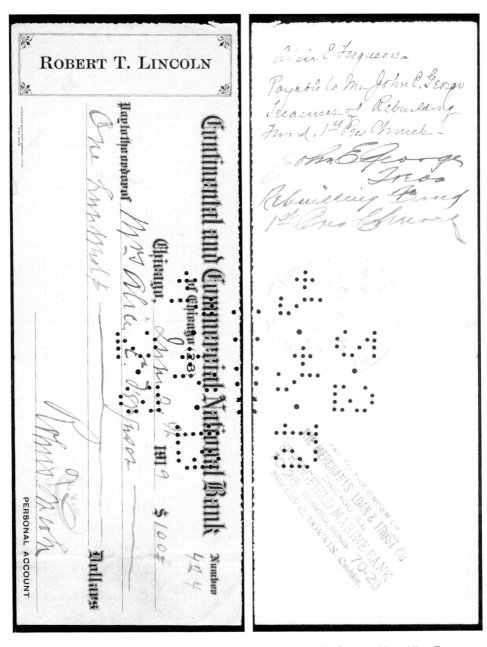

Robert T. Lincoln, on June 21, 1919, wrote a check for $100 to Mrs. Alice E.
Ferguson who, in turn, endorsed it to Mr. John E. George, Treasurer of the
Rebuilding Fund of the First Presbyterian Church in Springfield, Illinois.
Original in author's collection.

"What was the unit's number and what State were they from?" One of the marchers, not recognizing the President in his carriage, replied, "It is a regiment, you damned old fool!"

On the evening of July 25, 1926, Robert retired to bed, and a faithful servant discovered the next morning that he had died during the night. July 26 is thus taken as the date of his passing. A physician deduced that Robert had succumbed at his beloved "Hildene" residence in Vermont as the result of a cerebral hemorrhage. Had he lived to August 1, he would have been eighty-three years of age. As he would have wished, a very simple funeral service was planned.[157] Being in the New England States, the Congregationalists at that time were one of the most predominant denominations. The Rev. D. Cunningham-Graham, pastor of the Congregational Church in Manchester, Vermont, was asked to conduct the very informal rites in the presence of only a few selected mourners. This minister read the 23rd Psalm and a few other selections from the Bible. Instead of a eulogy, Alfred Lord Tennyson's "Crossing the Bar" was recited.

Those pallbearers in charge of the casket were Lincoln Isham, of New York; Robert Todd Lincoln Beckwith of Washington; Edward P. Isham of Manchester; Henry, John and Prentice Porter of Chicago; and Dr. Paul Collona of New York. Also present were Norman Frost and Fred Powers of Washington; Mr. and Mrs. George H. Thacher of Albany; and Mr. and Mrs. Horace G. Young of Greenwich, Connecticut. Pallbearers escorted the remains to a vault in Dellwood Cemetery at the foot of Ekwanok Mountain for a temporary burial. It had already been announced that the body would be taken back to Springfield for interment in the Lincoln Monument that autumn.[158] Robert had expressed a desire to be laid to rest there. He so informed Nicholas Murray Butler on November 15, 1922.[159] Anticipating the burial of Robert in the Lincoln Tomb at Springfield, a local newspaper there described the arrangement of the bodies already resting in the Monument. Tad Lincoln, the reporter related, occupied the first crypt; Eddie and Willie, the second; Mary in the third; and the fourth and fifth were empty and ready for the burial of Robert and his wife. Abraham Lincoln, II, reposed in the last crypt, but President Lincoln, after the complete reconstruction of the Tomb in 1901, lay under the floor of the burial chamber in twelve feet of concrete.[160]

Widow Mary (Harlan) Lincoln sent a wire to Mrs. E. D. Keys in Springfield informing her of Robert's death and telling her that the body would be shipped to Springfield in the autumn of 1926. By way of explaining this telegram, the editor divulged to his readers that Mrs. Keys was a cousin of Robert's and about the only relative of his remaining in Springfield.[161] Thereby hangs a tale which has never been told and deserves telling.

Mary (Todd) Lincoln had a brother named Levi Owen Todd (born June 25, 1817) who married Louisa Ann Searles on January 17, 1843. They had several children: Robert Stewart Todd, born May 11, 1844; Ellen "Ella" Lindsey Todd, born August 27, 1846; James Searles Todd, born May 23, 1849, died August 23, 1852; Edward Owen Todd, born March 25, 1853, died July 16, 1860; Louisa Howard Todd, born January 27, 1856; and Susan E. Todd, born August 10, 1858, died in 1912.[162] These offspring were cousins to Robert T. Lincoln and nieces and nephews to Mary (Todd) Lincoln. However, Louisa (Searles) Todd divorced Levi for drunkenness, cruelty and non-support; Levi died in October of 1864.

Unfortunately, on April 15, 1861, Louisa (Searles) Todd died, leaving several children to be cared for by others. Little Louisa—just five—and her older sister, "Ella," were taken up to Springfield, Illinois, to live with their aunt, Ann Marie (Todd) Smith, who had been married to Clark Moulton Smith in Springfield on October 25, 1846. The Smiths were then living on the southwest corner of Fifth and Edwards. When writing to President Lincoln on February 7, 1864, C. M. Smith mentioned to him that he had been caring for the children he had "taken to raise."[163]

Ann had been born in 1824, and like her older sisters, Elizabeth, Frances and Mary, had moved up to Springfield from Lexington, Kentucky. Now, another generation of Todd women were making their way to Springfield to search for husbands when the proper time came. However, little Louisa became so homesick for Lexington and her dear friends there, that she had to be taken back where she was cared for by an aunt on her mother's side of the family, Mrs. Susan Edge. There, she remained for an unknown period of time, but eventually returned to Springfield. Later she went to live with her sister, "Ella" Todd, who had married John C. Canfield on February 15, 1865, in the home of the C. M. Smiths.

John C. Canfield had been born October 8, 1842, in Sangamon County, the son of John E. and Susan (LaTourette) Canfield who were Episcopalians. As a single man, John C. Canfield boarded at the American House and worked as a salesman for the firm of Yates & Smith in which C. M. Smith was the junior partner, and where he, no doubt, met "Ella." After their marriage, Canfield struck off on his own and opened a drygoods store on the west side of the public square where he stocked fancy goods, notions, as well as millinery. The Canfields resided on the northwest corner of 4th and Allen. Because of the severe depression in the 1870's, the shop did not do well and Canfield went to Kansas in the fall of 1879 in an attempt to recoup his financial losses. A year later, on January 9, 1880, he died in Sterling, Kansas. Following the death of her husband, "Ella" (Todd) Canfield moved out to Bristol, Rhode Island, where she succumbed on September 4, 1893. With her passing, another of Robert's cousins had preceded him in death.[164]

Louisa Howard Todd—while living with her older sister, "Ella," and her brother-in-law, John C. Canfield—somehow met Edward Douglas Keys. He was the son of Capt. Isaac Keys, Jr., and Almira J. (Neal) Keys and had been born in Springfield on May 1, 1852. Capt. Keys had been a Deputy United States Marshal for the Southern District of Illinois before President Lincoln appointed him Provost Marshal for the Eighth Congressional District. He served in this position until September of 1865. Capt. Keys always supported Abraham Lincoln in his political races and seemed to have been close to the Lincoln family. His son, young Edward Keys, went to school with Willie and Tad Lincoln in a small institution at the northeast corner of 7th and Edwards. He remembered Abraham Lincoln coming by there upon occasion to participate with them in a game called "soak 'em." It was played with a hard rubber ball, but Keys gave no further description of the sport. Little Edward Douglas Keys was also present at the Great Western Depot on February 11, 1861, when President-elect Lincoln departed for Washington, D. C.

Until he married Louisa H. Todd on October 10, 1876, Edward Keys lived with his parents at the northwest corner of 7th and Edwards and worked as a bookkeeper for the Marine Bank. He was a Baptist and eventually became the President of the Farmers National Bank in Springfield. For her wedding gown, Louisa Todd wore a white corded bengaline dress with a full court train which Mary had purchased in Europe. Before leaving the United States in 1868, Mary Lincoln had asked the twelve-year-old Louisa what she wanted from Europe. It was eventually decided that Mary would bring her a set of coral. But on her travels Mary Lincoln later purchased a beautiful gown in England and determined to save it for Louisa. To preserve it, Mary packed the gorgeous dress in waxed paper and brought it back with her when she returned in 1871. Mary also gave Louisa a traveling dress of gray plaid camel's hair with pin stripes of blue. When Louisa Todd married in 1876, she already had stored in her closet some very historical items for her trousseau.

A reporter later divulged that Louisa possessed "the Todd wit, the

Todd temper, and the proud Todd independence." Louisa always spoke well of Mary (Todd) Lincoln, although she readily admitted that Mary "was high spirited and no one could down her!" Of course, Louisa never had any personal contact with Mary Lincoln during the years the Lincolns lived at Eighth and Jackson. Louisa had not come to Springfield until after they had left for Washington. Yet she certainly saw Mary during those months Mary lived with the Edwardses and suffered from a very clouded mind and feeble health.

In Lexington, however, Louisa did get to know the noted Confederate General John Hunt Morgan. As a little tot, she often sat upon the lap of General Morgan's mother who fed her candy and petted her. She also saw this famous Rebel raider return to Lexington to accept a silk Confederate flag which had been fashioned by her cousin and two other young ladies. She may have had some sympathy for the Southern cause, although her father, Levi O. Todd, was a Unionist.

Edward D. Keys died at 9:20 a. m. on November 19, 1935, and the Rev. Vernon L. Shontz of the Central Baptist Church conducted the funeral service. Louisa Keys lived on in her residence at 603 South Seventh until she passed away there at 7:17 a. m. on May 30, 1943. Both were buried in Oak Ridge Cemetery. Louisa had lived well beyond her 87th year and was certainly one of the last Todds who had actually known Robert Todd Lincoln to some degree.[165]

But Robert Lincoln's body was not transmitted to Illinois in the autumn of that year. Despite his own wishes, Robert T. Lincoln was destined not to rest in death within the Lincoln Monument at Springfield. His widow determined to bury him permanently at Arlington National Cemetery instead. Perhaps Mary (Harlan) Lincoln suddenly decided that she did not desire to spend eternity beside her beloved husband if he lay in the same catacomb with Mary (Todd) Lincoln. Or perhaps she finally decided that the Lincoln Monument was too much visited by crowds of tourists, although she must have known that Arlington is also a tourist mecca. There does not seem to be any other ready explanation since their son, Abraham Lincoln, II, already reposed in the Lincoln Tomb. She had the casket of Robert removed from Dellwood and transported to Washington. Being very shy and wishing to shun any public notice of Robert's final burial, Mary (Harlan) Lincoln sent her daughter, Mary (Lincoln) Isham, to bring the Rev. Dr. Joseph Richard Sizoo to her home in Georgetown. Upon being admitted to Mrs. Lincoln's residence, he met Robert's widow—all dressed in black—dress, shawl and hat. "Today," she said to Dr. Sizoo, "I am your mother and you are my son. We shall go out and bury father." Without knowing where he was going, Dr. Sizoo put his arm around Mary (Harlan) Lincoln and walked her to the waiting car. They drove out to Arlington where the automobile stopped beside a little knoll that Congress had presented to the Lincoln family.

Dr. Sizoo noticed that a new grave had been dug there and that Robert Lincoln's casket stood beside it, covered with the United States Flag. Waiting for them was the Supervisor of Arlington National Cemetery. Not even Robert's daughters were present. As they walked to the grave, Dr. Sizoo asked her, "Mother Lincoln, what do you want me to do?" She replied that was entirely up to him. Rev. Sizoo recited the 23rd Psalm, gave a prayer and closed with the standard Presbyterian benediction, since this clergyman was the pastor of the New York Avenue Presbyterian Church where the Presidential family had gone and where Robert had attended. Upon the conclusion of this very private burial service on March 14, 1928, Mary (Harlan) Lincoln turned to the minister and asked, "Do you think father would appreciate what we have done?" Dr. Sizoo on this very beautiful day replied, "I am sure that he would be happy at what we have done." Then, concluded Mrs. Lincoln, "Let us go home." While the casket was lowered, side by side, they retraced their solemn steps to the car and were driven back to her home in Georgetown. Robert T. Lincoln had been quietly and secretly laid to rest among the war heroes of the Nation.

The Lincoln family had not severed their connections to the New York Avenue Presbyterian Church with this brief funeral service. In that same year, Mary (Harlan) Lincoln donated enough money for the construction of the Lincoln Memorial Tower at this church. It was designed after one done by Sir Christopher Wren. This fine tower was dedicated on May 26, 1929. Mary (Lincoln) Isham donated the Westminster chimes for the tower. When the old church edifice was torn down and a new building constructed in 1951, the Lincoln Tower was also reconstructed. This memorial tower, with its chimes and four clock faces, was built in memory of Abraham Lincoln, "a pewholder and regular attendant at the services of this church while President of the United States." The chimes had been cast at Troy, New York, by the Meneely Bell Company which had family ties with Nancy (Hanks) Lincoln. The biggest one is a replica of the Liberty Bell preserved at Philadelphia. President Lincoln would have appreciated that historic gesture. He had based so many of his principles of freedom upon the Declaration of

Independence, and he had—we know—spoken at Independence Hall on February 22, 1861.[166]

After having placed her deceased husband in Arlington, Mary (Harlan) Lincoln finally determined to move the body of their son there, also. She applied for official permission to withdraw "Jack's" casket. When asked, the State of Illinois, which controlled the Lincoln Monument, gave its permission, and the City Health Department of Springfield issued a permit on May 22, 1930. That very afternoon, T. C. Smith's Sons appeared at the Lincoln Monument and withdrew the body. They took it to the Smith Funeral Home where it remained until put aboard a car of the Chicago & Alton Railroad at 12:50 a. m. on May 26.[167] Sometime during May 27, "Jack's" body was interred at Arlington close to Robert's grave, so say the cemetery records there.

Although Oak Ridge Cemetery had lost a rather noted figure when "Jack" Lincoln's body was transferred out to Arlington, it had received the remains of an even more famous person eight years before this. Ellen Wrenshall Grant, only daughter of General and Mrs. Ulysses Simpson Grant, was born on July 4, 1855. Eugene Field had once even written a poem about "Nellie" Grant. During her father's years as President, "Nellie" married Algernon Charles Frederick Sartoris in the White House on May 21, 1874, and returned with this British Army officer to England. When her husband died February 3, 1893, "Nellie" soon returned to the United States and on July 4, 1912, married Frank Hatch Jones, a banker and politician whose home was in Chicago. After suffering for nearly ten years from the effects of a partial paralysis, she died from a cerebral hemorrhage at her Chicago home, 1130 Lake Shore Drive, on August 30, 1922. Since Frank H. Jones had originally come from Springfield, Illinois, he took his wife's body back there for burial in the Jones' plot. There, on September 1, 1922, the Rev. Dr. John T. Thomas of the First Presbyterian Church conducted a graveside service for "Nellie" in Oak Ridge Cemetery.[168]

When Robert Todd Lincoln Beckwith learned the law had been amended at Arlington so that minor children might have their names placed upon monuments, he saw to it that Abraham Lincoln II's name was cut upon the marker there in 1983. That would be one of his last services to the Lincoln name. Beckwith died on Christmas eve two years later. He followed the teachings of the Christian Science Church.[169]

Mary Eunice (Harlan) Lincoln led a very secluded life. Only rarely did photographers catch her likeness with their cameras. She appeared very shy and reserved, and she disliked appearing in public. After Robert T. Lincoln died in 1926, Mary, nevertheless, made philanthropic contributions to various organizations. She had been born in Iowa City, Iowa, on September 25, 1846, and died March 31, 1937, when she passed away quietly at her home, 3014 N Street in Georgetown, attended by her daughters, Mrs. Charles Isham and Jessie Randolph. She was well past ninety years of age. Being a member of the Christian Science Church, there was only a very brief and private funeral service for Mary (Harlan) Lincoln. Then her body was taken to Arlington and buried beside that of her husband. Thus passed from view the last of the direct line of Lincolns who had actually known the Great Emancipator. Prior to her death, she had donated what pieces of Lincolniana she possessed to The Library of Congress. She had also given a portrait of Mary (Todd) Lincoln to the White House for its collection.[170]

Yet, the Lincoln saga continues. Nearly every site even remotely connected to Abraham Lincoln has become a shrine of sorts. Lincoln publicly exhibited his religious feelings in various church buildings across this land. Despite these diversities, he practiced religion in its purest form, giving credit, prayer and thanks only to his Maker and largely ignoring the specific doctrines and unique procedures followed and exercised by the many diverse denominations which touched his heroic-but-tragic life. He eventually accepted God, but avoided committing himself to any other holy figure associated with Him. Abraham Lincoln certainly came to realize that God was the one common denominator agreed upon by all denominations which he knew and explored by observation. We must conclude that Abraham Lincoln was indeed a most religious man and expressed his reverence for God in an unadulterated matter and very openly.

References

1   *Illinois Daily State Journal*, May 6, 1865, p. 3, c. 3. See also David B. Chesebrough, "Just Shy of Sainthood," *Lincoln Herald*, XCIII, 40-44 (Summer, 1991). See also article in *ibid.*, XCIII, 125-128 (Winter, 1991).

2   Henry A. Nelson, *Two Discourses Delivered at the First Presbyterian Church, Springfield, Illinois* (Springfield: Baker & Phillips, 1865).

3   He called them "The Divinely Prepared Ruler" and "The Fit End of Treason." The latter was based upon Second Samuel where King David's son, Absalom, became a traitor and rose against his father in battle only to be slain by Joab, faithful leader of David's army. Likewise, "that miserable stage-player," Booth, "accustomed to act tragic scenes, morbidly brooding over those dark plots and desperate actions which form so large a part of the material of his trade, aspiring to the fame of pre-eminence in crime, fooled probably by dreams suggested by a name of historic and tragic eminence in his family, heartily sympathizing with the great conspiracy against the noble government, whose protection he still accepted and enjoyed, accomplished the premeditated murder successfully." Rev. Nelson thought that "no other profession is so well adapted to produce just such a character as J. Wilkes Booth." In other words, actors were not in an honorable profession. Booth, declared Nelson, was shot "by the faithful soldier, but whose bullet, God, in marvelous exactness of retribution, guided to his brain." "But," explained Nelson, "it is not personal bitterness nor malignity which most firmly and most sternly demands the due punishment of treason." *Ibid.*

     The *Illinois Daily State Journal*, May 8, 1865, p. 3, c. 3, duly reported the first sermon given by Dr. Nelson but did not mention the second one, evidently having no reporter at this later service.

4   Hamilton and Ostendorf, *Lincoln In Photographs*, 242.

5   R. J. Oglesby to Wm. H. Herndon, Springfield, Ill., Feb. 5, 1866, copy in Oglesby Papers, Ill. State Hist. Lib.

6   Ward H. Lamon to Rev. Henry Ward Beecher, Jan. 31, 1874, in Dorothy Lamon Teillard, ed., *Recollections of Abraham Lincoln*, 334.

7   Bates, *Lincoln in the Telegraph Office*, 216, 202.

8   Nicolay and Hay, *Abraham Lincoln: A History*, VI, 339.

9   Calendar found in room of David Davis upon his death. *Illinois State Journal*, June 29, 1886, p. 1, c. 4.

10   Basler, ed., *The Collected Works*, VI, 256. This is but a single example of the many that could be cited.

11   *Ibid.*, I, 178.

12   Turner and Turner, eds., *Mary Todd Lincoln*, 67.

13   *Illinois Daily State Journal*, Apr. 18, 1865, p. 2, c. 3.

14   The style of the Masonic regalia painted upon Lincoln's portrait is typical of the apparel worn in France. Alphonse Cerza, "Lincoln and Freemasonry," *Bulletin of the Illinois Lodge of Research*, I, No. 2, pp. 79-82.

15   *Daily Illinois State Register*, May 3, 1865, p. 4, c. 3.

16   Mary Lincoln to Dr. P. D. Gurley, Washington, D. C., May 22, 1865, in Edgington, *A History of The New York Avenue Presbyterian Church*, 252-253; Mary Lincoln to Alexander Williamson, Chicago, Ill., Dec. 1, [1865], Turner and Turner, eds., *Mary Todd Lincoln*, 290-291.

17   Turner and Turner, eds., *Mary Todd Lincoln*, 272.

18   Neely, *The Abraham Lincoln Encyclopedia*, 322, 50.

19   Cole and McDonough, eds., *Benjamin Brown French Journal*, 479.

20   Reminiscences of Mrs. B. S. Edwards, MS., Lincoln Library, Springfield, Ill.

21   Cole and McDonough, eds., *Benjamin Brown French Journal*, 483-484, 498.

22   Quotes from Browning's diary in *The State Journal-Register*, Mar. 2, 1994.

23   Turner and Turner, eds., *Mary Todd Lincoln*, 682.

24   *Ibid.*, 453-454, 256.

25   Ruth Painter Randall, *Lincoln's Sons* (Boston: Little, Brown & Co., 1955), 232; Turner and Turner, eds., *Mary Todd Lincoln*, 605, 424-426.

26   Chicago *Tribune*, July 17, 1871, p. 4, cc. 1-2.

27   Washington *Evening Star*, Oct. 5, 1868, p. 1, c. 1.

28   Chicago *Evening Journal*, July 15, 1871, p. 4, c. 2; N. Y. *Tribune*, June 21, 1871, p. 5, c. 2.

29   Turner and Turner, eds., *Mary Todd Lincoln*, 577.

30   N. Y. *Tribune*, May 11, 1871, p. 5, c. 5.

31   *Ibid.*

32   *Ibid.*, May 18, 1871, p. 5, c. 3.

33   *Illinois State Journal*, May 20, 1871, p. 2, c. 1

34   Turner and Turner, eds., *Mary Todd Lincoln*, 580-581; Helm, *Mary, Wife of Lincoln*, 272-274; Neely and McMurtry, *The Insanity File*, 162.

35   *Edwards' Annual Directory: Chicago* (Chicago: Edwards & Co., 1871), 206. This "hotel" moved about quite a bit.

36   Turner and Turner, eds., *Mary Todd Lincoln*, 588.

37   *Illinois State Journal*, July 7, 1871, p. 1, c. 1

38   *Ibid.*, July 17, 1871, p. 2, c. 2; Chicago *Tribune*, July 16, 1871, p. 3, c. 2.

39   A. T. Andreas, *History of Cook County, Illinois* (Chicago: A. T. Andreas, 1884), 640.

40   Chicago *Tribune*, July 17, 1871, p. 4, cc. 1-2.

41   *Daily Illinois State Register*, July 17, 1871, p. 4, c. 2.

42   *Ibid.*; Norman Williams, Jr., was an incorporator of the Pullman Palace Car Co. of which Robert Lincoln later became President.

43   *Ibid.*; *Chicago Evening Journal*, July 17, 1871, p. 1, c. 3.

44   Deed Record, XLV, 13, Sangamon Co. Bldg., Springfield.

45   *History of Sangamon County* (Chicago: Inter-State Pub. Co., 1881), 673-674; *Springfield City Directory 1871-72*, 53, 64.

46   *Daily Illinois State Register,* July 17, 1871, p. 4, c. 2.; *Illinois State Journal*, July 18, 1871, p. 4, c. 2.

47   "Interments at Oak Ridge Cemetery," I, n. p., MS., Oak Ridge Cemetery, Springfield, Illinois; *Illinois State Journal*, Sept. 20, 1871, p. 4, c. 2.

48   *Chicago Inter Ocean*, May 20, 1875, p. 1, c. 1.

49   *Illinois State Journal*, July 17, 1882, p. 6, c. 1.

50   Rodney A. Ross, "Mary Todd Lincoln, Patient at Bellevue Place, Batavia," *Jour. Ill. State Hist. Soc.*, LXIII, 5-34 (Spring, 1970); Neely and McMurtry, *The Insanity File*, 120-121; N. Y. *Times*, Oct. 1, 1876, p. 12, c. 4; Turner and Turner, eds., *Mary Todd Lincoln*, 617-618.

Edward Lewis Baker, Jr., had been born in October of 1858 in Illinois. He later moved to Omaha, then Lincoln, Nebraska, and died in Baldwinsville, N. Y., on Feb. 22, 1923, as a result of heart disease. In Nebraska, he worked in the printing business. U. S. Census 1900, Lincoln, Lancaster Co., Nebraska, ED 68, p. 8, l. 67; *Lincoln Star*, Feb. 23, 1923, p. 2, c. 6. Courtesy of Andrea I. Paul.

51   Keckley, *Behind the Scenes*, 104-105.

52   Neely and McMurtry, *The Insanity File*, 68.

53   *Chicago Inter Ocean,* May 20, 1875, p. 1, c. 1.

54   Neely and McMurtry, *The Insanity File*, 37.

55   Dated Feb. 20, 1897, MS., SC 923, Ill. State Hist. Lib.

56   R. T. Lincoln to Isaac Markens, Washington, D. C., Apr. 6, 1918, in Paul M. Angle, ed., *A Portrait of Abraham Lincoln in Letters By His Oldest Son* (Chicago: Chicago Hist. Soc., 1968), 58.

57   John Carroll Power, *Abraham Lincoln: His Life, Public Services . . .* (Springfield: H. W. Rokker, 1889), 413.

58   William H. Townsend, *Lincoln and His Wife's Home Town* (Indianapolis: The Bobbs-Merrill Co., 1929), 44-53.

59   Levi O. Todd Family Bible, formerly owned by Alvin S. Keys, Springfield, Ill.; copy of family data in author's possession.

60   William H. Townsend, *Lincoln and the Bluegrass* (Lexington: Univ. of Kentucky Press, 1955), 317-319.

61   Elizabeth Edwards to R. T. Lincoln, Springfield, Ill., Aug. 13, 1875, in Neely and McMurtry, *The Insanity File*, 66.

62   Condemnation proceedings to acquire more State House land, Apr. 3, 1878, MS., State House File, Illinois State Archives.

63   Turner and Turner, eds., *Mary Todd Lincoln*, 187-188. E. L. Baker, Sr., was appointed U. S. Consul to Buenos Aires, Argentina, on December 8, 1873. He left for this post in March of 1874. *Illinois State Journal*, Mar. 25, 1874, p. 4, c. 1. While there, he was injured in an accident on June 21, 1897, and died there on July 8. His body was finally returned to Springfield, Illinois, during the early morning hours (7:00 a. m.) of August 25, 1897. With the Rev. Dr. Frederick W. Wines, former minister of the First Presbyterian Church, offici-ating, Baker's funeral was held in the Lincoln Home at 10:00 a. m. on August 26. His brother-in-law, Albert S. Edwards,was the custodian of the Lincoln

Home, having taken over this post on July 1,1897. Burial was made in Oak Ridge Cemetery. *Ibid.*, July 10, 1897, p. 6, c. 3, Aug. 25, 1897, p. 5, c. 2. Julia (Edwards) Baker went to Chicago to live with her daughter. There, she died on July 29, 1908, and her body was returned to Springfield where her brother, A. S. Edwards, also held her funeral on July 31 in the Lincoln Home. *Ibid.*, July 31, 1908, p. 6, c. 4, Aug. 1, 1908, p. 6, c. 4. Julia was an Episcopalian.

64 Death Record No. 14376, Morgan Co., MS., Ill. Dept. of Public Health: Vital Records, Springfield; Temple, *By Square and Compasses*, 112.

65 *Leshnick's Jacksonville City Directory 1921-1922* (Peoria: Leshnick Directory Co., n. d.), 3, 180, 193.

66 Death Record No. 12652, Morgan Co., MS., Ill. Dept. of Public Health: Vital Records, Springfield; Registration No. 8350, Registration and Education Records, MS., Illinois State Archives; *Seventeenth Annual Report of the State Board of Health of Illinois . . .* (Springfield: Ed. F. Hartman, 1895), 146, 225. At this time, Dr. Norbury was President of the Morgan County Medical Society.

67 Turner and Turner, eds., *Mary Todd Lincoln*, 627.

68 N. Y. *Tribune*, Oct. 17, 1889, p. 12, c. 5.

69 *Ibid.*, Oct. 28, 1880, p. 8, c. 4.

70 *Illinois State Journal*, Oct. 29, 1880, p. 1, c. 2. The N. Y. *Herald* reported that she was "in good health" on Oct. 28, 1880, p. 6, c. 6. She lied, of course, to the reporters and told them she intended to proceed to Florida. That was very typical of Mary Lincoln. She generally tried to mislead them and retain her privacy.

71 *Illinois State Journal*, Nov. 4, 1880, p. 4, c. 3.

72 Turner and Turner, eds., *Mary Todd Lincoln*, 709; Dorothy Meserve Kunhardt, "An Old Lady's Lincoln Memories," *Life*, XLVI, No. 6, pp. 57-60 (Feb. 9, 1959). This is the reminiscences of Mary (Edwards) Brown, daughter of Albert S. Edwards.

73 *Life*, Feb. 9, 1959, 57-60.

74 *Illinois State Journal*, Oct. 6, 1881, p. 6, c. 3.

75 *Ibid.*, May 30, 1881, p. 4, c. 3, p. 6, c. 3.

76 *Illinois State Register*, Oct. 6, 1881, p. 3, c. 2.

77 *Illinois State Journal*, Oct. 6, 1881, p. 6, c. 3.

78   *Ibid.*, Oct. 13, 1881, p. 5, c. 3.

79   N. Y. *Tribune*, Oct. 12, 1881, p. 8, c. 4.

80   Mary Lincoln to Mrs. Albert S. Edwards, New York, N. Y. , Oct. 23, 1881, MS., Ill. State Hist. Lib.; Turner and Turner, eds., *Mary Todd Lincoln*, 694.

81   David A. Sayre to Mrs. Mary Lincoln, Lexington, Ky., Dec. 4, 1863, MS., examined by the author while in the possession of King V. Hostick, Springfield, Ill. This letter bears Pres. Lincoln's endorsement on the back.

82   *Illinois State Journal*, Nov. 26, 1881, p. 4, cc. 1-2.

83   Dumas Malone, ed., *Dictionary of American Biography* (N. Y.: Charles Scribner's Sons, 1935), VIII, 403; *Who Was Who in America 1897-1942* (Chicago: A. H. Marquis Co., 1943), I, 1084.

84   Turner and Turner, eds., *Mary Todd Lincoln*, 709.

85   N. Y. *Tribune*, Nov. 22, 1881, p. 8, c. 2.

86   *Illinois State Journal*, Nov. 26, 1881, p. 4, cc. 1-2.

87   Quit Claim Deed of Mary Lincoln to Robert T. Lincoln; it was never recorded but was still a legal document. Mary thus knew that investigators could not find it in a courthouse and prove her a liar. Document in private hands but examined by this author.

88   *Illinois State Journal*, Nov. 29, 1881, p. 1, c. 5.

89   *Ibid.*, Nov. 26, 1881, p. 4, cc. 1-2.

90   *Ibid.*, p. 6, c. 3.

91   N. Y. *Tribune*, Nov. 30, 1881, p. 4, c. 5.

92   Turner and Turner, eds., *Mary Todd Lincoln*, 710-712.

93   *Ibid.*, 711.

94   W. A. Evans, M. D., *Mrs. Abraham Lincoln* (N. Y.: Alfred A. Knopf, 1932), 342, 344; *Chicago Daily Tribune*, July 17, 1882, p. 2, c. 4.

95   *Congressional Record-Senate*, 47th Congress, 1st Session, p. 402 (Jan. 16, 1882).

    For the records of the physicians, see *The Medical Register of New York . . . For the Year 1882* (N. Y. : G. P. Putnam's Sons, 1882), XLII, LVI, 48; N. Y.

Times, Apr. 21, 1902, p. 9 for Dr. Clymer; N. Y. *Times*, Dec. 14, 1913, p. 6, c. 3 for Dr. Knapp.

96   Turner and Turner, eds., *Mary Todd Lincoln*, 711.

97   *Ibid.*, 714.

98   *Ibid.*, 715.

99   *Ibid.*, 715.

100   *Ibid.*, 716.

101   *Illinois State Journal*, Mar. 25, 1882, p. 6, c. 3.

102   *The Round Table* (Springfield, Ill.), Mar. 25, 1882, p. 5, c. 3.

103   *Illinois State Register*, July 18, 1882, p. 3, c. 3; Herndon and Weik, *Herndon's Lincoln*, III, 434-435n; Wallace, *Past and Present of the City of Springfield . . .* , II, 1277; *Chicago Daily Tribune*, July 17, 1882, p. 2, c. 4.

104   Wallace, *Past and Present of the City of Springfield,* II, 1274-1278; *Illinois State Journal*, Apr. 28, 1907, p. 6, c. 1, Apr. 29, 1907, p. 6, c. 4. He married Margaret Doremus on November 28, 1865. She was a native of Louisiana and perhaps greatly influenced Dresser to join the Confederate Army. He had to have met her while residing in New Orleans prior to the Civil War.

105   Quoted in Willard L. King, *Lincoln's Manager: David Davis*, 74.

106   Basler, ed., *The Collected Works*, VI, 275-276.

107   O. H. Browning to Capt. N. W. Edwards, Washington, D. C., May 26, 1865, MS., Chicago Hist. Soc.; Doris Replogle Porter, "The Mysterious Browning Letter," *Lincoln Herald*, XC, 20-23 (Spring, 1988).

108   Basler, ed., *The Collected Works*, I, 466; A. Lincoln to Dr. Stone, Washington, D. C., May 26, 1864, published in *Jour. Abraham Lincoln Assoc.*, XIII, 55 (1992).

109   Herndon and Weik, *Herndon's Lincoln*, III, 434-435n.

110   *Life*, Feb. 9, 1959, pp. 57-60.

111   Mary L. D. Putnam to St. Clair and Clement Putnam, Dec. 8, 1882, copy in Ill. State Hist. Lib.

112   Ruth Painter Randall, *Mary Lincoln: Biography of a Marriage* (Boston: Little, Brown & Co., 1953), 442.

113   *Illinois State Register*, July 16, 1882, p. 3, c. 3, July 18, 1882, p. 3, c. 3.

114   *Ibid.*, July 16, 1882, p. 3, c. 3; *Illinois State Journal*, July 17, 1882, p. 6, c. 1.

115   *Illinois State Journal,* July 17, 1882, p. 6, c. 1.

Herndon and Weik, *Herndon's Lincoln*, III, 434-435n. Contrary to the statements of several authors, Dr. T. W. Dresser did not file a death record with the County Clerk of Sangamon County, although he should have by law. The State Board of Health was created on May 25, 1877, and in force July 1 that year. Paragraph 4 made it the duty of physicians, etc., to report births and deaths to the county clerk within ten days. They were to be kept in a bound volume. Failure to make such reports called for a fine of $10 if the physician was charged for his neglect. *Laws of the State of Illinois Passed by the Thirtieth General Assembly* (Springfield: D. W. Lusk, 1877), 208-210. It would appear that the Edwardses did not wish any more publicity about Mary Lincoln's mental state and perhaps asked the physician not to file. Finding the law unsatisfactory, the Legislature passed an act June 22, 1915, requiring original copies of birth and death certificates to be sent to the State Board of Health in Springfield. *Laws of the State of Illinois Enacted by the Forty-ninth General Assembly* (Springfield: Ill. State Journal Co., 1915), 660-670. Beginning in 1916, the birth and death records were much better kept but not perfectly recorded in all cases.

116   Evans, *Mrs. Abraham Lincoln*, 342, 344.

117   *Illinois State Register*, July 18, 1882, p. 2, c. 3.

118   *Illinois State Journal*, July 17, 1882, p. 1, c. 6., July 19, 1882, p. 6, c. 1, Mar. 29, 1882, p. 5, c. 1.

119   *Ibid.*, July 18, 1882, p. 6, c. 1; *The Round Table*, July 22, 1882, p. 4, c. 2; *Illinois State Register*, July 20, 1882, p. 3, c. 3.

120   *Illinois State Journal*, July 20, 1882, p. 1, c. 5; *Life*, Feb. 9, 1959, pp. 57-60; *Illinois State Register*, July 18, 1882, p. 3, c. 3.

121   *Illinois State Journal*, July 20, 1882, p. 1, c. 5.

122   *Ibid.*, p. 6, c. 3.

123   *Ibid.*, July 19, 1882, p. 6, c. 3; *Illinois State Register*, July 19, 1882, p. 3, c. 3.

124   Only once did a black band appear and that was at the top and bottom of a notice announcing that the funeral would begin at 10:30, a time that proved incorrect. *Illinois State Journal*, July 19, 1882, p. 6, c. 1.

125   James A. Reed, "The Later Life and Religious Sentiments of Abraham Lincoln," *Scribner's Monthly*, VI, 333-343 (July, 1873).

126   *Illinois State Journal*, Dec. 13, 1873, p. 4, c. 1.

127   James A. Reed, the son of a lawyer, was born May 22, 1830, in Huntington, Pennsylvania. He attended Milnwood Academy before entering the sophomore class at Jefferson College in 1853. Next, he went to Western Theological Seminary in 1856 and graduated in 1859. He was ordained in the First Presbyterian Church of Wooster, Ohio, in 1860. After Dr. Gurley died on Sept. 30, 1868, he preached supply at the New York Avenue Presbyterian Church in Washington, D. C., where the Lincolns had rented a pew during the Civil War. While preaching from that pulpit, Pres. Andrew Johnson was often in his congregation. Eventually, Rev. Reed came to the First Presbyterian Church at Springfield. Then, in 1874, Wooster College awarded him an honorary Doctor of Divinity degree. He was married to Cornelia M. Ker, daughter of the Hon. John Ker of Huntington, Penna., in May 1859. Dr. Reed resigned from First Church in 1888 and traveled to Europe for rest. Upon returning in 1889, he located at Chicago where he died of peritonitis at his residence, 584 Fullerton Avenue, early on the morning of February 7, 1890. His body was returned to Springfield where Rev. T. D. Logan preached his funeral service in the First Presbyterian Church at 11:00 a. m. on February 8, with burial in Oak Ridge Cemetery. He and his wife had no children. *Illinois State Journal*, Feb. 8, 1890, p. 4, c. 1, Feb. 10, 1890, p. 5, c. 6.

128   *Illinois State Journal*, July 20, 1882, p. 1, cc. 5-6, p. 6, c. 1.

129   Helm, *Mary, Wife of Lincoln*, 295.

130   Allen Thorndike Rice, ed., *Reminiscences of Abraham Lincoln . . .* (N. Y.: North American Review, 1888), 442.

131   *Illinois State Register*, July 20, 1882, p. 3, cc. 3-4.

132   *Ibid.*; *Illinois State Journal*, July 20, 1882, p. 1, cc. 5-6, p. 6, cc. 1-2. At this time, the south door to the Tomb led only into Memorial Hall. To enter the Catacomb, one had to go around the Monument to the north door. There was no inside connecting corridor from one chamber to the other. Only after its two rebuildings was the Lincoln Monument redesigned with passageways from the south to the north, and then the north door was permanently closed.

133   Turner and Turner, eds., *Mary Todd Lincoln*, 257.

134   John Carroll Power, ed., *History of An Attempt to Steal the Body of Abraham Lincoln* (Springfield: H. W. Rokker, 1890), 76-87.

135   *Illinois State Register*, July 21, 1882, p. 3, c. 1.

136   John S. Goff, *Robert Todd Lincoln* (Norman: Univ. of Oklahoma Press, 1969), 92. See also Robert's letter published in Fred. B. Perkins, *The Picture and the Men* (N. Y.: A. J. Johnson, 1867), [191].

137   *Illinois State Journal*, Aug. 26, 1876, p. 1, c. 1.

138   *Ibid.*, Feb. 12, 1895, p. 3, c. 3.

139   Basler, ed., *The Collected Works, Supplement 1832-1865*, 49; Page, *Abraham Lincoln in New Hampshire*, 111-112.

140   Goff, *Robert Todd Lincoln*, 42.

141   Pease and Randall, eds., *Diary of Orville Hickman Browning*, I, 657.

142   Washington *Evening Star*, Sept. 26, 1868, p. 1, c. 3.

143   Erne R. and Florence Frueh, *The Second Presbyterian Church of Chicago: Art and Architecture* (Chicago: Rohner Printing Co., 1978); Register [of Members], 1842-1942, pp. 286-287, MS., Archives, Second Presbyterian Church, 1936 S. Michigan Avenue, Chicago, Ill. 60616.

144   Trustees' Minutes, MSS., Archives, Second Presbyterian Church.

145   Allan Nevins, *Henry White: Thirty Years of American Diplomacy* (N. Y.: Harper & Bros., 1930), 72-73; *Illinois State Register*, Mar. 6, 1890, p. 1, c. 4, dispatch from London; Ruth Painter Randall, *Lincoln's Sons*, 307-308; Death Certificate by Dr. John G. Nagle filed in Death Records, II, 40, Sangamon Co. Clerk's Office, Springfield.

146   *Illinois State Register*, Mar. 6, 1890, p. 1, c. 4; *Illinois State Journal*, Mar. 7, 1890, p. 4, c. 4, Mar. 8, 1890, p. 3, c. 1.

147   *Illinois State Register*, Mar. 8, 1890, p. 1, c. 6, Nov. 9, 1890, p. 6, c. 5; *Illinois State Journal*, Mar. 8, 1890, p. 3, c. 6, Nov. 9, 1890, p. 4, c. 1.

148   Session Minutes of the 2nd Presbyterian Church of Chicago, 1856-1887, 201-280, MS., church office.

149   Nevins, *Henry White*, 72-73; *Illinois State Journal*, Mar. 8, 1890, p. 3, c. 6.

150   Basler, ed., *The Collected Works*, IV, 87.

151   Wallace, *Past and Present of Springfield*, I, 406; Death Record No. 6545, Ill. Dept. of Public Health: Vital Records, Springfield.

152   Ill. State Hist. Lib.

153 *Illinois State Journal*, Nov. 7, 1890, p. 4, c. 2, Nov. 8, 1890, p. 4, c. 1, Nov. 9, 1890, p. 4, c. 1; *Illinois State Register*, Nov. 9, 1890, p. 6, c. 5.

154 Edgington, *A History of The New York Avenue Presbyterian Church*, 187.

155 R. T. Lincoln to C. L. Conkling, Chicago, Ill., Jan. 14, 1907, MS., Conkling Papers, Ill. State Hist. Lib., kept in special vault.

156 Original check in author's possession.

157 *Illinois State Journal*, July 27, 1926, p. 9, c. 5; *Chicago Daily Tribune*, July 27, 1926, p. 6, cc. 1-4.

158 *Illinois State Journal,* July 29, 1926, p. 1, c. 5; Randall, *Lincoln's Sons*, 340.

159 Butler Papers, Columbia Univ. Lib., N. Y., N. Y.

160 *Illinois State Journal*, July 27, 1926, p. 1, c. 4.

161 *Ibid.*

162 Entries in Levi O. Todd's family Bible, copy in possession of the author; *The Lexington Kentucky Cemetery* (Lexington: Hisel's Headstones & Kentucky Tree-Search, 1986), 42.

163 *Sangamo Journal*, Oct. 29, 1846, p. 2, c. 6. This residence would later become the home of Dr. Nicholas Vachel Lindsay. R. T. L. Coll. No. 30277.

164 *Illinois State Journal and Register*, Aug. 23, 1942, p. 2, cc. 4-8; Levi O. Todd Bible; Power, *Early Settlers of Sangamon County*, 176-177; *Williams' Springfield Directory For 1860-61* (Springfield: Johnson & Bradford, 1860), 65; *Illinois State Journal*, Jan. 10, 1880, p. 3, c. 3; Sept 5, 1893, p. 5, c. 5; *Springfield Directory 1877-78* (Springfield: M. G. Tousley & Co., 1877), 20.

165 *Illinois State Journal and Register*, Aug. 23, 1942, p. 2, cc. 4-8; Power, *Early Settlers of Sangamon County*, 426-427; *Illinois State Journal*, Nov. 20, 1935, p. 3, cc. 2-4, June 1, 1943, p. 6, cc. 1-2. Death Record No. 44809 and 21457, Ill. Dept. of Public Health: Vital Records, Springfield.

166 Edgington, *The New York Avenue Presbyterian Church*, 266-268, 218-219.

167 *Illinois State Journal*, May 23, 1930, p. 1, c. 2, May 26, 1930, p. 5, c. 4.

168 *Ibid.*, Aug. 31, 1922, p. 8, c. 3, Sept. 1, 1922, p. 4, c. 1, Sept. 2, 1922, p. 5, c. 4; *Jour. Ill.State Hist. Soc.*, XV, 760-761 (Oct., 1922-Jan., 1923); Death Record 21182, Chicago, MS., Ill. Dept. of Public Health: Vital Records, Springfield.

169   Joseph Gallagher, "A Lincoln Day Without a Lincoln," *Lincoln Herald*, LXXXIX, 134-135 (Winter, 1987).

170   *Chicago Daily Tribune*, Apr. 1, 1937, p. 16, c. 1; *Illinois State Journal*, Apr. 1, 1937, p. 12, c. 6.

Photo of New York Avenue Old Church at the time Lincoln worshipped there.

Photographer unknown

Note:
In addition to the pages referenced in the index,
the reader may want to examine the wealth of information
included in the notes at the end of each chapter.